D1497073

DISPOSED OF
BY LIBRARY
HOUSE OF LORDS

Rethinking Domestic Violence

Domestic violence, men's abusive power and control over women in intimate relationships, is a widespread but still largely hidden problem. *Rethinking Domestic Violence* explodes the myths concerning its nature and causes and explores how the responses of social workers and probation officers to the women, children and men involved need to be far better co-ordinated and more effective. Women experiencing violence and abuse are actually encountered in every social work setting but, to date, their needs have largely been ignored.

The opening chapters of the book look at men's violence to women as a worldwide phenomenon, known in all cultures and through all ages. Traditionally dismissed as a man's right, as part of what women must endure in marriage, as the result of the man's drinking or as an occasional aberration in men who are psychologically ill, domestic violence has only recently been accepted as a criminal behaviour that must not be tolerated by a civilised society. Social work often became hooked not only into all the myths listed above but into another kind of unhelpful 'explanation' that violence was part of the dynamics of a relationship. This view may be particularly hard to shake off in facing up to men's responsibility for their abusive behaviours.

Rethinking Domestic Violence goes on to explore the opportunities and challenges, in every context of social work and probation practice and policy making, to meet the needs of abused women and their children and to confront abusive men. In some areas of work, such as child protection and groupwork with male perpetrators, domestic violence is already widely recognised as a major contemporary issue. This recognition urgently needs to spread to all areas of work – community care; mainstream probation practice; the whole of child care; duty rota responses to women with emergency needs; hospitals, day centres and family centres – everywhere where women may seek help.

Audrey Mullender is Professor in Social Work at the University of Warwick, Coventry.

Rethinking Domestic Violence

The social work and probation response

Audrey Mullender

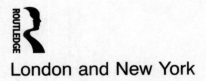

London and New York

First published 1996
by Routledge
11 New Fetter Lane, London EC4P 4EE

Simultaneously published in the USA and Canada
by Routledge
29 West 35th Street, New York, NY 10001

© 1996 Audrey Mullender

Typeset in Times by Keystroke, Jacaranda Lodge, Wolverhampton
Printed and bound in Great Britain by Clays Ltd, St Ives plc

All rights reserved. No part of this book may be reprinted
or reproduced or utilized in any form or by any electronic,
mechanical, or other means, now known or hereafter
invented, including photocopying and recording, or in any
information storage or retrieval system without permission
in writing from the publishers.

British Library Cataloguing in Publication Data
A catalogue record for this book is available from the British Library

Library of Congress Cataloging in Publication Data
Mullender, Audrey.
  Rethinking domestic violence : the social work and probation
response / Audrey Mullender.
     p.   cm.
Includes bibliographical references and index.
  1. Wife abuse—Great Britain. 2. Abused women—Counselling of—Great
Britain. 3. Abused wives—Counselling of—Great Britain. 4. Social work with
women—Great Britain. 5. Domestic violence—Great Britain—Prevention.
6. Abusive men—Counselling of—Great Britain. 7. Abusive men—Great
Britain—Rehabilitation. 8. Probation—Great Britain. I. Title.
HV1448.G7M85   1996
362.82'92'0941—dc20   96–2572
                                CIP

ISBN 0–415–08054–1 (hbk)
ISBN 0–415–08055–X (pbk)

To my sister,
Lesley,
with love

Contents

Preface   ix
Acknowledgements   xi
Introduction   1

1 The terms of the debate   3
The record of social work   6
Terminology   8
Other forms of abuse in intimate relationships   11
Conclusions   17

2 What do we know about domestic violence?   19
What is domestic abuse?   19
Where does abuse take place?   26
When did abuse start?   29
How widespread is domestic abuse?   30
Why does it happen? The myths (and facts) of causation   36
Theories about men   37
Theories about women   45
Conclusion   63

3 Social work as part of the problem   65
The research evidence   66
The way forward   81

4 Developing good practice in social services departments   82
Best practice   83
Duty work   92
Child protection and child welfare   95
Conclusion   106

5 Responses to domestic abuse in health and adult care settings   107
Primary health care settings   110
Mental health   116
Hospital settings   124

Work with older women   131
Women with physical disabilities and/or learning difficulties   133
Conclusion   138

6 The needs of children living with domestic abuse   139
The impact on children   141
Links with child abuse   144
Work with children in refuges   153
Direct work with and for children   159
Conclusion   167

7 Social work and probation practice with families   169
Family work and violence: a fundamental change of perspective   170
Family court welfare work   185
Child care work, families and the courts   191
Conclusion   201

8 The probation service and domestic violence   203
Current attitudes   203
The probation role with women   206
Work with men   210
Supervision   214
Throughcare and aftercare   216
Ways forward: action on a service-wide level   219
Conclusion   220

9 The men who abuse: what kind of intervention in groups?   222
The current British context   223
Methodology and philosophy   225
Accountability to women's safety, perspectives and priorities   235
Efficacy   242
Resourcing   245
Conclusion   247

10 Working together for change: the wider context and the
     empowerment of women   249
Inter-agency forums   250
Public education   259
The overall aim: the empowerment of women   266
Conclusion   276

Notes   278
References   280
Name index   303
General index   309

Preface

Researching and writing this book has not been easy. It is harrowing to be immersed in graphic accounts of physical and sexual assaults and of emotional degradation over a long period of time, as all those living and working with these realities know. Like other authors before me (see Kelly, 1988b, pp.15–19 for a powerful and intelligent account of all that is involved), I have been put in touch with painful memories – and I have been unable to avoid at every turn questioning all the male and female constituents of the relationships and assumptions, as well as the social backcloth, of my daily life. I could not have survived without the strength of the women's networks and the female academic community of which I count myself privileged to be a part. I emerge more determined to add my small influence to all those who survive – and work to help others survive – the harms inflicted in an abusive society.

The acknowledgement in this book that social workers have traditionally been 'part of the problem' for women experiencing abuse is also chastening for me, as I am a social worker by training and experience and now a social work educator and writer. Yet this book is certainly not intended as another 'social work bashing' tome. My continued involvement with the profession rests on the belief that we are one of the best hopes for the enlightened recognition of human resourcefulness and potential for change. Women living with abuse are not hopeless victims and men inflicting it are not individual monsters for whom the only solution is to be locked up for ever and the key thrown away. The reality is at once more hopeful – because people *can* change (given a conjunction of justice, confrontation, support and motivation) – and more difficult, because the root of the problems is embedded deep in our society and involves all of us in confronting painful truths about our lives and ourselves. Social workers have never fought shy of such recognition, however. All our work demands that we engage with complex social problems mirrored in personal vulnerabilities. At our best, we seek to learn about the intricacies of such issues so that we can be better equipped to empower people to tackle them. It is high time we turned this best practice in the direction of domestic violence and its impact on women and children. This is the aim that underscores this book.

Acknowledgements

I should like to thank all those who have taken considerable time and trouble to share ideas and read drafts; the University of Durham, for research leave; the National Children's Bureau, for a Mia Kellmer Pringle Fellowship which funded a trip to the USA and Canada to study services for child witnesses of woman abuse; John, for all the sacrifices made for the sake of this book; and the media, for both competent and incompetent reporting of women's experiences which enraged me afresh every day and kept me to the task.

In time honoured fashion, enormous help came from all the above but errors and inadequacies are mine.

Introduction

Effective action in any social sphere is impossible without an adequate understanding of the nature and extent of the problem. Chapter 1 analyses the terminology of domestic abuse and the record of social work in this field, whilst firmly establishing the fact that the greatest amount of violence is inflicted by men on women. Gay and lesbian relationships are referred to, but the main concentration is on abuse within heterosexual relationships. Chapter 2 explores information on the incidence and theories of the causation of domestic violence. In so doing, it exposes common myths – that drink causes domestic violence, that women seek or provoke the violence, and so on – which have percolated into social work practice. It seeks to replace the myths with the actual stories of women's lived experience. The common themes that emerge – for example that men must take responsibility for their abusive behaviour and that women must be heard, believed and empowered – constitute the strongest evidence on which to base appropriate professional intervention. Social workers need, too, to understand the complexities of women's attempts to escape: the use by male partners of all forms of abuse to prevent this; the interaction between the emotional impact of the abuse and the difficulty of negotiating the maze of legal and welfare services; above all, the crucial need for advocacy, self-help and support services to empower women through this process on their own terms.

Chapter 3 examines research into social work involvement in domestic violence in the past and why the profession has had such a bad image in the literature. There has been shown to be widescale neglect of the issue by practitioners. The most common traditional response, that of 'keeping the family together', may have been replaced by insisting that the woman goes into a refuge or seeks an injunction – but with no less a failure to support her in her own perceptions and choices in a highly dangerous situation, and no less a tendency to redefine cases as 'child protection' as if women subjected to abuse were not themselves also preoccupied with protecting their children. Chapters 4, 5 and 6 show that this is slowly beginning to change, with good practice across some whole social services departments (or equivalent around the UK) and in some specialist settings including duty teams, child care work, and health and community care contexts. This is contrasted in Chapter 7 with a widespread failure by social workers and probation officers to recognise that working with a couple or family together is unsafe, though policy covering probation practice in family court welfare work is giving a lead. Chapters 8 and 9 move the focus to the remainder of probation practice, in general workloads, and in special programmes for abusers.

The book closes by advocating a woman-centred, crime preventive and public education perspective. Core responses that can be of assistance in developing a new approach are identified, with much hope for the future resting on the need for interlinked services to give women choices and to help them and their children to be safe. Though organisational obstacles to confronting male power and empowering women remain strong, practitioners can find alliances and trends for positive change – inceasingly through inter-agency forums (Hague *et al.*, 1995) – and equip themselves with the necessary analysis and skills to be part of the solution rather than part of the problem.

Chapter 1

The terms of the debate

In recent years there has been a growing intolerance in Britain of the abuse by men of their wives, girlfriends, partners and ex-partners. This can be measured by increased media coverage as well as by changes in policing policy to recognise much of the abuse as criminal behaviour, a rise in the number of domestic violence inter-agency forums intended to co-ordinate practical responses, and belated Government attention – though, at the present time, the latter has yet to be backed up by serious resourcing or legislative change.

These developments have been surprisingly slow to come, as a result of which, although Britain began to originate a nationwide refuge movement as early as 1972 (Dobash and Dobash, 1992, pp.63–7), we currently lag behind parts of the USA, Canada and Australia in giving women and children real hope for safety through adequate public funding of services. The intentions and philosophy of the early feminist campaigners have held firm (pp.87–90), despite public neglect, and the results are there to be turned to: by women experiencing abuse for life-saving assistance, and by statutory professionals for guidance and example. The four Women's Aid federations of England, Scotland, Wales and Northern Ireland hold the nation's expertise on men's abuse of women. They are well-established voluntary organisations which undertake campaigning and offer support to independent, collectively run local refuges[1] and related services which conceptualise their committed work for women's safety within broader goals of personal and social empowerment. There are no bureaucratised refuges run by or employing professional social workers or psychologists in this network as one finds in North America; women living in Women's Aid refuges make their own decisions, continue to look after their own families, and are supported by workers, still normally in collective structures, who have often been through similar experiences themselves. This keeps UK refuges highly woman-centred.

Women's organisations in Britain, in a second wave of feminism with roots in the nineteenth and early twentieth centuries, have fought for over twenty years for a national funding base for refuges, for effective rehousing policies, economic and social support for women forced to leave their homes, legislative protection, and effective law enforcement. None of these battles has yet been fully won. It has always been an uphill struggle to get women's danger and distress taken seriously. In particular, Government has lacked or resisted a comprehensive understanding of the problem that could underpin action across a range of fronts. The Children Act of 1989 (implemented in 1991) makes no mention of domestic violence, for example, yet contact orders made under the Act (see Chapter 7, this volume) can involve men being given details of their ex-partners' whereabouts. Furthermore, the lack of comprehensive national planning means that gains for women in one area are frequently accompanied by losses in another. Recent research by Malos and Hague (1993), for instance, indicates that proposed improvements in legislation on homelessness have been accompanied by cutbacks in funding for local government housing departments that make rehousing harder than ever. There is also an interplay (or perhaps a vacuum) between agency responses that is counterproductive for women. Many housing departments now expect women to obtain injunctions through the courts, for example (ibid., pp.36–7).

In the mid-1990s, however, Britain does at last appear to be in the midst of a wave of serious attention to the issues at national level,[2] however sceptical one may remain about the political motivation underlying some of the moves or the extent of real change they have achieved (Morley, 1993). The police were amongst the first public bodies to set the trend towards change. In 1987, the Metropolitan Police introduced a force order on domestic violence, advising all officers to utilise their existing powers of arrest, since 'an assault which occurs within the home is as much a criminal act as one which may occur in the street', followed in 1990 by a set of best practice guidelines. The Home Office (Circular 60/1990) and Scottish Office advised similar improvements for the whole of Britain, based on 'showing the victim that she is entitled to, and will receive, society's protection and support [by always considering t]he arrest and detention of an alleged assailant'. Most local police forces (now police services) responded, and the publicity received by such moves, together with pressure on women to report assaults (see Chapter 10, this volume, on public education campaigns aimed at women), increased the numbers of women calling the police and the number of assaults recorded as crimes (see Chapter 2, this volume). Other positive measures mooted in the Home Office Circular that have been widely implemented are police involvement in inter-agency forums, and the establishment of designated Domestic Violence Units (DVUs) or of specialist units combining responses to domestic violence and child sexual abuse. Informal feedback from Women's Aid does seem to reflect some overall improvement in police responses to women reporting abuse, though remaining problems include inconsistencies between individual officers and continuing feelings on the part of many Black[3] women that the police use domestic violence to keep them and their communities under surveillance (Mama, 1993, p.135). Prosecution of abusive men, and for sufficiently serious offences, remains difficult to achieve (e.g. Kennedy, 1992, pp.84–5), and pressure on the police and the Crown Prosecution Service (or equivalent; Procurators Fiscal in Scotland) in this regard continues. Current concerns are that charges are more, rather than less, often being reduced to common assault; that women's behaviour is too often seen as an aggravating factor, and men's apparent contrition as a mitigating factor in the situation; and that arrests, charges and imprisonment have all failed to increase as one might have expected (Glass, 1995) despite the changes in policing policy.

The police have not been alone in giving domestic violence greater prominence and, gradually it has come to public attention. Three Appeal Court decisions in 1992, for example, which resulted in the release of women imprisoned for killing violent partners, gained widespread media coverage.

Nineteen ninety-two, in fact, was arguably the pivotal year. It also saw the beginning of inter-ministerial co-operation administered by the Home Office (House of Commons, 1992a, para. 132; see Chapter 10, this volume), and the commencement of a Home Affairs Committee enquiry (which reported in House of Commons, 1992a and 1992b) focusing largely on policing and civil remedies. Lest we were becoming too confident in the likelihood of the establishment setting the pace, however, the Government's reply to the Home Affairs Committee report (Home Department *et al.*, 1993) was cautious and disappointing. But, before the end of 1992, the issue had become unstoppable. A national inter-agency working party from a voluntary organisation had issued a much cited report which set the probation service, amongst others, on the path towards change (Victim Support, 1992), and Southall Black Sisters – the group that campaigned for the release of Kiranjit Ahluwalia, one of the women driven to kill her abusive husband – had achieved their aim and been awarded a civil liberties prize by a national charity. The issue of women who kill their abusers later went on to occupy a major storyline in a soap opera (Channel 4's *Brookside*) for several months – culminating in a trial and a not untypical life sentence for the fictional wife in May 1995 – and was picked up throughout the media. All these developments, over a period of several years, combined to rekindle general interest in the issue of domestic violence in national news and current affairs reporting and were accompanied, at local level, by a growing interest in establishing multi-agency forums to co-ordinate existing statutory and voluntary responses (see Chapter 10) and to identify what else needed to be done.

Most recently, the Labour Party's (1995) 'Peace at Home' initiative (which proposes a national strategy on domestic and sexual violence, including strengthened legislation, a funding framework for refuges, improved police practice and housing provision, and more effective public education) has placed domestic abuse more firmly on the national political map. In Europe, Ministerial conferences have drawn up plans of action to combat violence against women. Globally, the Beijing World Conference on Women in 1995, also included this matter as a critical area of concern, with the abuse of women increasingly now being seen around the world as an issue of basic human rights (Bunch and Carrillo, 1992).

As 1995 and 1996 have seen the release from prison of Emma Humphreys (following an appeal) and Sara Thornton (after a retrial led to a conviction for manslaughter rather than murder), it does seem that the tide of popular opinion may be turning towards justice for women who experience abuse, even those who kill as a result. Certainly, the media are becoming more willing to report cases from the perspective of the domestic violence involved, rather than glossing over this. There is still a long way to go, however, both in achieving changes in the law so that it is less punitive towards women (making manslaughter pleas and provocation defences easier, lessening the emphasis on women's mental health and ending mandatory life sentences for murder) and in switching the focus from women who kill to the far larger number of women who are themselves killed.

THE RECORD OF SOCIAL WORK

Social work has not been at the forefront of any of the positive moves for change, though probation and social services are represented on most of the local inter-agency forums which are springing up. Probation services have begun to respond to the need to work with abusive men through special programmes (see Chapter 9, this volume), but neither probation officers nor social workers have routinely re-examined their workloads to consider how they might use their role and influence to hold abusive men to account for their actions in other ways or – crucially – to help women achieve safety and a greater possibility of caring for their children as they would wish. Furthermore, though probation has a national position statement (Association of Chief Officers of Probation [ACOP], 1992, under revision in 1996), only relatively few local probation services, social services departments, and social-work based voluntary organisations have tackled the issue at a policy level, leaving it to individual practitioners to be more or less concerned – as their personal awareness, their life experience, or their training dictate.

Social workers and social work agencies urgently need to learn more about domestic violence, to understand its seriousness, and to rethink their typical responses in order to achieve greater consistency and a more helpful approach. They need to do this in a context that perceives power and control as exercised not only through gender oppression but also through racism, homophobia and heterosexism, as well as unequal treatment on the grounds of class, disability and age. At the same time, they need to find ways to project a more positive image – so that women subjected to abuse do not simply avoid statutory help for fear of having their children taken into care, their ex-partners enabled to recommence their harassment, or their own experiences discounted.

Social workers and probation officers come into contact with very large numbers of abused women and abusive men, and arguably they are in a better position than many other professionals to take constructive action because they are trained to look for concealed problems, to understand issues in a wider social context, to offer interpersonal support or challenge to achieve personal change over time, and to harness a range of forms of practical and emotional help. Too often, they fail to use the opportunities available to them to identify or respond adequately to women experiencing abuse or to confront abusive men. At the same time, the role of the social worker remains blurred – is it to promote family life, to protect children, to help women and children reach safety or, if a little of all of these, then where is the cut-off point and who decides? Contact with abusive fathers is just one area in which these possible roles can come into conflict. Probation officers, too, are being required to be more concerned with the safety and interests of the victims of crime and the nature of offending behaviour but without effective guidance as to their precise role in relation to abuse. Both groups, social workers and probation officers, have commented to researchers and at conferences that they lack skill and confidence in this area of work owing to lack of essential knowledge (see Chapter 3). They need to know what research can tell us about the realities and causes of abuse, what statutory and community-based resources provide the most appropriate answers, whether particular ways of intervening may increase the dangers and what their own involvement should be. Policy makers need to support their staff with adequate training, resources and information, clear guidelines, and systematic co-operation with other agencies right across the statutory health and welfare, criminal justice, and independent sectors. Where these improvements have been made, there has been a noticeable increase in attempts to tackle men's abuse of women consistently and effectively.

This book will attempt to engage with all these issues and to help practitioners meet their practical and moral responsibilities in ways which put women and their children at less risk and leave abusive men less likely to continue inflicting harm. It is addressed to all social workers, care managers, probation officers and related professionals, as well as to their managers and those who make the policies and laws that they implement. The term 'social services' will be used to embrace social services departments in England and Wales, social work departments in Scotland, and health and social services boards or trusts in Northern

Ireland. The text is seen as relevant, not only in these settings, but in the far wider context of health and welfare provision in this country.

TERMINOLOGY

The term 'domestic violence' has been used in the title of this book because it is in common everyday and professional use and was judged most likely to alert readers to the book's content. This is of particular importance in respect of a topic that has been widely neglected in social work and that could not, therefore, afford to lose attention through misunderstanding. Nevertheless, the term has been criticised on several grounds and the author shares all of the following concerns about its inadequacies.

The word 'domestic' is challenged for its links with the trivialisation of abuse in the past when, for example, the police would not respond on the same level to an assault if it was 'just a domestic' as they would to an assault in a public place. The problem has been a private trouble for too long; it now needs to become a public issue. Today's 'domestic' is too frequently tomorrow's murder.

The word 'domestic' is also inaccurate in the context of domestic violence for three reasons. Firstly, there are other crimes in domestic settings, such as child abuse, that are not encompassed by it. This book will not deal with defining or responding to other forms of family violence such as child abuse and elder abuse, except to explore the overlaps – for example where the same men abuse partners and children, or where women continue to be abused into later years. Secondly, the abuser and the woman he subjects to abuse may have had a relationship but need not actually have lived together. The Victim Support national report (1992, p.6) gives an example of 'Jolita', whose long-standing boyfriend had keys to her flat and often stayed there although they had never cohabited. He was jealous and violent; she became depressed. She did not dare to confront him about his behaviour or know where to obtain help. A conceptualisation of domestic violence as relating to husbands and wives or live-in partners would not help women like Jolita to know where to turn. Thirdly, harassment and violence often continue after the woman has attempted to end the relationship and either she or her partner has left. Many murders are committed by ex-partners.

The word 'violence' conveys an incomplete impression, since men's ill-treatment of women takes many forms which combine together into a pattern of intimidation, humiliation and control. It encompasses physical violence, psychological terrorisation, sexual abuse of all kinds including rape, and actual or virtual imprisonment. Economic domination and abuse of male privilege also feature strongly, as does using the children against the woman and abusing them or harming pets to frighten or threaten her. In this book, the term 'abuse' will tend to be preferred to 'violence' or 'battering' since it covers both the physical and sexual assaults and the emotional and mental torment to which many women are subjected by their male partners, including the threats of repeat incidents. Many accounts by women tell of physical attacks interspersed with gestures or glares, for example in public when the man feels he cannot actually hit his partner, which contain the threat of renewed violence and are enough to elicit submission; as a social work student said in a women-only discussion in class: 'How could I go to anyone for help and tell them "He looked at me"? – that's not a crime and no one else would even notice it, but it was enough.'

We should beware of working within male definitions which outlaw only the grossest and most public forms of abuse. Even though prosecutions and breaches of court orders, for example, must remain for the time being couched within legal language constructed by men, social workers and probation officers have opportunities for professional conversations with women which, with sensitivity and support, could work from women's understandings. We know, for example, that marital rape has been recognised by the courts in England and Wales as a criminal offence only since an Appeal Court ruling in March 1991 (previously a woman was 'deemed to have consented to sexual intercourse on marriage': Maynard, 1993, p.102). Kelly (1988a and 1988b) broadens our understanding of sexual abuse in intimate relationships beyond the purely legalistic by listening to women's own accounts. Sex can be coerced, unwanted, or consented to under the pressure of continual fear without satisfying legal definitions of rape; the woman feels sullied and demeaned but may be aware that no crime has been committed, may see herself as performing her wifely duty or fulfilling her female destiny, or may lack the language to conceptualise her experiences as abusive (as indeed we all did until Kelly's and related groundbreaking work). The social expectation upon her to regard behaviour that feels abusive as normal and inevitable will contribute to the feelings of worthlessness and isolation and the suspicion of going crazy engendered by all the other abuses and taunts. The social work, police or health professional who understands abuse as part of a continuum of unwanted, coercive, cruel and gendered behaviours – that is, who thinks along woman-centred lines – is more likely to appreciate what a woman has been through and is also better able to give her a model for survival.

Finally, the term 'domestic violence' has been criticised because it masks the fact that the socially condoned abuse that makes up the clear majority of these behaviours is inflicted by men on women:

> I reject all . . . titles and descriptions that obscure the real nature of the violence; that it is violence committed by men against the women they live with, have lived with or are in some form of emotional/sexual relationship with . . . . giving any form of violence a name which does not address its nature and causation diminishes its importance.
>
> (Maguire, 1988, p.34)

Maguire calls for a name to define the violence and acknowledge the power relationships. In co-ordinated inter-agency work in London, Ontario, for example, the term 'woman abuse' is preferred, but even then the perpetrator disappears and the focus is on the woman he victimises. Pahl (1985a, p.5) regards as significant the discussion of 'battered wives' rather than 'violent husbands'. Not only does this mask 'who is the victim and who the perpetrator' (Smith, 1989, p.1) but it causes the search for solutions to be directed at victims rather than instigators (Pahl, 1985a, p.5) and can feed into victim-blaming attitudes (see Chapter 2; see also Dobash and Dobash, 1992, pp.221–30). In Leeds, community care planners have accepted responsibility for providing services for 'women experiencing violence by known men'. This term has clearly been chosen with care by activists in Leeds for the fact that it, firstly, names the perpetrator, secondly, draws attention to the gendered nature of his unacceptable behaviour and, thirdly, clarifies that the policy relates to men's abuse of women in current or past intimate relationships albeit within a broader awareness of broader issues of physical, sexual or emotional abuse such as stranger rape, pornography, obscene telephone calls and sexual harassment in the workplace.

Although we can understand men's abuse of women adequately only if we conceptualise all its forms together within an overall social system of male control of women (e.g. Stanko, 1985; Kelly, 1988b, p.41; Maynard, 1993, pp.99 and 114), the abuse of women within relationships demands its own attention in social work policy and theorising. It requires particular understanding by social workers and court welfare officers, for example, because it is right in the heart of the home and family – where they do their work and where they face the dilemma of how to approach 'the social institutions of marriage and family ... [as] special contexts that may promote, maintain, and even support men's use of physical force against women' (Bograd, 1988b, p.12, in the context, as here, of justifying a whole book on the topic of 'domestic violence' rather than sexual violence more widely defined).

Although the term 'domestic violence' will still sometimes be used here (particularly in reference to British professional contexts where it still predominates, and sometimes to differentiate violence from other kinds of abuse), this book will talk as often as possible about men as abusers and about women who experience or are subjected to abuse. 'Abused woman' is not ideal because it appears to encapsulate women in terms of their abuse, rather than their survival or the rest of who they are, but it will sometimes be used to keep sentences shorter. Similarly, 'victim' terminology is frequently undesirable because it makes women sound inherently passive, but it is widespread in criminal justice contexts and may occasionally be used here (regarding probation responsibilities in relation to the victims of crime, for example).

OTHER FORMS OF ABUSE IN INTIMATE RELATIONSHIPS

Not all abuse or violence in relationships is perpetrated by men against women. Some women abuse men, some relationships involve abuse on both sides, and same-sex relationships can also be abusive. Let us consider each of these situations in turn.

Do women abuse men?

The popular media regularly attempt to draw attention to a supposed social problem of women abusing men, often, it would seem, to dilute or deflect the meagre attention paid to the abuse sustained by women. They create smokescreens by claiming that men are too ashamed to seek help with a problem which, it can therefore be speculated, could be quite wide-spread. There has never been any substantiation through research of the alleged 'battered husband' phenomenon. One study of medical notes at Leicestershire Royal Infirmary (Smith *et al.*, 1992) claimed to have found almost equal numbers of men and women who had been assaulted, but the researchers had, in fact, counted all assaults in the home and not only those in intimate relationships (Barron and Harwin, 1994, p.5). They included stranger attacks and fights between teenaged men in their sample, for example. On closer examination, far more women than men had been assaulted by a spouse or partner (85 as against 17) and no information was given as to the meaning or circumstances of the attacks – for example, whether they were part of an abusive pattern or a one-off retaliation (p.6).

No doubt there *are* some women who physically and/or emotionally dominate their male partners but there is no evidence that this is a common situation. Whereas, whenever a women's refuge opens, it is typically full almost immediately and having to turn frightened women away to other, less secure places, it appears that the isolated attempts to open men's 'refuges' have failed to uncover a widespread need. Furthermore, they have faced the serious problem that men with recorded histories of very serious abuse (e.g. men who have been excluded from their homes under the civil law) have moved in as part of a ploy to portray their partners in a negative light – as 'abusers' – in contested court cases involving children. At the least, they aim to create a scenario that minimises the impact of their own behaviour – which many abusers do not regard as abusive in any case (see Hearn, 1994 and forthcoming, and Chapter 9, this volume). The men who have made the one or two experiments in establishing such places have lacked the experience to foresee these difficulties and have not, for example, run checks on whether men had ever abused the children they took there (source: personal communication with a men's group worker). Consequently, they have found themselves caught in the middle, working with aggressive men and controversial issues for which they have no training or support. One man operated a so-called 'refuge' from his own home in London until his estranged wife took High Court action to have it closed, on the grounds that 'the place had become unfit for her children' (*Community Care*, 'End to battered men's refuge', 4th February 1993, p.2). The organisation Families Need Fathers has also attempted to convey the impression that women's violence is a common cause of marital breakdown (ibid.), but by voicing allegations rather than undertaking research.

Enormous publicity has been given to the fact that there *are* women who kill their partners, less to the fact that they do so in far smaller numbers than men kill women. Women are almost five times as likely to be murdered by a male partner or ex-partner as the other way round (Home Office, 1990, Table 4.4b), and typically in a different pattern of behaviour. Women tend to kill in self-defence or after enduring years of abuse (Kennedy, 1992, Chapter 8; Women's Aid Federation England, hereafter may also appear as WAFE, 1992a, paras 7.9–7.15). Research by Stout and Brown (1995), in a small study in the USA, showed that women killing their partners had a higher level of fear and were more likely to need medical attention for injuries to themselves than were men killing partners – indicating that women killed after being seriously assaulted themselves (and, in other cases, of course, women may kill because they are justifiably fearing such attacks) – yet the women were more harshly sentenced. American juries have sometimes been advised of the need by smaller and terrified women to use weapons to repel their attackers (Saunders, 1988, pp.99–101) which, of course, can lead to serious injuries or to death in situations where men would be able to use more controlled amounts of force – and, of course, would not be undergoing repeated assaults in the first place. The law makers and the courts in Britain have been more reluctant to recognise the particular circumstances in which women tend to kill, with the result, for example, that women are found guilty of murder rather than manslaughter and have less access to the partial defence of provocation (e.g. Kennedy, 1992, Chapter 8). This is the subject of active campaigning by organisations such as Justice for Women and Rights of Women, which are seeking changes in the law (see, for example, *ROW Bulletin*, Autumn/Winter 1994, pp.39–40) and the release of individual women imprisoned for killing their abusers.

No evidence has been produced from any quarter, then, of any female-on-male equivalent of the pattern of coercion, terror and virtual imprisonment to which women are not infrequently subjected by men. There are no case studies in the literature or in the media of women treating men as women have been treated by men, the latter in numerous horrifying examples encountered in every text and, of course, in every refuge and every helping agency in the country. There are claims that men might be too ashamed to report such treatment, but many women feel embarrassed, guilty and ashamed and yet untold numbers of woman abuse cases come to light (in addition to those which remain concealed). No social phenomenon could be that well hidden.

Mutual fighting

More worrying is the assumption or alleged 'fact' that a second scenario, that of mutual danger in the heterosexual household, is commonplace. This allows terms such as 'spousal violence' or 'marital abuse' to be used which mask the domination of men and make the problem look like 'mutual fighting' or 'equal combat'.

Straus *et al.* (1980) and Straus and Gelles (1986) (see also summaries in Saunders, 1988; Smith, 1989, pp.11–13; and in Dobash and Dobash, 1992, pp.258–63) claimed to have discovered from two national representative self-report surveys that wives committed almost as many assaults as husbands (Straus *et al.*, 1980, p.36). The existence of a hidden problem of 'battered husbands' was hailed and was given a great deal of air-time by the American media. Less reported were the findings that wives assaulted less repeatedly and caused less damage through their smaller size and less dangerous and injurious behaviour than did the husbands (p.43), and that considerably more husbands than wives justified violence as a necessary or good feature of a relationship (pp.47–8). The research was flawed in many ways: for example in counting acts rather than consequences, such as injuries actually inflicted; in the complete overlooking of the meaning of violence in the relationship, including motivation, build-up, other forms of abuse, and social context (see Carlson, 1992, p.97); and in making probably risky projections from 2,143 husbands and wives in the sample, albeit a carefully constructed one, to the 47 million couples in the entire USA. Straus (1980) actually conducted further analysis of the data, his qualitative impressions from the work having been different from the apparent quantitative findings, and concluded that husbands were three times more likely than wives to make severe attacks on non-violent spouses, whereas wives resorted to severe violence only after a virtually continuous stream of minor violence. The apparently more equal figures in the overall study findings were blurred by including couples' behaviour in normal rows, such as throwing things. It is crucially important in any such work to include motive and consequence. Resisting assault, for example, is not 'mutual fighting' (McGibbon and Kelly, 1989, 3.1). In Saunders' study of 52 couples where abuse had taken place (1988b, pp.102–9), violence was overwhelmingly initiated by husbands, with women 'fighting back' in self-defence. Women sustain far more numerous, and far more serious injuries than men (Pagelow, 1992, p.109, summarising Berk *et al.*, 1983).

There *are* women who strike the first blow, but the context in which they do so is usually one in which they have been abused before (in this or another relationship) and they hit as a usually futile coping strategy to stop themselves from being hit again. For example, one young woman in Relate counselling hit her husband after growing up being abused with fists and a belt and firmly believing that this destined her to be an abuser. Furthermore, there is no excuse for retaliation from the man who, firstly, has other choices and could, for example, simply leave the room (two wrongs do not make a right); secondly, is likely to be larger and/or stronger than the woman so that he will do damage out of all proportion to what he has suffered; and, thirdly, in striking a woman, commits an action that has a different social meaning and, because his domination has been challenged, can too easily slip into regular, socially condoned woman abuse: 'She slapped me across the face hard. It hurt . . . . And that did it. Then I slapped her, and punched her, and kicked her, and knocked her down. I mean, I just let her have it' (Ptacek, 1988, p.144). Her action was offensive, but he could have brushed it off; his was life-threatening.

In fact, very few women hurt their partners. Dobash and Dobash (1980, cited in Pahl, 1985a, p.6) found 0.4 per cent husband assaults as against 25 per cent wife assaults in 34,000 police records studied in Edinburgh and Glasgow in 1974. Indeed, very few women hit anybody. Only 7.37 per cent of all the assaults in this study, both inside and outside the family, were identifiably by women, as against 85.48 per cent by men (and just over 7 per cent not specified). Taking the spouse assaults alone, over 98 per cent are by men against women. Self-reports by men of personal crimes against them are overwhelmingly by non-intimates (who, from the above, may be taken to be mainly other men), whereas half of those against women are by intimates – primarily husbands (Worrall and Pease, 1986, pp.121–2 drawing on Hough and Mayhew, 1983). Women are far more likely to be murdered by a male partner or ex-partner than the other way round (see above). Dobash and Dobash (1992, pp.264–5) review extensive evidence from the USA and Canada that men are disproportionately the perpetrators of assault and homicide, with 90–96 per cent of domestic assaults dealt with by the police and courts being committed by men against women. Self-report in large, intensive national crime surveys in those countries has revealed almost identical figures to the above, with figures for male victims of women too low to handle reliably in the statistics or to amount to any real degree of risk. This is despite the fact that men are more likely to report incidents and to press charges (so much for 'embarrassment' in this research), often, it seems, in an attempt to bring their partners into line or to prevent them from leaving. Furthermore, repeated assaults and worse injuries were shown to be a feature for many women.

Police in areas of the USA with mandatory arrest policies in cases of domestic violence do sometimes tend to arrest both partners (Saunders, 1995, p.147). Of course, assault is wrong whoever does it (this is one of the reasons why refuges do not allow violence or violent toys and have nosmacking policies), but issues arise of whose word is believed by the police, of the man calling the woman's self-defence an attack on him, or using counter-allegations to minimise his own behaviour and sentence, and so on. Also, this is one way in which police officers can obey the letter of the requirement to arrest without needing to understand or agree with its spirit. Both partners may then be convicted, and courts are beginning to mandate very small numbers of women to attend women-only batterers' programmes (source of information: study visit to Duluth). On talking to the workers in such a group, it emerged that they had only ever seen two young women whom they regarded as inherently aggressive. (I observed one of the two in court; she was wearing an electronic tag and presenting a 'hard' image. The criminal justice system appeared to be treating her as a prize specimen proving that women can be as bad as men.) All the others either denied violence or had used it only in self-defence after long periods of abuse. Consequently, the first two did not fit into the group, which was run for the others using the same self-help model as all the project's groups for female survivors (Pence, 1987) . It should be remembered that we are talking here of a society that glorifies violence in its media and where possessing hand-guns is commonplace.

The surprise should, perhaps, be that the overwhelming majority of women are not violent, even under the most extreme provocation. Many no doubt sense that, without self-defence training, fighting back typically leads to an escalation of the violence and worse injuries (e.g. Bowker 1983, pp.68–9). Serious violence is still what men inflict on women and on each other. Sustained severe abuse, adding sexual and emotional torture to physical harm, is what men do to women. All the above means that practitioners can safely learn to work with men as perpetrators and with women as typically the victim-survivors of abuse (but see below on lesbian abuse). Mutual combat (like the battered husband syndrome) is a myth, and mutual undertakings – sometimes substituted by courts when women seek to use the civil law to restrain men – an insult. Without men's aggression, let alone rape and other sexual assaults, there would be many redundancies in the criminal justice system.

Lesbian and gay abuse

Finally, let us turn to lesbian and gay relationships, which can certainly be abusive (e.g. Island and Letellier, 1991; Renzetti, 1992; N.B. neither book is completely free of pathologising explanations). All the kinds of behaviours perpetrated by men against women – including physical attacks, coerced and abusive sex, and emotional cruelty and humiliation – can be perpetrated by women against women (Burstow, 1992, p.167; Renzetti, 1992, pp.20–4, who found psychological abuse to be most common in this context) and by men against men (Island and Letellier, 1991, pp.26–32), though they cannot be fully understood as a 'just-like-them' parallel to men's abuse of women (Kelly, 1991, pp.13 and 19; Burstow, 1992, p.167). Reasons why such abuse has been slower to receive attention (Island and Letellier, 1991, pp.9–12) may include the likelihood that, within the already taboo topic of domestic violence, gay and lesbian partners experiencing abuse are even less likely to have approached or told the truth to helping agencies – fearing both an individually hostile response to themselves and their abusers and that they will be adding 'fuel [to] the fires of anti-gay discrimination from the heterosexual world' (p.10) – whilst the agencies are even less likely to have asked the right questions, or heard or been trusted with requests for help, unless they have worked hard at awareness raising (Research Committee and Staff of London Battered Women's Advocacy Centre, 1993; Champagne *et al.*, 1994). Since lesbian histories, in particular, render inadequate 'women good/non-violent, men bad/violent' perspectives on intimate abuse – which may previously have represented an attractively simple way of summarising feminist explanations (confronted by Kelly, 1991; Hall, 1992) – it may have been difficult to hear them, including within the lesbian community itself.

Yet it would be amazing if abuse did not occur between men and between women. We are still in the lifetime that is making the first real attempts at developing cohabitations of any kind on something approaching an egalitarian basis, and, while there is evidence that lesbians work particularly hard at rejecting traditional roles (summarised by Renzetti, 1992, pp.45–6), this is no easy matter:

> We are not born knowing how to form equal, non-destructive relationships, so we borrow from heterosexual models, which is how most of us begin to learn about relationships. Having been restricted and controlled all our lives, the option seems to become, control or be controlled.
>
> (Hall, 1992, p.40)

Not only this, but same-sex households are only now beginning to be formed against a background of organised attempts to win social acceptance for this life choice. A patriarchal society fails to provide models for equality; it is also hostile and homophobic in ways which can compound abuse:

> Growing up in a lesbian-hating society, we are very aware that society does not legitimise our relationship. As an abused woman this silenced me further. For my abuser · the fear of being labelled as a lesbian increased her need to control me, to stop me talking to anyone. The fact that this is abuse underpinned by fear rather than something which men take as their right, does not lessen the pain, but without explanations it can increase isolation.
>
> (ibid.)

Feminists and pro-feminist men in the health and welfare professions need to face up to this fact, and to develop a more complex analysis of patriarchal oppression inextricably interlinked with homophobia, racism and other societal abuses of the power to define and pathologise (but still gendered: Kelly, 1991, p.15). Otherwise, we risk giving inadequate help (Research Committee and Staff of London Battered Women's Advocacy Centre, 1993; Champagne *et al.*, 1994; Burstow, 1992). Of crucial practical importance in emergency situations, for example, is the need not to jump to conclusions. One graphic example (Research Committee and Staff of London Battered Women's Advocacy Centre, 1993, p.9) is of the woman taken to casualty by her female abuser who is assumed to be a friend the injured woman has taken along for support, thus denying the latter the opportunity to disclose the true situation in privacy – and hence to seek safety from an abuser who happens to be a woman. In the all-woman context of a refuge, different problems arise. The woman fleeing abuse is not automatically safe from her abuser there, as she would be from a man. Her abuser may pursue her, claiming that she has also been abused and requires help. Staff, pursuing a policy of believing women's accounts, can be placed in a difficult position – although one remedy is to offer both women places in different refuges.

In longer-term work, Burstow (1992, pp.66–71 and 167–71) gives an affirming account of the need for feminist counsellors to work within (and through raising awareness of) an understanding of the additional social and personal pressures facing lesbian couples: ubiquitous homophobia and internalised lesbophobia; the fear of being 'outed', in the absence of employment protection rights, for example, which can also be used as a threat by the abuser; the greater ease of self-defence which makes the victim blame herself as a co-abuser; and so on. She calls for practitioners to be aware both of the similarities and the differences between heterosexual and gay abuse (ibid., p.167). Hammond (1989), for example, teases out, on the one hand, the equal need in all relationship work to take abuse seriously and to avoid victim blaming and, on the other, the additional need for heterosexual counsellors seeing gay and lesbian clients to work on their own homophobia and for gay or lesbian counsellors to ensure that they do not overlook safety issues in their enthusiasm to affirm same-sex partnerships.

CONCLUSIONS

Numerically, by far the greatest incidence of abuse is perpetrated by men against women and it has been men through the ages who have perfected the techniques of terror and domination as well as the rationale that under-pins them. All abuse can still be understood in the context of gendered power relationships where the traditions of masculinity that dominate society are rooted in interdependent sexism and homophobia. Hyper-controlling heterosexual men are controlling and demeaning the feminine side of themselves as well as the women in their lives. (This may be one of the reasons why lesbian women are abused by *male* partners, particularly when the latter have discovered their partners' sexuality.)

This book will engage primarily with the issue of men's abuse of women, and will root its analysis of abuse in an understanding of the patriarchy and of interconnected oppressions. Lesbian and gay abuse will be mentioned from time to time, especially where practitioners need particular awareness, and readers are urged to become more knowledgeable about it by drawing on a growing literature (Research Committee and Staff of London Battered Women's Advocacy Centre, 1993; Champagne *et al.*, 1994; Burstow, 1992). The need to improve professional responses to lesbian and gay service users should be borne in mind at all times, even though the text that follows will primarily use terminology relating to men as abusers and women as those who are victimised by men and who attempt to survive (with an awareness too of the impact on children). The only alternative would be to resort to non-gendered language – as applicable to both genders of abuser and victim/survivor and to both heterosexual and gay relationships – but this cannot be done without sliding into the apparent neutrality associated with 'mutual fighting' which was rejected above *and* into the 'just-like-them' over-simplifications of lesbian and gay abuse exposed by Burstow (1992, e.g. p.167). Readers are asked to work extra hard, then, to hold on to these complexities.

Men's abuse of women is condoned and even applauded by society as natural, understandable, tolerable, deserved, the natural order of things, inevitable, women's lot, part of the price of the marital bargain. Women who attempt to expose or escape it, and social workers and related professionals who attempt to help them or to work with their abusers, will not find it easy because they are swimming against a historical and global tide (Radford and Russell, 1992). The tide may be beginning to turn but plenty of women are still drowning.

Chapter 2

What do we know about domestic violence?

Any book concerned with men's abuse of women must clearly begin by focusing on what women go through and what help can be offered. Women's personal accounts can make one feel overwhelmed and hopeless but they also point to practical and supportive things that social workers can do, like emphasising safety and believing what women say. Better practice starts with listening to a woman's own account and respecting her choices, recognising that they are made under pressure. Only by developing a keen awareness of abuse as a widespread but criminal behaviour, together with a sustainable model for understanding its patriarchal roots, can professionals avoid being part of the problem and help women take power over their lives. There is a long way to go. Although domestic violence is everywhere in the media at present – studio discussions on morning television, tabloid articles on how to spot a controlling husband, radio interviews with prominent researchers – and professions like the police can point to much improved responses, no one is yet mentioning social workers or probation officers as key sources of help. The extent of the problem indicates that we need to ally ourselves with the heightened activity and awareness.

This chapter will explore what is meant by men's abuse of women in relationships, together with the geographical, historical and statistical evidence of its endemic nature – attempting to answer the what, where, why, when and how much questions. It will then go on to explore the who questions, which involves looking at common myths about the causation of abuse and the information available to counter these.

WHAT IS DOMESTIC ABUSE?[1]

Physical abuse

The most familiar form of abuse men inflict on their female partners is physical violence. We are not talking here about the odd slap, though, in the view of the author, there is never any excuse for men hitting women. Furthermore, this is the point at which women should start to get worried.

In an estimated 90 per cent of cases (Hanmer and Stanko, 1985, p.366), assaults begin in this way but continue over time, during which they become more frequent and more severe. Dobash *et al.* (1985, p.144) also found this, with early slaps and punches that resulted in cuts and bruises giving way to being knocked to the floor, kicked and punched. (See also studies listed by Smith 1989, p.16.) More severe injuries then become common, such as fractures, burns, miscarriages caused by violent attacks, internal injuries, attempts to strangle and drown, being pulled around by the hair and having clumps of hair pulled out. Pahl (1985a, p.4) lists damaged eyesight, a ruptured spleen, stab wounds and a fractured skull and cites accounts recorded by Binney *et al.* (1988, p.3) of 'being pushed into fires or through glass, thrown against walls or down stairs, being punched or having hair pulled out'. One woman (in Pahl, 1985a, p.31) describes her head being banged repeatedly against a cupboard so that she needed stitches and an X-ray. She was six months pregnant, was preparing her daughter's birthday party at the time, and her sister was present. Inflicting injuries with objects and weapons of all descriptions also becomes more likely over time: just under a quarter of all incidents in the Islington crime survey (Jones *et al.*, 1986) involved bottles, glasses, knives, scissors, sticks, clubs and other blunt instruments. They inflict terrible injuries, such as those listed in the following record by a woman who was abused for sixteen years until she left her husband:

> I have had a knife stuck through my stomach; I have had a poker put through my face; I have no teeth where he knocked them all out; I have been burnt with red hot pokers; I have had red hot coals slung all over me; I have been sprayed with petrol and stood there while he has flicked lighted matches at me.
>
> (House of Commons, 1975, para. 10)

Ptacek (1988, p.135; also for a series of references) elicited admissions from abusers themselves including: 'dragging by the hair, throwing objects . . . bodily throwing, choking, "beating up", threatening with a knife, and rape' from a group of only eighteen men, a third of whom also admitted to breaking bones or inflicting other substantial injuries. All had been in touch with a men's counselling agency, a third having completed its full programme, but many were still heavily denying, justifying and minimising their abuse; in other words, this account was, if anything, likely to constitute an understatement. Hoff (1990, p.137) includes a description from a man whose violence began with slaps, controlled so as not to hurt too badly, 'but as the beatings got on I just lost my temper and just got hateful toward her'. Hoff suggests (ibid., p.138) that he wanted to control his partner with his violence, and that it was socially acceptable for him to do so. Over time, his inhibitions against hurting her became weaker and he injured her more seriously.

Over the course of a relationship, only 3 per cent of assaults on average are 'low' in physical severity the rest are 'medium' or 'high' in roughly even numbers (Dobash *et al.*, 1985, p.146, reporting research on a refuge sample). Binney *et al.* (1988, cited by Pahl, 1985a, p.4) report 30 per cent of their refuge sample as having experienced life-threatening attacks or having ended up in hospital. The injuries are horrific:

> There was one woman in the refuge we visited in Edinburgh, we were told, who had been 'thrown out of the window by her husband and she had her back broken. She was in hospital for six months, and her husband came to the hospital whilst she was in traction to assault her again.
>
> (House of Commons, 1975, para. 11)

The violence also continues for extended periods. Studies by Pahl (1985a) and Binney *et al.* (1988, p.5) both found that a majority of women in refuges had been subjected to violence for over three years (62 and 73 per cent respectively) and 25 per cent in the latter study had endured it for ten years or more. Often, it goes on until the woman goes into hiding or is killed. A vicar who had abused his wife for 46 years finally took two hours to bludgeon her to death (Dobash and Dobash, 1992, pp.5–6). Women who leave without hiding are at increased risk because their ex-partners pursue them; one constantly violent man stabbed his wife, who had made several attempts to escape, in front of their 6-year-old daughter and claimed in court that he was provoked by his wife's threats to take the child abroad (ibid.).

Browne (1987, cited by Burstow, 1992, p.149) lists warning signs that, together with escalating violence, indicate men who are most likely to end up killing their partners: threats to kill; bringing a knife or gun into the house following threats to kill; locking the woman in the house; multiple injuries inflicted in each attack; killing her pet. A fifth of all homicides are men killing female partners and ex-partners (Morley and Mullender, 1994b, p.2, citing Home Office statistics for 1983 to 1990: see below).

Sexual abuse

Sexual and physical violence frequently become combined in dominating behaviour which includes marital rape (Russell, 1990) – now criminalised, as we saw in the last chapter, under the usual narrow legal definition, but still likely to lead to few cases reaching court – and a wide range of pressurised and coercive sexual activities (Kelly, 1988a and 1988b). These include imposing any kind of intimacy while the woman is still hurting from the violence (i.e. sexual behaviour to which she might consent at other times), and other acts to which the woman does not consent or which she finds degrading or disgusting, such as being photographed in sexual positions against her wishes (Burstow, 1992, p.151), or being forced to have sex with others, with or without her partner watching (ibid.). Physical and sexual abuse may be combined in various ways, as in injuries to the breasts and genital area (Pence, 1987, p.37: sexual abuse segment of the power and control wheel). Frieze (1983) demonstrated this link between sexual and physical abuse with a third of the women in her sample reporting being raped by their violent partners, often accompanied by a beating. (This may be high, as only 9 per cent are reported in Brand and Kidd, 1986.)

Emotional abuse also overlaps with sexual abuse through, for example, taunts about sexual undesirability, openly taking other partners and voicing negative comparisons, and other forms of sexual humiliation and degradation. Hoff describes a man who attacked his wife, aroused her sexually, and then sat and laughed at her (1990, p.60).

Fleming (1989/90), a woman who survived twelve years of rape and forced penetration with objects, in a context of violent abuse, explains in a graphic and moving account that she never told the whole story, even in a refuge, in case the woman she might tell was shocked or disbelieving or thought she had enjoyed it even a little bit. It was only books she was given to read there that taught her the difference between consensual, enjoyable sex and rape. She is now able to work through Women's Aid with women who have had similar experiences to hers. The rationale and the aim of sexually abusive men is to treat their partners as sex objects over whom they exert domination. Fleming's account describes both the lengths to which such men will go, and the strength women can find to survive.

It is only relatively recently that women like Carol Fleming have been given a vocabulary to name sexual violence inflicted by known men and it is still neither known to all nor easy to apply to one's own experiences. One result of this is that surveys will always result in an under-reporting of sexual violence. One form of sexual abuse that is now more widely recognised because of changing public attitudes is marital rape. Of the women in Hall's large London sample (1985, p.33) who had ever been married or lived in a common law marriage, 15 per cent reported having been raped in that relationship. In a similarly large American study (Russell, 1990, p.57) with a random sample, a comparable figure of 14 per cent of those women who had ever been married admitted having been subjected to completed or attempted rape (not including attempted rape during sleep where the wives woke up and stopped it, because this was considered to be so common that it could lead to disbelief and discounting of the figures). The author points out (pp.58–9) that the 14 per cent is an underestimate for other reasons, too, not only because of unwillingness to disclose – and the absence from the sample of high-risk groups who have been killed, have committed suicide, or who are in psychiatric, shelter (refuge), and other institutional settings – but because so many women do not even have a concept of choice concerning sex with their husbands and would not therefore describe it as rape. Even so, husbands and ex-husbands are the commonest category of rapist (p.64; counting only completed rapes). They also repeat their rapes more frequently than any other category of rapist (p.67), for some women hundreds of times, and their rapes are as traumatic as those inflicted by strangers (Chapter 14). Figures for rape amongst self-selected samples (women who all are or have been in abusive relationships) are higher, for example 34 per cent in Frieze's study, rising to 43 per cent when the question was worded as 'forced sex' rather than 'rape' (Frieze, 1980, Table 9, cited in Russell, 1990, pp.61 and 121–2). The most violent, tyrannical men were found in this study to be the most likely to rape.

When given time and support to reflect, women are clear about sexual activity they did not want (Kelly, 1988a, pp.121–2). The threat of violence from a man who has used it before but who, on one particular occasion, does not employ actual physical force or physical resistance, as well as the fact that sex has previously been consensual and may be so again, can confuse definitions for professionals or the courts (ibid.; Maynard, 1993, pp.101–7) and can also lead to minimisation of the problem, regardless of the impact on women themselves. Social workers and probation officers need to learn to listen to women and not to impose rigid categories on what they ask or hear. Women themselves may resist thinking of their partners as rapists (Kelly, 1988a, p.123) but can often clearly describe sexual assaults that are experienced as rape. Skilled and sensitive interviewing, as with all forms of abuse inflicted on all age groups, is crucial not only because of the sensitive nature of the material but because women's coping mechanisms include suppressing incidents they could not name, understand or bear at the time.

Suppressed memories also return to students in class and to professionals attending training events, and therefore support mechanisms are crucial. Examples include: women-only discussions in classes, training events, and research projects; resource lists of outside support networks and referral points such as Rape Crisis and Women's Aid; warnings beforehand that the material is painful and of its possible effects; permission to be selective and self-protective in sharing personal experiences.

Emotional abuse

Constant severe assaults cannot be endured without emotional effects. Chronic emotional distress is a normal, not an abnormal, reaction to this kind of treatment (Dobash *et al.*, 1985, p.144).

Men who have been physically abusive also deliberately use psychological tactics to reinforce their control. Once the fear of further attacks is established, threats, gestures and glares will be enough to maintain the constant atmosphere of fear and necessity for the woman to try and predict his every whim to forestall another attack. Any behaviour that elicits fear can be used, such as shouting, hitting walls, driving recklessly, displaying weapons, stalking, prolonged silence, destruction of objects, injuries to children or pets (inflicting the double torture of making her watch, with the clear implication that she may be next). Women live in constant terror and fear for their very lives.

Men's controlling tactics also include emotional abuse, that is, all the words and actions designed to break the woman's spirit and destroy her self-image and self-esteem. Women survivors not infrequently describe the humiliation and degradation as the most damaging part of their ordeal: 'Physical battering may last from five minutes to two hours, but the mental battering is 24 hours, even while you're asleep' (WAFE, undated b); and: 'I remember one night I spent the whole night in a state of terror, nothing less than terror *all night* .... And that was *worse* to me than getting whacked .... That waiting without confrontation is just so frightening' (Kelly, 1988a, p.120). In Binney *et al.*'s national refuge study (1988, p.4), 68 per cent gave mental cruelty as one of the reasons they left home. It includes constant criticism of the woman and everything she does, both specifically and generally. She may be told that she is stupid, ugly and incompetent; she may be called degrading names and belittled through the ignoring of herself, her needs, her opinions and any previous agreements the couple had reached together; she may be embarrassed in public, constantly accused of actual or intended infidelity; and negative comparisons may be made with other women. At the same time as all this is happening, the blame is constantly shifted onto her, by a man who sees himself as always right and his partner as always wrong and who isolates her from any other influences who could challenge this – such as her family and friends, any education or leisure activities she might pursue on her own, and any professional help. Additional racist, class- or age-based, or disablist slurs will be added where applicable. Most commonly, the woman will be told she is crazy whenever she tries to disagree and this will be taken as proved if she resorts in desperation to any medical help for depression or other emotional result of the constant undermining.

His control also operates through his own moodiness, swinging from aggression to contrition (though the latter is variable, not a clear pattern as some suggest, e.g. Walker, 1977–8), and through possessive jealousy which may look like caring in the early stages of a relationship (giving her lifts everywhere) but becomes a total restriction on her freedom, accompanied by constant questioning of whom she has seen and what she has done, with gross physical 'punishment' for imagined infidelities. These are *his* behaviours and *his* choices. Though the woman may respond by trying to predict what he wants, by seeing love or caring in his better moments and in his jealousy, neither this nor her self-blame makes her equally responsible; nor does it succeed in stopping his violence.

Emotional and psychological abuse is devastating. It closely resembles the torture of hostages (Graham *et al.*, 1988) who are similarly stripped of all freedoms and deprived of sleep, never knowing when the next beating will be. The constant verbal degradation and brainwashing also resemble those used on political prisoners: the woman is constantly told not only that she is ugly, stupid and useless, but that everything she experiences she deserves and has caused. McConnell (1991) draws parallels between the coercion of domestic and sexual services from women by male partners and modern cases of involuntary servitude brought to court in the USA under a constitutional amendment originally designed to outlaw chattel slavery. The level and nature of coercion in three cases of domestic abuse she presents equals or exceeds that in contemporary involuntary servitude cases (ibid., p.32). The woman may have to beg for money to buy food for herself and the children (Pahl, 1993) and for permission to go out; she may even be kept a prisoner: 'I was allowed out occasionally and to pick up the children from school. I was timed, I was watched' (WAFE, undated b). One woman who made the national news in Britain a year or two ago had been discovered in the coal store where she had regularly been locked; the news item was treated as if it was completely unique and bizarre, yet refuges have regular reports of men locking their partners in rooms, cellars or cupboards. Dobash and Dobash (1992, p.270) summarise research findings of techniques of coercion and intimidation which often centre on virtual captivity in the home, complete economic dependence, and unfounded suspicions about any contact with men – including those who necessarily call at the house. Male social workers and probation officers should bear in mind that their presence at the door or in the home may be the cause of further beatings, and also that many women prefer to confide in a female worker.

Not surprisingly, women 'report symptoms of stress, such as lack of sleep, weight loss or gain, ulcers, nervousness, irritability . . . [and] thoughts of suicide' (e.g. Stanko, 1985, p.57). Depression and anxiety are common and make it harder to escape the abuse (ibid.), while self-esteem is damaged so long as the abuse continues, although it can recover (studies summarised in Smith, 1989, pp.18–19). Kennedy (1992, e.g. pp.86–7) describes the way women look who have recently been subjected to this constant emotional damage. They appear flat, devoid of affect, drained of energy and fight – quite unlike someone who has just come through a one-off attack, which may be what courts are used to seeing or how they envisage domestic abuse. This can be very misleading in the courtroom in convincing judges and juries what the woman has been through, but it can also mislead welfare professionals who may expect to see heightened fear or anger.

Women themselves may find emotional abuse particularly difficult to recognise as such at the time, or to name: 'Mental violence is something you can't pinpoint . . . you can't define mental torture. It comes in very funny ways' (Kelly, 1988a, p.120, quoting a woman survivor). Kelly further suggests that terminology is very relevant to help-seeking. If women know only the term 'battered wives', they may not apply the concept to themselves if they are cohabitees who are being mentally tortured. This is important for professionals to remember in their use of language, in their interviewing style (ibid., p.116 on the use of open-ended terms and questions), as well as in records and statistical categories. Abuse covers a range of behaviours, all of them harmful, and we need to bear this in mind when naming it. Specific terms are *not* helpful when they are used to label or blame women, as has happened with 'learned helplessness' (Walker, 1977–8) and 'battered woman syndrome' (Walker, 1983). Emotional damage can be survived and outgrown with appropriate help.

Through all the forms of abuse, it is the physical violence or the anticipation of it that keeps all the other forms of abuse in place. Consequently, the Domestic Abuse Intervention Project in Duluth, Minnesota (referred to hereafter as 'DAIP' or 'Duluth') has portrayed abuse as a wheel, with all the spokes kept in place by physical abuse and the central aim as power and control by the man over the woman (see Figure 1). Between the spokes are listed all the other forms that abuse can take which the Project aims to help women survive and men to cease (through an excellent multi-agency programme which will be returned to at various points in this book).

WHERE DOES ABUSE TAKE PLACE?

Woman abuse is both endemic and prevalent in all continents, cutting across racial, cultural and economic development lines (Dobash and Dobash, 1992, pp.9–11; Davies, 1994). Heise (1989, p.4) reports that 70 per cent of all crimes reported to the police in Peru are of women beaten by their partners; over half the married women in a Bangkok study (Skrobanek, 1986) are regularly physically abused, and Davies includes chapters from Argentina, Eastern and Western Europe, the USA, Pakistan, and Australia, amongst many others. Every piece of research confirms that the problem is also huge in scope. In Canada, one in ten men was estimated to have committed at least one assault against his partner during 1986 (MacLeod, 1989, pp.13–14). A survey of 2,000 women in New Zealand found that 16.2 per cent had been hit by their male partner, more than half of these on three or more occasions and a quarter requiring medical treatment (Gray, 1989, p.4). Statistics for Britain are reported in a later section.

Whatever weapons are to hand will be used, and particular variations on the abusive theme develop in particular cultures. In North America, widescale ownership of firearms lends its mark: all but one of the children in a group the author attended in second-stage (post-emergency) housing in Canada had seen their mothers threatened with guns, while a member of

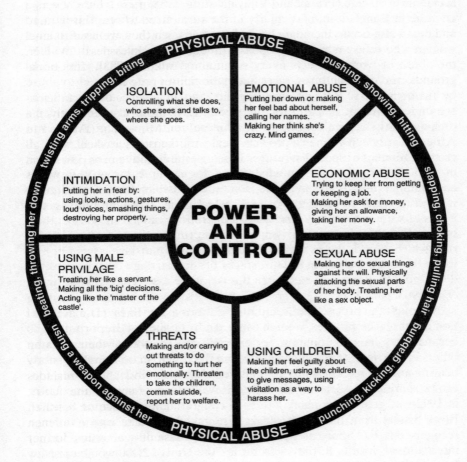

Figure 1 Power and control wheel
Source: Pence, 1987, p. 12

a women's group told of the family dog being shot in front of her with the words 'You'll be next'. Being pushed out of moving cars is also a feature of contemporary life for women experiencing abuse in North America. Kerosene is poured over young women and set alight by husbands and their families in dowry deaths[2] in India which are then passed off as kitchen accidents or suicide (Prasad and Vijayalakshmi, 1988, p.274). Dowry is also an issue in Bangladesh, particularly in the rural areas where ill-treatment and death also occur, including by acid-throwing, which is also used against women who refuse marriage proposals (Shefali, 1988, pp.3–4). In the UK, the abuse of women affects every community: women of all class backgrounds, and of all cultures, races and nationalities are subjected to abuse by male partners. Refuges in every city and in towns and rural areas are under constant demand for their help. Like those in other women's organisations, women's workers in Chinese centres, and in Asian and African Caribbean women's projects, deal with the problem constantly. A growing number of specialist refuges is being established to serve the needs of particular populations – understanding, for example, the ways in which communities may deny and hide domestic abuse, making it harder for women to admit to problems or seek help (Imam, 1994), and the special needs of women who may lose their immigration status if they leave their husbands within a year of arriving in Britain (under the 'primary purpose rule' which regards this as a way of proving that the marriage is genuine), or whose husbands tell them at later stages of the marriage that they will be deported if they leave, even though this is not the case (Home Department *et al.*, 1993, para.36).

Although the precise forms and justifications assumed by male domination differ across cultures, women can learn from one another's campaigns because they have in common, for example, the shaping of their roles by others in marriage, family and society, and the restrictions imposed by child bearing and the responsibility for children (Hanmer, 1993). Successes, too, can be shared: the release of Kiranjit Ahluwalia from prison in this country in 1992 was greeted by many letters of congratulations reaching Southall Black Sisters from India. The struggle to get the issue of men's violence recognised is, like abuse itself, universal. Wife abuse only became a formal international priority in the 1980s during the United Nations' Decade for Women (United Nations, 1986 and 1988; Heise, 1989, p.3; United Nations, 1994). In 1992, a UN Declaration recognised violence against women and children as a human rights issue, and the UN Platform of Action from the Fourth World Conference on Women, held in Beijing in 1995 (United Nations, 1995), built upon this by including violence against women as one of its critical areas of coneren. Domestic abuse is now clearly recognised as one of the major universal ways in which women are subjected to discrimination while men retain 'power, domination and privilege' (Davies, 1994, p.vii), and is being studied and responded to not only in dominant cultures but in native, immigrant and refugee populations (United Nations, 1994, p.2). Across the world, women are organising to take action to protect women from abuse and to work with them to rebuild their lives. Work to oppose men's violence is being undertaken, for example, in comprehensive research and curriculum and economic development work in Papua New Guinea (Bradley, 1994); in women-only groups drawing on spiritual and ceremonial traditions in a Native American reservation in the USA; throughout Zimbabwe by a voluntary project holding workshops; in the Philippines by shelter and counselling services for women (sources: personal correspondence and contacts); and in women's organisations lobbying for a law on protection orders in Malaysia (Ahmad, S., 1990). But wider and more determined action is needed to combat abuse. Mainstream agencies must add their efforts to achieve an integrated response to men's abuse of women. All societies still 'tacitly condone it through their silence or, worse yet, legitimize it through laws, customs, and court opinions that blatantly discriminate against women' (Heise, 1989, p.3).

Women from all over the world agree that the key factors in escaping the violence are income, housing, the civil law, and the criminal justice system. As we saw in the preceding chapter, the UK has seen a recent resurgence of activity, but advances in some of these areas are accompanied by public spending cuts and official suspicion of any work that appears to threaten 'family values'. Women's Aid has always struggled against chronic under-funding from central and local government and this has not changed. Britain has yet to prove that it 'owns' the issue fully, even though woman abuse is now acknowledged as a major area of serious and continual violent crime. Some pressure in this direction is coming from the Council of Europe which formed a Committee on Violence Against Women in 1994, following the issuing of a Declaration and a Plan of Action by its Third Ministerial Conference on Equality between Men and Women in 1993 (ROW Bulletin, Autumn/Winter 1994).

WHEN DID ABUSE START?

For as long as we have a detailed social history of life in this country (and others), it has included accounts of women experiencing abuse at their partners' hands and not being permitted to control their own lives. Subjection and submission were sanctioned by Church and State. Various historical studies are now available: Pleck (1987) for America; May (1978), Tomes (1978) and Clark (1988) for England; Dobash and Dobash (1992) for the history of the women's movement opposing male violence in Britain and the USA in modern times.

Freeman (1979, pp.128–9; see also Smith, 1989, pp.3–5; Maynard, 1993, pp.100–1, and Pahl, 1985a, pp.11–12) provides a brief historical summary. Smith tells how, in 1395, Margaret Neffield of York was refused permission by an ecclesiastical court to separate from a husband who, witnesses testified, had attacked her at different times with a knife and a dagger, had stabbed her in the arm with the dagger and broken a bone. Dobash and Dobash (1981) outline a husband's accepted prerogative and, indeed, perceived duty through the ages to dominate, punish and control his wife, although, if the attacks became too savage, local communities used to come together to shame and ridicule the man if his social standing was not too high. The legal right of a man to 'correct' his wife was not expressly abolished until 1891, with individual judges' pronouncements in court still condoning such chastisement or believing wives accepted it even as recently as the mid-1970s (Freeman, 1979, pp.177–8). The second half of the nineteenth century saw concerted pressure for change, largely from women, though with a tendency to view domestic violence as a working-class problem (as in novels by Dickens and Mrs Gaskell; Freeman, 1979, p.5). Frances Power Cobbe published a pamphlet in 1878 on *Wife Torture in England* which blamed 'incalculable evil and misery' on the notion of a man's wife being treated as his property and argued for separation orders from magistrates' courts. In the same year, the Matrimonial Causes Act gave wives the right to separation orders with maintenance if their husbands had been convicted of aggravated assault and their future safety was in peril.

The suffragettes were also concerned about domestic violence as a symptom of an unequal society, but it then disappeared off the social agenda until the first refuge opened in 1972. Women's Aid groups began to spring up all over Britain, working to establish refuges and later second-stage housing; most are now affiliated to the Women's Aid federations of England, Northern Ireland, Scotland and Wales. The House of Commons Select Committee on Violence in Marriage was established in 1974 (House of Commons, 1975). There are specific references to domestic violence in legislation relating to divorce, injunctions and housing, dating from the 1970s, and in policing directives from the 1980s (see previous chapter). The problem, then, is ages old but most of the solutions we recognise are relatively recent.

HOW WIDESPREAD IS DOMESTIC ABUSE?

Women are abused behind closed doors. There are remarkably few usable estimates of the extent of the problem, partly because it is so hard to be accurate but also because there has not been the political will to fund a large-scale incidence and prevalence study. There has never been a national random incidence study in Britain, in terms either of the number of relationships affected or the frequency of violent attacks in each case, let alone of the other aspects of abuse. What figures there are will be explored below. Estimates for marital rape were given above and suggest that at least 14 to 15 per cent of long-term heterosexual partnerships may be affected.

There are impressionistic sources of data. Numbers of women using refuges and homelessness services, for example, give only the broadest clue as to the numbers actually affected by domestic abuse nationwide, since provision is chronically underfunded and many women are redirected to other forms of provision; many more never hear of or reach such forms of help. The House of Commons Select Committee on Violence in Marriage in 1975 recommended a national minimum of one family place per 10,000 of the population as an initial target (p.xxvi). This has never been achieved and, indeed, the situation is felt to have worsened owing to public housing shortages (Malos and Hague, 1993, e.g. para. 6.2). Any refuge that opens is immediately full. Statistics from Scottish Women's Aid (source: conference hand-out) show 1,810 women and 2,886 children admitted to Scottish refuges during 1990/91, 3,898 turned away, and 11,549 given support and advice only. Between 1992 and 1993, Leeds Women's Aid Refuge did not have a spare bed space for more than one hour (Women Experiencing Violence by Known Men Service Planning Team, 1994, p.2).

We certainly know that domestic abuse is widespread. It affects women of every age and background: 'We've had a woman of seventy four in our refuge . . . we've had a girl of sixteen' (WAFE, undated b), both disabled and able-bodied, Black and white, lesbian and straight, and across all socio-economic classes: 'It seems to go straight across the board from all walks of life. We have a judge's wife, we've had social workers' wives' (ibid.). Evason (1982) found no difference in educational background or social class between single mothers in Northern Ireland who had experienced violence and those who had not. Middle-class women are under-represented in refuges but not amongst those seeking advice about violence (e.g. Pahl, 1985a, pp.47 and 81). More affluent women may be more able to conceal the abuse from public agencies – by using their own income or savings or the support of family or friends to escape – but may find it particularly hard to accept the definition of themselves as abused precisely because it is widely perceived as a problem of the poor. A conversation initiated by one woman who telephoned a refuge is reported as follows: '"I'm not sure if I am a battered wife, I've got a black eye, but I don't think I'm a battered wife" she said. "Why not?" I said, "Well, because I've got plenty of money, and a big car." [But] "I found it a tremendous relief – because I could stop blaming myself"' (ibid., p.82).

Dobash and Dobash (1992, p.5) cite cases in the USA that rocked public assumptions; in particular, it emerged that one of President Reagan's high-ranking officials had abused his wife for eighteen years, and a wealthy New York lawyer did the following to his well-educated wife: 'lumps of hair missing, clusters of small scabs on the bare scalp – were they cigarette burns? Deep ulcers on gangrenous legs. A bruise on the buttock the size of a football. Bruises on her back. A pulverized nose. Jaw broken in two places. Nine broken ribs, a cauliflower ear, a split lip . . . a ruptured spleen, removed in hospital, a broken knee, a bruised neck and innumerable black eyes – 10 in one year – and . . . doctors discovered minor brain damage (ibid., citing the *Guardian*, 2nd January 1989, p.15). Any woman can find herself living with an abuser. The abuse will not go away but will almost certainly increase in intensity and severity. Some men start during courtship, others appear to change on marriage (Pahl, 1985a, p.48), as if they regard the marriage licence as a licence to hit.

Research evidence: the statistics

Although it is incomplete, there is certainly research evidence to uphold the widespread existence of domestic abuse as defined in this book. In a representative sample, Andrews and Brown (1988, p.308), researching in Islington, found that 25 per cent of women interviewed had been abused during their adult lives, almost all severely (92 per cent) – typically punched, kicked and beaten up. Two-thirds reported violence by their male partner as a 'regular occurrence'. Research undertaken in Hammersmith and Fulham by locating women through doctors' surgeries and community women's groups found that 48 per cent had been repeatedly criticised, 35 per cent had been punched or shoved and 29 per cent hit, 29 per cent had been threatened with violence, 18 per cent had been beaten up, 13 per cent had been threatened with death and the same number forced to have sex, and 14 per cent had been threatened and 10 per cent attacked with a weapon (McGibbon and Kelly, 1989, p.26).

Probably the most useful study conducted in Britain to date is a random-sample survey undertaken in north London (Mooney, 1994, Table 5). In this, 30 per cent of women reported violence by a current or former partner or boyfriend more severe than being grabbed, pushed or shaken; 27 per cent had been threatened, 23 per cent raped, and 37 per cent had experienced mental cruelty. Only small differences were found by class or ethnicity (ibid., Tables 11 and 13). The author comments that these are disturbingly high figures in all categories and mentions the need for all agencies, including social services, to respond (ibid., p.23 and 27).

Research undertaken by surveying men also confirms that violence against women partners is commonplace. Mooney presented men with vignettes of potential conflict between partners; 63 per cent did not rule out using violence in one or more of the situations, about half said they would do so in up to two, and 17 per cent said they would do so in every example (ibid., p.63). Nineteen per cent of the men said they actually had used physical violence against their partner in at least one of the range of situations described. There were no appreciable class differences (ibid., Table 22); ethnicity was not reported.

Police statistics

The male abusers and their victims are a minority of a minority in police statistics; this reflects the few assaults reported to the police and the minority of reports recorded as crimes. Woman abuse is an enormously under-reported area of offending (Dobash and Dobash, 1979; Hanmer and Stanko, 1985; Worrall and Pease, 1986, p.123). Researchers who have interviewed victims estimate that between 2 per cent (Dobash and Dobash, 1979, p.164 – from 1980 edition) and 27 per cent (Jones *et al.*, 1986, p.88) of domestic assaults are reported to the police. The British Crime Survey of 1992 puts the figure at a fifth of all incidents (in Home Office 'Domestic Violence Factsheet', April 1995). It must be remembered, too, that only specific, identifiable *incidents* are ever reported as crimes. The constant terrorising that goes on between each assault is equally a part of living with male abuse but is not measurable in the same way.

Any crime that is chronic and all crime between intimates is under-reported. The reasons women do not report incidents to the police include reasons related to the police themselves, for example their failure to talk to the woman on her own so that she cannot say what has happened (Hough and Mayhew, 1983, p.21), or negative views and low expectations women hold of the police, e.g. because of anticipated racist and/or sexist responses (Mama, 1993, p.135; Stanko, 1985). Other reasons relate to the behaviour of the abuser – his threats, or his forcible confinement of the woman in the house and keeping her away from the telephone (Dobash *et al.*, 1985, p.153). Still others relate to the woman herself, though they must be understood within the context created by the abuser. She may feel ashamed (Hough and Mayhew, 1983, p.21), or partly to blame (Dobash *et al.*, 1985, pp.152–3); she may prefer to deal with the matter in another way (Worrall and Pease, 1986, p.122). She may wish to keep it private for her own or her partner's sake (Dobash *et al.*, 1985, p.153). She may be too badly injured or too distressed to call the police (Kennedy, 1992), and, early on, she may believe the man's promises that he will not do it again (Dobash *et al.*, 1985, p.150). Finally, she may not define the incident as abusive (Pahl, 1985a, p.82; Kelly, 1988a, pp.119 and 123–4), or as criminal (Hanmer and Saunders, 1984, p.33ff; Smith, 1989, p.7), or as serious enough to report (Hough and Mayhew, 1983). In fact, the assaults women experience are not less serious than those reported by men (Worrall and Pease, 1986, p.122).

In relation to the pattern of repeated assaults, it is clear that women are unlikely to call the police on every occasion and that, if either the response they receive or its eventual outcome (or both) is unhelpful, they may be deterred from calling again (although others, such as neighbours, may do so) – and, of course, it is for the woman to decide whether summoning the police is likely to make things better or worse. For these many reasons, then, domestic abuse is notably under-reported.

As the police take domestic violence more seriously, and publicise the changes involved, it appears that more women are reporting abuse. But large rises claimed by the police (e.g. a 66 per cent increase in reported domestic violence over a year mentioned by Inspector Shirley Tulloch of the Metropolitan Police on the television programme *The Time, The Place*, ITV, 22nd March 1993) start from a very low base and still probably represent a minority both of women and of incidents. Added to this, there are still major failings in achieving arrests and prosecutions, in prosecuting for sufficiently serious offences ('breach of the peace' and 'threatening behaviour' are far too common), and in attracting sentences that are likely radically to affect men's behaviour or women's lives (Glass, 1995).

Of those crimes that *are* reported to the police, only a minority are, in fact, recorded as crimes (Edwards, 1989, pp.201–6). Smith (1989, p.8) cites Edwards' study (1986a and 1986b) of two London boroughs in which 12 per cent of all reported cases were written up in a crime report but 80 per cent of those were later 'no-crimed', i.e. not pursued. And, since this figure starts from only the reported incidents (see above), this could be 2.4 per cent of 2 per cent – i.e. 0.048 per cent of all domestic assaults on women – or 2.4 per cent of 27 per cent – i.e. 0.648 per cent of all domestic assaults on women – and those figures still do not count other forms of abuse that would not always fit the definition of a crime but do form part of a pattern of control and intimidation. It is true that, since the improvements in policing domestic violence have begun to take hold (see Chapter 1, this volume), there has been a steep climb in recorded incidents. In the Metropolitan Police area, for example, these increased from hundreds in the mid-1980s to 11,420 in 1993 (parliamentary answer given by David Maclean, Home Office Minister, on 26th October 1994). Nevertheless, arrests and prosecutions seem not to be rising at so fast a rate which indicates that more work is needed both by the police and the Crown Prosecution Service (and equivalents around the UK). In fact, neither the official statistics on recorded crime or sentencing provide much help in arguing for improved services for women since they fail to identify domestic violence as a separate category, or to identify the relationship between offender and victim.

Recent research has gone further back than police recorded statistics to circumvent the gaps they leave in our knowledge. Some information comes direct from the general public, in research interviews about crime they have experienced – whether reported or not. The British Crime Survey found that one in four of the assaults it uncovered in 1987 was domestic (Davidoff and Dowds, 1989, p.14, cited in Morley and Mullender, 1994b, p.2), and that 56 per cent of all assaults on women were domestic as compared with 8 per cent of assaults on men. The 1992 British Crime Survey revealed that only one in five assaults was reported to the police ('Domestic Violence Factsheet', April 1995) – at most, since some of the same obstacles prevent women from confiding in research interviewers as from calling the police.

Another approach, adopted by a team at Manchester University, has been to go directly to police incident logs or message pads to find out about calls when they first come in to the police, before decisions are taken as to whether to record the incidents as crimes. Over 25 months from February 1989 to March 1991, nearly 12 per cent of all calls to the police in Norris Green, Liverpool were domestic (Pease *et al.*, 1991). Such calls also keep coming because this is a repeat crime: its incidence is higher than its prevalence (more crimes per head than victims per head of the population). Naturally, then, a proportion of women call the police on multiple occasions – unsurprisingly, as Dobash *et al.* (1985, pp.143 and p.164) report 109 women being assaulted approximately 32,000 times throughout their married lives, or about twice a week. Pease's team has logged calls to the police concerning domestic violence, demonstrating that 35 per cent of all households call again within five weeks and, after a second reported incident, 45 per cent call a third time within a further five weeks (Lloyd *et al.*, 1994, p.3). A household that has called twice is virtually certain to call again within a year (Pease *et al.*, 1991, p.4). The British Crime Survey also shows a clear pattern of repeated reporting of violence (Home Office factsheet). Clearly, this is a major area of work for the police and will increasingly be so for the probation service. The challenge is, firstly, to computerise police data so as to make links between calls but, secondly, not to let this mean that the police respond with less alacrity or concern to repeated calls. Women die as a result of escalating violence.

Domestic violence is rarely a one-off event. In a study by Andrews and Brown (1988, p.308), in London, two-thirds of those who reported domestic violence said that the assaults happened regularly. Attacks also tend to increase in frequency and severity over time (e.g. Hanmer and Stanko, 1985, p.366, summarising other studies). The violence consequently features heavily in women's reasons for ending their relationships. Figures ranging from 40 per cent amongst recently divorced people interviewed in Bristol by Borkowski *et al.* (1983, p.26), to 59 per cent of the divorced and separated women in Painter's UK sample (1991, p.44), reported violence in their relationships. Evason recorded 56 per cent in Northern Ireland (1982, p.7). Separating often does not end the abuse, however. After Pahl's sample of women left the refuge where she contacted them, 31 per cent were subjected to further violence by their original abusers (Pahl, 1985a, p.62) and 50 per cent had to call the police. Of the women in Mooney's north London survey (1994, p.38, Table 10 and p.39) who had experienced 'more severe' physical violence, 34 per cent were no longer living with their partners when the last incident occurred and, for 6 per cent, the violence started only after the breakdown of the relationship. Women are often at greatest risk when they are attempting to leave or seeking outside help with a view to doing so (e.g. Browne and Williams, 1989). Men track down ex-partners who have gone into hiding, for example using contact with the children as a means to trace their mothers and continue their violence (see Chapter 7, this volume). It is terrifying for women to be pursued and to live in this constant danger (Browne, 1987, p.115). Almost a third of women murdered by male spouses in England and Wales in 1986 and 1987 had already separated (Edwards, 1989, p.200). In other words, this is a highly dangerous time and should always be treated with due caution. Professionals should never, for example, disclose a woman's whereabouts to her ex-partner or his representative without her express permission – even for the most plausible of reasons concerning the children or solicitor's business – or pressurise her into accepting a meeting with him (see Chapter 7, this volume). We should trust women when they fear violent men at whatever point in the relationship. Each year from 1983 to 1990, between 42 and 49 per cent of all female homicide victims in England and Wales were killed by current or former partners or lovers, in contrast to between 7 and 11 per cent of male victims; and for most years during that period, about a fifth of *all* homicide victims were women killed by men in these categories (Morley and Mullender, 1994b, p.2, calculated from Home Office, 1992, p.88, Table 4.4b). Men are a major cause of women's deaths. Men are also, arguably therefore, a major cause of preventable deaths but only if we are prepared, as a nation, to accord the issue of domestic abuse far greater seriousness and to take more effective action to stop it.

Both social workers and probation officers have a role to play in this, as this book will attempt to highlight. Both professional groups also need to be aware that, when they interview a woman who talks about violence, the statistics lend weight to taking what she says very seriously indeed. The figures point, too, to the likelihood that, in work of any kind with populations of women, there will be a great deal of hidden abuse in their lives. Skills in questioning women directly about abuse, and helping them to work out the best alternatives, can contribute to preventing further abuse and saving lives.

WHY DOES IT HAPPEN? THE MYTHS (AND FACTS) OF CAUSATION

As we shall see in Chapter 9, which deals with direct work with abusive men, one of the most notable factors to emerge from talking to men who have abused their partners is the degree to which they are capable of denying responsibility for what they have done and minimising what they are prepared to admit about its impact (Hearne, 1994). Despite having been in contact with a men's counselling agency which aimed at confronting them to take responsibility for their actions, all but one of eighteen men interviewed by Ptacek (1988, p.142) for example, claimed diminished control over their actions. They blamed drugs, alcohol and uncontrollable anger – the typical stuff of anger management and alcohol abuse groups to which such men might easily be referred without ever needing to engage with the social structural issues underlying men's abuse of women. The danger is that abusive men will grasp at any excuse for their behaviour, and there are many half-baked theories of causation which give them ample scope. Like the abusers themselves, wider society – and the welfare agencies that serve it – tends too often to treat men as if they are less than fully to blame and women as if they share the blame for domestic abuse. The latter tendency can be summed up as 'blaming the victim' and – as a wider social trend that involves focusing on those affected by social problems instead of their macro-social structural causes – it is beautifully summarised in the book of that name by William Ryan (1971). Meanwhile, choosing to ignore the complacency and domination of men as a gender, there is a tendency for criminal justice and welfare agencies to regard the few men against whom action is unavoidably taken – those who take abuse to its logical conclusion and kill, for example, or who happen to come before the courts – as the few bad apples in the barrel. Action must be taken against them, runs the thinking, or they might turn the whole barrelful bad. In fact, the barrel – the patriarchy – is already bad and what we really need is a new barrel.

There are a range of these theories blaming the abuse on individual psychological or physiological factors in either perpetrators or victims, some with psychoanalytic or psychosocial and others with behavioural roots (Harway, 1993). They tend to have been formulated primarily in North America and to have coincided with attempts to dilute men's abuse of women into a depoliticised, individualised and professionalised issue (Pagelow, 1992, p.88), which is the proper province of therapists and clinical researchers rather than social and political activists and feminists. A selection of the most popular theories will now be explored. Their chief danger in Britain is that they tend to pervade popular and, too frequently, professional thinking in numerous direct and indirect ways.

THEORIES ABOUT MEN

Psychological theories

They are sick or mentally ill

'The conventional liberal/psychological view of male violence sees it . . . as the behaviour of a few "sick" or psychologically deranged men' (Maynard, 1993, p.109). Individual male pathology has been sought by researchers, sometimes in physiological areas ranging from organic or biochemical brain abnormalities to dietary deficiencies (summarised by Dobash and Dobash, 1992, p.236), and more frequently in psychological functioning, but no consistent patterns have been found (Bograd, 1988b, p.17). Ptacek (1988, p.139) makes the enormously telling point that such theories allow the male professional to carry out his work without questioning broader male/female relationships, including his own: 'In a traditional setting I would have more barriers to separate me from such men. They would be seen as borderline personality disorders, as suffering from psychological dysfunctioning, as deviant. This would keep me from recognizing the common background we share' (ibid.). He also realised that seeing himself as the 'good guy' and abusers as the 'bad guys' (the 'bad apples'), and wanting to protect women from them, were also symptomatic of distancing himself from the issue of men's control over women.

Psychological explanations are more common than physiological ones in the literature and tend to focus on allegedly uncontrollable anger which is seen as rooted in unresolved family conflicts, primitive aggressive reactions, the submerged fear of the bully, insecure dependence on women, or any other form of internal stress (summarised by Dobash and Dobash, 1992, p.237). The man is mad or sad rather than bad; if he is emotionally disturbed, he is not fully responsible for his actions. He may believe he should be forgiven by society, his partner and himself; indeed, he can even gain the moral high ground by showing that he is willing to change by entering therapy (see Chapters 7 and 9, this volume). Maynard (1993, p.110) cites American studies which, in fact, failed to demonstrate particularly marked degrees of psychological disturbance in wife abusers. Above all, woman abuse is too prevalent to be the deviance of a few; it is far more likely to exist on a continuum with the psychology and actions of all men (Bograd, 1988b, p.17).

Sin

A variation on the above theme is sinfulness: the sickness of the soul.

> [M]y priest never really gave me any out, no other way to look at it. He'd just talk about how we both had to pray for Jack because he was a lost soul. . . . It was as though no one talked about what he was doing or why he was doing it. It was like some sin in him that he had nothing to do with.
>
> (An abused wife quoted in Pence, 1987, p.34)

This is dangerous because it made Jack feel he was 'rotten to the core', which is not a good basis for working on change. Also, he enlisted his wife's sympathy for this state of being and she, who knew 'He was mean and he could be very violent, but he wasn't really rotten to the core', was encouraged to boost his male ego. Neither her safety needs nor his actions were confronted and no links were made with the widespread nature of abuse in society.

Loss of control

This is a very popular notion amongst abusers themselves and must be confronted. A groupworker describing men introducing themselves and their reasons for attendance to a court-mandated abusers' group wrote:

> The first man said he was there because he had a short fuse. The next said he was there because he had an anger problem. Another said he exploded. . . . I began to wonder to myself if this was a batterers' group or not. Aren't these men here because they beat up women?

> (ibid.)

Ptacek (1988, pp.142–52) also has some very characteristic quotations from men talking in these terms:

> When I got violent, it was not because I really wanted to get violent. It was just because it was like an outburst of rage.

> [A]nything would set me off. Anything. I was like uncontrollably violent. I would slap her, knock her down, choke her, and call her a slut and a whore.

> A blowout is where I lose, I just lose everything. I would just blank out, more or less. You know, like there would be a gap in between where I wouldn't actually remember. You know, like all I could remember seeing is like white, little twinkled white, red, like lights. That's all I can remember. That's a blowout.

Anger management groups positively encourage men to think in this way (see Chapter 9, this volume). Consequently, they teach men refined excuses and a kind of pop-psychology rationale for their behaviour. There is no difference between the concepts that Ptacek quotes from abusive men and those in the clinical literature, except that the latter use longer words:

'I had no control over myself' = 'poor impulse control'
'eruptions' and 'blowouts' = 'paroxysmal rage attacks'

> (based on Ptacek, 1988, p.152)

Any loss of control model fails to explain target choice: why men hit women, in private, rather than other people whenever they feel annoyed. In Ptacek's interviews (1988, p.143), 17 out of 18 men claimed loss of control, but only 5 out of 18 were violent outside of the family as well as in it. Furthermore, abusers contradict themselves: 'While the men claim that their violence is beyond rational control, they simultaneously acknowledge that the violence is deliberate and warranted' (p.153). The abuser wants to hurt and frighten his partner who, he claims, provoked him, and he feels entitled to punish her for not being a good wife (pp.144–50). He is usually able to stop short of killing, unlike someone in a frenzy of rage (Bograd, 1988b, p.17), and even to choose his level of violence (e.g. Straus *et al.*, 1980, pp.45–6, describe a man who considered it acceptable to hit but not to stab) and to place his blows on parts of the body that do not show. Further contradictions include the later playing down of the injuries and the woman's fear – unnecessary if he was blameless – and the failure of 'loss of control' to explain other admitted actions that take time to perform, like writing a series of threatening letters, or lying in wait for the woman and her new boyfriend (Ptacek, 1988, pp.145–7 and 151). Abuse is indeed all about control but, far from being loss of control, it is about controlling the will of another – the woman being abused (McConnell, 1991, p.3).

Transgenerational transmission, or the 'cycle of violence'

The Select Committee on Violence in Marriage (House of Commons, 1975) was particularly interested in the supposed intergenerational transmission of violence because it sat in the era of Sir Keith Joseph's 'cycle of poverty' when there was major research investment in trying to blame 'problem families' for continually recreating their own misery and disadvantage (see also Ryan, 1976 edition, p.7). Erin Pizzey, creator of the first refuge in Chiswick but quickly the despair of the refuge movement for her non-feminist views, gave the Select Committee what it wanted to hear when she spoke of 'the violence that actually transforms a generation of children into another generation of wife batterers' (House of Commons, 1975, vol. 2: 3; see Dobash and Dobash, 1992, pp.114–18 for a fuller account).

Since then, a number of careful reviews of the research literature have appeared which reveal the reality to be far less simple (see, for example, Pagelow, 1984, Chapter 7; Stark and Flitcraft, 1985, pp.151–8; Okun, 1986, pp.59–63 and 110–12; Kaufman and Zigler, 1987; Widom, 1989). The over-all conclusion from this work is that empirical studies that have actually compared adult perpetrators or victims with those believed not to fall into these categories do often find some difference in the expected direction, but that the differences tend to be small and the studies flawed (see below) and over-deterministic. Furthermore, whatever they may or may not have established about the aetiology of abuse, they are of no predictive value in individual cases in practice. It is of crucial importance to explain this to families with members who were brought up with violence or who are currently abusive. Human beings *always* have choices (and hence responsi-bility for their behaviour); we are not pre-programmed like a machine. Indeed, people who have lived with abuse may have more motivation for avoiding it later in life since they have seen the damage it can inflict.

Reviews of the research have shown it to be methodologically flawed. Very often, in the studies on which the claims for a 'cycle' have been founded, percentages of adult perpetrators or adult victims of abuse found to have had violent childhoods fall below 50 per cent. This means that, in many studies, the *majority* of current abusers and victims come from backgrounds defined as non-violent so, clearly, some other factor or factors in the past or present must be of more importance. This is almost always true of studies of women – who clearly have as much chance of rejecting their supposed destiny as of meeting it. The findings are clouded by the fact that we do not know for certain the prevalence of violence in the general population (see above). Male abuse is common enough, though, to be perpetrated in large numbers of women's adult relationships whether they expect it to or not, and none of the studies has established cause and effect between the past and the present. We can, therefore, virtually discount any notion of a transmitted 'cycle' affecting women.

Turning to studies of men, there is at first sight more reason to believe in the cycle of violence hypothesis – but clearly in relative rather than absolute terms since percentages, though higher on the whole, still vary widely between studies and can *never* be used in a predictive fashion for a particular individual (nor to excuse any particular man's behaviour). A range of methodological flaws in the research, however, means that it cannot be trusted even to indicate a general truth about men. Many studies use samples from clinical populations (i.e. those receiving treatment or help of some kind) so are likely to be unrepresentative; the interpretations implied by the men having sought professional help, and by the form that help may be taking, also affect the responses they give to research questions (rather like dreaming Freudian dreams for Freudian therapists). Studies often lack control groups so cannot claim to have established cause and effect. Those that do have comparison groups tend to find *small* differences in the predicted direction but remain unable to establish cause and effect with certainty since any number of other factors could be clouding the picture. Furthermore, the research questions people about the past; retrospective data are suspect not only because people may not remember clearly, but because those questioned have had ample time to impose their adult understandings (contaminated by all the myths explored in this chapter) onto childhood events. Most damningly, there is such vagueness in deciding what counts as growing up with abuse that it is impossible to compare one study with another or to say that the researchers have clearly divided off an abusive population from one that most of us might fall into. Different studies include, for example, having experienced severe physical or sexual abuse, routine physical punishment, psychological abuse, physical or emotional neglect; or having witnessed fathers assaulting mothers and/or mothers assaulting fathers, or unspecified 'parental violence'.

Nevertheless, such strong claims are made by researchers that professionals need to exercise an equally firm influence in remembering that human matters are generally far too complex to be explained away with a single theory. For example, Straus *et al.*'s claim of 'striking evidence for the idea . . . that violence by parents begets violence in the next generation' (Straus *et al.*, 1980, pp.112–13) depends on data showing that the sons of the most violent parents have a rate of 'wife-beating' of 20 per cent compared to 2 per cent (p.101). But this could equally well be read as showing that the overwhelming majority from all the groups with violent childhoods are not now violent towards their partners – 80 per cent in the above example. Social workers and probation officers might well be more interested in what keeps this 80 per cent of men non-violent, and in using this figure to motivate abusive men to change their behaviour. Further, Stark and Flitcraft (1985, p.157) demonstrate from the Straus *et al.* findings that 'a current batterer is more than twice as likely to have had a "non-violent" rather than a "violent" childhood (a ratio of 7:3) and seven times more likely to have come from a "non-violent" home than from a home classified as "most violent"'.

Clearly, none of this bears out the thesis that 'the majority of today's violent couples are those who were brought up by parents violent toward each other' (Straus *et al.*, 1980, p.100) and abusive men cannot take refuge in such an assumption. Therapy and couples counselling are dangerous if they encourage men to focus on their family of origin as a supposed explanation for their violence (see Chapters 7 and 9, this volume): 'I know my husband used to tell me he beat me because he was working out a deep hatred he held for his mother and when he hit me it really had nothing to do with me' (in Pence 1987, p.34). This man has been given the perfect excuse for denying responsibility for his violence against his partner. Re-educational men's groups that confront violence using a feminist analysis will not allow family of origin work in group time; it has to be undertaken in separate therapy or counselling time. The 'cycle of violence' tries to blame family influences alone rather than a social context which is ineffective in tackling abuse and which, in much media and popular portrayal, still actively condones it. Influential family members may, of course, have upheld these negative attitudes towards women and, in that sense, have been part of the problem.

Drink

One of the most commonly held popular views of the cause of domestic abuse blames alcohol. Ptacek's self-report interviews with 18 abusive men excel in the 'demon drink' category of excuses:

> It was all booze. I didn't think. I didn't think at all. I was just like a madman. It was temporary insanity. I really, all's I really wanted to do was crush her. There was nothing there but – I wanted to cause pain and mess her looks up.
>
> (Ptacek, 1988, p.144)

In fact, there *is* a clear intention here to abuse, as well as inconsistency in the man's account. Drink may play a role in abuse but is certainly not a simple cause. Most tellingly, the same man may be violent drunk or sober (Pahl, 1985a, p.29) and roughly even numbers of sober as drunken men are violent: drinking accompanied violence for 48 per cent in Gelles' study (1974) while 52 per cent of abusers had drunk heavily in Pahl's work (1985a, p.39). Smith (1989, p.29) cites other studies that failed to demonstrate a link. Drink cannot therefore be a sufficient explanation.

> He was a drinker but drink didn't make it worse so it wasn't the drink. We look for something to blame. I've just found out his brother's the same.
>
> (woman in refuge, research interview by the author and co-researcher)

> These assaults did not just take place when he was drunk but at any time; early in the morning; late at night; in the middle of the night he would drag me out of bed and start hitting me.
>
> (Mrs X in House of Commons, 1975, para. 10)

Also, even if some studies do show more drinkers being violent to their partners (Kaufman Kantor and Straus, 1987, p.224: a national random sample survey in the USA reported under the memorable title: 'The "Drunken Bum" theory of wife beating'), this does not explain why many drunken men do not abuse (80 per cent of heavy and 'binge' drinkers did not hit their wives at all during the year of this survey: ibid.), nor why there is target choice in hitting a woman (see above). It is more likely that drink is, for some men, an intervening variable: men drink to give themselves dutch courage or permission to be violent, or to provide an excuse to call on after the event. They can deny any memory of the attack or say they lost control and did not really mean it (McGibbon and Kelly, 1989, p.3.2); some partners believe them and hope they will change if they stop drinking. But men are using drink to disinhibit inhibitors they have already decided to disobey (Gelles, 1974, p.117; Pahl, 1985a, p.40). Another one of Ptacek's interviewees explains this process:

> It's taken the edge off my self-control. That's what I will call it, being intoxicated. It's taken my limits off me and let me do things and become disruptive in a way I would not become. I can get angry with people, really violent, stone sober. But the more I was drinking on a day-to-day basis, the more easy that was to come across.
>
> (Ptacek, 1988, p.142)

This quotation is interesting in backing the view that the same man can be violent drunk or sober, and that he drinks to feed violence he has already chosen to pursue. Kaufman Kantor and Straus (1987, p.224) found that most incidents in their study took place with the abuser sober and concluded that alcohol was neither a necessary nor a sufficient cause of woman abuse; cultural approval of violence appeared to be heavily implicated for these men.

None of the above should be taken to suggest that men ought not be given help with alcohol or other substance misuse problems, but this needs to be undertaken quite separately from work on their abusiveness (without undermining the latter in any way) because alcohol treatment programmes will not stop abuse. Women experiencing abuse may also turn to alcohol or drugs to anaesthetise the physical and emotional pain. Here again, they may require help if their use becomes problematic but, for them too, this is a side issue to their need for an effective response to the abuse, including safety planning.

Psychosocial theories

A variation on the psychological approach is to claim that men become individually abusive in response to social and environmental pressures on them in the form, for example, of poverty, bad housing, poor living standards, unemployment or exploitation in the workplace, racism, educational underachievement, unfulfilled aspirations in a consumerist society, and/or a lack of hope for the future (Gelles, 1983; Smith, 1989, p.25). These pressures are considered to lead to frustration and stress which, in turn, lead to abuse. The corollary would be that more affluent and successful men would not abuse, whereas this is not the case (Mooney, 1994). It is also not the case that men stop abusing when pressures are lifted; the typical pattern is of an escalation of violence once it has begun (see above).

This is not to say that material problems do not matter, or even that unemployment, poor housing and poverty might not act as contributory factors to violence (perhaps, for example, because they threaten men's dominant role in the household: Pahl, 1985a, p.43; see also Smith, 1989, p.26), but they cannot take away men's responsibility for their own actions or explain why many men facing poverty and unemployment are *not* abusive. One methodological problem is that much research has taken refuge-based samples of women who tend to come predominantly from poorer backgrounds (Pahl, 1985a, p.47; women with savings, an income or more affluent familes can sometimes escape in other ways) and who, not surprisingly, speak of issues such as money and inadequate housing exacerbating stress and rows (e.g. ibid., pp.41, 42–3, and Smith, 1989, p.15). Furthermore, as with so much of the research claiming to establish cause and effect in domestic abuse, samples are often small and unrepresentative, and comparison groups are not used (Maynard, 1993, pp.110 and 112). Nor can backing for the theory safely be derived from the disproportionate numbers of men from lower socio-economic groups, including Black men, who are arrested for abusive assaults and who appear in criminal statistics since this may say more about policing practices; the police tend to police the poor and Black communities (Mama, 1993, p.135). This may be one reason why Mooney (1994, p.50) found that working-class women called least upon the police of all class groupings in her study, and had higher reporting rates to other agencies. The police already represent a negative presence in their lives and in the lives of their communities so poor women and Black women may tend to avoid calling the police when they need help. Violence is grossly under-reported in all social strata and women with higher social standing are more likely to keep it hidden both from the police and other agencies (ibid.); their abusers may take more care that the bruises do not show or may favour psychological abuse (Pagelow, 1981). When general populations are interviewed, class differences virtually disappear (Andrews and Brown, 1988, p.308, note 1; Mooney, 1994, pp.40–2; Pagelow, 1981).

Also, the psychosocial theories fail to explain *why* stress should lead to violence and, in particular, to gendered violence: why it is virtually always men who hit, why those men hit women particularly (Walby, 1990, p.134), and why they hit women who are their social equals not their class enemies (Maynard, 1993, p.113). The latter factors can be understood only by taking a feminist view of gender inequalities in society: women are disproportionately the targets of men's physical abuse and coercion (Bograd, 1988b, p.19). This is also the only explanation that can satisfactorily encompass both the persistent and escalating nature of abuse (as men increasingly exercise their domination), and its combination of physical, sexual and emotional control – a pattern that simply does not equate with sudden loss of anger under stress. Hearn's interviews with violent men suggest that men are 'knowledgeable actors, able to reflect on their violence' (1994, p.52). Violence is not a problem for men unless it evokes a negative reaction from other men (ibid.). Only when it starts to have an adverse impact on their own lives – in criminal or civil justice or employment terms, for example – are they likely to exercise the choice to stop it.

THEORIES ABOUT WOMEN

Blaming the victim

The equivalent of 'bad apple' theories about men, which deflect our attention from wider social tolerance of abuse, are 'blaming the victim' theories about women. Women are seen as inviting violence in many and various ways which will be explored in turn below. Maynard (1993, pp.110–11) points out the naivety and insidiousness of any view that ignores both male domination and power and the prevalence of male abuse by substituting men as the victims, either of their own supposedly sick or

vulnerably aggressive natures or, here, of women's alleged unreason-
ableness. It should be noted, then, that blaming the victim not only
implicates women as at least partially responsible for their own abuse, but
also invites us to feel sympathy for their abusers. This may sound bizarre,
but will be familiar to anyone who has listened in court to the defence
lawyer (and sometimes the judge) during a case of sexual violence.

It is worth tracing the concept of 'blaming the victim' back to Ryan's
original formulation (1971). Victims get blamed for the failings of their
social superiors, and the solutions favoured by the powerful to tackle the
resultant social problems compound this tendency by focusing also on the
victims. We have become somewhat more subtle over the years. Just as our
society has progressed from believing in an innate inferiority of Black
people to blaming the socially deprived Black child for not learning
anything (even in a grossly under-resourced school with an irrelevant
curriculum where racism is rife), we no longer believe that women are
chattels without a separate existence in the law – but we still ask why
women are abused even though they are routinely treated as second-class
citizens by men who hold economic and social power. Too often, research
questions and practice solutions are applied *as if* individual victims were to
blame: they focus on the educationally underachieving child or on the
woman experiencing abuse rather than on schools and the school system
or on abusive men and male/ female relationships in their social context.
One result is that women themselves are encouraged to believe the victim-
blaming messages from their abusers and from wider society, and to feel
guilty enough to go on enduring the abuse. A key part of any intervention
with a woman experiencing or attempting to leave abuse – whether by a
duty social worker or a women's support group facilitator – has to be to
emphasise that she is not responsible for the abuse and that her abuser is
guilty of criminal behaviour that society will no longer tolerate.

She deserves it/she provokes it

Women are frequently portrayed as inciting abuse by their own behaviour
– typically nagging or, as Dobash and Dobash put it (1979, p.133):
'continued discussion once the husband has made up his mind'. Joseph
McGrail received a suspended sentence for manslaughter on the grounds of
provocation because his wife had, for ten years, drunk heavily and then
insulted and sworn at him. In February 1991, he kicked her so hard that she
died of internal bleeding. The judge commented that living with his wife
'would have tried the patience of a saint' and allowed this to lessen his
culpability for the killing (Kennedy, 1992, p.205). Similarly with Rajinder
Bisla who, in March 1992, strangled his 'nagging' wife in front of his three
children. Courts are equating women's words with, and regarding them as
deserving of, men's (fatal) violence . As Ptacek argues (1988, p.145), in the

view of the courts 'his retaliatory behaviour is acceptable, her verbal excesses are not'. Other common 'provocations' cited are adultery and failing in wifely duties (the latter explanation for abuse accepted by husbands and social workers alike in Maynard, 1985, pp.133–5). Yet, as Ptacek (1988, pp.150–1) asks, if men are being provoked to do something against their better nature, why are they so able to talk about their intentions and so callous about the injuries inflicted? (See also Hearn, 1994.) Women's groups campaigning for a change in the law on provocation want to see both 'adultery' and 'words alone' specifically disallowed, and 'long-term domestic abuse' included in definitions used by the courts (*ROW Bulletin*, Autumn/Winter 1994, p.40).

Abusers, of course, readily adopt this male explanatory model of provocation to excuse their behaviour to themselves and to others because it feeds into their pattern of denial and minimisation. They also incorporate it into the abuse: 'He cracked a bone in my nose and I had to tell him I was sorry for making him do it' (research interview with a woman in a refuge). Men are still seeing it as their right to expect women to perform in the kitchen and bedroom:

> it just became too much . . . . I certainly, you know, didn't think I was wrong in asking not to be filled up with fatty foods

> I did strike her, and for basically the same reason. I just tried making love, and making love, and she couldn't do it.
> (Ptacek, 1988, p.147)

Husbands will blame any form of action or inaction by their wives for their own abusive behaviour, and frequently cite exact opposites at different times, as Scottish Women's Aid (1989a) has so graphically summarised in the following piece:

> We're always reading in the papers that women who get battered not only like it really, but ask for it. If only you'd behaved differently, it would never have happened to you! In line with this way of thinking, Women's Aid are now proud to present their new guide:

> *How Not to be an Abused Woman*
> DON'T dress up when his friends come round. He'll say you're making up to them.

> DON'T look a mess when his friends come round. He'll say you're trying to show him up.

> DON'T ask your friends round. He won't want the house full of chattering females.

> DON'T not ask your friends round. Are you ashamed of him or something?

DON'T have supper on the table when he gets in. He'll think you're getting at him for being late.

DON'T let supper be late. The least he deserves when he gets in after a hard day's work is to have his supper on the table.

DON'T let the children stay up till he gets home. He'll be too tired to be bothered with a lot of screaming kids.

DON'T send them to bed before he gets there. Do you want them to forget their father?

DON'T ask him what sort of day he's had. You should be able to see just by looking at him that it's been dreadful.

DON'T forget to ask him how his day was. A woman should show some interest in what her man's doing.

DON'T tell him about your day. He doesn't want to hear a lot of complaints when he's just got in from work.

DON'T not tell him about your day. Are you sulking or what?

DON'T put on a sexy negligee at bedtime. You look ridiculous, and anyway, whose money do you think you're spending?

DON'T go to bed in your pyjamas. It'd be nice if a man had something attractive to sleep with occasionally.

DON'T put your arms round him in bed. When he wants it, he'll ask for it.

DON'T turn away and go to sleep. You frigid, or what? And lastly . . .

When he hits DON'T fight back. You'll make it worse. And DON'T, whatever you do, cower away. It'll make him feel guilty, so he'll hit you more.

That's it then. Women's Aid can promise that if you follow these few little tips, you'll never get battered again. Unless, of course, you ask for it . . .

It is crucial that all those working with women, including social workers and probation officers, see the nonsensical nature of blaming women for their partners' abuse. The woman can never win because the more she gives, the more the man wants and, if she tries to read his cues, he changes the rules at every turn until he has an excuse for a violent assault: ' No one has to "provoke" a wife-beater. He will strike out when he's ready and for whatever reason at the moment. I may be his excuse but I have never been the reason' (from a letter published by Martin, 1976, pp.1–5 and cited in Schlesinger *et al.*, 1992, p.10). (This is a crucial message for those undertaking systemic family and couples work: see Chapter 7, this volume.) There is not something 'wrong' with battered women but with the institution of intimate relationships between men and women (Bograd, 1988b, p.22) and the way it is mediated in society. Men are encouraged to be dominant and controlling and the logical extension of this is abuse.

In fact: 'No one "deserves" being beaten up or mentally tortured, or the abuse women coming to refuges have received' (WAFE, undated b). How would provocation explain women being attacked while asleep (Scottish Women's Aid, undated a)? How could anyone 'deserve' marital rape or forced anal sex, or being imprisoned in a coal store for days on end, or being killed? It is time this nonsensical thinking was exploded for all time and, in its better disguised forms, rooted out of all professional practice.

She needs the violence, or enjoys it, or is addicted to it

There is also an abundance of theories that see the woman as psychologically deviant, rather than the man. These seek explanations for the abuse within women's own personalities (Dobash and Dobash, 1992, pp.221–8), in concepts such as masochism (Shainess 1984) – to explain submission and suffering as a way of life – or learned helplessness (Walker, 1977–8) which purports to explain why women do not leave abusive men.

Whether the theory is chiefly pyschodynamic or chiefly behavioural, the victim-blaming tendency is evident: 'I do believe that the victims of violent crime may sometimes play a part either in triggering or exacerbating those crimes' (Shainess, 1984, p.125). The woman is also implicated in Lenore Walker's 'cycle of violence' (not intergenerational transmission but three stages of build up, explosion, and a 'honeymoon' phase of contrition) because she is supposed to participate in it as a learned behaviour, because it binds her to the abuser, because it distorts her view of what is normal, and because, it is claimed, she does not believe that anything will make the batterer stop and will not respond to offers of help (Walker, 1977–8, p.530).

It is relatively easy to indulge in circular arguments that present the combined effect of physical threats and terror with the restrictions of a patriarchal society (e.g. lack of child care, low pay, housing cuts) as shortcomings in the women themselves. Dobash and Dobash (1992, pp.224) list over thirty personality failings attributed to abused women – from 'low ego strength' to 'manipulativeness' and from 'self destructiveness' to 'avoidance of confrontations' – many of them mutually contradictory along passive/aggressive or indecisive/domineering lines. This kind of theorising is encouraged by entrenched individualistic traditions in American psychological research and clinical practice, and by the fact that being diagnosed as suffering from something like 'battered woman syndrome' or 'post-traumatic stress disorder' (e.g. Kemp *et al.*, 1995) may be the only way a woman in America can qualify for insurance-funded health or counselling help. In Britain, such terms have been used as a defence or mitigation in court when a woman has killed her abuser (Kennedy, 1992, Chapter 8). As Dobash and Dobash (1992, pp.228–30) point out, there are problems with these labels because they portray passivity and psychological damage rather than justifiable self-defence, but the current state of the law on murder allows women few options, so lawyers use what they think will be helpful. A defence of self-preservation (*ROW Bulletin*, Autumn/Winter 1994, pp.39–40) would be far more constructive and would focus on the man's abuse rather than any supposed 'sickness' in the woman.

Psychological testing has been unable to find significant differences between women experiencing abuse and others (summarised in Dobash and Dobash, 1992, pp.223–4). Many studies are conducted in clinical contexts with biased samples, researchers who already operate from a particular stance, and an absence of controls (Maguire, 1988, p.35; Bograd, 1988b, p.17). Even if differences are demonstrated in women who have been abused, these could be an effect rather than a cause of the abuse. Hoff (1990, pp.22–4) asked nine women to administer a self-evaluation schedule which showed that all experienced damaged self-esteem and felt suicidal only while the violence continued.

A variation on the theme of implicating women's psychology in the violence is the representation of women as going from one relationship to another, seeking out abusive men each time. The Select Committee on Violence in Marriage was told by Erin Pizzey that 'there is a high percentage of women who go from one [abusive] marriage into another' (House of Commons, 1975, vol. 2, p.6) and by Dr J. J. Gayford that they 'seek violent men' (ibid., p.37; see also Gayford, 1975 and Pizzey and Shapiro, 1982). A more recent variant is the claim that women 'love too much' (Norwood, 1985 and 1988) and are addicted to the excitement and danger of violence which they allegedly seek in successive relationships. The evidence points against this. None of the women in Pahl's refuge sample (1985a, p.62) who moved on to new stable relationships had experienced repeated violence (in strong contrast to those who returned to their abusers in this study and that by Binney *et al.*: see above). Only three of the 32 women in another, representative, survey who had lived in more than one relationship had been subjected to violence in more than one of them (Andrews and Brown, 1988, p.308). One explanation that Kelly (1988, p.201) found for violence sometimes starting up in a new relationship was that the women had told their new partners of the previous abuse before it happened again. Somehow, this may have stirred abusive inclinations, or planted the idea in minds attuned by society to be receptive to them – particularly if there had been no serious consequences for the previous abuser. There *is* some reason to believe that *men* go from relationship to relationship being violent. Pahl (1985a, p.5) reports that every refuge knows of men like this. In Pagelow's study (1981, p.62), 57 per cent of previously married men were known to have been violent before. These are dangerous men and should be treated with due caution by social workers and probation officers as well as by their partners. Just as there is an argument for a shift away from registering children at risk of abuse to keeping a register of known abusers, and tracking them as they move around the country, so a greater emphasis on monitoring the continuing propensities of violent men to be violent (as opposed to those of women allegedly to continue 'seeking' violence) might help women and children to be safe. Some women's campaign groups do attempt to follow the progress of men who have killed women through the prison system. Keith Ward, who has killed twice (see Chapter 8, this volume), is now thought to be corresponding with another woman he was introduced to through a letter-writing scheme for prisoners. A women's organisation has been in touch with her to try and warn her. Probation officers may feel that this has relevance to current debates about responsibilities to victims of crime and to the wider community.

Far from loving too much, women find that violence kills their love even for men who bring them gifts and apologise profusely: 'And when they start knocking you about and you start losing teeth, and they start scarring you, and you break your nose and all that – just slowly the love dies out and you don't want to know' (Pahl, 1985a, p.48). Similarly: *'In our experience of helping over 10,000 women we have never encountered a woman who enjoyed being beaten'* (Scottish Women's Aid, undated a). Women's active attempts to seek help (see below) also belie any suggestion that they choose to be abused: 'I know that I do not want to be hit. I know, too, that I will be beaten again unless I can find a way out for myself and my children' (letter quoted by Martin, 1976, cited in Schlesinger *et al.*, 1992, p.10).

She learns to live with it

There is as much truth in this as there is in the fact that hostages 'learn to live with' their captivity – in other words, women draw on whatever reserves of courage and coping strategies they personally possess to survive from day to day in an atmosphere of terror. This does not equate with learning to tolerate the abuse; it never ceases to be dreadful. One pattern seems to be that women will find ways to survive untold agony and distress for themselves but leave the man when they discover an adverse effect on their children: 'Often it was when the eldest child started to notice what was going on that women decided that it was time to leave home' (Pahl, 1985a, p.49; see also Chapter 6, this volume, on the impact on children of living with abuse). It is not, as Women's Aid stresses, 'part of the "normal give and take" of family life' to be regularly assaulted (in House of Commons, 1992b, Memorandum 22, para.2.4). A woman may stand by her partner through illness or ill-luck but the man must take responsibility for abuse. Nor should others fear to intervene between husband and wife under these circumstances (though not in opposition to what the woman believes to be safest). Such men do kill and if the woman is scared she no doubt has excellent reason to be.

They put up with it, it's their culture

This is a variation on the theme of 'learning to live with it' and is sometimes heard, for example, amongst police officers reluctant to intervene in Asian communities and encouraged by male elders not to do so. It is certainly true that women with origins in the Indian subcontinent may have been brought up within a system of values that emphasises the acceptance of their lot in life without complaint, holding the family together, and preserving *izzat* (family pride) at all costs. However, this does not mean that Asian women find abuse any easier to bear:

> The culture into which I was born and where I grew up sees the woman as the honour of the house. . . . In order to uphold this false 'honour' and glory she is taught to endure many kinds of oppression and pain in silence. Religion also teaches her that her husband is her god and fulfilling his every desire is her religious duty. For ten years I tried wholeheartedly to fulfil the duties endorsed by religion. For ten years I lived a life of beatings and degradation and no one noticed.
>
> (Kiranjit Ahluwalia, quoted by Kennedy, 1992, p.203–4)

Rather, they may face particular difficulties in obtaining help or in leaving home (Imam, 1994).

Family and community supports may depend on the code of behaviour being strictly followed. Although religious and cultural beliefs give Asian men reciprocal responsibilities, there may be few alternatives for women whose husbands ignore them – particularly if the wife has travelled alone to Britain to marry and lacks the support of her extended family grouping, or if she faces deportation on leaving a violent husband in the first year of marriage before she has permanent residence rights or the right of recourse to public funds (Alibhai, 1989; *ROW Newsletter*, July 1995: Southall Black Sisters are gathering accounts of relevant cases). There have been recent instances of social services employees in this situation, for example Prakash Chavrimootoo, a home care worker in Birmingham (*Community Care*, 22nd December 1994–5th January 1995, p.6). Other women, who do not know the law, may wrongly believe – or be told by their husbands – that this deportation threat remains in place throughout marriage (Home Department *et al*, 1993, para.36); the Home Office states that it would like them to be better informed but it is not willing at this time to budge from a case-by-case treatment of the problem and considers researching it to be methodologically impossible (ibid.). Economic dependency, together with a lack of knowledge about benefits and housing services – which, anyway, are inadequate and frequently racist in operation – makes leaving home as good as impossible for many more minority ethnic women (Jervis, 1986, p.7). Male religious and community leaders, including doctors and lawyers, may side – or be expected by the woman to side – with the husband, or may regard claims of violence as simply an exaggerated response to the influence of white feminists and the white media. One woman's male Asian solicitor effectively destroyed her case in court. Male elders may also tend to adopt more traditionalist views for official consumption here, for purposes of community conservation (ibid.), than in the subcontinent where a greater range of options may be developing or where a more natural process of change may have been possible than in a small, oppressed and highly visible community.

Asian women's voluntary groups in Britain, including campaigning groups like Southall Black Sisters (1990; Farnham, 1992) and a growing number of refuges and resource centres, are showing that Asian women have safety needs and want abuse to be tackled, just like all women. It is racist stereotyping that causes white agencies to *expect* Asian women to want to stay in their marriages, rather than exploring options as they might do with white women whilst also understanding the particular difficulties and dangers. Whilst most women, Black and white, initially hope that reconciliation will be possible, it cannot work miracles and may be dangerous (e.g. the fatal stabbing of Vandana Patel by her husband in Stoke Newington police station in 1991). The case of Kiranjit Ahluwalia (see Chapter 1, this volume) reminds us of the protracted and severe violence to which Asian women may be subjected if they do stay, either not knowing where to turn for help or finding civil remedies totally ineffective (a campaigning leaflet, 'FREE Kiranjit Ahluwalia', reported that two injunctions went unheeded). Campaigning efforts have had to be concentrated on taking up such cases and on providing immediate safety through establishing specifically Asian and other specialist refuges (Guru, 1986).

Too little direct work has yet been undertaken with the police or courts, or with welfare agencies, in relation specifically to their treatment of Asian or other minority ethnic women. There can be a tendency for white social workers and probation officers to 'freeze' in the face of an Asian woman, not wanting to do the wrong thing and cut across cultural norms. This is the new inverse racism, sometimes compounded by a little anti-racism training and a lot of ignorance. Every woman has the right to safety, to skilled services, to emergency assistance, and to effective communication – using appropriate interpreters where necessary. Black women's groups are always an important source of advice and help, both to women experiencing abuse and to professional workers.

It cannot be that bad or women would not stay/return/have the man back

The question 'why doesn't she leave?' is victim blaming in itself, both because it puts the onus on the woman to act and because it is the question most commonly asked; it is rare in comparison for people to ask 'Why does he abuse?' Criminal justice and welfare agency officials get side-tracked by the question and not infrequently allow one of its variants to reduce their helping efforts – particularly if the woman has left before and they begin to see her as unworthy of help or as having let them down: 'there is a brutal but common misconception that if women do not leave, the violence they are enduring cannot be all that intolerable' (Victim Support, 1992, p.7). Yet children as young as 8, in a Canadian group for children who had accompanied their mothers to second-stage housing, could instantly comply with a request to do a drawing of reasons why their mothers had stayed. One child drew a huge fist entering from the side of an otherwise blank sheet of paper; another drew a darkened house with one figure threatening another in the only lighted window at the top of the house. These children understood perfectly that 'Women stay in violent homes for reasons ranging from love to terror' (WAFE, undated b).

When abuse first starts, it may seem like an accident or a 'one-off', and perhaps not particularly serious. Only in retrospect, of course, is it the beginning of a pattern. Nevertheless, as many as 40 per cent of women do tell someone at this stage (McGibbon *et al.*, 1989, p.27) although the response is often not believing or helpful. In the early stages, most women want the abuse rather than the relationship to end because they still love their partners or feel a commitment to the marriage and to shared parenthood (e.g. Hoff, 1990, p.33 and elsewhere, drawing on nine very detailed life histories). The gaps between the incidents of violence give the woman the hope to try again, backed up by the man's promises that it will never happen again – that he will change (ibid.). As the abuse escalates, some couples and some men seek therapy which may encourage them both to see him or the relationship as in some way sick, but curable (see Chapters 7 and 9, this volume, on the inadequacies of therapies that do not confront the abuse as criminal behaviour). Typically these do not work but may trap the woman for longer in the relationship and may even increase the danger.

One obstacle to leaving and to help-seeking is that, as we know from research, women underdefine themselves as abused. Women completing questionnaires may tick specific forms of abuse, including even 'threatened to kill', without ticking a direct question about physical abuse (McGibbon *et al.*, 1989, p.24). It is hard for a woman to name herself as an woman experiencing abuse and her partner as an abuser. The terminology she knows, such as 'battered woman' or 'marital rape', may not fit her precise circumstances, or she may interpret it in a very specific way that does not include herself: 'I don't get beat up every day' (ibid.). Women also consciously or unconsciously suppress their awareness or memories of the abuse as a coping mechanism: 'I'm sorry but it's too painful and difficult to explain. I can't even think about it' (ibid.). A woman may not be aware of knowing anyone else who has ever faced what she is facing so may never try to put a name to the experience. She may have received religious, cultural and/or family messages that this is just a part of marriage and that she should not put her own safety or needs first.

Gradually, over time, the abuse worsens: 'After the third time he said "This is getting easier and easier to do"' (woman in refuge, research interview by the author and co-researcher). The woman may not realise the danger she is in for some considerable while: 'It was only when he started hitting my head against the wall that I began to think "this is serious"' (McGibbon and Kelly, 1989, para.2.2). By this stage, there may seem no possibility or no point in seeking help when 'she believes nothing will prevail upon her husband to stop, and that any challenge to him will destroy her' (Kennedy, 1992, p.90); all too often women are right to believe this and are maimed or killed by their abusers. Threats and psychological abuse may leave the woman frozen and isolated in the face of power and control tactics, rage and possessive jealousy. Often, women who try to leave are pursued or tracked down, and not infrequently killed, in a bid to continue the domination of their lives. Ann Jones (1980, p.299, cited by Dobash and Dobash, 1992, p.9) considers that we should ask not 'Why do women stay?' but 'Why don't men let them go?' She gives examples of women who were continually tracked down, beaten and raped; hospitalised seven times by an ex-husband who kept coming back with a gun; and made to watch while her grave was dug, the pet cat and horse were killed, after which she was pursued and brought back with a gun held to her child's head (ibid., pp.298–9). The women in Jones' study were driven to kill because there literally was no escape. Others kill themselves or attempt to do so as a form of release (Maynard, 1985, p.132; Prasad and Vijayalakshmi, 1988, p.275; Dobash and Dobash, 1992, p.8).

Throughout the experience of abuse, there are major practical obstacles to leaving (e.g. Barnett and LaViolette, 1993, Chapter 2). Often, the woman has nowhere to go or does not know that there are places she can go: 'I had two kids, nobody had room you know, didnae know where to go and look for a house' (woman quoted in Scottish Women's Aid, undated c). She may well have no money of her own and may not know her entitlement to benefits or may justifiably fear poverty and isolation as a single parent. She may be worried about losing her home and all her possessions if she leaves; if she is disabled it may be an adapted home or she may have special aids without which she cannot manage – indeed, her abuser may be her main carer on whom she relies. She may fear that she will lose her children – if, for example, she takes them without a proper home to go to, or has to seek outside help, or leaves them behind with her partner, or takes them into a lesbian relationship against which the courts are known to be biased (Rights of Women Lesbian Custody Group, 1984) – or she may consider that, as a single parent, she could not give them the life she would wish (Pahl, 1985a, p.50). It may be particularly hard to leave, in practical terms, if she has several children, and she may see it as her role to keep the family together. Her partner may threaten the children in order to make her stay. Women from minority ethnic communities or particular religions may face additional obstacles (see above) such as forced reconciliation, the likelihood of being disowned by family and community, proscriptions against divorce, dangers or fears of deportation, and the racism of the wider society which manifests itself, for example, in hostile attitudes and in practical barriers such as a lack of interpreters and of translated information materials. Many women, from every kind of background, feel so trapped in abusive situations that they see suicide as the only way out (e.g. Stark *et al.*, 1979, p.468; and as a recurring theme in British research, e.g. McWilliams and McKiernan, 1993, p.80).

Women are right to feel that there are practical obstacles to leaving, as will be outlined below. (Social workers and probation officers need an up-to-date knowledge of all these practicalities, and should call upon their agencies to assist with training. What follows is a summary of the situation at the time of writing; the problems confronting women fleeing abuse tend to transmute over time, but not to be resolved.)

Housing

Government-imposed spending restrictions have forced housing authorities into policies that narrowly define their statutory duties to rehouse women fleeing abuse (and have prevented them from using receipts from rents or council house sales to end shortages of public housing). This situation, together with inconsistent and sometimes hostile attitudes from some authorities and some staff, means that women may be put under pressure to return home, or be referred back to the local authority in their home area, or required to furnish detailed proof of violence, and/or to wait inordinately long for decisions to be taken as to whether they are in priority need, not 'intentionally homeless', and eligible for local help (Malos and Hague, 1993, p.83). Thus, although women's legal rights have been somewhat strengthened in housing legislation over the years, women still often have to return home for reasons connected with accommodation, as they did in Pahl's study ten years ago (1985a, p.41).

Furthermore, the Government is actively considering reducing rights to permanent rehousing (e.g. WAFE, 1993/94, pp.6–7), so that the local authority duty to those in priority need would be merely to provide temporary accommodation for a limited period – and that only after the claim of homelessness had been assessed and accepted. It is not clear where anyone forced to leave home in an emergency is intended to live, other than on the street. There would be no duty to help families already in any form of temporary accommodation, such as refuges and hostels. Unless they could get the abuser excluded from the family home (which is extremely difficult – see below), women heading homeless families would be obliged to join the waiting list for public housing on the same basis as anyone awaiting rehousing, or, if they could scrape together a deposit and the rent, to take their chances in an inadequate and poorly regulated private rented sector (which could give the abuser grounds to argue in contested proceedings concerning the children that the woman had failed to provide them with a suitable home). At the same time, the Government proposes to cut housing benefit entitlements to a local average level, as opposed to the actual rent charged by the private landlord or landlady – and regardless of the quality of the property (*Shelter News Release*, 14th June 1995).

Some housing authorities and housing associations *are* still working to good practice guidelines or developing particular policies to help women fleeing abuse (Malos and Hague, 1993, Chapter 6), and inter-agency forums may help this to spread, but funding remains a huge problem even when attitudes change. It is a dreadful irony that the same Government that has funded a public education campaign about domestic violence (see Chapter 10, this volume), and encouraged increased police activity, is pursuing policies in the welfare field that are so wholly bad for women experiencing abuse and their children. Three to four thousand of the families currently accepted as homeless each quarter (11 per cent) are recorded as having left their last place of residence because of domestic violence (Home Office 'Domestic Violence Factsheet', April 1995, citing Department of the Environment Bulletins 237/92, 160/93, 178/94). More are concealed behind categories such as 'overcrowding', having gone first to family and friends. Homelessness (like constant moves and bad housing) affects women's and children's physical and mental health and children's safety, emotional development and schooling. It is an indictment a so-called civilised society.

Injunctions

The limitations of injunctions and related court orders, always assuming women can overcome the obstacles to obtaining them, are summed up in the title of Barron's research study (1990): *Not Worth the Paper*. (See also North Eastern Legal Action Group Women's Section and N.E. Women's Aid, 1992.) These obstacles include unsympathetic solicitors (Evason, 1982, p.40), tight definitions, the need to furnish evidence, unsympathetic courts, and the substitution for action by the court of undertakings by the parties which are easily broken and leave the onus on the woman to take further action. Even where the court does make an order men regularly ignore injunctions and they are rarely enforced. Powers of arrest and orders excluding the man from the home are particularly difficult to obtain. (It is crucial that the injunction is actually served on the man and that a copy of any power of arrest reaches the police.) Yet legal proceedings are stressful and can lead to reprisals from the man. Not all women know about entitlement to Legal Aid so some never get to court. To make matters worse, funding again impinges, with regional ceilings on Legal Aid budgets being proposed by the Lord Chancellor. These may well ration or limit Legal Aid and thus deny many women the skilled legal help they need to pursue their rights effectively. Law centres and Citizens Advice Bureaux may be expected to cope with excess demand.

Improvements in respect of the civil law almost came in the Family Homes and Domestic Violence Bill, which would have introduced a unified set of remedies offering more women, including ex-wives and former cohabitees, greater protection (though some groups, notably those never cohabiting and those without children, would still not have been covered) but this was withdrawn at the tail-end of the parliamentary session in 1995, under right-wing Tory pressure not to allow unmarried women, as they saw it, to force men out of their homes. At the time of writing, in the 1995/96 parliamentary session, a new Family Law Bill has been introduced which combines some aspects of the former Bill with proposals for divorce; Part III deals with 'protection from violence'. The streamlining of earlier measures still seems likely to occur, but cohabitees with no existing legal rights to occupy the home are deliberately denied equal remedies for themselves and their children. They will only be able to apply for a temporary occupation order, lasting a maximum of one year, and the 'balance of harm' test between the parties will not be allowed for these women to override other factors, such as respective housing needs and financial resources. Currently, moralistic groups in both Church and State are putting up a rearguard action to have the 'commitment of marriage' (clause 36 of the Bill) recognised as vested in the marriage certificate rather than in the emotional, physical and financial investment made over a period of years. Abusive men may refuse to marry their partners, refuse to include them in ownership or tenancy rights to property, and rely on the fact that leaving will render them penniless and homeless as a way of closing the trap of the violence. The current proposals ignore this, and will make abused women suffer further for being unmarried and for lacking legal rights in their home. They are seen, in effect, not only as being less deserving than married women, but as less deserving than their abusers (WAFE, 1995, in its briefing on the Bill).

Social workers and probation officers can help all women experiencing abuse by recording, or advising the woman to record, any injuries that might help her to obtain a non-molestation or occupation order under the intended Act, by being aware in broad terms of the remedies available and when they may or may not be obtainable, and by knowing of sympathetic and well-informed solicitors in the locality.

Refuges

The problems here are simply hearing about the refuge and finding space, given a national picture of gross underfunding (Ball, 1994). In 1994, there were around 35 per cent of the places deemed a minimum in 1975 by a Parliamentary Select Committee on Violence in Marriage (House of Commons, 1975), since when estimates of the need have almost doubled (Ball, 1994). The women in refuges who were questioned in Binney *et al.*'s survey (1988, p.6) had mostly wanted to leave from the first year of their marriage but many had had nowhere to go, especially those who had not heard of refuges at that time. Similarly:

> I wish I'd known about Women's Aid years ago because I would have left then. I'd been married to my husband for 21 years. He'd always beaten me up but he became so violent that I knew he was going to kill me.
>
> (woman in a refuge, quoted in McGibbon and Kelly, 1989, p.7:1; see also Ball, 1994, p.1)

Some women told Binney *et al.* (1988, p.8) of spending the night in a telephone box or public lavatory or on a park bench. Two-thirds had tried staying with families or friends, but were easily found and gave in to pressure to return home which not infrequently involved physical force or threats. By the time they found the refuge, they had been subjected to violence for periods ranging from a few months to thirty or forty years (ibid., p.5), with the average being seven years. Women's aid and other women's refuges provide safety for many thousands of women and their children who otherwise would be further abused or killed by violent men. The need for refuges is proven by the fact that they are always full and that women speak positively of what they offer. Eighty per cent in the survey by Binney *et al.* (ibid., p.21) had found Women's Aid useful, often because:

> For the first time, women had safe accommodation for as long as they needed it, together with practical help and advice on how to organise a permanent separation.
>
> (Binney *et al.*, 1985, p.171)

Women who have used refuges rate them more highly than any other agency, despite sometimes poor and overcrowded premises (Smith, 1989, p.99). Part of their success lies in the empowering philosophy of Women's Aid which emphasises:

1 The central importance of the abused woman's perspective in the provision of support and services.

2 The need to enable women to regain control of their own lives. Women's Aid services are provided by women and for women.
3 The value of mutual support from other women who have similar experiences.
4 A commitment to caring for the emotional, developmental and educational needs of children affected by domestic violence.

(WAFE, in House of Commons, 1992b,
Memorandum 22, para.1.4)

Having nowhere to go is the main reason why some women never leave (McGibbon *et al.*, 1989, p.28), so it is important to continue increasing the publicity given to refuges, helplines and other emergency options, though not to put pressure on women to use them. Provision increasingly includes specialist refuges – for example, those specifically for Asian, African Caribbean, Latin American and Chinese women (see also Ghattaora, 1992) – which work to meet a range of needs most appropriately. One problem in increasing publicity and demand, of course, is that there is still no national funding base for Women's Aid (see Ball, 1994, for detailed costings and argument), despite the fact that it plays the most crucial role in making women safe and is already under intense pressure. The Government has promised 'inter-departmental discussions on refuge provision' (Home Department *et al.*, 1993, para.103), but so far without concrete result.

Other obstacles

Other difficulties encountered by women attempting to leave include the fact that the police, the Crown Prosecution Service and the courts still fail to take action against many men who pursue and harass partners – or take minor action which trivialises the offences and is consequently ineffective – and that so many women who leave encounter the complications of dealing with income support, housing benefit and child support. WAFE (1993/94, pp.10–11) has received reports that the provisions of the Child Support Act 1991 that cover confidentiality and women's rights to refuse the Child Support Agency permission to pursue an ex-partner are not always publicised or implemented as intended, even though they were hard won to protect those at risk of violence. If women on benefits are disbelieved when they cite violence as the reason for withholding an ex-partner's name, their benefits may be reduced. Furthermore, as we shall see in later chapters, women pay the price for the failings of health and welfare agencies in meeting their and their children's needs both before and after they leave relationships. For women to face all this when their partners have consistently told them that they are stupid and useless, and when their self-esteem may be at its lowest ebb, is particularly hard. This is why helping agencies need to develop sensitivity, consistency and a believing and non-blaming approach to the women who approach them. They could help a woman in danger to develop a safety plan involving others (for example, neighbours and family to check regularly on her safety, employer to block abusive calls at work, religious leaders and co-worshippers or other respected contacts to make it clear to the abuser that his behaviour is unacceptable and is being monitored), and covering readiness to leave in an emergency with money for fares, all major documents, the house key, and a few clothes for herself and the children.

Women's persistence

Women, in fact, do make complex attempts to end the abuse and to seek help. Strategies (e.g. Dobash *et al.*, 1985; Pahl, 1985a; Browne, 1987; Kelly, 1988b, Chapter 7; Hoff, 1990; London Borough of Hammersmith and Fulham, 1991a) include trying to talk to their partner about the abuse; challenging his demands; fighting back; consulting family and friends; calling the police; seeking counselling or legal advice; and threatening to leave. Attempts to seek help typically increase over time (e.g. Bowker, 1983; Dobash *et al.*, 1985; Kelly, 1988b, p.182). The majority of women do cope by leaving violent relationships eventually, but leaving is often a long and painful process rather than a one-off event (e.g. Homer *et al.*, 1984; Kirkwood, 1993; Women and Children in Refuges, undated, pp.58–60). Studies have suggested, for example, that around 40 per cent of women return home after going to a refuge (22 out of 50 in Pahl's study, 1985a, p.26; 40 and 41 per cent respectively in studies she cites by Welsh and Scottish Women's Aid, both conducted in 1980, see Pahl, 1985a, p.54). But there is attrition over time. At Pahl's follow-up interview, approximately two years later (Pahl, 1985b), she found that nine women were with their partners but only two had stayed consistently and only one of them was happy (Pahl, 1985a, p.55). Binney *et al.* (1988, pp.102–4) also found only 11 per cent at home at the second interview and they were mainly unhappy. Pahl (1985a, pp.55–6) concludes that the marriages were dying but that they were dying slowly and painfully because a clean-cut ending was not a practical or socially approved option for these women. Both studies found that women attempted reconciliation initially for accommodation reasons; those who tried it after finding the refuge wanted to give the marriage another chance, sometimes out of pity or misplaced hope in husbands who put enormous emotional pressure on them to return (Pahl, 1985a, pp.57–60), or for reasons connected with the children, such as having been parted from them. Trying again for the sake of the children is also quite common: 'After all, he is the kids' father' (research interview conducted by the author and co-researcher). The stresses of an extended stay in a refuge or of making a new life can also drive women home (Binney *et al.*, 1988, p.10).

The first time women leave, they tend to go to family or friends (39 and 22 per cent respectively in Pahl's study, 1985a, p.41). Even assuming she does not encounter cultural or religious or personal objections to helping her leave her marriage, the woman will then often find herself in overcrowded conditions, with nowhere to move on to, and with her partner pursuing her with either promises to change or threats against her or her hosts; not infrequently, she returns home. The abuse restarts and frequently worsens. But refuge workers and other activists talk of women progressively growing in determination, confidence and practical skills in day-to-day living as a lone parent so that, each time they leave, they are one step closer to coping alone. Most of those who are not killed do make the break eventually.

Too often, the agencies the woman approaches for help along the way, however, fail to pick up the signals and underestimate what she is going through and the effort it has taken to try and get help (often not realising that there is already a long history), or else lack a clear policy and have gaps in what they are prepared or able to do. Too many professionals still fail to believe women, fall into the myths outlined above, omit to mention the key information women need (such as the existence of refuges), present too much confusing and conflicting advice without practical and emotional support to find a way through it, and/or give mixed messages about the woman's deservingness of help. All agencies are capable of giving a good service and sometimes achieve it; many are starting to take the issues more seriously (see Chapter 4, this volume, for good practice guidelines and policies). But all too often they still fail to give women the help they desperately need. There is a crucial role for advocacy, self-help and support services to empower women through the process of making their own decisions on their own terms. Women who survive abuse are strong, but surviving from day to day has often absorbed all their strength (McGibbon and Kelly, 1989, p.2.2). The cornerstone is to 'approach battered women as survivors of harrowing, life-threatening experiences, who have many adaptive capacities and strengths' (Bograd, 1988b, p.15) with which they can gradually be helped to move forward and rebuild their lives.

Women who do reach the empowering help of refuges or women's support groups reflect on the questions: 'Why did I stay? Why didn't I walk out?' (Pence, 1987, pp.31–5). Only then do they see the full picture of the controlling tactics used by their abuser, together with the institutional and cultural supports for abuse which helped him get away with it, and the lack of effective help which prevented them from leaving. Although there are now handbooks for women in abusive relationships, explaining what help is available (e.g. NiCarthy, 1990; Jones and Schechter, 1992), the obstacle is not a simple lack of knowledge – crucial though accurate information is. A complex interplay of personal and social factors is also implicated.

CONCLUSION

Theories that encourage welfare and criminal justice practitioners to blame victims or to look for 'bad apples in the barrel' will do little to engage effectively with the widescale problem of men's abusive behaviour towards women. Exceptionalist explanations do not fit universalistic problems (Ryan, 1971). The real problem is that *all* men are encouraged to be aggressive, competitive, unemotional, sexual and powerful in order to define their masculinity and their difference from women. These dominant and dominating characteristics are expected in their relationships with women as well as in other aspects of their lives. Popular culture and language reinforce the image, summed up in the American saying: 'My way or highway' (which translates as 'Do as I say or you're out').

Both masculinity and male sexuality are rendered synonymous with power and hence are socially constructed to be oppressive (Maynard, 1993, pp.119–20; Pringle, 1995). Men's abuse of women can be understood only in this context. It is an extension of normal, condoned behaviour in a context of social inequality, not individual deviancy. Feminist perspectives on woman abuse have shown that it can be understood only in its social context. Men wield power over women and all men benefit from this through 'differential access to important material and symbolic resources, while women are devalued as secondary and inferior' (Bograd, 1988b, p.14). This keeps men as the dominant group. Despite important class and race differences between them, virtually all men can use violence to subdue women and keep them subordinate if they choose or allow themselves to do so. Globally, this is played out in public and in private in ways that lead to the deaths and suffering of many millions of women, and yet that are condoned and regarded as normal (Radford and Russell, 1992; Davies, 1994).

Abusive men believe in and act out the inequality within the privacy of the home and the intimacy of relationships. Many are possessive, jealous and use abuse to enforce double standards by which they are free but their wives and partners are constrained: not allowed to come and go or talk to other people at will, deprived of money or control over money – including so that they cannot leave (Pahl, 1985a, pp.32–9; see also Evason, 1982). Abusive men are also more likely to expect a domestic and sexual slave. Evason (1982) found that 66 per cent of violent husbands favoured male dominance in marriage as against 34 per cent of the non-violent. Men also use the fact that women find it difficult to leave for practical, safety and psychological reasons. They play on women's feelings of terror, hope, affection, and responsibility for their children – for example by threatening to hurt the children unless she returns – and exploit women's frequent lack of money and housing options.

Domestic abuse is endemic and it is overtly or covertly sanctioned. In an official study in Massachusetts, judges, court clerks and police belittled what women had experienced and sided with the men. From police officers joking around with an abuser they knew personally – whose wife had just required hospital admission – to a judge telling a woman she had no reason to be in court if her husband did not drink, gamble, or run around with other women (Governor's Battered Women's Working Group, 1985, pp.8–9, cited in Ptacek 1988, pp.154–5), these officials of the criminal justice system shored up the ability of the men concerned to subordinate their partners, to justify their actions to themselves, and still to retain social credibility. We are not dealing with a few bad apples in the barrel but with the whole barrel.

Chapter 3

Social work as part of the problem

Up to now, the statutory welfare services have represented less of a success story for women's safety than refuges and related provision. Social workers have typically had a bad press as regards men abusing women, often being seen as not knowing how to respond or as having other priorities – typically child care. (Parallels in probation family court practice will be seen in Chapter 7.) Probation officers, equally, are seen as focusing on the men and ignoring women's safety (their record will be examined in Chapter 8; see also McWilliams and McKiernan, 1993, p.96).

According to any abused woman or women's activist one chooses to ask, the picture in practice is one of inconsistency, ranging from those practitioners who have somehow remained oblivious or become inured to the extent and degree of violence inflicted on women – and who see it as irrelevant to their work or some other agency's problem – through others who reflect the negative and unenlightened attitudes that blame women for their own abuse, to those individuals who are not only concerned for the women they meet in the course of their professional work but who also devote considerable amounts of their own time to working with Women's Aid or other women's groups to improve the help available in the community. Those workers who recognise that men's abuse of women is endemic and who believe that social work should respond to it are, however, in a minority (McWilliams and McKiernan, 1993, p.66). Greater consistency will come only through a co-ordinated approach to training and an overall departmental or organisational lead; but this is slow to happen. Even now, with domestic abuse currently receiving a high public profile, social services departments are not in the forefront of inter-agency responses (see Chapter 10, this volume). Probation services are rather more in evidence but their progress is patchy. This is *not* because woman abuse is rarely seen by professionals, either in duty referrals or in allocated cases.

In fact, abused women seek help from social workers in large numbers. Improvements in the ability of social services to offer them practical assistance and emotional support, and to help prevent further violence, would therefore have an immediate impact. This chapter sets the scene by examining the research evidence on social work involvement with women experiencing abuse.

THE RESEARCH EVIDENCE

The statistics: proportions of abused women seen by social workers

A number of studies have been based not on the general female population but on women contacted through Women's Aid. These samples are, of course, skewed towards those who have reached safety, at least temporarily, but are useful in that they are likely to include women who have been abused over long periods of time. Their experiences of social work intervention will therefore be of particular interest. Binney *et al.* (1988, p.19) record that over half their national sample of abused women living in refuges (54 per cent) had at some time sought assistance from the personal social services, this being second only to their rate of contact with the police.

Other studies record higher figures. Pahl (1985a, p.80) interviewed forty-two women during and after their stay in a refuge. Three-quarters (76 per cent) had asked social workers for help at some point before going into a refuge. This figure was higher than contacts with police and doctors and was exceeded only by social security at 93 per cent, although that agency was no doubt approached for money, not to advise on escape or stopping the violence (which is not to say that money is not a crucial key to future survival nor that DSS offices could not usefully carry leaflets and posters). A similar number (74 per cent) contacted social workers after leaving as had done so before.

Dobash *et al.* (1985, p.150) found that women were more likely to approach formal sources of help, including social workers, as the abuse persisted and worsened. Early in the relationship, when the violence started for women in this study (a fifth before even living together, almost half in the first year of doing so; ibid., p.143), they either hoped that it would stop or typically approached family and friends (p.150). All those involved with violence, personally or professionally, need to recognise that the abuse hardly ever stops at this stage or under these circumstances. Rather, it escalates over time. Hence, any concept of isolated incidents is misleading. This understanding needs urgently to permeate all social work and related professional practice. The 109 women in this Scottish research, most of whom were interviewed in refuges, had experienced around 32,000 assaults throughout their years with their abusers (p.164), or two attacks a week on average (p.143). These had graduated from kickings, slappings and punchings to severe burns, fractures, internal injuries, miscarriages, and attempted strangulations and drownings (p.144). A typical assault had an almost even chance of being of either medium or high severity (p.146). Only 3 per cent were categorised as of low severity. We must, in any case, guard against writing off the latter as unimportant. There can be no excuse for a man to use any degree of violence against a woman and, furthermore, all the attacks form part of a pattern of intimidation and terror.

Once again, three-quarters of the women (74 per cent) had contacted social workers for help at some point during the period of violence (p.148, Table 10.4). Although this fell a short way behind the police, doctors and relatives (at 82, 80 and 76 per cent respectively), it was extremely high in view of the almost universal access to the last three sources of help as against the more selective contact with social workers. (Abusive men may try to prevent access to all these forms of help, including social workers: McWilliams and McKiernan, 1993, p.65). The likelihood of contacting social workers rose over time, from 5 per cent of contacts after the first attack and 14 per cent after the worst, to 17 per cent of contacts after the last attack (Dobash *et al.*, 1985, p.149). By the time of the last attack, these contacts outstripped those with police and doctors at 13 and 12 per cent respectively. Bowker (1983) noted an even steeper rise in social service contacts (focusing on a different range of agencies, being in an American context) from 7 per cent after the first to 43 per cent after the last attack.

The present author has looked again at the Dobash *et al.* contact figures and calculated them as a percentage of women making contact rather than as a percentage of total contacts made. This makes a difference because women were trying on average two, three or four sources of help after any one assault. On this further analysis, the figures rise to 11.5 per cent of women making contact with social workers after the first attack, 40 per cent after the worst and 60 per cent of women contacting social workers after the last attack (based on Dobash *et al.* 1985, p.149). (Of course, the proportions relative to other sources of help remain constant.) Although no clear information is given, it is tempting to think that some of the contacts with social workers were of help since most of the women were in safety when interviewed. This is also borne out by women's appreciation of practical help (see next section). It may be that contact rates with the police will be rising now that officers around the country are being instructed to take domestic violence more seriously. The challenge to social services to do likewise should be overwhelming.

It must be remembered that the women interviewed in the Dobashes' research were struggling against extreme fear, shame and guilt to make these contacts. We can conclude from this and from the fact that 97 per cent sought help of some kind after the last attack (ibid.), that women genuinely need, desire and seek help. We can also assume that, when it is so hard to seek help because the man does everything in his power to prevent this, the woman who defies his threats and other forms of emotional subjugation – keeping her isolated, convincing her that it is her fault and that she deserves it – will be devastated if the person contacted at such personal risk is unable or unwilling to do anything. Such a failure to help can be extremely dangerous: 'the decision to approach a formal agency is a very difficult one. The initial contact is so fraught with misgivings and trepidation that the nature of the reponse can easily lead to discontinuation of contact' (ibid., p.155). The social worker whose help is sought needs to bear this in mind when gauging the urgency and extent of the need for help. More recent work (McGibbon *et al.*, 1989, p.60) suggests a recognition by some social workers that women contact them in desperation and as a last resort, also that this is likely to be particularly true for some particular grouping, such as Asian women, who frequently have additional family and community obstacles to confront in seeking help (see Imam, 1994).

Proportions of women contacting social workers are lower among Black women but are still significant. There is an urgent need to make this contact a more successful route to help for them. Mama (1989, p.93) used links with refuges and Black women's organisations in London to locate a hundred Asian, African Caribbean and African women who had experienced housing problems related to domestic violence. On average, a third of them had had contact with social services, rising to half the Asian women in the sample. None of the African Caribbean women described social services contact as 'positive or supportive', although some of the Asian women interviewed did.

Numbers on current caseloads

The next set of studies took general samples of social work service users rather than specific samples of abused women. Leonard and McLeod (1980, p.44) recorded 13 per cent of overall caseloads as definitely involving woman abuse, according to the workers concerned, rising to 18 per cent amongst child care cases. Borkowski *et al.* (1983, p.18) similarly obtained information from 36 social workers about the number of cases of domestic violence within existing caseloads. They estimated that known cases of domestic violence are likely to constitute 10.5 per cent of a social worker's caseload. Adding suspected cases brought the total to 12.5 per cent, very close to the Leonard and McLeod figure for the generality of work. The total number of known and suspected cases held by Borkowski *et al.*'s 36 workers over the previous 12 months was 141, of which 107 were said to be *known* to involve violence. The highest number on any one caseload was 45 and the lowest 15. This would seem to offer considerable scope for helping abused women, given the right forms of training and support for the social workers involved, especially as the figures are far higher than for the other settings and groups listed – hospital accident departments, health visitor caseloads, and three local voluntary organisations: the Citizens' Advice Bureau, Marriage Guidance (now Relate) and the Council on Alcoholism – perhaps because social workers see people in their own home circumstances and work predominantly with women.

Maynard (1985, p.127) went beyond asking social workers to make their own estimates to examining their files herself, when she found one in three of a sample of all current cases with 'direct references to domestic violence'. One of the most recent figures available, from a study in a multiply deprived London borough, cites one in five of currently allocated cases (London Borough of Hackney, 1994, p.36). Added to this, at least a third of the children on the child protection register for the area had mothers who were being abused (ibid.). Thus, although most social services do not collect routine statistics on woman abuse, there is ample evidence that it features heavily in everyday work, particularly in child care but also more generally. Social workers are thus in a good position to offer help.

The good news

Referrals by social workers to Women's Aid

We know that social workers do refer many women to safety through Women's Aid. Binney et al. (1988, p.20) found that 37 per cent of women in refuges were referred by social workers. Scottish Women's Aid (1989b), in their leaflet 'Social Workers – Working with Abused Women and Their Children', state that, of the 5,000 women and children given safe refuge by them in the preceding year, more than a quarter were referred by social workers. (The present author found averages of 28 per cent and 30 per cent recorded in the late 1980s by one urban and one rural refuge, based on unpublished figures.) All these studies and Pahl (1985a, p.84) recorded social workers as by far the commonest source of referral to refuges. In a Canadian study, Home (1991–92, p.158) found that social workers did better than the police in this regard, and were generally more safety conscious, which she attributed to greater knowledge of available forms of help even after the police had begun to take domestic violence more seriously.

It should be remembered that all the above (except the work by Home) are based on samples of women already in refuges, whereas other studies of women on general social work caseloads (particularly Maynard, 1985 – see next section) found far fewer appropriate referrals. There is room here, then, for only guarded optimism. Furthermore, a referral to a refuge may represent an exploitative use of a community resource looking as if it is willing to take over a problem. This could be one reason why Tayside Women and Violence Group (1994, p.51) found that social workers working with women experiencing abuse contacted Women's Aid more frequently than any other agency – they knew there would be a consistently constructive response. Seeking to use refuges as if they were simply hostels, however, with social workers in the assumed role of gatekeepers, ignores the underlying feminist principles and methods of working of Women's

Aid refuges – which help women make their own decisions and choices and rebuild confidence through mutually supported self-help (see Chapter 2, this volume). No one, in fact, has to 'refer' a woman to Women's Aid, although they may usefully tell women that refuges exist and how to telephone them for advice or practical assistance. Women need to make their own choices about the action they wish to take; social workers can help enormously by supplying essential information and support without taking over the decision making. Nor should there be an automatic assumption that the woman and her children will leave home in every instance rather than the abuser, who perhaps could be confronted instead through the criminal or civil justice system, depending on the viewpoint and the safety of the woman concerned.

Women's views on help from social workers

There is, again, limited good news in women's evaluation of social work help. According to Binney *et al.* (1988, p.20), 52 per cent of the women in their refuge-based sample who contacted social workers found it useful, usually because some form of practical help had been offered. Pahl (1985a p. 80) records 56 per cent of an admittedly small sample of 42 finding social workers helpful before a stay in a refuge, mainly through direct assistance in getting to the refuge, rising to 74 per cent afterwards. Perhaps this indicates that social workers are more at home helping women with the practicalities of settling into a new life – 'knowing the system' well enough to advise on and negotiate with other services according to Pahl – than they are in confronting, stopping or helping women escape violence. A similar contrast was found by Dobash *et al.* (1985, p.160) between supportive counselling which social workers *were* able to offer (though not from a feminist base which would effectively challenge the woman's blaming herself) and confronting the violence, which they avoided. More recently, in a sample gathered through NCH Action for Children family centres (Abrahams, 1994, p.85) lower figures were recorded for positive feedback: 36 per cent of mothers had found social workers helpful, as against 15 per cent who had not. This sample, having presumably been identified as having child care needs, may have been particularly wary of social workers, although two or three had positively sought continuing social work support (or protection for a child during contact visits with a violent man) which had not been forthcoming, and, most worryingly, one child had told a social worker what was going on at home and had not been believed (ibid.). In similar vein, Tayside Women and Violence Group (1994, p.52) found only a handful of women who considered social work responses 'effective' – when they led to a child care place or information on where to get assistance – or 'helpful' in terms of supportive listening and constructive advice. A sympathetic manner alone was not enough. The worst case was where a male worker revealed that he knew the woman's husband socially but did not offer her the opportunity to see someone else. Interestingly, in this study, social workers assessed themselves as overwhelmingly effective and helpful (p.51). McWilliams and McKiernan (1993, p.66) recorded less than a third of women in their sample in refuges and in contrasting communities in Northern Ireland who had found social workers helpful. Of particular note in their account, however, is the difference a good social worker can make: one woman's needs had been neglected for years but a change of worker brought questioning about the scars she bore and immediate information about refuges. Not surprisingly, respondents in this study recommended a say for women in choosing consistent workers with specialist knowledge about domestic abuse (ibid.). At present, only the lucky few can say: 'the one person that really helped was a social worker. ... She was really, really, good – really helpful ... ' (Tayside Women and Violence Group, 1994, p.52). This social worker had given the woman her contact telephone number to use whenever she needed to.

Taken overall, then, the success of *some* social workers in offering the right kind of help means that practitioners are wrong if they feel there is little they can do, and that other professionals are wrong to think this about them (Borkowski *et al.*, 1983). They may be the crucial link that helps get a woman to safety and stops further violence being committed against her, but too much is left to chance. Social worker comments that they lack skill and confidence in this area of work (Leonard and McLeod, 1980, p.53; Borkowski *et al.*, 1983; Mama, 1989, p.93), together with the research finding that their intervention depends on their level of knowledge (Binney *et al.*, 1988, p.20), are worrying and relate to a lack of training and agency support (see, for example, Tayside Women and Violence Group, 1994, pp.51 and 53 and Chapter 4, this volume). Qualifying and post-qualifying training programmes also urgently need to make changes. Curricula that by no means consistently cover background information on domestic abuse or how to respond to it, too often touch on it – if at all – in a tangential area of the timetable rather than in the mainstream coverage of work with families, children, and adult service users, and leave students ill-equipped to cope with the frequent instances of abuse they encounter on placement.

The development of more appropriate training and services needs to be based not only around domestic abuse but also on anti-racism. Mama (1989, pp.93–4) encountered entirely negative views about social services amongst African Caribbean women, but did find some young Asian women who had been helped by social workers to escape from violent husbands. One positive story (ibid., pp.99–100) concerns a young Asian wife who was helped to escape to an Asian women's organisation by a social worker who also scrupulously guarded confidential information about her whereabouts and, at the same time, helped her stay in touch with her family by passing on letters. This seems a particularly hopeful account.

Firstly, the social worker was not called in to work with the young wife but possessed the knowledge and skill to spot her distress while visiting the household of her husband's family. Secondly, the social worker does not appear to have fallen into the ethnocentric trap of assuming that anyone would wish to escape an arranged marriage, since such clear efforts were made to preserve family ties.

Most of the above research focused on women trying to leave abusive and destructive relationships to start a new life. It is particularly encouraging to see that sometimes social workers so appropriately assist women in this life-preserving aim.

The bad news

The bad news is that in Binney et al.'s refuge-based sample (1988, p.19), 48 per cent of the women had not found social work contact useful. The unhelpful social workers had shown little interest and had been unable to offer constructive help. Pahl (1978) came up with exactly the same figure. There are various ways in which matters appear to go badly awry.

Failure to identify abuse

Firstly, there has been evidence to suggest that social workers are failing to use the information available to them to identify or respond adequately to abused women. They consistently underestimate the proportion of their own cases involving domestic violence, for example (Johnson, 1985, p.115, reviewing other studies referred to above). Maynard (1985) provides the best insight into this. She read a one in ten sample of case files (103 cases) and, based on this information – which was, by definition, available to the workers themselves – identified over a third of the open cases (34 cases, or 33 per cent) as containing direct references to marital violence having taken place at some time, including 27 during the previous year. The social workers, however, viewed only three of these cases as centrally concerned with domestic violence; these were the only three where home visits were made because of the violence to the woman. Maynard estimated that at least 340 cases of domestic violence existed across the whole town and not the one or two that management had said she would be lucky to find (Maynard, 1985, p.127).

Ignoring the woman as a person in her own right

The main reason given by women interviewed by McWilliams and McKiernan (1993, p.65) for finding social workers unhelpful was that their own needs and perceptions were ignored, however urgent: 'She never asked how badly I was hurt'. As noted earlier, only three of the cases

Maynard read took abuse of the woman as their central concern. 'Of the others, the vast majority had children's and family welfare as their main focus. . . . Whatever the nature of the presenting problem, social workers regarded the woman in her role as wife/mother as their primary contact' (Maynard, 1985, p.133). If the woman was absent at the time of a social work visit, this was remarked on in the files, whereas the man's absence was not and, indeed, his potential role in resolving any problems in the family did not appear to be recognised. Paradoxically, although the woman is expected to assume sole responsibility for family matters, she is not treated as an individual. Her problems are considered only when they have an impact on other family members: 'Indeed she is frequently encouraged to suppress her own fears and emotions for the sake of these others. Women are treated as appendages of their families rather than as individuals in their own right.' (ibid.). This is actually at odds with social work values, whether of the dignity of the individual and self-determination era (Miles, 1981, p.15), or deriving from contemporary anti-oppressive, anti-sexist thinking. There is a particular irony in this neglect of issues affecting women, given that most employees in the lower echelons of social services are themselves female (Department of Health Social Services Inspectorate, 1991 and 1992). The presence of large numbers of women in an occupation does not, of course, guarantee that the work will be based on a feminist analysis of male power. Employees are expected to buy into the existing values and priorities of the organisation for which they work, and these are determined within a male ethos.

Being interested only in the children

Social workers are often regarded as being interested only in the children. Researchers (Maynard, 1985; McWilliams and McKiernan, 1993, p.65) and women service users alike confirm that social workers are child focused. It is not the concern with children's safety or well-being that is at issue here, but social workers' apparent inability to look beyond these to the woman's safety, even when the violence to her is obvious and openly talked about, and even though tackling it safely will always leave the children in less distress and will often remove direct dangers towards them (see Chapter 6, this volume). Conversely, women who actually want social work help may be unable to get it unless the allocating worker sees a 'statutory' reason to become involved (Abrahams, 1994, p.85). Women know that social workers prioritise their children's interests above theirs and fear approaching social services in case their children are taken into care (e.g. Dobash and Dobash, 1979, p.200; McWilliams and McKiernan, 1993, p.65); several had actually had this threatened. Workers, in turn, recognise that women may be discouraged from approaching them: 'Social workers are more concerned about children. It is high profile stuff. So coming here does have implications for people' (McGibbon *et al.*, 1989, p.60). It will take a considerable change in attitudes, based on a recognition that helping women frequently coincides with helping children (see Chapter 6, this volume), before this barrier can be broken down. Ironically, there are accounts of social workers overlooking children's real interests because they refuse to listen to women, for example a mother who knew her partner had been physically abusive towards their daughter but could not dissuade the social worker from leaving her with him (McWilliams and McKiernan, 1993, p.66).

Expecting women to 'live with' the violence for the sake of the children

In the 1980s, failure to help women was often closely tied to an expectation that they should stay for the sake of the children:

> She was thinking of leaving her husband again. Pointed out that she had Christopher (son) to consider in this and her husband's feelings for the baby and herself. Reminded her that she had married and had to accept the consequences.
>
> (Maynard, 1985, p.130)

A quarter of the women in Binney *et al.*'s national refuge sample found social workers unhelpful because they attempted to stop them leaving:

> I rang social services because I was so desperate to leave and they said 'All we can do if you leave is we'll take the children off you and take them into care and we don't want that, do we?' so I said 'No' and that was it.
>
> (Binney *et al.*, 1988, p.19)

Dobash *et al.* relate a similar story:

> I went to the welfare to get somewhere to stay but they couldn't help me. Mrs Jones told me I would have to stay and I said, 'I just can't,' and they said, 'You'll just have to stay for the sake of the wee ones.' And at that stage I thought, 'My God all anybody can ever say to me is the wee ones, the wee ones, but what about me?
>
> (Dobash *et al.*, 1985, p.161)

and yet again:

> Patch it up. I thought I was going crackers with patch it up, patch it up, patch it up .... The Welfare all said to me ...: 'You've just got to stay in the home for the sake of the children. You've just got to keep the home together.' And of course there was little else I could do because they wouldn't help me to get a house or anything. Just the usual, you know, just try and talk it over, try and patch it up.
>
> (ibid., p.162)

The typical advice to women on how to do this, at that time, was either just to cope with the violence or to change their behaviour to placate their husbands: 'I advised Mrs Blank not to argue with her husband too much and said that I would pop in to see her in a week or two' (Maynard, 1985, p.130). The social worker played no active role other than handing out this insultingly simplistic and dismissive advice. Sometimes, though, workers did intervene to attempt to assist reconciliation through marital or family work (Binney *et al.*, 1988, p.19) which carries its own dangers (see Chapter 7, this volume).

In the 1990s, this rigid attitude appears to have been replaced by another, equally rigid, which expects women to leave their partners for the sake of the children. McWilliams and McKiernan (1993, p.65), found both attitudes co-existing – 'get rid of him' and 'get back together and talk'. The move towards expecting women to part from their husbands has probably arisen from a greater awareness of the adverse effects on children of living with domestic violence (see Chapter 6, this volume) but still ignores two salient issues: the difficulties and dangers associated with leaving, and the fact that women need to be empowered to make their own choices – otherwise we only replace one set of controls with another. Furthermore, it falls into the victim-blaming trap of continuing to put all the onus of change onto the woman, rather than emphasising criminal justice and other confrontative responses to the abuser, the result of which might mean that he or the danger he poses could be removed from the household.

Blaming the victim

The victim-blaming analysis seen in Chapter 2 was detected by Maynard (1985, pp.133–5) in the heart of social work recording. She found entries in case notes describing women as inadequate in their wifely and motherly roles: 'House is in a shocking condition. I insisted she should get it cleaned up before I called again' (p.133); 'She always has full make-up on but the house was in a tip' (p.134). When the supposed reasons behind the violence and triggers for specific incidents are mentioned, men's complaints about their wives' failings in the kitchen and the bedroom are simply echoed in the case recording as if they explained everything: 'Mr Blank describes her household management as appalling'; 'Her husband complains of her neglect of him and the children'; 'Apart from domestic incompetence, she is also failing to meet his sexual demands' (ibid.). The last quotation is interesting: *he* makes demands (with what kind of controls we can only imagine) but *she* is failing. Maynard sees social workers here as finding ways to understand (whether or not they condone) the violence and hence colluding with it (pp.134–5). It follows from this that the best way for women to avoid further beatings is to conform to men's expectations, to please them, to avoid disagreeing with them. A woman whose 'nagging' was seen as 'the trigger for his violence' was beaten with a shillelagh, punched and kneed. There are also accusations of lying – for example, levelled at a woman whose head had been split open with a gun the week before. There are implications of women accepting, responding to and even enjoying the violence (p.136). Thus the violence may be made to sound natural and the social workers' inactivity less bizarre. These grossly oppressive and unjust reactions to women's experiences have cast social work into widespread disrepute. The fact that social work records are now largely open to their subjects, and therefore less likely to include harshly judgemental comments about them, does not mean that wrong-headed views are not still held by some or even many social workers.

Women are perfectly able to interpret these messages without seeing them in writing, too, and can see that they, rather than their abusive partners, are being blamed for the situation: 'He was all right, he could do what he liked to me but nobody ever tried to help me. It seemed to me that the social workers and the doctors were blaming me for it' (Dobash *et al.*, 1985, p.160). Victim-blaming attitudes are not peculiar to workers who are dismissive of women as people. It is the meaning of their experiences that is dismissed through the lack of an adequate understanding of male violence: 'The social workers were sympathetic but it was a case of, if he did that to me, I'd have done this to him and I'd have done that to him. So it was my fault, and I think they believed him' (ibid.).

Failure to work with or confront the man

Nor did Maynard's sample of social workers take a stand against the male abusers, confronting them about their actions, telling them *they* could lose *their* children if they did not stop, as wives were told could happen if they left. Indeed, men's actions were often minimised: 'And although he beats his wife frequently he rarely hits the children' (Maynard, 1985, p.131). Men's parenting abilities were rarely examined (McGibbon *et al.*, 1989, p.57). This is not surprising since they were frequently not seen and almost never fully involved: 'social workers had made it clear that contact with ... the men who carried out the violence rarely occurred' (Leonard and McLeod, 1980, p.22). That this has remained the case is confirmed by McGibbon *et al.* (1989, p.59), who also comment that 'the possibility of stopping men being abusive was seldom addressed'.

Of course, social workers could be in danger if they confront men (Dobash *et al.*, 1985, p.160; Cervi, 1993, p.5) and, if the workers are women, they may be pulled into the same controlling mechanisms as the men's partners (Hanmer and Statham, 1988, p.81). Hanmer and Statham (ibid.) point out that agencies are becoming more aware of violence generally, with training, paired visits, and so on. Other common measures include personal alarms, staff notifying departure and return times when they make home visits, seniors waiting until everyone is back from visits before leaving the office, and a range of security measures to protect reception and social work staff in social services offices. This growing sensitisation to violence generally could be used as an opening for raising the profile of domestic abuse in social services and may, suggest Hanmer and Statham (ibid.), be a way of beginning to rethink practice with abused women. Social workers could then do more to acknowledge men's role in families and their criminal responsibility for abuse.

Feeling unable to help

There are, of course, social workers who have a better understanding of domestic abuse than those cited above and who want to give active help to women but cannot see how to do so. McWilliams and McKiernan (1993, p.65) met women who had been directly told by social workers that there was nothing they could do. Hanmer and Statham (1988, pp.79–81) highlight the fact that it is not surprising if social workers feel 'frustrated and defeated' by a problem that sees women complaining about 'the very nature of marriage itself': that is, the control of women by the men with whom they live or have previously lived. In their view, social workers *do* feel a desire 'to assist unhappy, depressed and even desperate women' but screen out or minimise the issue because they simply do not know what to do. The Black social workers in Mama's study (1989, p.93) illustrate this frustration: 'very much aware of domestic violence as a problem, but did not have any clear idea what sort of assistance they might provide'. It must be admitted however, that there are also some social workers who tell women there is nothing they can do in a dismissive manner which belittles them and what they have been through (Binney *et al.*, 1988, p.19; McWilliams and McKiernan, 1993, p.65).

Not knowing how to respond to Black women

Mama's research (1989, pp.93–4 and 100) indicates that African Caribbean women and many Asian women do not find social workers helpful. This accords with other work showing social services as punitive rather than supportive to Black women (Bryan, *et al.*, 1985; Ahmad, B., 1990). At the same time, the needs of some groups, such as Chinese and Vietnamese women, tend to be completely invisible to social services departments, while professionals 'freeze' in the face of women of Indian, Pakistani and Bangladeshi origin, not wanting to do the wrong thing and cut across cultural norms. This is the new 'inverted racism' or 'cultural racism' (Ahmed, 1986) which seems to have followed in the wake of brief racism awareness training in agencies. Many workers are now aware that a colour-blind response is not enough, since Black families are somehow 'different', but have not yet learned what to put in its place. This can lead to inappropriate forms of intervention or to none at all, often grounded in stereotypical assumptions about cultural practices. The following quotation is from a white male worker (author's research interview) who had had basic racism-awareness training and some experience of working with Asian families:

> Asian people are quite suspicious and really don't understand what a social worker is offering as the options. It goes over their heads and culturally there's a world of difference between white expectations of the norm and theirs. It's the same with West Indian families. The male figure in the household will be the strictest; he will deal out punishment and say what should happen. The women are often subservient. They do what they're told when they're told and that's the end of the story.

It will not be the end of the violence, however. This is a gross dismissal of the difficulties for Asian women in escaping violence (Imam, 1994) and an unhelpful generalisation of what individual women may want or need.

A lack of support agencies for minority ethnic communities in some areas is likely to mean that any service set up will be eagerly grasped as a resource to call on in all types of case, regardless of its theoretical under-pinnings and attitudes towards women. A family conciliation service may thus be widely supported by social workers making referrals to it, irrespec-tive of the fact that safe conciliation is highly unlikely where persistent abuse has developed. Black refuges and women's organisations are far more likely to understand the risks and to be able to help (Southall Black Sisters, 1990; Ghattaora, 1992; Imam, 1994). Most white social workers still lack subtlety of understanding and sensitivity in helping Black women find the best solution.

Every woman has a right to safety whether she is Black or white. This does not mean imposing white cultural norms on Black people or assuming that white society is superior. All communities and societies experience domestic violence so none can claim cultural superiority on that score. Nor is any culture monolithic. Every community has a range of views within it, held by people striving for different goals – including those who oppose men's control and abuse of women. In all countries, there are groups work-ing for women's safety in the face of misunderstanding or hostility from other sections of the community. In England there are groups of women with origins in the Indian subcontinent working towards the same end and facing the same reactions (Southall Black Sisters, 1990; Imam, 1994). Hanmer and Statham draw attention to Jewish, Muslim and a range of other women's groups and women's analyses of religious writings and teachings:

Claims that male control of women is validated by religion [are], like culture, contested from within. Social workers should not be put off from meeting the requests of women for help by accusations that they are attacking religious beliefs by doing so.

(1988, pp.78–9)

Male community leaders may attempt to exert pressure to keep women in the home and in line. Social workers should not accept this any more unquestioningly than they would accept white men speaking on behalf of white women. The key is to work to woman-centred agendas across communities. This will only be possible if interpreter services are readily available, and services aimed at women's safety are widely known about and advertised in a range of languages. Some white social workers do refer women to specialist Black refuges but feel that more women could be helped if there were greater numbers of Black female staff in their own agencies (McGibbon *et al.*, 1989, p.61). It can also help if white male officials and professionals talk freely about male abuse with Black male community leaders, and emphasise that safety measures and women's organisations need to be supported in all communities (personal communication with Asian woman activist).

Failure to provide the woman with effective help

Despite having personally observed severe injuries, some inflicted with weapons, and being told of death threats, the social workers in Maynard's study had done little actively to help the women concerned. They did not take effective action to remove from women's lives the intimidation and fear they were undergoing, but appeared more concerned with keeping marriages together and with concentrating on the needs of the children rather than those of their mothers. Maynard (1985, pp.129–32) found three referrals to Marriage Guidance (now Relate), two immediate admissions to mental hospital (plus eight other women who had had in-patient treatment and one deemed to need it who refused to go), one woman being advised to take a holiday, seven instances of women being dissuaded from separating or leaving, twelve women described as 'depressed', most as lethargic or lacking in energy, and five having made suicide attempts. Only two social workers suggested separation or divorce and these options do not, of course, guarantee safety. Even if the social workers expressed sympathy to the women that they failed to record on paper, as Maynard generously suggests may have been the case (p.131), there is no escaping the fact that they gave no practical help to stop or escape the violence.

Researchers consistently find that women want practical help (Binney *et al.*, 1988, p.20; Pahl, 1985a, p.80) and want the abuse to stop (McGibbon *et al.*, 1989, pp.34–5). Women's support organisations of various kinds are also viewed positively (ibid.). Those who receive constructive help experience it positively (Binney *et al.*, 1988, p.20), but those who are left to continue living with the violence find intervention of little help.

Being seen by women as unable to help

Women from all communities quickly get the message that effective help is not available from social workers and that they have other concerns: 'I knew about the social work. I knew they existed but not for this type of thing. To me the social work was for families and homeless and things like that.' They also fear unsympathetic intervention which will merely introduce new pressures and controls into their lives. 'I felt that when you get in tow with these people they interfere too much in your home life and with your kids, and the running of your house, which I didn't think was necessary' (Dobash *et al.*, 1985, p.154). Hanmer and Statham (1988, p.79) warn that women will be silenced if they see 'that no one can help or that no one wants to help' and, crucially, that this turns the problem back upon them. It becomes even more their personal trouble: it is their responsibility in every sense of the word and even less likely to be defined as rooted in public issues of social inequality between men and women.

Making the woman feel worse

The problem is that a lack of help does not have a neutral impact on an already desperate woman. Bowker (1983, p.90), in dealing with a range of counselling agencies, highlights the dangers of poor intervention. In addition to prolonging the violence, it may further damage the woman's self-esteem, thus leaving her feeling still more depressed and trapped (see also Dobash and Dobash, 1979, p.205), or help to strengthen the husband's sway over his wife. One specific way in which social workers can make women feel worse is by not taking them seriously: 'Everybody seemed to think I was exaggerating every time I said anything about him' (Dobash *et al.*, 1985, p.162). A number of women in Binney *et al.*'s survey (1988, p.19) felt social workers showed little interest in their desperate situation. This showed most clearly in the passing of off-hand remarks: 'They said the only way I could get out of my situation was by winning the pools'. At base, the failure to develop an adequate understanding of men's abuse of women leaves women to carry the can: 'I felt everybody was up against me, even socially. I felt inadequate as a woman' (Dobash *et al.*, 1985, p.160). Social workers are often experienced as being 'against' women when this need not be the case by virtue of anything the women have done.

THE WAY FORWARD

Much of the previous section has consisted of material which we, as social workers, find hard to read because it is critical of our practice as a profession. We have to accept, though, that social workers' involvement in the lives of abused women is not neutral. It will either hinder or help the woman in her attempts to marshal the authorities and her own coping strategies to stop the abuse. The next chapter will concentrate on exploring ways in which social services can be of positive assistance, first through agency-wide initiatives and then in specific areas of practice. There is an urgent need for new research to look at the reorganised social work and care management specialisms, to trace the extent of – and responses to – domestic abuse in those settings. In the meantime, we can be sure that large numbers of abused women could be reached by social workers, both those already on caseloads who are being abused but who are currently hidden behind every possible category of work, and those who come forward as new referrals.

Chapter 4

Developing good practice in social services departments

Some social services departments have begun to recognise domestic abuse as an issue in its own right and to take action to help social workers, and the whole department, to make a more appropriate response. Clearly, the research summarised in Chapter 3 has shown over a period of time that there is a desperate need for this, but, in fact, it has largely had to wait for pressure from local authority women's units and from inter-agency groupings before any change has been put in hand. That the profession of social work is not taking a lead is illustrated by the disgracefully thin Memorandum of Evidence submitted by the British Association of Social Workers to the Home Affairs Committee (House of Commons, 1992b, Memorandum 9). This makes only six points, including two aimed at other agencies and one about elder abuse. It says nothing whatsoever about what social workers can do to confront abuse or assist women, and admits responsibility only for cases involving children and older people.

Typically, those social services departments which have taken a more positive approach have started with the introduction of an overall policy (for example in the context of community care planning or a corporate stance on taking domestic violence seriously) and/or a set of guidelines that outlines good practice and gives an indication of the standard of service women should expect to receive. A range of examples will be given in this chapter. Coherent policies and consistent guidelines represent a major advance over individual workers either ignoring the problem entirely, or taking inappropriate action, or happening to be able to give useful assistance but without consistent support from their agency. There have been moves within the Department of Health's Social Services Inspectorate (SSI) to encourage such progress. Two conferences were held during March 1995, in London and Leeds, to urge social services directors to take an urgent and co-ordinated approach to the issue of domestic abuse (Ball, 1995).

After exploring agency-wide developments, this chapter will go on to consider what good practice looks like in duty and child care settings. Further attention will be paid to the needs of children in Chapter 6 and, in relation to family court welfare work, in Chapter 7. Prior to that, other social services work, in care management, health and adult care settings, will be examined in Chapter 5.

BEST PRACTICE

Recent best practice examples, showing what can be done, are the development of an inter-departmental corporate policy (e.g. Hammersmith and Fulham, Hackney, Islington, Newcastle), the inclusion of domestic violence in community care planning (e.g. Leeds City Council *et al.*, 1992/93 and updates since 1993/94; London Borough of Newham, 1993–96, pp.99–102; see also Chapter 5, this volume), and the issuing of detailed guidelines. The latter may either cover all relevant groups of staff, with a section addressed to social services (e.g. London Boroughs of Islington, 1992, and of Hackney, 1994), or be written specifically for the social services department (Nottinghamshire County Council, 1989; Leeds City Council Department of Social Service, undated). From the voluntary sector, good advice for social workers has come in publications from Family Service Units (Winfield, 1988; see below) and NCH Action for Children (Abrahams, 1994, pp.16–17), as well as Women's Aid (Scottish Women's Aid, 1989b; see also the publications list of the Women's Aid Federation, England, based in Bristol).

Good practice guidelines

Family Service Units were among the first on the scene with their *Domestic Violence: A Step-by-Step Guide for Social Workers and Others* (Winfield, 1988). Drawing on the input of a range of other professions and organisations, their booklet gave a very full account of the legal protection available to women (as it then stood) and considered the role of social workers, as well as the police, housing and benefit officials, the medical professions, and Women's Aid. The task of the social worker was seen as helping the woman feel safe, believed, and able to use the appropriate services if she so chose. An opening list of 'Eight Things To Do Immediately' covered the following imperatives:

1. Create a safe place for the woman. (E.g. With an interpreter if needed; providing a female or male, and Black or white worker according to preference; interviewing apart from the abuser if present.)
2. Attend to any injuries. (Also to emotional state; obtain medical treatment if needed; medical/police/social work documenting of all the foregoing for any legal action.)
3. Find out if there are any children. Are they safe? (Scottish Women's Aid, 1989b, adds getting a colleague to look after the children, if present, during the interview.)

4. Identify sources of immediate support.
5. Find out the legal position. (Current injunctions, powers of arrest.)
6. Cultural factors must be taken into consideration. (They may compound the dangers and other consequences.)
7. Individual factors must be taken into consideration.
8. Be clear about your own attitudes and values. (Based on Winfield, *op. cit.*, pp.7–8)

The booklet provided space to write down the details of: temporary accommodation locally, including for minority ethnic groups; sources of financial aid, including charities; community support groups and resources; and sympathetic solicitors, doctors and health visitors, housing and DSS officers, including the languages they speak. All duty and out-of-hours teams (and anyone else on duty rotas, for example in hospitals or care management settings) still need to gather this information and make it available to all team members, along with details of the more recent addition of the police domestic violence unit or any local equivalent and, of course, Women's Aid. The booklet is dated by its failure to warn of the dangers of marital and family work where there is violence (see Chapter 7, this volume); it also strays into the assumed 'cycle of violence' (see Chapter 2, this volume, for the failure of research findings to bear this out) as a major reason for helping children, but, in other regards, its message to social workers to challenge societal attitudes by higlighting abuse as unacceptable and as the man's, not the woman's, problem remains of crucial importance. Social work support is seen as potentially very helpful to the woman in allowing her to pause, take stock of her options, and reach the difficult decision whether to leave home or not, with all the attendant risks in both situations.

Nottinghamshire County Council's Social Services Department (1989) was one of the first to provide advice for its own staff on an agency-wide basis with its *Domestic Violence – Guide to Practice: Practice Guidelines to Assist Staff Dealing with Situations Involving Domestic Violence* (followed later by its booklet: *Putting a Stop to Domestic Violence: A Practical Guide for All Advisers*, Morris, undated). Social workers were given advice on: how to respond to initial referrals – including those received in relation to statutory child care, mental health, services for older people, or other categories where the violence might not be immediately mentioned; how to give advice and practical help to women; how to work appropriately and in a non-exploitative way with refuges – for example, not passing on financial or child care problems that the social worker could have solved or accepted responsibility for; and how to deal with violent partners. The latter section stressed risk to the woman, children and worker, and the need to maintain confidentiality and to avoid any collusion with the abuse.

Brief mention was made of the particular needs of Black women,

women whose first language is not English, older women, disabled women and lesbian women. Appendices contained practical information about housing, legal and financial rights – seen as the typical problems with which women would seek advice and help – as well as a resource list of refuges and other specialist voluntary organisations. The *Guide* mentioned that staff in family centres and day centres, as well as community workers, would be working with women experiencing abuse, but was primarily directed towards field staff. The latter were seen as likely to offer long-term involvement only if there was a statutory reason to be involved.

The Nottinghamshire *Guide* built on the kind of awareness outlined in the opening chapters of this book. The key advice to social workers was to put aside their own feelings about domestic violence, gender roles and the family, and to listen to what women were actually saying. There was an important recognition that women were likely to have been subjected to abuse for some time, and would have needed to summon up considerable courage to approach the Department at all. The type of reception received there could influence – and perhaps jeopardise – any future help-seeking efforts. The most helpful approach would include: a private interview with a woman worker (see Downey, 1992, on the potentially negative effect of not being able to choose to see a woman worker), based on hearing the full circumstances without rushing into offering advice; a believing approach, emphasising the seriousness of domestic abuse and raising the possibility of reporting it to the police as criminal behaviour; avoidance of any hint of victim blaming; assistance to the woman in making her own choices and beginning to take control over her situation; encouragement to return to the Department if future help was needed; and good record keeping, with details of injuries, in case confirmation of these should be needed to support the woman in court, housing applications, or other official contacts.

In 1992, the Women's Equality Unit of Islington Borough Council drew up *Working with Those Who Have Experienced Domestic Violence: A Good Practice Guide* (London Borough of Islington, 1992), which was updated in 1995. Section 7 of this borough-wide advice focuses on social services in relation to child care, duty work, contact with violent men, and mental health work. The aim of any social work intervention is emphasised as being 'to maximise the opportunities for women to take control of their lives'. Male responsibility for abuse is emphasised, and concepts such as 'dysfunctional families' and women provoking violence are explicitly rejected. Women's safety is stressed, for example by reminding staff that women have been murdered while left alone with their abusers in the offices of statutory agencies. Clear recording that the abuse has been reported to the Department, and preparedness to write letters of support, are seen as potentially important later, for example in respect of child care proceedings, injunction applications, rehousing, DSS Crisis Loans, and so on.

More recently, there has tended to be a sharing of information between the more active local authorities so that many of the same themes arise across their documents. Hackney Council's Women's Unit, for example, in producing *Good Practice Guidelines: Responding to Domestic Violence* (London Borough of Hackney, 1994) builds on the work of others including the Nottinghamshire and Islington Guides, the FSU booklet, and a policy report from Lewisham. The *Guidelines* contain one section for social services and others for education, housing, and managers across the borough's services whose own staff may be being abused, as well as material on equal opportunities and on the law. Women's own pacing and choices are again strongly emphasised in decision making (p.38), with the social worker helping the woman to take control rather than imposing views or alternatives on her. A believing approach is the basis for this, extending here to not asking for verification of physical assault before offering help (in recognition of emotional, sexual and other forms of abuse).

Awareness of the interlinking nature of many forms of oppression is reflected in mentions of the impact of women's immigration status, caring responsibilities, and/or of reduced access to housing, money and information for many groups of women. Black women's wariness about approaching the police or social services is recognised, and the suggested response includes giving information about complaints procedures whilst, at the same time, increasing access to non-racist, non-racially stereotyping services. Absolute confidentiality is again stressed for all women, with a reminder that disclosing details which reach the abuser can lead to a woman's death.

The Guidelines stress the fact that workers right across a social services department, from office receptionists to nursery nurses, from care managers to approved social workers, will be working with women who are being subjected to abuse. Particular attention is paid to staff on duty in area offices and to the most helpful response to initial referrals. Whilst it is recognised that this will usually involve referring women on to other agencies for practical help rather than allocating the case internally, it is suggested that this whole process be fully explained, that recording be openly shared, and that the woman be supported throughout her approach to the other agencies – if not by the social worker then by a relative or friend.

Leeds City Council Department of Social Service (undated; this also built on the Islington and other materials), working as one of the funders of a large inter-agency project (see Chapter 10, this volume), has produced *Good Practice Guidelines* for its own staff in working with women experiencing violence from known men, or with their children or abusers. They contain general background material about abuse and very helpful principles covering all intervention – including confidentiality, sensitivity, and maximising the woman's control over the situation – as well as the specifics of working with spoken and sign language interpreters and of practising in particular situations such as on duty, or in child protection, mental health, or work with older or disabled women (the last three of these will be returned to in Chapter 5, and the others below). Wider anti-oppressive issues are well integrated into the material presented.

The general principles in these *Guidelines* go into a great deal of useful detail. Under 'safety and confidentiality', for example, pointers are given such as not recording the woman's address on official papers 'except where essential and with her permission', never passing on the address or even letting the abuser learn that the department knows how to contact the woman – since this puts both her and staff at risk. It is also recognised that Black staff who are members of the same community as the woman may be at particular risk, with specific supervision and safety needs. In addition to practical advice, the *Guidelines* also strongly emphasise sensitivity to women's feelings. This is apparent in everything from urging workers to be trustworthy and respectful of the woman's wishes, as well as knowledge-able about abuse and able to ask the right questions, to encouraging the placing of posters and other materials with imagery and wording/languages representative of the local area in social services premises to let women know that they are not alone and that they can expect support from the staff working there.

There is also a useful section for managers (Leeds City Council Department of Social Service, undated, Section 6). In addition to their role in ensuring that all staff are familiar with and act in accordance with the *Guidelines*, and are adequately trained and supported, this draws to managers' attention their responsibility for creating an environment in which services for women are publicised and men's violence is viewed as a crime, not tolerated through jokes or dismissive comments. There is also a clear recognition that staff are amongst those at risk in their personal and professional lives, and that managers can be key people in making confidential advice and support available. We might go further than this and urge managers, for example, to block physical or telephone access by abusers to staff where this would be helpful and, if it is the abuser who is the employee, never to shield him or condone his behaviour or attitudes. Indeed, his abuse could be regarded as wholly relevant to the question of continued employment in a social work or social-work related setting unless there is evidence of very real efforts to change.

Agency-wide standards

At the agency-wide level, the compilation of statistics, provision of training, and co-ordination of services, including through the funding of specialist staff, are all ways of seeking to develop a better quality of service for all women who are experiencing abuse and who are in contact with social workers.

Statistics and policy development

Typically, social services departments do not know how many of their adult female service users are being abused (Leeds City Council *et al.*, 1992/93, p.9), even where the abuse is the main reason for seeking help land even in authorities where there has been the most activity targeted at the issue. This makes it difficult to argue for more resources or to distribute them effectively. It could also allow 'backlash' claims that few women are abused, or that men suffer equally (see Chapter 1), to be used against moves to increase resources for women. Domestic abuse should be included as a specific category in referral and assessment forms, and intake or duty records, and should feature in all agency monitoring exercises on the work being undertaken by staff (McGibbon *et al.*, 1989, p.15). Currently, people are operating with widely differing guesstimates which can vary even within one office (McWilliams and McKiernan, 1993, pp.67–8). Statistical information about cases involving abuse is lost behind every category with which it may coincide, notably child care and mental health but by no means only these (see Chapter 5, this volume), and even consultations by women seeking specific help in duty settings are often recorded under general headings such as 'family problems' (Leeds City Council *et al.*, 1992/93, p.13) or 'family work' and 'other adult cases' (McGibbon *et al.*, 1989, p.57). This makes it far harder to improve services for women experiencing abuse since information cannot be pulled together until agreed terminology and recording practices are in place. Both duty workers and staff engaged in planning, research, information management and policy development will require guidance in the use of whatever new recording term is chosen, including a basic understanding of the forms of abuse and relationship categories to be included under it.

We know from the research summarised in Chapter 3 that social services departments encounter large numbers of women who are experiencing abuse. We also know that the abuse tends to persist and escalate over time, which means that an effective response early on may actually save agencies work in the longer term. McGibbon *et al.* (1989, p.15) suggest that this merits a full-scale policy approach, recognising that appropriate help given at the stage of a first referral or early engagement with a new service user may prevent resource-intensive statutory child care and/or mental health intervention at a later stage. In cases the author has come across, a woman in a residential unit designed to undertake intensive assessment of her ability to care for and keep her young children, who was receiving psychiatric out-patient treatment after years of being called a 'mad woman' by her abusive husband and his family, had never been listened to when she had talked about violent and other abuse at earlier stages of her contact with the department. Similarly, the child protection social worker faced with meeting the practical and emotional needs of a family of children, one being seen by a child psychiatrist and another by an educational psychologist, whose father was in prison for killing their mother, may well have wished that the woman had received a more constructive response from any sources of help she had attempted to tap at an earlier point. Both these cases went on to absorb large amounts of staff time and other resources from social services. Managers, politicians, and others involved in influencing policy could take an entirely pragmatic approach to improving the response to such women in the early stages, regardless of their personal views on women's social status or on family life.

Training

A Women's Aid worker, asked to comment on the quality of help offered to women by social workers, replied: 'Very mixed. Some social workers seem to be great – others not. They need training.' Consistency of appropriate help, including in taking abuse seriously as soon as a woman begins to mention it in any of its forms, can only come from raised awareness. Both intensive team-level training and inter-agency training can offer good models; the latter should also improve liaison between relevant services. The Leeds Inter-Agency Project and the Cleveland Domestic Violence Co-ordinator both began their work by stressing the need to train the trainers in social services so that there can be a cascade effect of knowledge through the agency (pers. comms). Otherwise, the sheer numbers of staff needing to be aware of the issues is overwhelming. There is no member of a social services' workforce in direct contact with the public who does not need some awareness. Subsequent sections will demonstrate this in relation to duty teams, approved social workers and other mental health staff, and child care practitioners, for example.

Probably the most widespread training link to date is that between local Women's Aid groups and social services in relation to child protection, from which both stand to gain through pooling expertise. Even a modest approach can be valuable; inviting a Women's Aid speaker to a team or area meeting, for example (McGibbon et al., 1989, p.15), can improve working relationships and heighten sensitivity to women's needs. Child protection specialists in some departments are organising multi-disciplinary training events on children and domestic abuse, for example in Cheshire and in Inverness during late 1995. These localised events are particularly helpful in opening up debate between professionals who must work together in the context of difficult cases and set policy for the future. Other targeted training has included that offered by the Leeds Inter-Agency Project – on the incidence and impact of domestic violence – to residential and day care workers in mental health, and to area office staff. All training must counter the myths outlined in Chapter 2, which generate complacency and adverse attitudes towards women, and replace these with the best available skill-base and knowledge.

Front-line workers themselves would warmly welcome more training, which might usefully include meeting their own needs in coping with the impact of abuse on others or sometimes on themselves – perhaps through some single-sex component to the training event (McWilliams and McKiernan, 1993, p.67).

In qualifying training for social workers, there is an *ad hoc* approach to the inclusion of material on domestic abuse in the curriculum (ibid., and wide personal experience), even though reading the practice learning accounts by any cohort of students will reveal its presence in the work they encounter on placement. There is also the danger that the eclectic way in which the curriculum is assembled will mean that conflicting messages cancel each other out – for example, a lecture on domestic abuse might be juxtaposed with teaching on couple or family work that does not emphasise the dangers of seeing couples together where there is violence (see Chapter 7). In this way, students are actually learning dangerous responses.

Overlapping training needs include: the development of appropriate services for women from ethnic minorities; the use of interpreters; legal, financial and housing rights; and comprehensive assessments of women's needs, including women who are older and/or disabled and/or lesbian.

Liaison and co-ordination

One development that can certainly help to keep domestic abuse to the forefront of planning is the establishment of specialist posts. Typically, the post-holders concentrate on improving liaison with Women's Aid and other relevant women's groups, including those for Black women, as well as working to develop their department's own response. The London Borough of Newham, for example, has created two social work posts to work half time in Social Services and half time in the voluntary sector – Newham Asian Women's Project and Newham Action Against Domestic Violence – one post designated for an Asian woman and the other for an African Caribbean woman. The posts combine a practice-based role, aimed at supporting and empowering women through direct work with them and their children, with an inter-departmental policy development and liaison role. Nottinghamshire Social Services has a funded refuge liaison worker. In Bradford, a community care officer, whose post is split half time with Keighley Domestic Violence Forum, has her funding base in a health trust which gives her greater freedom to argue for change both in social service and in health provision. Similarly, the Leeds Inter-Agency Project has established a post of Partnership Adviser, jointly funded by the Health Authority and Social Services, in order to pursue progress in both settings. In Social Services, for example, she has a training and developmental role.

One aspect of this has been to offer two-day courses on the incidence and impact of domestic violence targeted at two groups of employees: mental health and residential and day care staff and managers, and those in and responsible for area offices. Key reference points for her work include the Gender Equality Officer in Social Services and the Leeds Inter-Agency Project (Women and Violence), including for line management.

Liaison within and between the statutory and voluntary sectors is crucial. In inner-city areas, for example, support teams working with women in bed-and-breakfast provision, hostels and homeless families units all need to be brought into the picture. Co-ordination needs to build on strengths already in place, particularly in women's organisations with their twenty-year history of assisting women subjected to abuse. There can be a tendency, despite their poor record, for some social services departments to act as if they have just invented the issue of domestic abuse and to fail to respect external expertise, including in the field of child protection (Singh, 1991, pp.4–5) – where, after all, it was women's groups who were amongst the first to 'hear' and believe survivors' accounts of child sexual abuse. Where social services departments fund posts in the voluntary sector, or contract for services, there can be vexed questions of control over resources and policies. Confidentiality, for example, may be viewed differently by a women's organisation, which wishes to support women in choosing whether to report past child abuse where the child is not in current danger, as against local authority policies which expect automatic reporting even though successful prosecution rates may be low and investigations very intrusive and traumatic for children (Debbonaire, 1994, pp.150–1). A financial stake in the organisation may carry with it an expectation that local authority policies will automatically be adhered to. It may also give rise to tensions if the social services department funds posts on local authority terms and conditions, and within a hierarchical career structure, and seconds them to women's organisations which have traditionally run along collective lines.

Membership of a multi-agency forum may be the best way in which a social services department can formulate policy and clarify its own role in conjunction with others, and also set in place processes for effective inter-agency liaison (see Chapter 10, this volume). The Area Child Protection Committee is another useful forum for developing a co-ordinated strategy in respect of woman abuse and its impact on children. This needs to draw on a subtle and creative understanding of what can be done to empower women and work with them to make children safe, not resort over readily to registration of children in households where there is abuse, which may help neither them nor their mothers (see section on child protection, below).

Local authorities also need to ensure internal consistency of response to domestic abuse. Hammersmith and Fulham, for example, in 1989 launched a corporate domestic violence programme as a component of its community safety strategy. The most comprehensive of its kind in the UK at the time, it sought to ground the work of every relevant department in an analysis of women's needs in situations of abuse and was accompanied by membership of a Multi-Agency Domestic Violence Group to extend co-ordination beyond the authority. A number of other authorities have since introduced corporate policies, or authority-wide Zero Tolerance stances against domestic violence (see Chapter 10, this volume).

We will now move on to explore how workers in specific areas of practice can improve their awareness of domestic violence.

DUTY WORK

Much of the good practice advice contained in the various sets of guidelines outlined above is of particular relevance to duty workers – whether in field, out-of-hours or specialist teams – and will not be repeated here. The key priorities are attention to safety needs (backed by confidentiality, including in any future telephone, letter or personal contact agreed with the woman), together with a sensitive and believing approach which stresses that the violence is not the woman's fault, that she is not alone in experiencing it, and which treats it as a crime. It is also important to ask directly, though sensitively, about abuse (McWilliams and McKiernan, 1993, pp.68–9) and to be alert to hints the woman may drop to test out whether she will be believed and helped.

A woman coming into a social services office, including for other reasons initially, will pick up important messages and information straight away about sympathetic attitudes and help available if multi-lingual posters and leaflets on emergency helplines and other domestic abuse services, including for Black women, are displayed in reception and waiting areas (and in social services day nurseries and other premises). There also needs to be handy information on legal measures, benefits, housing, immigration and nationality issues – both for women to pick up and for duty officers and other staff to hand out and explain. Helpline telephone numbers on posters need to be in large enough print for women to read them without having to walk over and identify themselves as interested (thus drawing the attention of the abuser if present). Similarly, leaflets should be displayed in amongst others so that a woman can take a handful of different ones without drawing undue attention to herself. Publicity material and advice given need to make clear that women can telephone Women's Aid and Black women's projects for advice and support without necessarily leaving home and without a referral.

There need to be play facilities for children and another member of staff available to look after them during a duty interview with a woman. She may need to describe distressing physical and intimate sexual assaults when she tells her story, so private and soundproof interview space is also important. The woman should always be seen alone for at least part of the interview if abuse is suspected. Her abuser may be with her and may be female – it cannot just be assumed that the woman has brought a friend with her. The abuser may be very plausible and pleasant in reception and in any joint interview, but the woman may be completely unable to disclose the abuse in her abuser's presence.

The Leeds *Good Practice Guidelines* (Leeds City Council Department of Social Service, undated, Section 5 under 'Duty Desk') are particularly strong on ascertaining the woman's physical safety and that of her children, both at the time of the interview (which may need to be relocated) and subsequently, when police help may need to be summoned. Other staff in the office, including those in administration, also need alerting to the questions of confidentiality and safety.

A woman interviewer needs to be available: a Black woman where the caller prefers this, and with interpreter support for any Black or white woman who speaks a first language in which the interviewer is not fluent. The gender of the interpreter may be important to the woman, as may potential problems with confidentiality or objectivity if they come from the same community. The Leeds *Good Practice Guidelines* (Leeds City Council Department of Social Service, undated, Section 4) include a whole section on using spoken and sign language interpreters. In addition to basic good practice in working with interpreters, this stresses the need for a shared understanding of what confidentiality means and of its importance. The worker is reminded to check fluency in a shared language and dialect, as well as the existence of two-way acceptance: by the woman concerned of this particular interpreter, and by the interpreter of the need to translate exactly the message the woman is conveying. It is not appropriate to use children or relatives as interpreters. Duty officers also need to be alert to the particular issues for women who are recent immigrants and should seek expert advice (ibid., Section 5), since their right to stay in the country and their access to services may be in question and may be affected by leaving home.

Clear and full records, openly shared with and agreed by the woman, are always essential. It should be remembered that they may afterwards need to be drawn on in support of legal proceedings, or a homelessness or other application, as well as to pass on information to colleagues or other professionals who may subsequently be involved and who may be called on to respond in an emergency. The Leeds *Good Practice Guidelines* (undated, Section 3) stress that, without asking women to prove or give unnecessary accounts of their experiences, it is useful for the above purposes to include in the record, firstly, a description of how the woman appears physically and emotionally – including the emotional, behavioural and physical signs that she is experiencing violence – and, secondly, the precise words she uses: e.g. 'My husband hit me with a bat' rather than 'Client has been abused'.

Safety planning with the woman, for herself and her children, is an immediate priority and may focus either on reaching safety now or on being able to do so in a future emergency, by keeping some cash, key documents and other essentials in an easily accessible place, for example. Women are generally very good judges of when they are unsafe in intimate relationships and may, for example, know when an attack is brewing. If they say they need immediate help then they do. They may be in danger of losing their lives. It is important, though, to listen to what women want and not to assume that one course or pace of action suits every situation, even if there are outward similarities. As with any duty interview, it is important to discuss options and possible consequences, other sources of help and how they can be accessed. It goes without saying that duty officers need a basic working knowledge of injunctions and legal aid/law centres, home-lessness legislation and local practice, how to help women contact the DSS, and what Black and general women's resources exist locally. Women's Aid will know where there is a refuge with disabled access but it may well come under heavy demand and may be some distance away. It can help a great deal if the duty officer takes personal responsibility for following matters through, to ensure that the woman gets the help she seeks from other agencies, for example. The officer giving the woman their name also helps her to follow up her contact with them if she wishes. Now that the advent of care management has meant that social services departments are taking advantage of computer packages for conducting benefits checks, there is no reason why these could not be used to assist women who may have left, or be considering leaving home. A comprehensive benefits check is, in any case, good practice.

Most duty responses do try to meet immediate needs. A woman who leaves home and/or who telephones an emergency duty team will, we should be able to assume, be listened to, helped to find emergency accommodation, and to obtain some money and food. The police and Women's Aid can both be called on a 24-hour basis, if needed. If the children's well-being is in question, the case may be allocated to a social worker for longer-term involvement, whereas this will normally only result from concerns about the woman herself if she is assessed as having needs that fit into a category such as mental health, disability, learning difficulties, or services for older people (and by no means always then). Otherwise, any assistance will probably be on an emergency or short-term basis – but it should never be perfunctory or dismissive.

Problems can arise, on occasions, in giving even a basic response in a bureaucratic departmental context where resources and staff are under pressure. It is crucial that duty workers take a sympathetic, believing and serious approach to domestic abuse, no matter how many times the woman may have sought help or what her circumstances. One social services duty officer, for example, interviewed a young woman with three children under 5 who had walked out of a refuge during an argument the evening before, after a stay of several months, and had slept overnight on a friend's floor. The woman was very distressed and described still being continually harassed by her ex-partner. She did not want to go back to him (he still occupied the family home and refused to leave), and she had nowhere else to go. The duty team manager felt there was nothing that could be done and wanted to refer the problem back to the refuge, although the woman did not want to return there. The duty officer, however, who had a good knowledge of domestic abuse and considered the children to be at risk of continued distress and now homelessness, argued strongly and persistently for a section 17 payment under the 1989 Children Act to meet immediate needs and for practical emergency intervention. She accompanied the woman to the relevant office of the housing department and persuaded them to admit the woman and her children to the homeless families' unit the same day. She also put the woman in touch with a solicitor. The duty worker happened to have personal and professional experience of domestic abuse and fought this woman's corner until something practical was achieved. Various other people in the same department had attempted to pass the buck and there was no departmental policy or guidance to follow. It is crucially important not to give up on women who may appear not to have made 'good use' of earlier help. Everything about domestic abuse makes taking control of one's life difficult – it is intended to – and slipping into woman-blaming colludes with this.

Social workers should avoid sending women from agency to agency without support and should do as much as possible from the office while the woman is there. Social workers have emerged from research (e.g. Pahl, 1985a, p.80; Home, 1991–92, p.158) as being very good at knowing the system and being aware of available services. This makes them a valuable resource to women, whether still living with their abusers or having left, in co-ordinating the efforts of others. It is never helpful to despair and feel the problem is just too big for one busy professional to be of any help. He or she may be a life-line, including to women who come to the office because they have the fewest options (through lack of money, for example) and the fewest supports. Good inter-agency liaison will help the worker to feel that he or she and the woman concerned are not facing the problem alone, and sympathetic contacts in other agencies, preferably known by name, may be especially useful.

CHILD PROTECTION AND CHILD WELFARE

Until very recently there has been a complete split between services for abused women and those for abused children, with a profound ignorance on the part of many child care workers about woman abuse and its relevance to their own work. When directly asked whether the issue of children living with domestic violence arose in her work, for example, one member of a child protection team asked for the question to be repeated and then enquired 'Do you mean whether they grow up violent?' Not only is this 'cycle of violence' link based on spurious assumptions (see Chapter 2), but it adversely labels the children in question and offers them and their mothers no constructive help in their current circumstances.

The impact on children – moral panic or effective help?

Increased attention to the emotional impact upon children of living with woman abuse, and to the heightened risks of direct child abuse where the mother is being abused (see Mullender and Morley, 1994, and Chapter 6, this volume), means that there is beginning to be proper social work concern about the well-being of the children of women who are experiencing abuse. Local authorities have a responsibility, under section 47(1) of the Children Act 1989, to enquire into the welfare of any child who may be suffering or be likely to suffer 'significant harm', and then to decide whether they need to take any action to safeguard or promote the child's welfare. Intervention involving the courts will be examined in more detail in Chapter 7, since the legal provisions overlap with those used following separation and divorce. This can lead to child protection investigations, sometimes resulting in case conferences, in respect of children in a household where an abused woman is or has been living, or whom she has brought out of the household with her. Without more training, there will continue to be a tendency for these enquiries and decisions to be made without a full understanding either of the phenomenon of men's abuse of women or of the most effective ways to help women and children where the woman is being abused. Discussions by Area Child Protection Committees (inter-agency co-ordinating forums), about the need to consider children living with domestic violence, have also sometimes veered towards similarly blanket and punitive suggestions (pers. comms and conference workshop discussions). More often, the topic has simply been overlooked (Abrahams, 1994, p.17).

The statutory duty covering children has no equivalent relating to women, whatever the danger they are in. A few departments have formally accepted responsibility to offer assistance to women through their community care plans or other policy development (see above and Chapters 5 and 10); most make a more *ad hoc* response. This results in children's needs often being considered somewhat in a vacuum, and women being seen as instruments for meeting children's needs rather than as people in their own right who may be impeded in offering their children the care they would choose unless their own needs are met. There is a consequent danger that, as the awareness of the impact on children of living with domestic violence rises, social work concerns could lead to well-meaning and apparently child-focused but actually intrusive and unhelpful interventions.

The risk is that these could cut across the care non-abusing mothers would offer were a little more assistance, and a true partnership approach, to be made available.

Placing the children of abused women too readily on child protection registers, or threatening to remove them if their mother – unassisted – is judged as failing to meet some form of externally imposed and possibly unrealistic expectation (such as leaving home by a fixed date), comes under this heading of intrusive and unhelpful interventions. In one county, for a time, whenever the police were called to an incident of domestic violence, they routinely contacted social services if there were children living in the house. This led to large numbers of children being registered – 'not', as one worker put it, 'because we doubt Mrs X's parenting skills, but because we are worried in case the children get caught up in it and accidentally hurt'. Policy and practice development needs to be far more subtle than this and child protection planning needs to build on the wider understanding of men's abuse of women conveyed in earlier chapters, emphasising partnership with the mother, since she has done nothing to cause the abuse she has experienced. In this hypothetical case of the X family, for example, placing the children on the child protection register would do nothing to make them or their mother safer, and would ignore Mrs X's probable capacity to care perfectly adequately for the children if someone took, or helped her take, action to end the abuse. As so often, the perpetrator appears scarcely to figure in the equation and we might well ask why involvement has not led to more effective intervention with him by social service or criminal justice agencies.

Child protection cases – the relevance of woman abuse

Rethinking of current approaches to domestic violence is necessary not only where the abuse of a woman comes to social work attention and raises concerns about her children, but also in cases where social workers are already involved because of child abuse. Recent research by Farmer and Owen (1995) has revealed both ignorance and disregard of men's abuse of women which could actually have major relevance as a measure of risk and as a helpful focus of intervention. An intensive follow-up study of 44 families with one or more children on the child protection register revealed domestic violence (in all but one instance here meaning men's violence to female partners), known to social workers in 12 cases and not known to them in another 11 (ibid., p.79; see also Chapter 6, this volume, for a summary of the strong research evidence of an overlap between child abuse and woman abuse). Reasons why these 11 women had not disclosed the abuse they experienced to social workers may have included the control rather than care nature of the social services' involvement (ibid.), sometimes the continued presence of the abusive man in the household (p.240), or perhaps – we may surmise – because the right questions were not asked by the practitioners concerned. Case conferences, in any case, did not place significant weight on men's violence to women (p.138) or diverted it from the agenda (p.172). The study revealed this as dangerous since entrenched patterns of woman abuse were associated with poor outcomes in terms of child protection and carer support (pp.302–6).

In continuing work with the families concerned, social workers left cases to drift because they did not know what to do about domestic violence (p.306). Social workers treated it as beyond their control (p.303) and simply worked with whatever else seemed more accessible, which included working with women because they were more amenable and available than the men (p.319 and see Chapter 7, this volume). Workers thus diverted their efforts from considering or confronting the man over his abuse of mother and child(ren) – in one case dropping work to exclude him from the home – onto another focus such as the woman's performance as a mother or 'failure to protect' her child, the child's behaviour, other family problems such as finances, or family of origin issues (pp.225–6). As a result of this 'absence of a clear focus on abusing behaviour' (p.226), social work involvement and understanding of risk were rendered far from effective. Workers appear to have been more influenced by whether the woman was co-operative with them – in which case they felt the child was relatively safe (p.306) – than by the continued presence of, and abusive control exercised by, the man. Yet, in the next to worst category by outcome (where children had failed to be protected), the risk posed by the man to the child was the reason for involvement in the cases, and severe and prolonged violence towards the woman provided continuing evidence that he had not changed (p.303). The women concerned were left to regulate the actions of their partners (p.319) because the social workers failed to do so. The women in turn felt blamed for inadequate child care (p.305). In one case, the child eventually became subject to a care order, following injuries and neglect, and the woman was still left without assistance with the abuse to which she was being subjected, or now with her grief at the loss of her child (p.304).

In fact, the Guidance accompanying the 1989 Children Act (vol. 1, para. 4.31) recommends that, where possible, the child abuser rather than the child should be removed from the home and imaginative ways could be explored to facilitate this. The local authority has powers under Schedule 2, paragraph 5 of the Act to provide financial assistance which could pay to accommodate the abuser if he is willing to leave. If he is not willing, and assuming that the criminal law cannot provide an answer or is felt by the woman to be inappropriate, the woman may have a strong enough case to pursue under civil law to attempt to remove the abuser. Section 76 of the Children (Scotland) Act 1995 now gives statutory powers for the abuser of a child to be excluded from the home under certain, very tightly circumscribed circumstances. These include there being reasonable cause to believe that the child will cease to suffer significant harm (or the likelihood of significant harm) if the abuser leaves, the order being necessary to protect the child, and its being more likely to safeguard the child's welfare than removing the child from the family home. There must also be a named person in the household who can care for the child, who is likely typically to be the non-abusing parent. An amendment to the 1989 Children Act, along similar lines (but here providing for a requirement excluding the abuser from the home to be included in an emergency protection or interim care order in respect of the child), fell with the withdrawal of the Family Homes and Domestic Violence Bill in 1995 (see Chapter 2, this volume). At the time of writing, the Family Law Bill has picked up the same provision to exclude an abuser (in Schedule 6) but its passage through parliament is controversial in relation both to its measures on divorce and those on domestic violence. It remains to be seen, therefore, whether exclusion orders become law in England and Wales. Of course, neither the man nor the woman leaving home guarantees that the man will stop abusing and, even if he is excluded from the household, further safety measures will still need to be considered by the woman for herself and the children, perhaps with social work help.

Indeed, one way in which men who abuse women frequently continue their abuse and their attempts to control the situation following separation is by manipulating family law provisions to allege unsatisfactory care by their ex-partners (London Borough of Hackney, 1994, p.44; Leeds City Council Department of Social Service, undated, Section 5), or to pursue contact or residence orders at all costs as a means of access to, or revenge against, the woman regardless of the wishes of the children (see Chapter 7, this volume). Physical and/or sexual abuse of the woman or the children may continue more readily under these circumstances, and women would be enormously assisted by a more believing attitude from social workers and courts at such times. As it is, the social work focus on mothers (see above) provides fertile ground for abusers' allegations.

Professionals in this country need to be more aware of the dangers of abduction of children by abusers. They could, for example, work out a safety plan with a child's mother and school (Loosley, 1994) to reduce this risk. The Hackney *Guidelines* (London Borough of Hackney, 1994, p.42) also discuss the need for social workers to advise and support mothers in: not leaving children unsupervised where abduction has been threatened; warning teachers and carers; seeking legal advice; and keeping passports and recent photographs in a safe place. Similarly, the Leeds *Guidelines* (Leeds City Council Department of Social Service, undated, Section 5) cover these matters and advise social workers how to alert the Passport Office and all ports via the police that an abuser may seek to take the children overseas.

Good practice

It cannot be overstressed that arguments in cases where men violently abuse women and children should not be framed around mothers' level of co-operation with social workers. This is not the point at issue. Men's violence is the issue. Social workers need to learn how to accord it more weight and how to confront it actively and safely, so as to work for the protection of children and women with due regard for their views. In all the sensitive practice situations outlined above, workers with a specialist knowledge of domestic abuse can offer advice and a useful input into case conferences and reviews. Their long experience of men's abuse of women and children should be respected as a useful tool in decision making. Women's Aid groups constitute a nationwide source of such support in respect of any woman who has sought their assistance, and some local authorities now have their own specialist domestic violence co-ordinators in women's or equivalent units or, less often, workers with a specialist link to the social services department, for example in Leeds and Cleveland. Their advice and the training they offer could lead to an immediate sharpening of assessment and intervention in some of the most difficult cases.

Inter-professional discussion can also raise the level of debate when those with active experience of woman abuse are involved, as can conferences such as the Nottinghamshire Inter-Agency Domestic Violence Forum day in February 1995 on the links between domestic violence and child abuse. Multi-disciplinary events are now being held in many areas. For example, a day organised by Cleveland Area Child Protection Committee in March 1996, to launch its practice guidance on domestic violence (Cleveland Area Child Protection Committee, 1995), was attended by social service, housing, education, probation, police and health professionals, together with the NSPCC and local refuge workers.

More positive interventions by social work and other child care professionals are certainly possible. At the policy level, the general duty of social services departments 'to safeguard and promote the welfare of children within their area who are in need' (section 17(1)(a) of the Children Act 1989), by providing an appropriate range and level of services, has been used to back an argument that children living with, or who have lived with, domestic abuse are, by definition, 'in need' and that social services should consequently fund child work in Women's Aid refuges and associated outreach and follow-up work. (Being 'in need' relates to the child's health and development, including mental health and emotional development, and is defined in detail in section 17, subsections 10 and 11 of the Act.) This has happened in some local authority areas and, since it keeps children with their mothers while the latter work to forge a new life, could be said to be particularly well in tune with section 17(1)(b), which emphasises promoting children's upbringing by their own families where possible, as well as with 17(5)(a), which calls on local authorities to fund services through voluntary organisations. In general, recent research funded by the Department of Health (1995, p.55) suggests that local authorities need to establish a better balance between child protection work – which consumes considerable resources, often with little practical result – and support under section 17 to assist families to cope better with the pressures they face. There is also a reiteration of the finding that social workers do little to intervene in a child care case when they know that a woman is being abused (Department of Health, 1995, p.63), despite the negative impact both on her and her children. The requirements to develop Children's Services Plans may be another pressure towards policy-level awareness of the needs of children living with domestic violence.

In direct work, social workers on duty or dealing with allocated cases can in fact give mothers and children help to choose how to leave or survive abusive situations, including through cash payments under section 17(6) of the Children Act, or can take action against the perpetrator as outlined above. Given that social workers and the courts are required to consider all other alternatives to court orders concerning children (under s.1[5] of the Act), there may be much to gain from exploring all the alternative ways to remove the man or to confront and change his behaviour, and to help the woman and her children be safe – either where they are (e.g. s.17 money for new locks or a telephone to summon help), or elsewhere (e.g. fares to a refuge, assistance in getting rehoused). Women need to be given full and accurate information about their legal rights in respect of their children, sometimes to counteract what the abuser may have told them (Leeds City Council Department of Social Service, undated, Section 5), and to be advised to take the children with them if they leave and to see a solicitor (ibid.). In the best examples, the needs both of women and their children are considered, both immediately and in the longer term. McGibbon *et al.* (1989, p.71) report, for example, that the mothers of children who had been sexually abused were offered membership of a support group by Hammersmith and Fulham Social Services and that, since the same man not infrequently abuses both the woman and the child(ren), this enabled women to raise issues concerning their own abuse. It also meant that safety planning could be co-ordinated for all those at risk.

Working with women's fear of social workers

Women are often, in fact, deterred from seeking social work help for themselves and/or their children precisely because they fear a heavy-handed approach that may lead to the removal of the children or some other reaction that labels them as bad mothers. Sometimes women conceal the abuse to which they are being subjected, as a result of these fears, and refer to vaguer difficulties in coping – not realising that this portrays them, rather than their partners, as the problem and can still lead to adverse comments in social work records and perhaps unnecessary statutory intervention.

One way of countering such fears, and allowing women to speak openly about the dangers they face, is for workers to be perfectly open about their statutory powers and duties and the circumstances under which these do and do not have to be applied. Child care research has shown that parents prefer social workers who 'put their cards on the table' (Fisher *et al.*, 1986, p.112). The child protection worker and the mother can often work together to avoid escalating the level of intervention, and this is more likely to be possible if they adopt the partnership model required by the Children Act. Workers can do much to make this happen by adopting a more informed and sensitive approach to domestic abuse. Removing children from their mother's care, just at a time when they are distressed and need her most, is often not the best solution for them and, in the longer term, it may leave the woman unable to apply for rehousing where she can make a new home for the children. Needless to say, it overlooks her safety needs and leaves the situation to escalate, almost certainly to cause more pain and distress for everyone involved, especially when it culminates in the woman's death.

Understanding the issues

What is urgently needed is a clearer analysis of domestic abuse in the minds of child protection workers, with a firm distinction between the abusing and the non-abusing parent and a clear awareness that the abuser may be abusing the children as well as the woman (see Chapter 6). Opportunities can then be maximised, even where there has had to be a formal child protection investigation or other statutory intervention, to work with the non-abusing parent to meet both her and her children's support and safety needs. At present, there is a tendency not only to overlook the dangers to women *and* the predictive value of the severity of woman abuse in relation to child abuse (Bowker *et al.*, 1988; see also Chapter 6, this volume, and O'Hara, 1994), but also to waste the enormous resource of the potential of non-abusing parents to be perfectly capable, caring parents if supports can be directed towards them: 'so in fact, supporting the single parent (mother) was a good social work priority. Because when she wasn't being abused and in a messy abusive relationship, she actually cared for her daughter a lot better' (McGibbon *et al.*, 1989, p.57).

Even if the primary focus remains on the children, the most effective way to protect the largest number of them is to support their mothers in doing so. We need to recognise the superhuman efforts that women experiencing abuse typically put into shielding and protecting their children, giving them the best care they can manage under the circumstances, and keeping the abuse focused on themselves rather than their children when they can. Domestic violence specialists in local authorities tend to have a more sophisticated understanding of the measures women take to protect their children than do social workers and health visitors, who may be inclined to want to 'play safe' through surveillance or intervention in every case. (This is frequently the reaction to any new form of 'moral panic', which the impact of woman abuse on children is currently threatening to be.) An example of the more discriminating judgement that can be made comes from a local authority domestic violence co-ordinator who accompanied a social worker to a case conference convened to decide whether the children's names should stay on the child protection register. The children's developmental milestones and educational achievement were not in question, and the mother was undoubtedly caring, but she continued to be subjected to severe assaults periodically. Some of the professionals present were arguing for registration to continue. The co-ordinator's approach was to ask the health visitor to score the woman, as a mother, on a scale of 0 to 10. She scored her at 8. Then, argued the co-ordinator, given that women experiencing domestic abuse start from, say, minus 4, this woman – to have achieved an 8 – must be an excellent mother. In particular, her children are very safe because she knows when the domestic abuse is coming and gets them out of the house. She stays there and either faces the abuse alone, or waits while her partner wrecks the house. As the children are not present at these times, there is even a doubt about an emotional impact on them. The children were removed from the register.

There are a number of wider issues stemming from cases such as the above, all of which interlink and which are of far wider relevance. Firstly, professionals need to become more accustomed to debating the precise implications of domestic abuse for children so that they can judge levels of risk more accurately. Secondly, this depends on training, including at the highest levels and informed by the kind of woman-centred ethos outlined throughout this book. The domestic violence co-ordinator in the above example, for instance, took from the case conference the message that all principal officers in the social services department needed to be trained about domestic abuse without delay, since the quality of day-to-day decision making was in question. Thirdly, as is now beginning to be recognised nationally (Department of Health, 1995, p.55), there is a need to make a shift from a predominantly 'section 47' child protection emphasis to a greater balance with 'section 17' family support. In other words, the time and effort being swallowed up in child protection work, often of a precautionary nature with little practical outcome for families, is grossly outweighing the resources devoted to a broader, preventive approach to recognising children's needs and families' capacities to cope if they have adequate support. The woman in the case example above had been judged rather than supported – her achievements in coping and keeping her children safe had been a result entirely of her own efforts. If social workers and case conferences could become aware of safety planning, they could not only assist more women to plan emergency strategies – and recognise the use of these as positive evidence of effective protection by the non-abusing parent – but also build into the planning a constructive role for agencies in supporting the woman.

Furthermore, when abusive men do drag the children into the misery, degradation and hurt of abuse, this is their responsibility and not the woman's. It is also the abuser's responsibility when he cuts the woman off from family, community and health and welfare agency supports that could help with child care (London Borough of Hackney, 1994, p.43), when he controls the finances so that food, clothing and treats are less than she would want to provide, and when children dare not ask friends home or when their school work suffers.

One immediate action that professionals can take is to change their style of recording so that perpetrators are clearly indicated as such and there is no more talk of 'violent' or 'dangerous' families (see Chapter 7 on the bankruptcy of interactional thinking in these circumstances). Yet again, today, I have read a local newspaper account (*Northern Echo*, 11th February 1995, p.4) of a man imprisoned for murdering his wife after a 'stormy' marriage with constant 'rows'. We may expect no better than this falsely neutral reporting from the press – failing to emphasise that *he* was 'intensely jealous', and that *he* killed while *she* died – but there is no excuse for social work recording to be conducted in this vein. Let us call a spade a spade, and an abuser an abuser. We will then have a much clearer assessment of the dangers and protective resources presented by the two parents in a particular case, and can also look at the complex ways in which these may be supported or blocked by members of the two extended families. Similarly, we should beware of sexist and oppressive questions in the language and thinking we adopt, such as 'What is their mother going to do to protect the children from this?' – asking, instead, 'How has the man caused this to happen?' and 'What are we going to do to support and inform the woman so that she can now protect herself and the children?' In short, empowering women protects children (see Chapter 6).

Women as abusers

It must be recognised, of course, that women themselves may be abusive towards their children, and sometimes this will require statutory intervention, but there is no evidence that women who are themselves abused are any more likely to abuse their children. Heightened suspicion is misplaced and unfairly punitive, the more ironically when so little practical help is forthcoming.

It can also overlap with other stereotypical assumptions such as those grounded in attitudes towards Black and/or single mothers. Mama (1989, pp.95–6), for example, describes a situation in which a Black woman who had been homeless for well over a year, during which she had put constant pressure on the housing department to help her, had finally been offered dilapidated and unsuitable accommodation. At this point, she lost heart and remarked to the housing department that she no longer cared what happened to her or her children, since clearly no one else cared. Housing reported her situation to social services, perhaps because of the remark she had made. She could not see the relevance of this to getting rehoused so did not stay in to keep the appointment she was sent. When she returned, the social worker had arrived with the police, who had broken down the door of her temporary flat and gone away leaving it open and unlockable. Mama (p.96) describes housing departments 'coercing women into relationships with social services, against their wishes . . . [which] may add to the oppressions of violence, homelessness and racism by further disempowering rather than supporting the woman', while others who could have benefited from social work help did not know about or could not get it. Black women received threats that their children would be removed if they did not leave the violence (with no understanding, for example, that some would risk deportation if married for less than a year). Social workers need to be aware that, as 'an arm of the state' (p.100) they can compound the oppression of women, and of Black women in particular. Empowerment, including working with Black women's organisations, is called for, as is providing good quality information about social work and other services, in a range of languages, and then delivering what we say we will.

Where women have actually abused or neglected their children, it is always important to ask how much of this has been coerced by the male abuser, or has in other ways directly resulted from his behaviour, since, where this is the case, it may immediately, or with help, stop in his absence. For example, if the woman, under the strain of persistent abuse, has been impatient with and has sometimes hit her children, might she be supported in renewing her parenting skills if she chooses life as a lone parent or if criminal legal action against her partner removes him or results in his changing his ways? She may need particular counselling help if one or more of the children is identified in her mind with the abuse (London Borough of Hackney, 1994, p.44) (consider, for example, the child who has been forced to participate in her or his mother's abuse, or who has been conceived through marital rape, or who looks or behaves like the abuser); but, again, untold numbers of women cope with these extraordinary pressures and many others may benefit from professional or voluntary agency support in being better able to do so. Child protection and child welfare agencies in North America (in places such as London, Ontario, where there is a fully co-ordinated response to child witnesses of woman abuse) are careful to work with and through the lone mother as the caring parent following woman abuse, and to boost her confidence by consulting her and doing nothing that undermines her role and responsibility (see, for example, Mullender, 1994a and 1995).

In situations where the woman's own ordeal has left her, at this juncture, unable to care adequately for her children then, of course, there may need to be statutory intervention by social services. The way that information is imparted to her and procedures followed, with openness and involvement, can still pursue an empowering philosophy and should certainly never replicate the belittling and controlling behaviour of the abuser. A further element of good practice (Leeds City Council Department of Social Service, undated, Section 5) is to tell the woman her rights and to help her make contact with a women's organisation and/or family rights or advocacy group which can support her through what is bound to be a painful time when she may feel she has failed as a mother. Her family may also be available to be involved to support her and/or care for the children. Even where the local authority takes care proceedings, under the 1989 Children Act they now share parental responsibility with the legal parent(s), so there may be positive ways of continuing to involve the woman in her children's lives and perhaps of helping her to resume their care at a future date, whilst also handling the abuser's level of involvement with extreme caution. Above all, this requires keeping in touch with the woman and updating her on developments, as well as remaining concerned about her continuing safety and that of the children.

CONCLUSION

In this chapter, we have begun to see how social services departments, in duty and child care work as well as through wider training and policy initiatives, can make a positive response to women experiencing violence and to their children. A number of authorities have adopted measures that present a stark contrast to the unfavourable research findings about social work outlined in Chapter 3. We will now turn to look in more detail at the ways in which community care, child care and family work settings can be geared towards a safer, more empowering approach for women experiencing abuse.

Chapter 5

Responses to domestic abuse in health and adult care settings

Social workers and care managers working with all adult user groups, including workers taking referrals from health settings, need training on domestic abuse and how to respond. They may, for example, come across older women who have been subjected to abuse for years, women with disabilities caused by their abuse or which compound the difficulties of escaping from it, women who have developed mental health problems as a result of abuse, or others who misuse alcohol or other substances to deaden its impact. There is no area of practice where a knowledge of domestic violence and skill in working with women to assess and improve levels of safety are not relevant, and no setting in which messages cannot be sent to women – through posters and leaflets in all locally spoken languages, and other means – telling them that they will be taken seriously if they disclose abuse. Social services, as the lead agency for community care, needs to recognise its special responsibility to ensure that the needs of women subjected to men's violence have been actively considered wherever they may present for help.

Traditionally, it has been said that social workers are only likely to become fully involved in a situation of domestic abuse if they have a statutory reason to do so under the child care or mental health legislation. In the preceding chapter, an argument for wider-scale interest in children living with violence as being 'in need' under the Children Act 1989 was mentioned, as well as the general requirement to work in partnership with parents – including abused mothers – to safeguard and promote the welfare of children. A similar argument can be made that it is no longer possible simply to say that social services has no statutory authority for domestic violence in adult services. Since the problem is already present in all settings in cases where there is a duty to assess, care managers and planners at both individual and authority-wide level need to know how to recognise and respond to it. Furthermore, since local authorities are now involved in drawing up their own definitions of need through local community care plans – with the legal questions concerning failure to meet need, once identified in individual cases, still unresolved at the time of writing – the issue is more complicated than perhaps it once was. Certainly, the formulation of community care plans under the NHS and Community Care Act, 1990, is being used by some local authorities to take a positive step towards writing domestic abuse into the areas of work for which they accept shared responsibility. (See, for example, City of Bradford *et al.*, 1995/96, pp.101–7; Derbyshire County Council, 1993/94, pp.42–4; Leeds City Council *et al.*, 1992/93 and 1993/94; London Borough of Hackney, 1993/94, pp.131–4; London Borough of Newham, 1993/96, pp.99–102; London Borough of Southwark, 1993/94, Volume 7; Nottinghamshire County Council Social Services *et al.*, 1993/94, Section 5.8, pp.169–77; Wolverhampton Council, 1995, pp.31–2. NB Dates here indicate volumes consulted, not necessarily most recent volumes.) In the areas where the work is most developed, there are specially appointed staff to move the work forward, for example a Community Care Officer in Bradford. Although some of the other published plans do little more than list what is already happening in their areas, and/or include domestic violence as a short section near the end of the document, all such initiatives represent an important placing of the issue 'on the map' of the statutory services. They may point the way forward for ending the long-term neglect of women by health and welfare agencies, including social services. They can also mean over time that the needs of women in particular communities in the locality concerned, including minority ethnic women and travelling women, and those with particular health care needs or disabilities, can be considered in detail. In Newham, for example, the Asian Women's Project has identified a need for an Asian health advice and policy worker (London Borough of Newham *et al.*, 1993/96, p.102). In Wolverhampton, the Domestic Violence Forum employs a part-time Asian worker to network with appropriate women's and other community agencies and with the police domestic violence unit, and has joined with the police to set up an Asian languages helpline.

Typically, it is inter-agency forums and women's units in local councils that are bringing health and social work professionals into conjunction, alongside others such as Women's Aid, to plan a more proactive and coherent response to women experiencing abuse. There has been a traditional neglect of adult survivors of all forms of abuse by the health and welfare services. Health professionals have no better record than social services in this regard, so a good deal of progress is needed across both sectors of care. Even though almost all women experiencing domestic abuse come into contact with their general practitioner, and many of them with hospital or dental services as a result of their injuries, and/or with mental health services because of the emotional impact of the abuse, very few as yet receive the necessary practical safety advice, continued support or most appropriate care. It should also be noted that women who have left abusive relationships also have continuing health needs, for both themselves and their children, including in recovering from physical injuries and psychological distress. Social workers could play an important role, both directly in taking and making referrals through community care and health-related routes, and indirectly in targeting health settings (for example through inter-agency discussions, see Chapter 10) as a major untapped resource for collaborative efforts in abuse prevention. This could help prevent women's deaths as well as years of continued abuse. As abuse continues and escalates over time, so do the number of sources of help that women approach (Binney *et al.*, 1988, p.12). A majority who reach refuges have been to doctors or social workers or both at some point (Pahl, 1985a, p.80; Dobash *et al.*, 1985, p.148). The challenge is to make those contacts instrumental in working effectively with women, with safety as the goal.

Domestic violence incurs enormous health care costs. The United Nations (at the Fourth World Conference on Women in Beijing in 1995), the World Health Organisation, the World Bank (Heise *et al.*, 1994) and work at national level – in the USA and New Zealand for example – are all beginning to indicate the global impact on women's health and on the call made upon the health, disability and care services by the injuries and stress men's abuse causes to women. Examples do exist, both overseas and in Britain, of multi-disciplinary and/or multi-agency planning that has identified men's abuse of women as a health issue of major proportions. Kurz (1987, pp.69–70), writing in the American context, refers to the profile of woman abuse being raised amongst health and related professions by conferences, publications, the development of information systems for use by health care personnel, training initiatives, mandatory reporting of statistics on woman abuse in some States, and a continuing debate about the best means of producing change. This led to the launching, in 1991, of a major campaign by the American Medical Association to educate the public and health care professionals about domestic violence (Health Gain Commissioning Team on Domestic Violence, 1995, p.1). The Joint Commission on Hospital Accreditation in the USA also issued new standards requiring comprehensive training and protocols (codes of practice) on responses to all forms of abuse which, in turn, led to many more women being identified as having experienced it (ibid.). In 1992, the Surgeon General of the US Public Health Service (Novello *et al.*, 1992) gave important backing to these efforts by issuing a call to health care providers, in a special issue of the *Journal of the American Medical Association*, to 'take an active, vigorous role' in identifying and tackling domestic violence.

The proliferation of private health care schemes and local trusts in Britain will not help the consistency of efforts that might be attempted here, but we do have a range of national and local initiatives targeted at positive health care which could be used to improve services for women experiencing abuse, as well as some important localised developments. At the national level, Government-backed health standards such as those in the *Patient's Charter* and *The Health of the Nation* could be developed to encompass situations of abuse if the political will existed. The Home Office research study on domestic violence (Smith, 1989, p.96) suggested that improved medical responses could come through training, codes of practice, guidelines for interviewing women known or suspected to have been abused, improved inter-agency liaison and referral, data collection, and careful recording of individual consultations and injuries. Locally, some useful work is beginning. In Wolverhampton, health promotion finance has been used to fund work on domestic violence supported at health authority level, with local GPs also fully involved. There is work targeted at both the purchasing and providing of health care, in Glasgow and Leeds for example. In Glasgow, a Health Gain Commissioning Team on Domestic Violence (1995, p.1) has been established to 'improve the management of abused women presenting to a number of health service settings in Glasgow and to produce a series of recommendations for inclusion in the 1996/7 contracts'. This involves auditing current numbers and responses, reviewing and costing alternatives for better detection and responses, and making recommendations for purchasing (ibid.) (see later in chapter for further details). Interestingly, it is building on the suggestions in the Home Office study (Smith, 1989). In Leeds, the United Leeds Teaching Hospitals NHS Trust (1994) has issued *Practice Guidelines* covering all health care staff involved in providing services for women experiencing violence from known men. Though relatively short, these are an excellent tool for identifying violence both from medical signs and confirmed through confidential and concerned interviewing of the woman (through an appropriate interpreter if required), employing direct questions like 'Do you ever feel afraid of your partner?' and 'Has your partner ever hit, pushed, shoved, slapped or grabbed you?'. The *Guidelines* also list relevant helping agencies and recommend the formulation of an emergency strategy if the woman chooses to return home. It should be remembered, however, that there will be yet higher resource needs in voluntary agencies such as Women's Aid and Black women's groups, against a background of already inadequate funding, if they receive increased calls upon their help as a result of others' raised awareness. It is important to argue for secure funding.

This chapter will consider what best practice in tackling abuse can and does look like in health and community care settings, with women who fall into a range of key service user groups.

PRIMARY HEALTH CARE SETTINGS

General practitioner (GP) services and primary health care teams

With the spread of fund-holding general practice partnerships, there may be a rise in the number of social workers based in or attached to surgeries – a setting in which the effects of domestic abuse are frequently seen. Leeds

City Council *et al.* (1993/94, p.40; see also Women Experiencing Violence by Known Men Service Planning Team, 1994, pp.5–6) report on two sessional counsellors (one Punjabi-speaking) based in surgeries in Leeds one day a week. They operate under the neutral title of 'Advice Workers' to preserve confidentiality (including when a woman makes an appointment at the reception desk) and see women who require advice and support as a result of violence. Confidentiality extends to not reporting back to the GP, except in specific circumstances involving harm to self or others which are clearly explained to all women using the advice service. One attached social worker saw 14 young women over a six-month period; 11 eventually took out injunctions and a twelfth sought rehousing in a secret location (Leeds City Council *et al.*, 1992/93, p.14). Almost all insisted on remaining anonymous, with no notes kept, and said they would not have sought help from the GP or social services directly for fear, for example, of having their children removed.

Such workers can have a special role in responding to, and educating their medical and nursing colleagues about the social aspects of medical consultations, including those resulting from or involving woman abuse. Joint training for the whole team could be especially valuable as it could include action planning for an improved response, perhaps based on the use of agreed procedures to follow when a woman consults the GP or any other member of the primary health care team (Leeds Joint Planning, 1994/95, p.42). As very often happens, the self-employed GPs are proving one of the hardest of all groups to involve in inter-agency efforts, so changes of this kind focused on their workplace might be more effective. In the mainstream of social work, the care management arrangements introduced by the NHS and Community Care Act, 1990, mean that social services departments (SSDs) have forged new assessment links with GPs to manage care in the community and could build on these to offer a more co-ordinated response to women experiencing abuse (whilst also respecting confidentiality, women's choices, and their inevitable suspicions of the SSD as an agency that also carries child protection functions).

Large numbers of women do consult their GPs following incidents of abuse, although there are few recent statistics. Family Health Service Authorities, which are responsible for GP services, could help by undertaking monitoring of the level of consultations involving acknowledged or suspected abuse and considering the specific provision that should be made (Leeds City Council *et al.*, 1992/93, p.10). There have been some relevant research studies. Pahl (1979, pp.120–1), in a sample of 50 quite young women in a refuge setting, found that 32 had talked to their GP about the abuse. Just over half of these had found the consultation helpful because the doctors listened, were sympathetic, and gave appropriate advice extending beyond purely medical concerns. Dobash and Dobash (1980, pp.180–1; see also Dobash *et al.*, 1985, p.148) found that, although only

3 per cent of beatings experienced by the women in their sample were reported to a doctor, 80 per cent did go to the doctor at least once during the violent relationship, which made their rate of contact with the doctor second only to contacts with the police (at 82 per cent) and higher than relatives (at 76 per cent). They were more likely to go to the doctor than to the police or social services after the *first* attack (18 per cent as against 11 and 5 per cent respectively – more than half go to family, friends or neighbours at this stage) and even more likely after the *worst* assault (22 per cent went to doctors but only 14 per cent to the police or social workers) (Dobash *et al.*, 1985., p.149). All three formal sources of help became more likely to be consulted as the violence persisted (p.150). This suggests that GPs and social workers on GP attachments would be well placed to identify women in need of help if they were more aware of what to look for.

Very many of these consultations happen despite male partners' direct demands that the woman either not go or remain silent about the cause of the injury. To protect himself, he is likely to have invoked the woman's silence by threats of increased violence (ibid., pp.153–4), by convincing her that she has deserved the attacks and that they are nobody's business but their own, or by accompanying her to the surgery (Pahl, 1979, p.121) – the latter especially if the doctor is male. Women, then, do not always have unfettered access to medical help and nor is the help they receive always objective. Dobash *et al.* (1985, pp.158–9) recorded instances of doctors refusing women assistance unless they left their husbands, while Mama came across Asian women registered with GPs within their own communities who knew and allied themselves with husbands and families in the advice that they gave:

> Mumtaz . . . had an Asian GP who told her that 'women should not try to leave their husbands'. Meena, a 42 year old mother of two also sought help from her Pakistani GP who sided with her husband and kept her addicted to tranquillisers instead of helping her.
>
> (Mama, 1989, p.172)

Although Mama's study also found a proportion of GPs who were helpful to Black women, medical services are amongst the many that make too little or unskilled use of interpreters. Other women may have a restricted choice of doctor or limited access to a surgery, for example in rural areas.

Johnson (1985, p.118) reviews the statistics on rates of medical consultation; all the British studies listed by him reveal women's reluctance or difficulty in consulting medical services, yet over half of abused women do so at some stage. Women's criticisms of GPs are consistent. Dobash and Dobash (1980, p.183) report that 75 per cent of GPs treated only the injuries and did not discuss their origin, even though most women had either told the doctor this or suspected that it was known. Where the cause remains unrevealed, expensive misdiagnosis can result. The Scottish Women's Aid leaflet (undated) entitled 'To – General Practitioners' cites the case of a woman who underwent tests for headaches throughout nine years of being beaten, during which time she was too scared to admit the truth and her doctor never asked. Those GPs approached in the Bristol study (Borkowski *et al.*, 1983, pp.23–5) certainly appeared to be under-diagnosing violence. An earlier American study revealed that only four women in a sample of 120 referred for psychiatric help had been identified as abused by the family doctor making the referral, whereas 50 per cent reported themselves to the researcher as having been battered (Hilberman and Munson, 1978). Also in the USA, doctors referring for emergency surgery had diagnosed only 4 per cent of the abuse likely to have caused almost half the injuries (Stark *et al.*, 1981, in Lent, 1991, p.1).

It is, of course, odd to talk of under- or misdiagnosis in this context since the women concerned know perfectly well what is wrong. The doctor has only to ask in the right way. It is crucial for medical practitioners to give the right openings and to show that they understand something of the issues in order that women will feel able to trust them. Although women experiencing abuse do frequently complain of headaches, of 'nerves', of sleeplessness, or of being at the end of their tether, prescribing pills (Dobash and Dobash, 1980, p.191; Borkowski *et al.*, 1983, p.6) or referring women for psychiatric help (Dobash *et al.*, 1985, p.158) will not get at the root cause. Tranquilliser use is actually contra-indicated in cases of domestic abuse (Dobash and Dobash, 1980, p.192; Stark *et al.*, 1979, p.469). Reasons include the heightened risk of attempted suicide (already associated with abuse), the fact that the woman needs to be able to think clearly while trying to make a crucial life decision, that domestic abuse is a chronic problem whereas these drugs are effective only in short-term use, that the woman is not sick but abused, and that trying to help women 'live with the problem' does nothing either to make them safe or to strive towards an eventual solution. It is also a waste of money for the health service if drugs are used unnecessarily, especially over a long period of time. Social workers could offer women advice not to accept drugs other than in brief periods of heightened stress. Women are unlikely to volunteer the truth to their doctors unless they are confident of a response that is helpful, sympathetic and does not lapse into victim blaming or misogynist myths, or offer impractical advice such as telling the woman to leave without telling her how (Dobash *et al.*, 1985, p.159) or offering support. Displaying Women's Aid and other useful contact and help-line numbers in surgeries, in reception or waiting areas – or perhaps in the women's toilets in case the abuser is present and watching – with leaflets and posters in a range of locally spoken languages, as well as explaining to women in confidence how to use the help, would be a good beginning. In Leeds, for example, information leaflets and posters in five community languages, with telephone numbers of key agencies, have been produced for use in health, social services and related settings (Leeds Joint Planning, 1994/95, p.39).

Social workers and care management teams, in discussing individual cases or in planning and reviewing wider-scale services, could educate primary health care professionals to be more aware of the need for well-informed help and of the circumstances in which it is sought. A not untypical pattern is for the attacks to have been increasing in number and severity before women consult professionals; they may well already have exhausted their own attempts to sort the problem out with their male partners, and they are likely to be feeling fearful of the response they will get from the professional, which can therefore set a pattern for future help-seeking efforts (Dobash *et al.*, 1985, pp.149–53). Research (ibid.) also shows that GPs are seeing:

- the tip of an iceberg;
- some of the earliest injuries when many more years of escalating abuse could be prevented;
- some of the worst injuries, when the woman is most in need of adequate help;
- many women who have endured worsening abuse for years; and
- women who have had to evade their violent husbands, or risk retaliation, in order to seek help.

The response they get may be improving somewhat as new generations of GPs emerge from vocational training schemes (about half of whose members are now women, although they can find it harder to become established in the profession) better trained than their predecessors to listen to their patients but probably still with too little knowledge of domestic abuse.

There is good advice from the Ontario Medical Association (1990) on introducing the topic into the curriculum from the medical undergraduate stage onwards (since it is useful in all specialist medical areas), including recognising the need to help women make an effective safety plan, but we currently lack such a thorough-going approach in Britain. Also in Ontario, there is officially sanctioned advice available on what family doctors should expect and how to respond (Lent, 1991, pp.2–3). The typical course of repeated and worsening attacks before help is sought is explained, as are the typical injuries of hits, slaps and kicks building to fractures and dislocations, concussion, internal bleeding, perforated eardrums, injuries to the head, neck and trunk (often on both sides which typically would not happen in an accident), and to the chest, breasts and abdomen of pregnant women. Injuries caused by weapons are not mentioned although they are also common. Inconsistent explanations and a tendency to play down the seriousness of the injuries are listed as danger signs, as are repeated incidents, unexplained persistent conditions such as insomnia, fatigue, backache or palpitations, suicide attempts, and substance abuse in women.

Doctors are advised (ibid.) to give women permission to confide, to demonstrate a willingness to listen, ask direct questions, be prepared for denials until the woman is ready, and to share the plain facts about violence in a non-judgemental manner: chiefly that it is a crime, is not her fault, will not go away without intervention but is likely to escalate, and that it can have an adverse effect on her children. The doctor is also advised to give practical information about local agencies offering safe housing and to encourage notifying the police. Finally, full written records including the nature of the complaints and extent of the injuries, as well as photographs of the injuries where possible, are seen as helpful for any future court action. (The same is true in emergency health settings.) In Britain, medical evidence can help in court proceedings for separation, divorce, an injunction or other order against the man, prosecution for assault and claiming criminal injuries compensation, and can also help with rehousing. As Pahl points out (1979, p.122), this may prevent the woman from taking more beatings while she waits to gather adequate evidence. If the woman has a social worker, the latter could help her request the documentation she needs from the doctor.

Social workers or probation officers can also encourage women to ensure that they find an understanding GP who will not collude with the tendency to locate the problem with the woman herself. Under care management arrangements, social services departments are expected to work more closely with primary health care teams. This could be used as an ideal opportunity for joint training and awareness raising on this issue. Perhaps eventually we will reach the stage where family doctors will not only protect women and children from male violence but also confront the abusive men in clinical consultations, as doctors in Ontario are given detailed advice how to do, while using their status in the community to oppose male violence and to support services designed to combat it and help women reach safety (Lent, 1991, pp.13–21).

Other potentially important sources of constructive help for women would be settings related to antenatal, maternity, and baby and child care. The majority of women enduring long-term abuse are routinely visited by health visitors during part of this time (90 per cent in Pahl's study, 1982, p.529), and we know that abuse frequently starts or worsens during pregnancy (it started then for 33 per cent in the Pahl study, ibid., and see the section on obstetrics below). It is important to involve health visitors and midwives in training on domestic abuse and to create effective inter-professional links. In Leeds (Leeds City Council *et al.*, 1993/94, p.38) the midwifery service is one of the health specialisms that was involved in developing good practice guidelines on responding to woman abuse. Older and disabled women may be in regular contact with a range of health professionals who need to remember that domestic abuse is not only a problem of the young and able-bodied (see later sections of this chapter).

MENTAL HEALTH

There is much that social workers in all mental health settings can do to identify and assist women subjected to abuse, as statistics gathered in American studies indicate. Warshaw (1989, p.506) cites estimates that up to 64 per cent of female psychiatric in-patients have been physically abused. Lent (1991, p.1) reviews North American research revealing high incidences of abused women in psychiatric in-patient and out-patient populations. The sources cited include one in which 50 per cent of women referred for psychiatric help reported themselves as having been physically abused, as against just over 3 per cent identified as such by the referring doctor (Hilberman and Munson, 1978).

Not surprisingly, women who are regularly assaulted by their partners often feel depressed, confused, fearful and overwhelmed. Terror naturally causes anxiety, while feeling controlled and powerless not infrequently leads to depression, and unremitting psychologial abuse leaves many women with little sense of themselves or their own strengths (Ingram, 1993/94, p.19). McGibbon *et al.* (1989) report social workers talking about the risk of more serious mental health problems developing from these initial feelings of isolation, desperation and depression where there is no preventive work being done to identify and support women experiencing abuse:

> Men grind women down to a certain extent and then their self esteem goes. You often only pick this up when it gets to the extreme stage or when a woman is sectioned. We don't cater for women in these situations at all.
>
> (McGibbon *et al.*, 1989, p.69)

Suicide and suicide attempts are, sadly, far from rare (Hanmer and Saunders, 1984, p.89; McWilliams and McKiernan, 1993, p.80), with one study estimating almost a third of all suicide attempts as being by women experiencing domestic abuse (Stark *et al.*, 1979). Other results of the stress induced by abuse, all of which may be seen in mental health settings, include agoraphobia, eating disorders, and alcohol and other substance misuse. One woman in a residential drug and alcohol rehabilitation project, for example, had begun drinking because of domestic abuse but had received no professional help until she lost her job following repeated warnings; she could not cope with life in a refuge, so workers had helped her to move on to the project and to remain in hiding from her partner there. Whether or not women require symptomatic relief through medication or other psychiatric intervention, they will also require non-medical solutions which social workers are well placed to offer. Treatment can be effective only if the woman's safety needs have first been met, and it may be especially helpful to offer the woman involvement in an empowering women's group (see Chapter 10), at this or a later stage, to highlight that she is not the only one to be subjected to abuse and that it is not her fault.

Yet it is often easier for the mental health professions, including some social workers, to treat the causes of women's distress as if they lie in the individual, rather than in the society and in the abusers, and not to acknowledge that women's problems may have had another source and may actually increase once they become labelled as psychiatric patients or as having mental health problems. For example, it will become more likely that their ability to care for their children will be questioned if they are labelled as 'unstable' and they may even lose their children. This situation can be manipulated by an abusive husband if child care proceedings are involved. Inappropriate physical or chemical treatments (ECT and drugs) have side effects, and these treatments may be avoidable through more accurate identification of underlying problems (Hanmer and Saunders, 1984, pp.89–90). The misleading individualising in women of a society-wide, male-instigated problem is the chief objection to psychological constructs such as 'battered woman syndrome' or 'learned helplessness' (Walker, 1979; see critique by Dobash and Dobash, 1992, pp.221–35 and rejection of implication of women in causality, Chapter 2, this volume), though it is hard to condemn lawyers for resorting to these and other labels as sometimes the only way to defend women who have killed their abusers (see Dobash and Dobash, 1992, pp.228–30; Kennedy, 1992).

Social workers and probation officers can act as women's advocates to influence assessment and intervention so that violence is taken far more seriously, as a crime for which the abuser is solely responsible and as an understandable cause of stress for women, without labelling women as sick. Women's own needs could then be met in a less victim-blaming way, and positive support given with child care if this is actually needed – without social work intervention becoming the cause of yet more problems and stresses for a woman who has already survived untold abuse through no fault of her own. One woman, after a spell as a psychiatric in-patient, had come to be regarded by a range of involved professionals as a burden on her husband, for whom they all felt sorry. Her elder son's school considered that both children might need to be removed, because their father worked long hours and their mother was unable to cope. The social worker they called in was the first to listen to the woman's accounts of the abuse to which she had been subjected. In addition to offering emotional support, she was able to arrange day care for the baby and to help the woman use a local law centre to learn about her legal rights to protect herself, as well as giving her a refuge number for use in an emergency.

Rosewater (1988) concludes that much of what is inappropriately diagnosed as psychotic illness, neurosis or personality disorder in women is actually a reaction to prolonged and frequent violence, with the accompanying mental torment. The title of her paper stands as a warning: 'Battered

or schizophrenic? Pyschological tests can't tell'. This has obvious implications for approved social workers (ASWs) who need to find safe ways of
talking to women separately from their partners, and to respond appropriately when abuse is disclosed – based on a good basic grounding in the
impact of woman abuse and effective ways to offer practical and personal
help. ASWs need to exercise particular care when consulting partners as
'nearest relative' under the Mental Health Act 1983. The London Borough
of Hackney's *Good Practice Guidelines* (1994, pp.48–9) point out the need
to differentiate between a man who is genuinely describing his partner's
symptoms of mental distress and one who is abusing his power to control
her by choosing to define her as 'mad' and compounding this by seeking or
agreeing to have her admitted to hospital, thus attaching the label perhaps
irrevocably. The advice is given that interviewing the woman in a suitable
manner, using interpreter services where needed, to obtain the woman's
own perspective – and disclosure of any abuse – becomes particularly important. The guidelines (as do those from Leeds City Council Department of
Social Service, undated, Section 5) also mention that a known abuser could
potentially be displaced as nearest relative by the County Court if he is not
acting in the woman's interests. A similar knowledge of the impact and
implications of surviving other forms of sexual violence, such as child sexual
abuse, is of course also needed (McGibbon *et al.*, 1989, p.15), alongside an
awareness of local women's and survivors' organisations to draw on, perhaps
as an alternative to hospitalisation.

Since ASWs are required to go through special training programmes, at
post-qualifying level, there is ample scope for including a proper awareness
of the dangers facing women subjected to abuse, and of the high incidence
of domestic abuse, so that all workers are apprised of the relevant information. Social services departments are responsible for organising or buying
into the courses and, consequently, could ensure that they were updated
to include this information as part of a department-wide policy to take
woman abuse more seriously. There is now ample resource material to use
(Andrews *et al.*, 1994; Good Practices in Mental Health, 1994), as well as
background reading to recommend (e.g. Ussher, 1991; Barnes and Maple,
1992), to re-examine mental health and psychiatric services from a woman-
centred perspective whilst also integrating awareness of other forms of
oppression. In Leeds (Leeds City Council *et al.*, 1993/94, p.38; Leeds Joint
Planning, 1994/95, p.44), community mental health teams are developing
policy and good practice guidelines to raise the profile in their work of the
impact on women of men's abuse. Teams will undertake special training
sessions and will benefit from a training package specifically designed for
health care settings. In November 1995, the Community Mental Health
Trust will launch a Trust-wide protocol on women and violence to cover
both mental health and learning disability services.

McGibbon *et al.* (1989, p.70) point out that women experiencing depression as a result of abuse are already using a wide range of social services, including day centres and nurseries, and could be offered help through that route. The Partnership Adviser in Leeds, for example, who is managed by the Inter-Agency Project (Women and Violence), has run two highly successful groups for women in mental health day centres which have specifically addressed men's violence. In the McGibbon *et al.* study (ibid.), nursery workers were asking for training and for designated workers – including a Black worker who could liaise with specialist refuges – to improve the work they were already doing in putting women in touch with refuges, law centres, counsellors and groups. This is good preventive mental health work. Social services nurseries sometimes offer a drop-in facility for mothers and so could either use this as a focus for information, support and confidence building, or help women to use other appropriate advice services or groups locally. Women-only days or drop-ins or group sessions offered by mental health workers in a range of statutory and voluntary settings always lead to discussion of abuse (ibid.) which needs to be followed up with appropriate practical information and one-to-one support. Again, this can be hugely important as a preventive resource – and such work could be widely replicated without new funding, provided that staff are given appropriate training in issues of woman abuse and how to respond, with a good knowledge of the women's organisations, women's health projects, and self-help groups available. This kind of approach always needs to be accompanied, too, by an awareness of the particular problems encountered by Black women in using pyschiatric services, both because their needs are not understood and because of racist stereotyping, and by access to appropriate Black workers and services (including Black women's groups and specialist refuges). Similar issues apply for lesbian women who are likely to encounter homophobia and heterosexism in using mainstream services and who may particularly value support from a lesbian advice line or project. There does need to be teamwork here, because there is a limit to the level of mental health problems which can be managed within refuges and women's groups without preceding or simultaneous medical help of an appropriate kind. Social workers, care managers and care programme key workers may have particular skills in drawing together this range of resources where there are complex needs. Specialist domestic violence workers can also offer an invaluable resource.

Empowering services for women can have a positive relationship with mental health. One refuge in a major English city – through the initiative of a social work student based there for her practice learning – negotiated with a community psychiatric nurse (CPN) from a local day centre to visit once a fortnight in a health education capacity. She was available to offer advice to refuge workers and for individual discussions with any residents who wished to see her, without being referred through a GP, to discuss any form of psychological problem from the aftermath of sexual abuse to long-standing depression or anxiety. For the rare woman who does have florid psychiatric symptoms, this kind of additional support may help either to make her stay in the refuge viable or to obtain more appropriate help, perhaps avoiding hospital admission and the children going into care. The CPN mentioned above also offered continuity of support to women moving on into the community, and held women-only groups on depression, post-natal problems, and so on, at a day centre. The overwhelming need was to reassure women that their feelings were perfectly normal and that they were not 'going mad'. Social workers and health visitors can also play a role in offering help, perhaps through or in conjunction with voluntary sector organisations.

Social workers, community workers or voluntary groups in other areas may be able to offer similar services, such as women's health education and awareness-raising groups in accessible community venues, or to liaise with mental health projects to identify unmet needs. For Black women, these may include isolation and the impact of racism, as well as the violence (Au and Banu, 1991). Being in a women's group or an all-women setting such as a refuge can promote positive mental health by reassuring women that they are not alone, that they are not to blame for the abuse, that they are good and caring mothers, and that they can rebuild their lives on their own terms and using their own skills (even though leaving the abuse and establishing a new life is made harder by cuts in housing, legal aid and other practical services). Since men's abusive control over women can feel like madness – being an intimidation similar to brainwashing – and since abusive men often encourage women to think that they are incompetent and crazy, these positive messages are crucial. Women may also be disbelieved once they have the label of mentally ill; one woman, who said her husband had set fire to her and that she was scared of him, was described as disorientated and paranoid in her records and was told that it must have been an accident as he was such a nice man.

Those advising women subjected to abuse may well want to check that local psychiatric services do have enlightened, community-based help available, and that they will not suck women into a pathologising model. This is, regrettably, still the norm in Britain, making psychiatric services an unsafe form of help for women to use routinely, despite the fact that women constitute a majority of mental health patients (58 per cent of all psychiatric admissions are women: Andrews *et al.*, 1994). Judgements of mental health and ill-health have always been rooted in stereotypical assumptions about an appropriate social role and demeanour for women. In 1970, Broverman *et al.* showed mental health professionals exhibiting sex-bias: in an experiment, clinicians attributed similar characteristics to a 'mature, healthy, socially competent' man as to an adult with sex unspecified, but they chose quite different words from a given list to describe a healthy woman. The greater emphasis on passivity, dependency, submissiveness, being emotional and excitable, and so on, that they expected to see in normal, healthy women showed both that the professionals' notion of an 'adult' equated with a man *and* that they were operating double gender standards in their definitions of good health. These could certainly lead to the misdiagnosis of women who failed to accord with the biased norms. Such attitudes still linger in those diagnosing and treating women who have been abused and who may be seen as either stereotypically passive and helpless or as unacceptably deviating from this norm if, for example, they resisted the abuse verbally or physically.

Recent criticisms of both the purchasing and providing arms of the psychiatric system have grown more trenchant in revealing, also, sexual harassment, abuse and rape within psychiatric settings, not only by therapists (Teevan, 1991) but also by other service users in mixed institutions (one of the 'Stress on Women' campaign issues: see below). This makes caution even more necessary, including for ASWs who may be involved in admitting women to such settings. It represents just part of a growing recognition in the literature and in practice that psychiatric services are generally failing women. In 1992, a MIND campaign and pack – 'Stress on women' – were launched (MIND, 1992; see also MIND, 1994). In 1993, a BASW day conference on 'Women and Mental Health' marked the earlier publication of the book of the same name by Marian Barnes and Norma Maple (1992). The MIND Breakthrough campaign with *Community Care* (e.g. the 19th–25th May 1994 edition) included a special focus on women's mental health needs, identifying the typical response to women as veering between neglect and over-treatment (p.14). In 1994, *Eve Fights Back* was published by MIND, and in March 1995 an 'Eve Fights On' conference was held. During this period, a number of relevant publications appeared (Gorman, 1992; Nadirshaw, 1992; Williams, *et al.*, 1993) which, amongst other things, contextualised the issues within the community care changes and tackled the specific needs of Black women. The wider context of gender politics was also highlighted in respect of women's mental health (Ussher, 1991). These efforts to achieve change build on a tradition in sociology (Miles, 1988) and social work (Corob, 1987) of trying to reach an understanding of how mental ill-health – notably depression – affects women and of drawing out some of the reasons in relation to family responsibilities, social isolation and female social roles. Although domestic abuse did not receive close attention in that work, it fits within the overall analysis. Some while before, Gove (1972) had demonstrated that marriage has a tendency to be good for men's mental health and bad for women's.

At the same time, there has been a focus on what woman-centred mental health services can and should look like, including for Black women, lesbian women, those with child care responsibilities, women with histories of offending or of substance misuse, older and disabled women, and those in these and other groups who have been subjected to abuse. Au and Banu (1991), for example, give an account of a group for Bengali women in East

London, run in a mental health day centre, where women who have been psychiatric patients can talk together about problems including domestic violence, and obtain emotional support combined with housing and welfare rights advice. There is a growing tradition of women finding their own solutions outside mainstream services (Ernst and Goodison, 1981; Women in MIND, 1986; Krzowski and Land, 1988). Such women's centres, groups, workshops and campaigns keep many women well – or at least reduce the need for them to use the psychiatric services where their needs are poorly understood and the treatments and attitudes they encounter tend to make them feel worse rather than better. It may be possible for a woman to draw on a range of women-only services. For example, a woman who has been on tranquillisers for many years to deaden and survive the impact of abuse might benefit from a tranx (tranquillisers) self-help group as well as support aimed at awareness raising, empowerment and confidence building in a refuge or drop-in setting.

Statutory mental health settings do also need to learn to provide woman-centred care, however, and not leave all the changes to women working in the poorly funded voluntary sector. An initiative taken by the European Regional Council of the World Federation for Mental Health (ERC/ WFMH) to identify and develop good practice in mental health services for women has led to the production of two training packs in Britain to date, with more work planned. A Good Practices in Mental Health information pack aims 'to make visible and celebrate the good work which is already being done and to provide inspiration and guidance to those who want to fill the gaps' (Good Practices in Mental Health, 1994, Introduction, p.2). The pack begins with a statement that women use mental health services more than men and yet do not consider that their needs are met. This extends from the most basic issues of service provision, such as a lack of mother and baby units in psychiatric hospitals and of crêche facilities in day hospitals, to the therapeutic issues of inappropriate treatments and the lack of an analysis of mental distress that takes account of causative experiences such as sexual abuse in childhood or violence and other abuse from adult partners. Mainstream provision is certainly still leaving gaps; the majority of projects featured in the pack are in the voluntary sector and many face funding problems. The pack does not fall into the danger of considering women as a homogeneous group; separate pamphlets focus, for example, on 'women of specific racial and ethnic origin', 'lesbians and bisexual women' and 'women in middle or later life'. Other categories of women whose needs are considered, in addition to those who have pamphlets specifically dedicated to them, include women in urban and in rural areas, young women, women who are carers, and women identified as offenders. Criteria for listing projects in the pack included ease of use, child care, available choice of a woman worker, channels for women to influence the service, and relevant training for staff.

A second pack, by Andrews *et al.* (1994), provides the basis of a one-day training workshop targeted at all mental health workers as well as at service users and carers where applicable. It aims to challenge stereotypes, promote good practice, and encourage planning for change. The materials again focus specifically on services for Black women, older women and lesbians, as well as working-class and disabled women. We learn, for example, that older women are prescribed more drugs despite greater risk of side effects, that professionals commonly still see lesbian sexuality as a cause of mental health problems, and that racist services affect both Black mental health workers and Black service users adversely, for instance through the lack of Black counsellors. The pack recognises that amongst the largest groups of women using psychiatric services are survivors of child sexual abuse and of physical and/or sexual abuse in adult relationships. It draws on a study (Jacobson *et al.*, 1987; see also Jacobson and Richardson, 1987) which found that, compared with self-report in research interviews, 100 sets of psychiatric admission case notes (half on women, half on men; 18 per cent overall were black in the American sense, meaning African American) missed 100 per cent of both childhood and adult sexual assaults, as well as 85 per cent of childhood and 90 per cent of adult physical assaults by known and stranger assailants (Jacobson *et al.*, 1987, p.387). One conclusion reached was that, frequently, people will reveal histories of assault and abuse only if directly questioned about their experiences (ibid., pp.388–9).

Social workers could be amongst those who begin to make the break-through in recognising and publicising the link between past or present abuse and a wide range of symptoms of mental distress, including those that emerge only after some lapse of time (London Borough of Hackney, 1994, p.48). Social services departments could also offer grant or service contract funding to voluntary sector groups responding to these and other pressures on women's mental health; other forms of assistance could include free premises for meetings, social worker co-facilitation or consultancy, or help with the resulting administrative work (ibid.). Key workers formulating care programmes for women about to be discharged from hospital, or meeting other statutory aftercare needs (under s.117 of the Mental Health Act 1983), can make a difference by routinely making an assessment of the woman's safety in her home environment (including by asking direct questions in confidence), by asking the woman herself what she wants and where she wants to live, and by drawing on the wide range of community-based services available for women (London Borough of Hackney, 1994, p.49). One woman, whose husband tracked her down in a refuge, had a breakdown after he forced her to return home, resulting in a period of hospitalisation. The community psychiatric nurse appointed as key worker formulated a plan to help her return home without ever asking her whether this was what she wanted. This did not constitute good practice.

HOSPITAL SETTINGS

Obstetric services

Helton *et al.* (1987) found that 37 per cent of obstetric patients were at risk of abuse during pregnancy and that this operated across class, race and educational lines. In Bowker and Maurer's sample (1987, p.34), 48 per cent of abused wives were assaulted while pregnant. Figures in other American studies range from 40 to 60 per cent (McFarlane, 1991, pp.136–8). McConnell (1991, p.62, n.104) reports an autopsy study in Los Angeles which found women killed by their abusers more likely to have been pregnant than other female homicides (thus resulting in two deaths per fatal incident, of course). Violence also tends to worsen during pregnancy and may double the risk of miscarriage or stillbirth (Andrews and Brown, 1988, p.311). Dobash and Dobash (1979, p.181) quote one woman who had had five miscarriages in this way. Premature birth and damage to the foetus are further risks. Typical injuries to pregnant women are to the chest, breasts and abdomen (Lent, 1991, p.2). Abusive men may block their partners' access to antenatal and postnatal services, in order to conceal injuries and/ or because of obsessive jealousy. In a television programme featuring interviews with women who had finally been driven to kill their abusers (*Women Who Kill*, broadcast on Network First, Yorkshire Television, 11th January 1994), one young woman spoke of her partner's aggressive behaviour in hospital during her first delivery and his use of a razor blade to deliver her second baby at home. It is impossible to imagine that someone could not have noticed the man's behaviour at the hospital on the earlier occasion and offered this woman help. Abusers' belief that they have the right to exercise complete ownership and control over women makes them a danger to their partners and to staff in such settings.

Yet a Midlands refuge (pers. comm.) was unable to obtain any reassurance that a resident's presence on the maternity ward would not be divulged to her abusive ex-partner, finding instead no apparent understanding of the implications, a lack of willingness to take them seriously, and certainly no formalised procedures for use in such circumstances. The same refuge, on trying to locate a midwife for the woman, was told that 'It's not really our responsibility'. The midwife eventually allocated refused to write to the housing department, at the woman's request, to tell them it was not ideal for her to return to this hard-pressed refuge with a newborn baby, even though she would routinely do so in respect of housing problems. (There is a particular irony in this, in view of some judges' readiness to use grounds of unsuitability of home circumstances for removing children from their mothers during a refuge stay: see Chapter 4, this volume.) The general assumption appeared to be that women in refuges would have all their needs met there and were undeserving of help. In fact, of course, a refuge is a temporary home, which should entitle a woman to receive the full range of health services serving that area.

Given that men who are violent to their children also frequently abuse their wives, and vice versa (see Chapter 6, this volume), staff in all obstetric and paediatric settings, including social workers, need to be aware of the issues and ready to respond appropriately. Loraine (1981) suggests making suitable leaflets available, for example in women's toilets and in new mothers' packs. In Leeds, as part of the co-ordinated community care and health care planning for women abused by known men, obstetrics and gynaecology staff have undertaken special training sessions, with midwives and others, and will also be able to use a training package specifically designed for health care settings (United Leeds Teaching Hospitals NHS Trust, 1994).

Accident and Emergency Departments (A & E)

A & E departments are open day and night, do not require appointments, and are more anonymous than GPs, who may know other family members including the abuser. They are also available late at night when many assaults happen (Lent, 1991, p.5). They will therefore be the medical service of choice for many women.

Nevertheless, domestic violence is frequently not audited or even recorded as such in these settings, and American research suggests that women tend to be given an inappropriate and unhelpful response when patients do inform medical staff of the cause of their injuries or would admit it if asked directly (Rounsaville and Weissman, 1977–78). External observers have arrived at far higher rates of detection of deliberate abuse as the cause of symptoms presented to hospital emergency settings than they find recorded in the medical notes. Warshaw (1989, p.506; see also Warshaw, 1993) reviews some of the earlier research and goes on to report her own findings from a study conducted in a large public hospital in the USA, serving a predominantly Black and Hispanic population. Her conclusion was not that abuse was difficult to detect but that there existed 'a lack of receptiveness and response by health care providers to the issues that a battered woman struggles with; issues that are vital to her life and well-being' (Warshaw, 1989, p.507; see also Stark et al., 1979, pp.466–7; United States Department of Health, Education and Welfare, 1980; Bowker and Maurer, 1987, p.27). The injuries are apparent, but medical personnel do not feel equipped to deal with social problems and so do not ask the key questions or pursue the matter. Social workers may be able to support them in this and, in Britain, it may be possible to work for change through community care planning or inter-agency forums. Certainly, the tradition of a medical/social divide has been an obstacle in the past: Pahl (1979, p.120) refers to a doctor who took a nail out of a woman's foot, saw that her feet were black and blue from running down the road barefoot, and put stitches in – all without speaking to her. Training and service planning need to take on board that treating only the physical and psychological effects of violence leaves the woman to conclude that staff do not care about the danger to which she is forced to return (Bowker and Maurer, 1987, pp.39–41). Social workers can join those who are arguing for, and helping to provide, a more safety-conscious and holistic response to women who are experiencing abuse.

Practical arrangements are also problematic, particularly in relation to confidentiality and safety. A small student study of an A & E department in a Midlands city in England elicited negative comments from women subjected to abuse, and from police and social workers about the complete lack of appropriate arrangements there for abused women. Women too frightened to sit in the waiting area by the main front doors were not offered anywhere else to go: 'You can't sit in here, love, we're busy'. One woman who had been X-rayed and was waiting to have a fracture plastered simply ran away when her partner appeared in pursuit. Nor was there any offer of anonymity, with surnames being shouted out as someone reached the front of the queue, and no one available to sit and talk to the woman while she waited or before she left. This A & E department did sometimes ask the police or social workers to help a woman get to a refuge, but this response was inconsistent. A more formalised procedure in the hospital, or availability of a suitably aware social worker on call (as has been success-fully tried in Canada: Barman, 1981), might have avoided the need for women to leave with their physical injuries treated but with no word having passed about their cause or likely repetition. No statistics about domestic violence were logged, and neither the reasons women gave for their injuries nor what happened to them on discharge were uniformly recorded.

Discharge diagnosis, on which treatment plans and future responses are based, failed to reflect explicit information or very strong clues in 92 per cent of cases in Warshaw's American study (1989). Agreed procedures were flouted in nearly all cases, most worryingly with 98 per cent of women receiving no information about shelters (the equivalent of refuges), and less than half the incidents being reported to the police. The style of interviewing did not include asking women who had abused them, whether it had happened before, or whether they had anywhere safe to go. Warshaw's comment that '[p]hysicians, in other clinical situations, would not discharge a patient with a potentially life-threatening condition' (Warshaw, 1989, p.510) perhaps best sums up the shocking nature of this abrogation of responsibility.

As in GPs' surgeries, some women do attempt to conceal the cause of their injuries, often owing to fear of reprisals, and here the same skills that are used to identify abusive injuries to children could be employed by medical and social work staff, not to impose solutions on women but to offer constructive help. Kurz (1987, p.70) lists a literature on signs and symptoms of domestic violence. Injuries, for example, may not fit the explanations given – such as bruising on both sides of the face being blamed on walking into a door (Stark *et al.*, 1979, p.465). As in child abuse, evidence of repeated past injuries (such as broken bones) can be looked for. Depression and 'nerves' are further common signs (p.463) which currently lead to drugs being frequently inappropriately prescribed. In hospital emergency settings, Stark *et al.* (p.474) found one in four women they considered had been battered receiving pain medication and/or minor tranquillisers as against one in ten of other accident victims. Thus, despite the fact that woman abuse was not being officially recognised or responded to in these contexts, it was receiving a different medical response – for no apparent reason other than doctors not knowing what else to do.

We know what a better response can look like from several North American authors, for example the account by Kurz (1987). Although the majority of doctors she observed were not asking about the woman's social circumstances or safety, across three emergency departments she found 11 per cent of cases where the abuse *was* taken seriously and given due time and attention.

> In addition to giving a battered woman medical treatment, staff note battering on the case record, speak to the woman about what happened, her current circumstances, her safety, and attempt to provide some assistance or give the card with hotline numbers. What distinguishes these responses from others is that staff attempt to follow through with a battered woman and ensure that when she leaves, something has been done for her.
>
> (ibid., p.72)

This was more likely to happen where the woman was seen to be in immediate danger, was not evasive about what had happened, was taking action to leave her partner (a factor which makes her more 'deserving' in the eyes of professional helpers), was not under the influence of drugs or alcohol, and was not acting in a bizarre or dramatic manner but was pleasant and normal. Yet the nature of domestic violence is such that women frequently cannot be open and honest about it, cannot leave their partners, and undergo extreme mental stress which may well affect their behaviour. Social workers in a multi-disciplinary team, and shared training involving Women's Aid, can help all staff to understand these factors.

There are other positive accounts. Lent (1991, pp.5–6), addressing all emergency department staff, stresses the need not to blame the woman, to tell her that domestic assault is a crime, and to give her the contact numbers of appropriate sources of help including shelters (refuges) and hot-lines. Loraine (1981), too, emphasises helping women to recognise that abuse is widespread and encouraging them to plan ahead – with the emphasis on their own and their children's safety – as well as building their self-esteem. Finally, Barman (1981) outlines a comprehensive approach to recognising and responding constructively to domestic abuse in a hospital emergency setting. All staff, including the admitting secretaries, are taught to recognise the signs. Files are always checked for repeat visits. Direct questions are asked and women's attempts to evade a direct reply are noticed. A social worker is on call 24 hours a day. A police escort home to collect children and belongings is guaranteed. Hospital staff do not give up until they find bed-space in a shelter when needed. Leaflets are in racks throughout the hospital and its associated clinic. Medical and nursing staff have developed expertise in collecting evidence for court (women are routinely asked whether they will agree to their injuries being photo-graphed), in raising women's consciousness, and in recognising that change may take time and repeated efforts.

We also know from published accounts some of the ways in which change may be achieved within hospital services to reach these high standards. Kurz (1987) reports on an emergency department with a good rate of positive responses to women. This was brought about by the enthusiasm and skill of one concerned medical staff member. Her feminist perspective made her 'strongly oriented toward referring women to battered women's services rather than to the mental health system' (ibid., p.79). She trained a group of eight other staff working with her to learn to identify, interview and refer even the more 'difficult' women appropriately, earning a 47 per cent positive rating in the research as opposed to 11 per cent across the three other departments studied. She developed a file card system through which abuse cases could be traced for referral to her or the social worker. Filling in the referral card helped the staff to overcome the feeling that there was 'nothing they could do', whilst the fact that the social worker followed women up after discharge meant that the referral 'had more meaning than just handing a woman a card with phone numbers of the relevant agencies' (Kurz and Stark, 1988, p.258). Some women decided to prosecute their abuser (p.257).

In Britain, the Accident and Emergency Department of Leeds General Infirmary is one of many groupings in that city that is responding to co-ordinated community care planning and inter-agency work to meet the needs of women experiencing abuse (Leeds City Council et al., 1993/94, p.38). There are also clear lessons from the above for any social work assess-ment or duty team (including out-of-hours teams). The justification for the additional work and changed priorities in the above example was that women would simply come back repeatedly unless given adequate help.

Other hospital services

It is typically not the assessment expertise that is missing in health care settings but the framework of responses in which women's experiences and needs can make sense. The present author (research interviews preceding the publication of Morley and Mullender, 1994b) heard from a senior social worker that domestic attacks were identified as the true cause of a wide spectrum of injuries and illnesses leading to treatment in one large urban hospital. These ranged from severe facial injuries treated in the ear, nose and throat department to fractures and stabbings dealt with on medical and surgical wards, and also included repeated presentations that defied diagnosis. It is worth remembering, too, that abusive men often drive dangerously to frighten or threaten their partners, which may result in a road accident. The multi-disciplinary assessment skill in evidence in the above example matches that called for by Lent (1991, pp.5–6). Identification depends on full history taking, a recognition that one incident of abuse is never the whole story, direct questioning about abuse, a suspicious attitude towards explanations that do not fit the injuries, finding a way to interview the woman away from her partner, and checking also on the safety of any children. Old injuries, including any that have gone untreated, may be indicative of abuse. Lent also alerts doctors to look out for burns from electric appliances, cigarettes or acids, and mouth injuries including broken teeth and jaws, as well as the typical psychological accompaniments of depression, anxiety, unexplained physical symptoms and a general feeling of being overwhelmed and at a loss (despite, of course, the resilience it takes to survive the experience of unremitting abuse). In a paper aimed at nurses in all hospital settings, Loraine (1981) also mentions tell-tale signs in women such as jumpiness and fear, flinching when their husband moves, and scattered wounds of different ages. She advises nurses how to ask direct questions about abuse.

What was missing in the British hospital mentioned above was, then, not the ability to identify abuse but a fully effective response once it was detected. Social workers were routinely involved when abuse was suspected by medical or nursing staff. Other cases were referred for advice on benefits or housing and emerged as instances of women wanting to leave home owing to violence. The team helped some women apply for housing transfers. They were not well informed about Women's Aid and were just as likely to refer to other voluntary agencies which did not have expertise in the field and could provide neither safety nor appropriate help with practical problems, let alone an empowering ethos for women. They were not proactive if the woman wished to seek legal remedies, but did refer her on to the local law centre. The social work record would mention domestic abuse but this would not feature in any collection or analysis of statistics. This is at variance with child abuse procedures which do have to be documented and counted in routine ways. In general, the social workers tried to list the options and help women look at their alternatives, but without a clear analysis of what domestic abuse actually is. Alcohol, drugs and cramped housing conditions were blamed, rather than male control and abuse of women.

Team members felt particularly perplexed as to how to make an appropriate response to Asian women, who they knew would have to defy family and community to leave, and did not feel able to work at variance with what appeared to be the dominant view of the local community (voiced by male elders) – so women were typically sent back into what was recognised to be repeated violence. White staff were noticeably fearful of acting inappropriately and tended to encourage women to attend a local Asian counselling and reconciliation service rather than intervening themselves. In fact, this newly established service had itself been shocked at the levels of violence and was, at the time of the research interview, attempting to renegotiate with community leaders over women's needs for safety. One Asian woman worker in a local centre who was attempting to work with women was seen, by her own report, as 'political, aggressive, unhelpful'. Yet some of the male community leaders were themselves known to have been violent. Attempts to recruit to the hospital social work department minority ethnic staff who might have been able to help find a way through these muddles and dilemmas had been blocked by spending cuts and no links were made with Asian women's groups further afield.

Women with other medical needs may also be being abused. Consequently, staff from specialities as wide-ranging as palliative care and paediatrics, geriatric medicine and genito-urinary services, need raised awareness and information about the help available to women experiencing abuse. Planning and policy making in these areas of health care does not generally take account of this area of need, and inter-agency forums can be important in calling for change. Family planning and 'well woman' settings, as well as gynaecology and maternity services, clearly serve large female populations. From the last two, alongside psychiatry, will be selected the sites of full-scale audits in Glasgow during 1996 to ascertain current proportions of abused women using these services and what responses they receive, to undertake staff training on abuse and work with them to develop and test a standard protocol for detection and management, as well as measuring the effectiveness of these changes (Health Gain Commissioning Team on Domestic Violence, 1995, p.3). This work will be preceded by similar exercises in 1995 in A & E in the west of Glasgow, and in family planning and sexual health, together with preliminary work in primary health care. To date, the Glasgow team has found that the only local routine collection of social histories, including experiences of domestic violence and other abuse, is being undertaken by the women's reproductive health service (ibid., p.2). Clearly there is scope for enormous progress to be made which could establish a model to be emulated nationally. The involvement of the Public Health Department in the Glasgow work is reminiscent of the great nineteenth-century successes in improving health by creating a cleaner environment. Perhaps the late twentieth-century equivalent will be the establishment of a clear link between better health and a *safer* environment.

WORK WITH OLDER WOMEN

Many older women have lived with abuse for years, throughout an era when the accepted view was that married women had made their bed and must learn to lie on it. Even if they called the police, they were likely to be met with the dismissive attitude that 'domestics' were trivial and not the concern of the criminal justice system. Only quite recently have these public and professional attitudes begun to change, and older women may either have given up trying to get help or may feel it is too late for them unless they are given the same time and attention to consider their options as younger women. There is also the problem that women's organisations and campaigns may appear to be directed solely towards younger women, in visual representations on posters and leaflets for example, and that older women may feel completely out of place in refuge and other women-only settings unless special efforts are made by staff to include and value them (Macdonald with Rich, 1983, pp.25–41; Hughes and Mtezuka, 1992, p.221).

The invisibility of older people in a youth-oriented society, and the stereotyped views of their lives as sexless, as well as the bureaucratised format of many care management assessments, may all mean that professionals fail to spot sexual violence experienced by older women. As society belatedly begins to wake up to the existence of marital rape, it does not picture the victim as being post-menopausal, for example. Marks of physical abuse may be attributed to older women having falls, and older male partners may appear particularly plausible and harmless when they give such accounts to cover their actions. Older women who are confused may be assumed not to be making sense when they talk about abuse. It is important that practitioners working with older people are as alert as in any other setting, that they listen carefully and observe, and interview the woman separately from her partner. All assessments of older women should include abuse by a partner (or someone else) as a possibility, and those discharging older women from hospital, respite care or other institutional settings should consider the possibility that they may face violence at home (Leeds City Council Department of Social Service, undated, Section 5). This involves asking the right questions: was the broken arm really caused by a fall and does the woman concerned actually want to return home?

Older women may encounter abuse in relationships that start in later life as well as in long-standing ones (one widow who sought to repeat the experience of a very happy first marriage was devastated by the treatment she received from her second husband), or their long-term partners may become abusive – sometimes when the older woman becomes frail or demented and more easily victimised. McGibbon *et al.* (1989, p.68) warn against making assumptions based on appearances, however, and highlight the need for careful assessment. A woman may strike back at her long-term abuser when he finally becomes frail and dependent on her, or a frail man may continue to dominate a now physically stronger wife by means of psychological and emotional ploys perfected over the years.

Older women have the same right to leave or to stay, to have action taken against their partners or not, as other women. A sensitive and believing approach may come as an especial relief after many years of hidden abuse or refusals of help, and a listening ear may be all that is wanted – including after a violent partner has died. An older woman may look back over an adult life restricted and impoverished by the control exercised over her; her regrets may be intensified by meeting younger women who have managed to leave violent men (London Borough of Hackney, 1994, p.49) and she may be at risk of depression, compounded by experiences of loss. She may also feel ashamed because of a belief that she provoked the abuse (see Chapter 2, this volume), or because she was unable to play woman's expected role of solving the 'relationship difficulties' (see Chapter 7, this volume).

Whatever the length of their marriages or their experience of abuse, however, some older women do determine to leave; it is never up to the worker to make this decision for them or to advise against it 'at your age'. One woman, aged around 60, who went into a refuge, changed in a week from being extremely nervous and emotionally unexpressive to laughing and telling the children stories (Pahl, 1985b, p.38). A woman of 81 in McGibbon et al.'s study wanted a final few years of peace and was rehoused away from her husband. Both women had undergone abuse for many years. Another woman in her eighties was admitted to a residential home from a hospital accident and emergency department by an emergency duty team worker; she had extensive bruising to her face and was malnourished. Her husband had a stroke soon afterwards. When social services staff went to the house where this man had 'ruled the roost', they found only the barest amount of food in a cupboard and drawers full of untouched pension payments.

The idea of separating from a partner after so long is a daunting one and may also be associated with the risk of losing independence or the partner's role in providing care (Leeds City Council Department of Social Service, undated, Section 5). Nevertheless, the risks of abuse may actually increase rather than decrease over time and complacence is certainly misplaced. McWilliams and McKiernan (1993, p.67) report on social workers coming across older women who had been abused for 40 or 50 years; one worker remarked that recovery from injuries can become harder as the woman becomes older and perhaps more frail (high rates of osteoporosis amongst older women could be relevant here, for example) and earlier coping strategies may no longer be available owing to poorer health or other altered circumstances (Leeds City Council Department of Social Service, undated, Section 5). Meanwhile, opportunities for the man to exert domination and control may increase as his wife depends on him to administer medication, help with mobility and transport, and/or gain access to pension or savings (ibid.). Older women may also be particularly reluctant to call the police or other public bodies to intervene with their partners, who may themselves now be frail or disabled (London Borough of Hackney, 1994, p.49), and, owing to class or cultural norms or simply the attitudes of their age group, many would regard this as humiliating and shameful: 'People that age, however much they suffer, they hate admitting it, they really do' (social worker cited by McGibbon *et al.*, 1989, p.68).

McGibbon *et al.* (ibid., pp.67–8) found particular sensitivity amongst social workers working with older and disabled people to their inevitably mixed emotions and to the difficulty of disclosing. Workers felt that taking the time to listen could lead to a woman talking about abuse, sometimes for the first time, to a professional who might have visited initially in connection with an entirely practical need such as a bath aid. Particular difficulties were noted in relation to assisting Black elders who were not being reached by still frequently inappropriate statutory sector services and whose view of social services was often very negative.

As women are in a majority in later years, there is ample scope for organising women-only groups and discussions which could give women an opportunity to talk about past or present abuse – and perhaps regain lost self-esteem and confidence, or take stock of life and make new choices. There is no reason why women in group and respite care, for example, should be offered craft groups at best and enforced idleness at worst. Women's groups would not be a new service drawing on additional resources but an imaginative use of existing staff time, requiring only training in domestic violence which, it is suggested, all those working with women already need.

WOMEN WITH PHYSICAL DISABILITIES AND/OR LEARNING DIFFICULTIES

An excellent example of good practice is the London Borough of Hounslow's booklet (1994): *Domestic Violence – Help, Advice and Information for Disabled Women*. It contains information on advice, help and support for disabled women experiencing all forms of domestic abuse, including those forms of abuse that relate to the disability itself – such as denying access to the toilet or help with bathing, using the disability against the woman by humiliating her or keeping her a prisoner by refusing help with mobility (taking away stick or wheelchair) and transport, or neglecting food, care or medication (ibid., pp.1–2). The booklet also confronts the emotional and social issues, such as the attitudes of others who think the disabled woman should be grateful for any partner at all, or who blame his abuse on the pressure of caring for her (p.3). The guide also remembers that the person being subjected to abuse may be a parent (pp.23–6), which is too often forgotten where disabled people are concerned since, firstly, they are often regarded as asexual and, secondly, they are seen as always taking rather than giving care. (The Leeds City Council Department of Social Service *Good Practice Guidelines* also point out that a disabled woman may fear losing her children if she separates from her abuser owing to the misconception, shared too often by social workers, that she will be unable to cope with them alone.) It is also recognised that the disabled woman, like any woman, may have additional health needs caused by the abuse – such as treatment for alcohol misuse or depression. Finally, the safety or crisis planning that is recommended takes account of particular transport needs (London Borough of Hounslow, 1994, p.30), and the resource list is longer than usual because it encompasses disability, transport and independent living organisations.

The first and most obvious link between domestic abuse and disability is that the abuser may himself have disabled the woman concerned. Ironically, this (or a disability with another cause) may turn him into her carer or her link with the outside world if, for example, she becomes physically dependent on him for transport, communication, handling finances, or in other ways. This increases his control over her and her difficulty in finding out about and using the options open to her. It also makes it much harder for her to report the abuse, both because outside communication may be physically difficult as well as closely monitored by the abuser, and because any action taken against him could lead to the loss of essential care if he is arrested or walks out in anger (McGibbon *et al.*, 1989, p.68). Alternatively, the woman experiencing the abuse may be the carer; she may feel too guilty to leave the relationship, knowing that her sick or disabled partner will not be able to cope without her, or she may feel under pressure from health or welfare professionals to stay, given their perception that she has tolerated the abuse up to now so must be able to go on doing so.

The oppression of disabled women and the exploitation of women carers are compounded if specialist workers in every field of disability do not know how to recognise and respond with appropriate urgency and sensitivity to domestic abuse or do not look for it. It may not fit our stereo-types of disabled people that they could be subjected to sexual violence or perhaps be victimised in any way – particularly by a carer. At the opposite extreme, such a woman may appear especially vulnerable and this may lead to other people – first the abuser, and then the well-meaning professionals – making decisions and choices for her. McGibbon *et al.* (1989, pp.68–9) point out the need to conduct an interview apart from the carer if there is an atmosphere of tension or suspicion of abuse, giving an example of a worker who returned when he knew the carer would be out; separate interviewing of the individual and her carer is also in keeping with good practice in care management (Department of Health Social Services Inspectorate and Scottish Office Social Work Services Group, 1991). McGibbon *et al.* (1989, p.69; and see Chapter 7, this volume) draw attention to the tendency of some of the workers in the social services department they studied to look for explanations of the abuse in the relationship itself and to offer respite care or other practical support to remove the supposed precipitating factors, rather than treating the abuse as criminal behaviour and focusing on the abuser's need to change and the woman's separate safety needs.

There is also a range of particular ways in which having a disability can compound the problem of domestic abuse unless information and help services are adapted accordingly. Women with sensory impairments may be less aware that help is available. Women who are blind or have sight impairments will not see posters and may require information in braille, large print, or on tape, although this would be hard to conceal from a carer. Deaf women may need a social worker who is able to converse in British Sign Language (BSL) or a BSL interpreter (who understands about confidentiality). They will not be able to use emergency telephone numbers unless there is minicom equipment available, as there is at the Leeds Inter-Agency Project, for example. Similar issues will arise with every agency each woman may need to access, from the DSS and housing department to the police and the courts, some of which are still ill-adapted in these regards. It might be especially helpful if the woman's needs could be met through a community care assessment, with an individual care plan paying, for example, for interpreter time as well as offering routes to independent living with all the necessary adaptations and assistance with personal care if required. A comprehensive assessment, to which anyone who is 'disabled' under the terms of the Disabled Persons (Services, Consultation and Representation) Act 1986 is entitled as of right (s.47[2] of the NHS and Community Care Act 1990), should include a full benefits check – all the more important as it takes six pages just to explain the basic entitlements in the Hounslow guide and the situation is constantly changing. Also, the silence might be broken for many more women if *all* community care assessments asked direct questions to check for abuse – confidentially and in circumstances that guaranteed the woman's safety.

Increasingly, though it is under pressure, refuge space is available that is accessible for women with limited mobility or who use wheelchairs, and Women's Aid emergency numbers will lead to appropriate information. Alternatively, or in the longer term, a full assessment of need in a care management context might lead to an application for some form of adapted housing and/or supported independent living for a disabled woman who has been subjected to abuse, whatever her age. The visibility of an obviously disabled woman, and the additional opportunities to trace her through the benefits system (Leeds City Council Department of Social

Service, undated, Section 5), may mean that she has to move more than once. If the woman is already living in adapted housing, this might be a particularly good time for the housing authorities or the civil or criminal law to consider removing the abuser instead (ibid.) – and exerting controls over his behaviour – or for social workers to pose him with this option if the woman so chooses.

Once again, there is a need for training and raised awareness here for professionals and their managers. The community care ethos is based on maintaining people in their own homes, which may be precisely where a woman experiencing abuse is least safe. Also, it can take several weeks for a community care assessment to be completed and there are typically waiting lists for suitable accommodation – none of which accords with a referral, or a suspicion arising from other work, indicating that a woman is facing immediate danger. The establishing of priorities in care management settings must take into account the ability to respond quickly, the fact that some women will require either temporary or permanent care away from their abusers and that, for others, an intensive safety plan will be necessary to support them in remaining at home. All social service settings in which disabled women receive services should carry relevant leaflets and posters, to convey the fact that there is help available and that a believing and supportive attitude will be encountered there. Crime prevention initiatives also have considerable ground to make up in identifying and meeting the needs of disabled women (see London Borough of Hammersmith and Fulham Environment Department Research Group, 1993).

Disabled women are increasingly coming together to empower them-selves and to recognise the issues that face them as disabled people and as women – for example, through the British Council of Organisations of Disabled People (BCODP) Women's Group, the Jewish Disabled Women's Group, and the newsletter *Boadicea* from the Greater London Association of Disabled People (GLAD) which regularly features specific information for disabled lesbian women, disabled older women, and disabled Black women. GLAD (together with the Association of London Authorities and the London Boroughs of Waltham Forest and Hammer-smith and Fulham) organised a conference in March 1995 on disabled women's safety issues (Greater London Association of Disabled People, 1995), including in relation to harassment and abuse. It has also undertaken research and action for change, funded by the Joseph Rowntree Found-ation (Ellis, 1994 and 1995), around disabled women's experiences of discrimination, including sexual abuse and domestic violence. One problem revealed was the difficulty in finding women's refuge or counselling services geared up to meet the needs of disabled women, or able to do so locally without cutting off entitlement and access to statutory services by moving the woman to another area. Other dangers highlighted are that services for disabled people can themselves create situations ripe for abuse (e.g. by drivers), and that women may be trapped with abusive informal carers. Disabled women who are being or who have been abused may gain strength from drawing on empowerment events and organisations in the fields both of disability and of sexual violence (provided the latter are accessible, including in communication), and it does appear that each of these 'interest groups' is beginning to recognise its interconnections with the other. One Women's Aid group, for example, obtained short-term social services funding to employ a specialist worker to identify needs and publicise resources for disabled women through the disabled people's network; these include an access suite (ground-floor refuge accommodation for a disabled woman or a woman with a disabled child) and information about accessible refuges elsewhere in the country.

Women with learning difficulties may be at particular risk of sexual violence if they have been deprived of sex education and of the opportunity to learn to make choices about their own lives and bodies or keep themselves safe in institutional or sheltered family contexts (McCarthy, 1991 and 1994; Williams, 1992). They may also be offered help even less readily than other women because they are seen by professionals as living a sexless life, or because they sometimes lack the concepts or vocabulary to describe their experiences easily, or because they are not listened to or believed. This happened, for example, to a young woman who was let down both by her sister and her social worker; they were so caught up in their competing views about the best form of care for her young child that neither paid any attention to her frequent complaints about the way her boyfriend was mistreating her. There may be particular difficulties, too, in pursuing action against an abusive man through the criminal law if the woman has learning difficulties. There is beginning to be a recognition in relation to sexual violence by strangers (Sone, 1995) that the Crown Prosecution Service may not consider a woman with learning difficulties (or mental health problems) as a credible witness – she is seen as likely to be incapable of testifying or of withstanding cross-examination, or to be regarded in a poor light in court – so the chance of a conviction is seen as low and the case is dropped. There may well be similar considerations in policing and prosecuting domestic violence.

As with other user groups, women-only discussions can be a source of strength for women with learning difficulties. There is now, for example, a national network of women service users, women staff and women researchers called Women in Learning Difficulties (WILD) which produces a newsletter and held its first conference in June 1994. Women-only self-advocacy groups give women with learning difficulties more confidence to voice their own agendas and talk about their lives, as in People First's 'Women First' group. The Powerhouse is a group of disabled and non-disabled women that is paying particular attention to all forms of abuse including sexual violence; it is working to raise awareness and to offer refuge, in Beverley Lewis House in London, for women with learning difficulties who have been threatened or abused (Hirst, 1996). Women-only groups, conferences, and days in drop-in and other centres are just beginning to be recognised as an important opportunity for women with learning difficulties to speak out about their particular experiences and needs, including those related to abuse. Without these opportunities they will remain doubly marginalised and doubly oppressed within a population of men and women with learning difficulties whose distinctive voice has only recently begun to be heard by the disabled people's movement and by the whole community.

Meanwhile, the criminal justice system often does not know how to cope with men with learning difficulties and may not charge them even when there is evidence of their abuse (not forgetting that they may more readily be reported than men in more powerful positions; see letter from Hilary Brown to *Community Care*, 4th February 1994, p.13). There are no published accounts of abusers' groups adapting their programmes to work with men with learning difficulties, although the Duluth-based groups (Pence and Paymar, 1986), and others derived from their ideas (e.g. in Lothian), use video triggers and other visual tools for re-education which could be appropriately reworked.

CONCLUSION

A full-scale response to domestic abuse in a health or community care context requires co-ordination and careful planning. There is only just beginning to be such an approach in Britain, so there is ample scope for professionals with energy and commitment to women's interests to make a real impression. The stance can certainly now be taken that the recognition of this area of need can and should be written into local health and community care planning. In addition, relevant professionals right across adult services require adequate training to be able to make appropriate assessments and responses – including by asking women direct questions about abuse they may have experienced, about levels of safety in the home and about their own choices for the future. As we shall see in the next chapter, children who have lived with the abuse of their mothers may also present with their own physical and psychological health care needs. Social workers and health staff in child health settings, as in all other health-related contexts, therefore need to be equally involved in under-standing and responding to the impact of woman abuse.

Chapter 6

The needs of children living with domestic abuse

There is a paradox in the fact that social workers in Britain, intervening in situations where women are being abused, appear often to be motivated chiefly by the presence of children (see Chapter 3) – and yet social work as a profession has not systematically recognised the issue of children living with domestic violence as a matter of concern in its own right. In situations where this *is* recognised, there tends to be a rather unsophisticated and sometimes punitive child protection response (see Chapter 4) as opposed to constructive work with the non-abusing parent – the mother – to help her and the children be safe. The child-centred responses to living with woman abuse in North America – disclosure work, children's groups, links with prevention in schools – are not seen in Britain and, despite the existence of a veritable industry of child protection agencies in Britain, it is left to Women's Aid to be the major national repository of expertise in such work. It is not even yet the case in Britain that child care professionals routinely ask questions to ascertain whether children newly referred with emotional, behavioural or other difficulties might be showing the impact of distress caused by living with the abuse of their mothers.

Britain is just beginning to see the development of literature, research and general awareness in this area – 1994 saw the publication of the first major text on the subject in the country, for example (Mullender and Morley, 1994). This was preceded by conference reports; the first to be published (though not the earliest conference) was from the London Borough of Hackney (1993) and was called *The Links between Domestic Violence and Child Abuse: Developing Services*. Others have followed, from Hammersmith and Fulham: *Suffering in Silence: Children and Young People Who Witness Domestic Violence* (Holder *et al.*, 1994), and from Scottish Women's Aid (undated): *Children, Equality and Respect: Children and Young People's Experience of Domestic Violence*. Previously, the only specialist literature had been from overseas – the best known source being the Canadian book *Children of Battered Women* by Peter Jaffe *et al.* (1990), which is limited by its clinically orientated, individualistic model. A further, much fuller North American book has just appeared (Peled *et al.*, 1995), as have three Canadian training packs: one on disclosure (Children's Sub-committee of the London Coordinating Committee to End Woman Abuse, 1994), the second on groupwork with adolescents to promote 'healthy' non-violent relationships (Wolfe and Gough, 1994), and the third on school-based anti-violence work (Sudermann *et al.*, 1994; a British educational pack from the London Borough of Islington was published in 1995). There is also material available from the USA. From Duluth, one of the most respected centres of co-ordinated work to tackle woman abuse, a manual entitled *What About the Kids?* (Pence *et al.*, undated) mainly concerns parents' groups, a visitation (contact) centre, and groupwork with young people who are already violent.

On the research side, an interesting new source in Britain is the study by NCH Action for Children (Abrahams, 1994) based on women and children using its own family centres, though it somewhat underplays the role of Women's Aid. The Women's Aid Federation (England) itself funded a nationwide pilot by a research team based at the universities of Bristol, North London and Durham (Hague *et al.*, 1996). This study explored the impact on children of both living with violence and moving to a refuge; the overlap with child abuse; the nature, impact and context of child work in refuges and beyond; and the extent of inclusion within it of agendas to combat racism, sexism, homophobia and violence. One key objective was to identify and help to disseminate best practice in direct intervention with children who have lived with violence, drawing on Women's Aid childwork as a key resource in this field. The same team plans more extensive research to examine children's experiences, agency responses, the connections between violence to women and violence to children, and any relevant preventative work. Another research team is examining the court-related practice of a range of professionals involved in questions of contact and residence in contexts of domestic violence (Hester *et al.*, 1994). Interviews with adults who lived in refuges as children and an analysis of calls to ChildLine from children currently living with abuse are both summarised in Saunders *et al.* (1995). Finally, there is a Nuffield-funded survey of the child protection policies and practices of social services departments, the police, and the court welfare side of the probation service as these relate to domestic violence – and no doubt there will be other work now that the field has begun to be recognised as worthy of study.

This chapter will draw on both research and practice to discuss what we already know about children and domestic violence – including its impact, the efforts that refuges and related services are making to help children, and what the professional child care response can be at its most positive (influ-enced by the North American work referred to above). The emphasis throughout is on the knowledge practitioners need, and the opportunities they can create for constructive intervention. The question of the cause for concern raised by Britain's inadadequate legislative framework, and by current social work and probation responses to abused women and their children, will be covered in the next chapter, which should be read in conjunction with this one.

THE IMPACT ON CHILDREN

It is rarely possible to conceal abuse from children or to prevent their being frightened and confused by it. The most recent British information on this comes from the Tayside Women and Violence Group (1994), with in-depth interviews covering 18 women with children (self-selected, recruited through press and radio), and NCH Action for Children (Abrahams, 1994), drawing on 108 questionnaires completed by a self-selected sample of women attending the charity's family centres (ibid., pp.19–20). Both samples are admitted to be under-representative, for example, of Black women. In Tayside, children in 16 of the 18 families had witnessed domestic violence; 15 had frequently heard it and 10 had frequently seen it (Tayside Women and Violence Group, 1994, p.34). In the NCH study, of the 86 mothers who believed their children had become aware of the violence they themselves were experiencing (Abrahams, 1994, pp.30–2), 73 per cent reported that the children witnessed and 62 per cent that they overheard attacks, 52 per cent that the children saw resulting injuries, and 99 per cent that they saw their mother upset or crying; 69 per cent said their children were conscious of living in an atmosphere of fear and intimidation. As many as 10 per cent of the whole sample of women had been sexually abused, and some have been raped, with children present. Only 13 women thought their children were unaware of the violence, and several of these, as in Evason's study in Northern Ireland (1982, p.45), were talking about children who were still babies at the time. In fact, it is likely that even the youngest children sense a tense atmosphere. Also, abusive men may adversely control the care the mother is able to give her baby or young child. In one refuge, a young mother described how her partner always insisted their toddler son must sit still and quiet for long periods of time. It was only when she moved into the refuge that the child could play naturally and run around with other children (author's research interview).

Dobash and Dobash (1984, p.279) found that almost 30 per cent of the incidents of domestic violence they analysed (i.e. not all the incidents throughout whole histories of abuse but specified attacks) took place with the couple's children present. Other work overseas has suggested that in 90 per cent of incidents of violence, the child is in the same or the next room (Hughes, 1992). Although women work hard to hide the abuse – 'women took great pains to protect their children from observing their father's brutality' (Hoff, 1990, p.204, commenting on her American research with mothers) – this is rarely completely possible. Interviews with children conducted by Jaffe *et al.* (1990, p.20) in Canada revealed that the majority could describe in detail assaults their parents were unaware they had witnessed. At the opposite extreme, some men force the children to watch the abuse and their mother's degradation (Tayside Women and Violence Group, 1994, pp.34–5) and/or to be implicated in it (Jaffe *et al.*, 1990, pp.17–18), knowing that this will be dreadful for her; naturally, it also adds to the distress and confusion of the children.

Women worry because they know that what they undergo personally has an effect on their children; 72 per cent of those interviewed in Evason's research in Northern Ireland (1982) felt there had been an adverse impact on their children. Children who witness attacks and live in the atmosphere they generate can hardly fail to be upset by it, though they show it in different ways. Of 96 respondents in the NCH Action for Children survey (Abrahams, 1994, p.35) answering a question on short-term responses to violence, 72 per cent said their children were frightened. What does this mean in detail? This study reports a range of behaviours indicative of distress, such as becoming quiet and clingy, or aggressive and disobedient. Evason (1982, p.45) cites 'bed wetting, asthma attacks, stuttering, insecurity, general nervousness, hysterics and nightmares'. Reports of emotional disturbance recur throughout the literature but do not describe a fixed syndrome or a single pattern of 'symptoms'. Clearly, children's responses are affected by factors such as their age, personality and circumstances – but the signs are there if professionals look for them. Sinclair (1985, p.88) sees pre-school children as more likely to demonstrate anxiety in physical ways, such as stomachaches or headaches, enuresis, sleep disturbances (including fear of the dark or resistance to bedtime – children may well have been woken from sleep by the sounds of the arguments and attacks), separation anxiety, whining and clinging behaviour, or failure to thrive. Medical services may undertake tests for physical symptoms that are actually the result of living with abuse (Tayside Women and Violence Group, 1994, p.35). Sinclair records children of primary school age as being likely to present broader-based fears and behaviours, such as fearing their own or others' anger, abandonment, being killed or killing someone else; eating disturbances such as over- or under-eating or hoarding food; trying to control the tension in the home; or becoming insecure and distrustful. Adolescents, according to Sinclair (1985, p.89), may escape into drugs, running away, early pregnancy or marriage, suicidal thoughts or actions, offending or violence.

Whilst age-related differences are clearly inevitable (within broad parameters), stemming from children's developmental stages and related life experiences, as well as the length of their exposure to the abuse (Tayside Women and Violence Group, 1994, p.36), sex-related categorisations are far more controversial. There has been a tendency in much Canadian and American research to over-emphasise differences between the reactions of girls and boys. In practice, both internalised reactions (anxiety, depression and somatic symptoms) and externalised behaviour (aggressive acting-out with, for example, bullying, fighting, frustration and tempers) can be observed, but not along stereotypically gendered lines. Indeed, one teenage boy began to feel suicidal because he could not fight his father as he thought he should, and reacted instead by shutting himself in his room feeling tense and miserable (author's research interview). Highly publicised findings of gender difference, for example 'that boys are more vulnerable to parental discord than are girls' (Jaffe *et al.*, 1986, p.76), have tended to be overstated. Less well publicised was the comment in the same study that showed it was not conclusive: 'A significant Group by Sex interaction was not found on any of the three factors, which suggests that the problems shown by both sexes were comparable.' (What *had* been found was a more marked difference between boys, as opposed to girls, from violent and non-violent homes, but there could be other explanations for this. Furthermore, this study took quite a small sample and had all the usual problems of trying to reduce the complexities of human life to a set of numerical representations.)

In fact, all forms of upset behaviour can be found in both sexes. Professionals need to be alert to every way of showing distress, including behaviours at opposite extremes. Sinclair (1985, p.89) cites these as including perfectionism and fear of failure at school on the one hand, and impaired concentration and poor school work on the other; hanging around the house to try and protect mother at one end of the spectrum, and avoiding home completely at the other. Despite flaws, the research to date is sufficient to confirm an adverse impact of living with abuse on the majority of children, but it is important to remember that the manifestation of distress in any individual child can never be predicted (see Morley and Mullender, 1994a, for both the broad research findings and a critique of methodology). Children react differently, even within the same family (Tayside Women and Violence Group, 1994, p.36).

Like every practitioner and every mother, each study and report has its own list of reactions to living with violence. The Women's Aid Federation England (in House of Commons Home Affairs Committee, 1992b, Memorandum 22, para. 4.2), from refuge-based observations, lists:

> stress related illnesses, confused and torn loyalties (i.e. to both mother and father), lack of trust, unnaturally good behaviour, taking on the mother role, an acceptance of abuse as 'normal', guilt, isolation, shame, anger, lack of confidence, fear of a repeat or a return to violence, and so on.

Hoff (1990, p.207), from her study of women and their children surviving abuse, states: 'A child's expression of anxiety takes many forms: aggressiveness, withdrawal, regression in toilet and eating habits, crying, demanding behaviour.' Nor do children stay fixed in one set of behaviours; their reactions change and develop over time (including as adult survivors of living with abuse), but we do not have longitudinal studies charting any of the trends involved. Some children are able to survive without any of the visible reactions, though not without unhappiness and grief. All we can say for certain is that living with violence has worrying effects on children and ought to concern us as much as the direct abuse of children themselves (which may present through remarkably similar signs and symptoms). Leaving violence, even though adverse memories and reactions can linger and making a new life is hard, often has a positive effect (source: accounts from refuge workers and Hague *et al.*, 1996).

LINKS WITH CHILD ABUSE

There is a demonstrable overlap between direct and indirect (that is, witnessed) abuse, and the impact of the two when they coincide may also be compounded. Hughes *et al.* (1989) compared 44 child witnesses of parental violence with 40 who had both witnessed and experienced abuse (both these groups came from 37 families recruited from a shelter) and also included 66 children from 45 families of a similar economic background who were thought, after a research check, not to fall into these categories. The children who had both witnessed and experienced abuse were seen as significantly more distressed, substantially so in their mothers' eyes, with the highest scores of problems in every age group; they were on the verge of needing clinical intervention by North American standards although they did not see themselves as more depressed and only felt a little more anxious than the control group. The non-abused witnesses fell between the other two groups. As does the present author, these researchers concluded that no one working with children can afford to neglect any kind of abuse in the home. This demands a new kind of awareness of woman abuse from professionals in child protection and child psychiatry settings who can work positively with women and their children to offer support and practical help (see Chapter 4, this volume):

> Just as it is vital to determine whether children in shelters for battered women have been physically abused, so it is essential for child protective service workers, clinicians, researchers, and others who identify abused and neglected children to assess the presence or absence of other types of violence in the home.

> (ibid., p.206)

The study just cited estimates the overlap between child abuse and woman abuse as being between 40 and 60 per cent, based on an overview of other research. British research also shows the two coinciding. Pahl (1985a, p.50) recorded 36 per cent of the women in her refuge-based study as saying that their husbands had physically harmed one or more of the children. O'Hara (1993, p.18) reports an Irish refuge-based study by Casey (1987) in which 28 per cent of women with children referred to severe physical abuse of the children by their own male abusers and 30 per cent to actual or suspected child sexual abuse. O'Hara (1992, p.4) also points to personal accounts as suggesting a link between domestic violence and child sexual abuse, and to the early role of refuges in drawing attention to its existence; children escaping their mothers' experiences of abuse were disclosing abuse against themselves which feminist workers were more inclined to believe than the then child care establishment. Reaching safety in a refuge is still not infrequently the first time a child feels able to speak about sexual abuse. In the recent NCH Action for Children study (Abrahams, 1994, pp.30–1), only 44 per cent of mothers said that their partners 'didn't touch the children', that is through deliberate abuse, and 13 per cent said that a child had been hurt by accident during an attack. This research did not discriminate between physical and sexual abuse of children.

Child sexual abuse

Broadly, there has been less information about the overlap between child sexual abuse and witnessing abuse. Starting from samples of sexually abused children, there tends to be a high proportion of mothers who have been abused in various ways (see Morley and Mullender, 1994a, p.32 for a summary). Worryingly, Forman's Scottish study (1995) affords further evidence that child protection workers have not only failed to note or respond to the further harm inflicted on the children by witnessing abuse, but have failed to help many women to recognise their own experiences as abusive (ibid., p.33) and hence to get help. This was despite the fact that every one of the 20 women in this study was able to recount abusive behaviour towards herself (p.21); for only three did this not include physical attacks (p.22), and almost half reported coerced sex (p.15). Only two had received help for themselves (p.23) and this came from voluntary sector organisations. Nine had found social services helpful with the children but had often felt that their own needs were ignored (ibid., and see Chapter 4, this volume). Despite their very difficult circumstances, the women had acted in whatever way was possible to protect their children when they discovered the sexual abuse (p.30); for three, their own abuse had been so severe that this had been possible only through leaving home.

Child physical abuse

There is more information relating to a clear overlap with child physical abuse. Risks to children include accidentally getting in the way of an assault upon their mother: 'She would stand there and get hit and just hold on and scream' (Hoff, 1990, p.204, reporting the words of a mother of a 2 year old). Others are hurt when they try to intervene. This had happened in a third of incidents reported by women in a study in West Yorkshire; the main exception was children who were too young, although even a 2 year old 'picked up a shoe and hit him with it' (Hanmer, 1990, p.26).

There are also risks to unborn children, because jealous and controlling men appear to increase their violence during pregnancy (Andrews and Brown, 1988, p.311; Bowker and Maurer 1987, p.34), frequently targeting the abdominal area. In a recent Scottish study (Tayside Women and Violence Group, 1994, p.34), in-depth interviews with 20 women recruited through press and radio advertising revealed that 11 were asaulted with kicks and punches to the abdomen while pregnant and several experienced abuse starting with the birth of their first child. In Pahl's study, a third of the women were pregnant when the violence actually began (Pahl, 1982, p.529). Unsurprisingly, then, women who have experienced domestic violence are more than twice as likely to have had a miscarriage or still-birth (Andrews and Brown, 1988, p.311; Bowker and Maurer, 1987, p.34). Furthermore, many women are prevented by domineering and jealous men from using antenatal and obstetric services (see Chapter 5, this volume). The combination of damage in the womb and damage caused by living with abuse and/or being directly abused presumably results in a dispro-portionately high number of children with disabilities, including learning and, of course, emotional and behavioural difficulties (Smith 1989, citing Pagelow, 1981).

There are two major studies of the links between men's abuse of women and of children; both were published in 1988 and both are American. Bowker et al. (1988, p.162) found that 'Wife beaters abused children in 70% of the families in which children were present.' They therefore suggest to child care professionals that they should 'assume that child abuse will accompany wife abuse in approximately 70% of the families in which children are present' (although this is an unsafe conclusion statistically since this was not a random sample including non-violent families). The authors felt even this was likely to be an underestimate (ibid., p.165) because the women respondents may not have known about all the abuse or may have been reluctant to report it, and because some forms of abuse were omitted, including child sexual abuse, neglect, and the torture and killing of children's pets.

The researchers had recruited a volunteer national sample of 1,000 battered women; only those who had had children with their abuser were studied (225 had not). In 543 families, the man physically abused both the woman and their children (p.162). The child abuse was, on average, less severe than the abuse of the woman but it included 9 per cent using weapons, and 16 per cent kicking, hitting or punching, amongst other severe attacks. The best predictor of abuse of the children was the severity of wife abuse (together with frequency of attacks and frequency of marital rape: husbands who had raped their wives over a hundred times were four times more likely to abuse their children than those who never raped). This reinforces the necessity for social workers to talk to women about their personal experiences, remembering always that they may initially lack the language to conceptualise or name these as abusive without skilled and woman-centred help (Kelly, 1988a and 1988b). Exposure to risk was also important in the Bowker *et al.* study; the more children, for example, the greater the likelihood of abuse – prevalence ranged from 51 per cent with one child to 92 per cent with four or more. The degree of the husband's dominance in the family was the next strongest predictor. Husbands who regularly got their own way perpetrated every kind of physical abuse more often than those who did not (Bowker *et al.*, 1988, pp.164–5). Husbands who had been physically abused as children were more likely to abuse their own children, but this was not as strong a predictor as the three just mentioned (see section below on the 'cycle of violence'). In other words, knowing what is happening in the relationship and family *now* is more likely to tell professionals what help children and women need than knowing about the past; furthermore, knowing that children need help for their own abuse will often coincide with their mother urgently needing help too. Wives in the Bowker *et al.* survey approached more sources of help when their children were abused as well as themselves (ibid.) – thus following the pattern set by professionals in neglecting women's needs – but did not find them particularly useful. Ending the abuse, for example, through removal of the abuser or escape from the abuse, will help everyone; there is no need to think about removing the children from their mother unless there is some other fundamental problem which will not be resolved by ending the violence against the woman and offering support.

A clear pattern of power and control emerges:

> violent and previolent men have high needs to dominate their wives and children. They achieve and maintain the level of dominance they consider appropriate by a variety of oppressive strategies, including wife beating, child abuse, marital rape, psychological abuse, punitive economic deprivation, and coerced social isolation.

> (ibid., p.166)

Professionals are not at present being trained to look for or recognise this pattern, or to help women and children to be safe from it. Early intervention when domestic violence first begins might prevent it from developing; action to confront the man and help the woman and children to be safe, working in conjunction with women's choices, is essential at any stage. The first step is acknowledging and naming men's actions as abuse and as unacceptable.

Stark and Flitcraft (1988; see also Stark and Flitcraft, 1996) approached their similar research aim of seeking overlaps between the abuse of women and that of children from the other way on: that is, by tracing abused women from information about their children. They were already convinced of a link from their earlier work (Stark and Flitcraft, 1985) which found that abused women were six times more likely to have a report or fear of child abuse noted on their medical records. They found indicators of domestic violence in the medical records (and family background notes) of 52 out of a sample of 116 mothers whose children were suspected of being abused and/or neglected. They comment:

> This frequency of at-risk women (45 percent) is 2.4 times greater than the frequency of battering among women presenting injuries to the surgical service (19 percent) and twice as great as the frequency of battering in the prenatal clinic (21 percent), making this the highest at-risk population yet identified. . . . It is also higher than for alcohol and drug misuse, attempted suicide, rape, divorce or mental illness.
>
> (Stark and Flitcraft, 1988, pp.104 and 107)

The 25 per cent of women who were positively identified as battered in this study had almost four and a half times as many injuries in their adult medical injuries record as a normal population (ibid., p.104; 4.9 as against 1.1), confirming that domestic violence is 'an ongoing process, not an isolated incident'. Their children were twice as likely as the children of non-abused mothers to have been identified for actual as opposed to suspected abuse (p.105). The child abuse appeared to have started after a pattern of wife assault had already become established (p.106) and fathers or father substitutes were three times more likely than anyone else to be the child's abuser where they also abused the mother. Yet the phenomenon of male abuse of women was not openly discussed in either the women's or the children's records (p.107). In a situation where women are trapped in violent and controlling relationships, including by the expectations and myths perpetuated by helping services, argue Stark and Flitcraft (p.101), men remain invisible as abusers both of women and of children.

Contrary to the myth of a cycle of violence (see below), the abused mothers of abused children were less likely than the non-abused to come from a disorganised family background and no more likely to have a family history of violence (ibid., p.105). Stark and Flitcraft regard the key factor in abuse as being 'Male authority . . . directly expressed in violent control over women and children' (p.97). They review literature (pp.99–100) indicating that, where men are present, they are many times more likely to abuse children than are women and that they are primarily responsible for serious child abuse, particularly fatal cases. Consequently, since women are typically the non-abusing parents, 'the best way to prevent child abuse is to protect women's physical integrity and support their empowerment. At a minimum, this implies close collaboration between child protective services and community-based shelters and a shift in child protection away from parenting education, therapy, and the removal of children' (p.102). It is a severe indictment of social work that abused women in this study were far more likely to have had their children removed (p.106) when the latter were abused than were non-abused women, a clearly punitive response and one which, purely in resource terms, means that all options have not been tried. Indeed, these are situations where there clearly *were* other options to try which could have helped a non-abusing parent to parent safely, unlike the other cases where there was no such obvious reason why the other parent has not protected the child. '[C]ase-workers and clinicians would do well to look toward advocacy and protection of battered mothers as the best available means to prevent current child abuse as well as child abuse in the future' conclude these researchers (Stark and Flitcraft, 1985, p.168). Abused women are, therefore, our greatest underused child care resource. Partnership with them is critically important. And there is, incidentally, no research evidence that abused women are more likely to abuse.

Individual cases also point to the dangers of social workers and other professionals overlooking domestic violence as an indicator of grave danger for children from the man in the household. There have been numerous deaths of children in households where their mother was being abused. One can read between the lines of published enquiries and commentaries upon them (O'Hara, 1994) to see social workers not addressing the issues or understanding their significance. The Bridge Child Care Consultancy Service (1991) was unusual in drawing stated attention to these dangers when reporting on the death of Sukina Hammond. There had been a pattern of physical abuse of Sukina's mother and younger sister, as well as of Sukina herself. Her mother, in fact, tried to stop the fatal assault (in 1988, when Sukina was 5) but was herself attacked. The report points to the social services' failure to accord sufficient weight to the persistent domestic violence as evidence of a threat to the children, as well as a failure to listen to Sukina – even though she was very frightened of her father and told several professionals that he hurt her. The children were removed from the child protection register only weeks after a grave assault on their mother – which involved professionals knew about – and only months before Sukina's death. The report cites research on the link between child abuse, particularly child murder, and men's subjugation of women and children through violence. The social workers fell into the same trap highlighted by Bowker *et al.* and by Stark and Flitcraft (both 1988; see above), as well as by the wider social work research (e.g. Maynard, 1985; see Chapter 3, this volume) of failing to single out the man's violent actions against the woman as particularly significant. They knew about the history of vicious domestic violence but recorded little about it and failed to make the links. (Since that time, further research has underlined these links still more emphatically – in demonstrating that woman abuse is present in many of the child abuse cases with the worst outcomes: Department of Health, 1995, p.63). There was no clarity in the social services' thinking about this man's dangerousness as an individual and as a man; rather, they saw the family as a whole as the problem – as an abusing family. The Bridge report itself in fact fails to make a gendered record of the abuse and talks about 'dangerous families'.

If the gender roles in the situation had been understood, Sukina's mother could have been seen as a source of potential protection and strength – which she tried to be even when in fear of her life – and action taken to remove her husband and stop his violence or to help her make her own escape. Hooper's research (1992) confirms that women are typically ready and willing to play a protective role, too, in cases of child sexual abuse. Creating the conditions in which non-abusing abused women are empowered and supported to protect themselves and their children (Kelly, 1994) should be a major feature of social work intervention. 'Many have done quite incredible jobs of raising their children in the face of horrendous odds' (Sinclair, 1985, p.85). Hoff (1990, p.204; see also Chapter 11 of her book) gives a detailed picture of women 'intensely devoted to their children, who were often the focus of their most acute pain and struggle', and this despite, for example, children being born from violent marital rape (Hoff, 1990, p.206). There were violent rows about pregnancy and discipline:

> Direct abuse of a child was often the occasion of violence toward the mother, particularly if she intervened on a child's behalf or protested against the father's harsh discipline of a child. One woman said that the most typical beating occurred when she defended her children. One time, for example, the man's glasses fell off while playing with their little girl. He blamed the child and kicked her across the room with his booted foot. This incident escalated into the final episode and near-fatal suicide attempt of the mother.
>
> (ibid., p.204)

Would social work reports have recorded this woman as needing help but still as displaying tremendous strength and offering an important resource to her children, or would she be written off as an inadequate and mentally unstable mother who 'failed to protect' her children?

In sum, the overlap between children living with abuse and those being directly abused points, not to children and domestic violence as the latest fashionable child care problem which should rival the few resources going to abused women, but, rather, to a situation where more resoures devoted to women will also help children. It is the abuse of women, including in its impact on children, that is still waiting to be recognised by many agencies in the social work field as a major social problem and as relevant to them.

The alleged 'cycle of violence'

The 'cycle' or intergenerational transmission of violence (see Chapter 2, this volume) is accepted by most people as reality and by some as a kind of destiny. One couple who sought marriage guidance counselling from Relate could not allow any kind of help or advice to work for them because they believed themselves predestined by the wife's abusive upbringing. They were also more concerned about the impact of their hitting one another on their young daughter's future development than about finding solutions to their present problems which were causing them all distress in the here and now. Many social workers and other professionals will mention the risks that they will 'grow up like it' as the one thing they 'know' about the impact of domestic violence on children, and refer to the need to prevent violence repeating itself as their primary motivation for intervention. Indeed one retired psychiatric social worker, when confronted over this, asked what would be the point of working with children in such circumstances if not to prevent abuse recurring. Leaving aside this callous disregard for the experiences of children living with violence in the present, and the high risk that they are being directly abused currently (see above), on what foundation does she base such a certainty that we can foretell the evils of the future?

First of all, it is necessary to pin down exactly what certainty we are talking about. Are we saying that children who *witness* domestic violence are affected, or children who are *directly* abused? Is this relatively more likely to happen or a virtual certainty – 'violence breeds violence'? Does it affect boys learning to be violent or can we talk about girls learning to be victims?

Like the public and the professionals, many authors assert or hint at some kind of 'cycle' without producing evidence that it exists or defining precisely what they mean. This remains true of recent North American output on child witnesses (e.g. all but one of the sources cited at the beginning of this chapter, at the very least, slip into talking about working with children for the sake of the future – the exception is the Duluth manual). It was shown in Chapter 2 that the research does not bear out such a rationale and our work with children should not need to depend on it. Work with child witnesses of domestic abuse should be offered because they need it now, and preventive work, in schools for example, should be undertaken with all children and with their local community, knowing that this will encompass currently abused children and children currently living with the abuse of their mothers (these two groups will overlap), as well as children who will and others who will not grow up to abuse or be abused. It cannot be predicted which children will find themselves in the latter two groups, so the work undertaken needs to be aimed at everybody.

Children as survivors

In all the discussion of adverse effects on children, it is important to remember that children, like their mothers, have their own resourcefulness and coping strategies. If a professional holds the image of a child living with domestic abuse as a passive victim, he or she may overlook both some of the dangers (children actively doing things that draw the violence towards them) and some of the personal strengths the child will be able to use to survive.

Many children try to offer protection or to seek help. Dobash and Dobash (1984) found that children observing attacks overwhelmingly supported their mothers either actively or passively. Responses, even from small children, included pleading with their fathers to stop, screaming, crying and trying to hide. As was mentioned above, older children may hit the man or try to get between the couple (Smith, 1989, p.20). Such behaviour is not gender specific. One woman in Hoff's study (1990, p.204) 'told of her 3-year old son coming to defend her, saying: "No, daddy, no!" And he came behind his father and started hitting him', while

> one 13-year girl was watching her father choke and beat her mother. She jumped on her father and choked him. He threw her on the floor, and dragged her by the hair across the street and told her not to come back.
>
> (p.207)

Children also try to obtain outside assistance.

> The 10-year old son of one woman called the police more than once. Often, the women were torn between wanting to protect their chil/dren from observing or having any part in the violence and needing to rely on them as the only human source of support available.
>
> (pp.204–5)

Children in Britain, too, telephone the police, ChildLine, social workers and other agencies (Tayside Women and Violence Group, 1994, pp.35–7). An Asian worker (in Imam, 1994, pp.195–6) noticed that children of the women she worked with in a refuge and women's centre setting had often tried to summon help – perhaps because they knew the system better than their mothers and were more used to dealing with people in authority, at school and elsewhere, and also because their mothers were often constrained by family and community from seeking help.

It is crucial that children who disclose experiences of living with abuse in this or other ways should find that adults are ready to believe them and to offer appropriate help (see section below on disclosure work). Help is not best offered by routinely placing children on the child protection register (see Chapter 4, this volume), for example, through a bureaucratic decision that living with domestic violence constitutes emotional abuse. It means working openly and constructively with children and their non-abusing mothers to make sense of all that has happened, and to help them draw on their coping strategies for the future. The sections that follow outline positive work undertaken, in Britain and overseas, with children who are living with or who have lived with the abuse of their mothers.

WORK WITH CHILDREN IN REFUGES

One setting in which the children of abused women have been receiving appropriate help for over twenty years is in refuges. Indeed, there are more child than women residents: 28,000 as against 17,000 in Women's Aid refuges in England alone (Women's Aid Federation England, 1993/94, figures for 1992/93; see also Debbonaire, 1994). Since, despite gross underfunding, childworkers keep in touch with many children after they leave – for example through follow-up work and invitations to special events – and undertake outreach work with families who do not enter the refuge, they are clearly helping many thousands of children every year. A comprehensive national resourcing base would enable them to do far more.

Typically, the younger children go with their mother into the refuge: Ball (1990, p.6) found the majority of children in nine refuges she surveyed to be under secondary school age, divided fairly evenly between pre-school and primary age children; if there are older children they may stay behind, go to friends or grandparents, or try the refuge for a time but leave again (Pahl, 1985a, p.50). Most refuges have policies against admitting older boys (the cut-off age ranges from 11 to 16), linked with their 'no men' rule. There are also particular problems for Asian women in bringing teenage girls to a refuge since it may be seen as compromising their family honour or *izzat* (Imam, 1994, p.197). Nevertheless, childworkers are skilled in offering a service to children and young people of all ages, including helping them understand what they have lived through and dealing with the fears to which it will have given rise and they work with a constantly fluctuating and wide range of ages.

Women's Aid groups, in refuges and second stage housing, increasingly offer specialised childwork and, indeed, represent the major British expertise in this field. Since 1988, a national support group has existed for children's workers in Women's Aid affiliated refuges in England, enabling them to share issues of concern and models of good practice, to identify and meet training needs, and to develop policy for children in refuges (Debbonaire, 1994, pp.147–9 and pers. comms). Facilitating the group is one of the responsibilities of the National Children's Officer. The other national Women's Aid federations in Scotland, Wales and Northern Ireland are also keenly interested in children's issues. Each develops guidelines and national policies but each refuge is separately constituted and also develops its own relationships with local child care agencies, schools, health visitors, solicitors, and so on.

As has been recognised earlier, refuge funding is always uncertain and childwork, like all other aspects of the work, relies on fundraising. The telethon-based charity, the BBC Children in Need Appeal, has funded a considerable proportion of the work in recent years; a few social services departments have also given assistance (Ball, 1994). Women's Aid argues that children in refuges should be classed as children in need within the meaning of the Children Act 1989 (Debbonaire, 1994, p.159) and that funding should therefore be automatic. This will be an important matter for consideration in the new local authority Children's Services Plans. Not all refuges can sustain paid childworkers and few can resource the work to the level they would like, relying on volunteers to provide valuable support, or to be the chief resource. It is a national disgrace that this body of expertise is being developed against a background of inadequate and unstable resources, including understaffing. As so often occurs, an enormous amount is being achieved through the sheer commitment and determination of a female workforce dedicated to the interests of abused women and their children.

What is childwork?

Playwork

Those members of the general public or child care professions who realise that work with children goes on in refuges at all, may think of it as a child-minding service or the simple provision of play facilities. They would be missing its main point. Certainly, play materials are provided and activities organised, there are outings and holidays, play schemes and day trips, festivals are celebrated. But refuges do not offer a childminding service, although residents do babysit for one another and there may be crêche or play sessions at fixed hours of the day, e.g. a morning crêche to assist women who are sorting out complex practical problems with housing, benefits, and so on, and after-school play while mothers are preparing the evening meal (meals are not taken communally in refuges – each woman buys and prepares food for her own family). Play can have value in itself: 'Constructive and creative activities help to restore balance to a child's life' (Women's Aid Federation England, 1992b, p.8), while building confidence and trust. Childworkers develop an understanding of the play needs of children of different ages and abilities, including disabled children and those with learning difficulties of various kinds. The comparatively fewer teenaged children also have particular needs, especially to talk (Ball, 1994, pp.6–7).

Play is used to help children understand all that has happened to them and why and, to develop new hope for the future together with their mother and any brothers and sisters. Specially designed play resources, such as *My Colouring Book of the Refuge* (Wilton, undated), are designed to help children comprehend and come to terms with the practical upheaval they have experienced: 'Your mum will cook your meals. Lots of other children stay here with their mums, and there will be toys for you to share' (accompanying multi-racial pictures of the kitchen and playroom). They also explain the associated emotions, as in the Scottish Women's Aid's leaflet (undated) for children *Going to a New House?*: 'Remember when you first came into the refuge – did you feel a bit frightened, upset or angry? . . . You might feel like you did when you first came in because you don't know what life's going to be like next.' Children's upset feelings are explained as quite normal – 'All change is a bit scary, even changes for the better' – and children are treated as resourceful survivors who have their own coping capacities on which to draw: 'You've been through this sort of thing before – when you came into the refuge – so you've had practice.' After going through so much together, mother/child relationships are also seen as a key source of support: 'You'll find that sharing your hopes and worries with your mum will also help you to settle in'; and in the companion leaflet to mothers, *Moving on with Your Kids*: 'If you and the kids feel this move is something you're in together, you've more chance of being company and comfort for each other in your new house . . . . admitting that you're worried can help a child to put into words how he or she feels.'

Individual and groupwork

The chief role of childwork in refuges is to meet the emotional and practical needs of children who are resident for periods ranging from overnight to over a year. This is achieved with children individually and in groups, underscored by a closer understanding of male abuse of women and children than is typically found in other child care settings.

Children's meetings are held in many refuges. These may make decisions about future activities, solve problems (for example, in the use of the playroom), voice issues and concerns, and feed into discussion and decision making by the adults in the refuge. Children's workshops have more of an educational function, including in relation to violence and anti-violence. Workshops and meetings, as well as individual work and discussion through play, also help children to talk about how they feel and to understand that other children also feel upset, depressed and angry. They experience torn loyalties and conflicting emotions about a father who has been abusive and a mother who has appeared unable to stop this happening. Children are also likely to be homesick and confused by new experiences, a new place with new people, and a new kind of life. Childworkers understand that children arriving will feel anxious after living with violence and the disorientation of a sudden move. Their mother is likely to be reacting to the crisis or may not know what to tell the children. Others may need to explain to the children where they are, that they are safe, and what is happening to them. Children benefit from explanations and from talking about their experiences. Often, other children will help with settling in the new arrivals. Children are taught the safety rules of the refuge (not to answer the door, not to go near the cooker, and so on) and they may test out the limits and who enforces them early in their stay. Once they settle in, many children like refuges (Hague *et al.*, 1996), often more than their mothers do (though see Saunders, 1994, for some of the negatives). They have other children to play with, toys and often a playroom or playspace, childworkers and/or volunteers; they are out of the violence and can relax and be children again.

Anti-oppressive work

Childworkers help children to understand the nature of violence and irrational hatred in society. A key value is to help children to learn to live peacefully together, to respect and not to make fun of one another. This includes understanding not only sexism, because it lies at the root of the violence, but also racism, homophobia and negative attitudes about disability. Children of a lesbian mother, for example, may have heard virulent verbal abuse from their father when he learnt of her sexuality, or may hear discriminatory remarks from women and other children in the refuge against a lesbian woman. They need to know that it is refuge policy to raise understanding and not to tolerate homophobic attitudes. This will also help any older girls or boys who may be discovering their own sexuality, which will not necessarily be heterosexual.

There are many Black families in refuges, not all in specialist Black refuges, and they may experience disproportionate problems in being rehoused (Mama, 1989). Ball (1990, p.7), in a survey of nine refuges, found that 145 children were identified by themselves or their mothers as belonging to minority ethnic groups, including all the children in three of the refuges, but this was visibly an underestimate as far as the others were concerned, the category having been rejected by some people. At least three refuges had children of travelling families in residence.

Just as the general refuge workers will raise anti-discriminatory policies in refuge meetings, so childworkers will use workshops and children's meetings to help children learn that women who love women, men who love men, Black and white people, children with disabilities and learning difficulties, are equally deserving of respect. Ignorance and prejudice have fed on the violence in these children's lives; the refuge has to be a place where they are challenged and refuted. Children are capable of quite sophisticated understanding; they can do quizzes on what the words gay and lesbian mean and learn not to be frightened of the unknown. They can

also have fun – in celebrating the festivals of different faiths, for example
– and take pride in developing their own policies, such as the following
actual examples, reproduced with permission:

Racism means a combination of white power and superiority over the
ethnic minority. This is our anti-racism statement!
1. Do not make fun of other people's accents.
2. Do not make fun of their religion.
3. Do not make fun of other people's food, and make noises about it.
4. Do not make fun of people's hair and what they look like, calling names
    etc.

!Anti-Sexism Statement!
1. We want boys and girls to play together.
2. Don't make fun of boys when they play with dolls and stuff.
3. Boys are not to take over the playroom.
4. Girls for football and rugby.
5. Club for both girls and boys.

Increasingly, there are positive play and learning resources available to
help children understand such matters in accessible language:

Racist jokes, name-calling and violent racist attacks happen all the time
and yet many people try to pretend that racism is not a problem . . . .
Racism means that some people make judgements about you without
bothering to find out what you are like.

(Grunsell, 1990, p.5)

Childworkers are encouraged through national support and training to
tackle racist attitudes regardless of the number of Black residents in a
refuge or the area in which it is situated, to offer positive images and play
and reading materials without racist content, and a clear understanding
about the nature of racism (Women's Aid Federation England, 1992b,
pp.35–7), and to build on different languages, festivities and customs as
part of the richness of sharing a home with others.

The anti-sexist character of playwork in refuges is not discernible only
in the fact that it builds continually on the need to find alternatives to the
violence of a male-dominated society. It is also developed through positive
images of women in play and reading materials, through avoiding gender
divisions in games, sports and play materials, through encouraging girls to
explore their abilities and ideas, creating girls-only time and space to build
girls' confidence in themselves and in their right to play and be as they
want. Childworkers also focus on the needs of boys and girls to learn that
domination and submission are not the only options, and that it is OK to
have feelings and to show them without hiding in aggression or withdrawal.
All children and young people in the refuge can actively discuss sexism and

its effects in children's meetings and can learn to make non-oppressive choices. (See also ibid., pp.32–4.)

Liaison with other agencies and advocacy

The childworker works as part of a wider network of agencies and services not only in relating to the statutory education, health, social services, civil and criminal justice authorities in their child-related capacities but also in locating and drawing on voluntary and community resources for children and families to enrich their time in the refuge. The childworker will often be the person who helps a woman to get her children into a local school. She will also work with local schools to ensure that children are comfortable there (for example, to help teachers be sensitive in setting family-related tasks in class and in talking to children about home and family) and also safe. There may be a risk of the child being snatched from school; staff there need to know if father has harmed or poses a threat to the child. Child-workers also work at creating positive relationships with health visitors and establish contact with the local social services where appropriate. Sometimes, other psychological, health or welfare services may be called upon where the child has particular needs, either pre-existing or caused by living with or directly experiencing abuse. Refuge workers were amongst the first professionals to recognise the existence of sexual abuse and to learn to hear and believe what survivors, both children and adult women, were saying about it. Like social workers, they follow the professional practices of not promising a child secrecy, knowing what signs and symptoms to look for, believing what children say, encouraging a mother to be involved in protecting her children, and, preferably through the mother, implementing procedures for formal investigation and action to remove any current risk of further abuse. In return, social workers and related professionals can value what refuges offer, work on building effective links, and respect their feminist philosophy and strict attention to keeping women's whereabouts secret, rather than regarding them as just another housing resource.

Childworkers also play a more general advocacy role. This implies understanding that a child may have needs different from his or her mother's (ibid., p.8), for example for extra time to be spent explaining things just when she has least time and emotional energy to spare. It also implies a relationship of trust being built up so that the childworker is there to speak up for children in the refuge and outside it, and to encourage children to understand and voice their own needs – including racial, cultural and religious needs, as well as those that depend on age and ability levels. In these ways, the childworker (or children's advocate in the USA and Canada: see Loosley, 1994, and Hughes and Marshall, 1995) is offering empowerment to children, just as all refuge workers aim to do for women.

Working through mother

Refuges work hard never to usurp any woman's parenting role. Consequently, the childworker will often work through a mother to help her child, building on their relationship where necessary and encouraging her in understanding both her child's needs and her own. Mothers are involved in play and planning activities, so that playwork is not seen as keeping the children occupied but as something positive. The worker will never undertake work with the child without the mother's permission. For example, when a children's group in a refuge was to have a session on sexuality that included gay and lesbian rights, only those children whose mothers consented participated. Both mother and children need to relearn, or perhaps to learn for the first time, to feel in control, to make decisions about what they want and what suits them, and to empower and support one another taking each other's needs into account. (See section below on mothers' groups.)

Refuges do recognise that some mothers abuse as well as fathers and that a woman's interests may at times conflict with those of her child. Although workers support the woman to meet her child's needs wherever possible, including by encouraging her to call on social work intervention if it is needed, they will take action themselves to protect a child if necessary and if the mother is not prepared to make the report. Refuges are actually very safe places, however. Because everyone there has lived with violence, refuges work very hard to help mothers develop alternatives to physical punishments and have written or unwritten 'no violence' policies. Women also provide each other with important mutual support.

DIRECT WORK WITH AND FOR CHILDREN

There are important lessons to be drawn by practitioners from the positive work achieved in refuge and related contexts (e.g. second stage and outreach housing). There is potential for child care and child protection agencies to undertake their own work to aid children's understanding of domestic violence and its impact on them, to meet their safety needs, and to assist schools in developing the personal choices of children and young people with respect to non-violent behaviour, as well as working with parents to meet their children's needs in overcoming the impact of living with abuse. Models for such work come chiefly from North America.

Disclosure work

A Canadian manual of responses to disclosures from children that they are currently living in situations where their mothers are being abused, to be used by all those working with children in professional, voluntary and community settings, has recently been reproduced in a British publication (Children's Subcommittee of the London Coordinating Committee to End Woman Abuse, 1994). It emphasises safety planning appropriate to the child's age. This covers how to get out of the dangerous situation and reach safety, and tells children not to try and stop the abuse but to go to a telephone or trusted adult elsewhere. It incorporates good practice for adults in communicating at the child's level, and taking into account feelings such as fear, guilt and shame. There are also tips on assisting the abused woman.

Groups for child witnesses of woman abuse

Like disclosure work, groupwork (Mullender, 1994a and 1995; see also Peled and Edleson, 1995) is underpinned by the need to help children understand that living with abuse is not their fault, and that they and their mother have a right to be safe. It goes beyond learning practical safety skills into work on feelings and comprehension. Individual work can also be of value in these respects but it does not give children the same opportunity to realise that they are not unique or to share their new learning with others. Children who are not given the chance to talk about their experiences keep their fears, confusions and family secrets bottled up inside. Persistent symptoms of having lived with and witnessed abuse consequently include intrusive thoughts and nightmares.

British child care professionals can build on skills they already possess to work through groupwork games and exercises on naming and under-standing feelings, dealing with anger, learning to keep safe from abuse, coping with conflicting feelings about family members, and accessing a range of community supports. They will need training to do the necessary work in children's groups on men's responsibilty for abuse (children need to know that women and children are not to blame), learning to keep safe from abuse, recognising the misleading nature of the myths about abuse with which we are all surrounded (see Chapter 2, this volume) and the fact that physically abusive behaviours are illegal. Children also need help to understand specific incidents as abusive and to understand the roles, and degrees of responsibility and control, of those involved in them.

The 'Community Group Treatment Program for Child Witnesses of Woman Abuse' in London, Ontario, is one of the best developed examples of using groups to meet the needs of children who have lived with domestic violence. The programme has seven agencies as members and uses a standardised referral process, including a risk assessment of the child's current degree of danger from the mother's abuser. A total of 100–125 referrals a year are accepted from social service agencies and also from mothers in the community. The Community Group Treatment Worker co-facilitates the groups with workers from member agencies; the children in any one group will not necessarily all have links with the same agency.

The programme is basically an extension of an earlier model (Wilson *et al.* 1986) which drew upon the research summarised by Jaffe *et al.* (1990). It has been developed in practice by a range of local agencies, including the major child protection agency. The groupworkers have broadened the age range from the original model and subdivided it, with perhaps five groupings across the gamut from 5 to 15 (taking into account, also, developmental and concentration levels). The younger the children, the smaller and more activity based the group; teenagers can cope with up to nine or ten in the group as they are more used to a discussion-style forum. Staff aim for roughly equal numbers of boys and girls in each group and will not run with only one boy or one girl because this would be too uncomfortable when working with essentially gender-based issues within a feminist framework of exposing sexism and gender power dynamics. There is a clear policy to separate siblings in the groups because they tend to interrupt each other, either to compete for space or to prevent disclosures happening at a pace they personally cannot handle. A pre-admission interview with mother and child decides whether the child is ready for the group. Children known to have been sexually abused are referred to a different group (and may eventually return to this one). The group is not aimed at those currently living with woman abuse; rather, it focuses on recovering from its impact. Children are given permission to talk about what have been family secrets; there is open acknowledgement that it is often painful to do the exercises in the group but there is also some fun and considerable learning – including estimates of the number of other children at school who may have had similar experiences. Group members develop a vocabulary and a set of understandings to talk about abuse, to know that it is wrong, and that it is not their fault. They are helped to start a new life, either without their father in the household or with him still present but working (through another groupwork programme and the criminal justice system) to stop his abuse.

Work in schools

A number of countries have begun to undertake work that relates to teaching young people about non-violent relationships, about the existence and impact of abuse arising from sexual inequality, and about ways to prevent and oppose it, as well as helping them to disclose if they are living with mothers who are being abused. Work of this kind in schools is far more developed overseas than in Britain, though Women's Aid groups have given many talks in schools and have joined with teachers to plan anti-violence work, sometimes in conjunction with work on bullying and/or racism (Higgins, 1994). Some local authorities, such as the London Boroughs of Hackney and Islington, through their Women's and Women's Equality

Units respectively, are currently developing programmes opposing male abuse which include curriculum development work for schools. The Islington pack (London Borough of Islington, 1995) includes background information on domestic violence, answers to teachers' concerns and reservations, activity sheets and other teaching ideas, resource and contact information. It tackles issues such as disclosure by children during use of the pack that they are currently living with abuse, the challenge to schools to be more proactive concerning domestic abuse, and the need for teachers to work on their own feelings and knowledge levels before using the materials in class.

Some of the most advanced preventive work in education has been carried out in Ontario, Canada (see Mullender, 1994b) though a change of political climate is threatening funding. An exciting amount has been achieved there and, as a general approach, it would be highly transferable to the British context. Beginning with training for school principals and key teachers, a pilot programme in five schools focused on an 'auditorium': a large-scale, day-long event with films, plays and speakers (including survivors of abuse), leading into guided discussion in the classroom. This was facilitated by designated teachers and workers from relevant agencies such as women's organisations. Other professionals with counselling skills, including social workers, were available to pupils who found the material upsetting or who made personal disclosures. In October 1989, 680 secondary school pupils and staff from 21 area school boards in the south-west Ontario region attended a family violence day workshop with speakers, videos and discussion groups. The overall conclusion reached was that school is a context in which it is possible to help child witnesses of woman abuse find out where to turn for help and to teach all children how to become non-violent adults. Topics included supporting and helping others to speak up; saying the right things to them and directing them towards appropriate services; setting up student-run hotlines, clubs and groups; displaying notices about services within and outside the school; and ways in which teachers can show more awareness and concern.

The Ontario Ministry of Education has supported the work because it recognises the adverse impact of living with abuse on children's ability to learn. It has issued a set of procedures to be followed when children disclose living with violence (a 'child witness protocol') as well as resource lists and policy statements. Social workers attached to schools are called on specifically to work with those who have experienced the effects of living with violence against their mothers. The Board of Education for the City of London has also committed itself to furthering a violence-free environment. It has, for example, published newsletters and leaflets for pupils, teachers and the local community that define physical, sexual, psychological and emotional abuse; discuss reasons why men abuse and why women are forced to stay; and list agencies to contact and ways in which readers can personally help children and young people who live with abuse or who may be becoming abusive, for example in dating relationships. The leaflets also outline common myths and counterpose these with researched facts, such as that the abuse happens across all classes and cultures, that alcohol is a common excuse but not a cause since not all batterers drink or not every time, and that women feel demeaned if others do not recognise the violence as solely men's responsibility.

The impressive activity in Ontario has also included a 'Health Fair'; a topic-based teaching programme; canvassing of support amongst parents and public bodies to complain to, and boycott, television channels carrying violent programmes in prime time; a group committed to listening to class-mates who have experienced or lived with violence at home or elsewhere; and a student assembly with a panel discussing aggression and sex roles. Other ideas include the use of films, videos, poster displays, theatre groups, 'magic circles' (basically discussion groups to develop listening skills and self-esteem), and a violence awareness week in school. The latter, at elementary school level, involved age-specific daily activities, exercises, and presentations on the topic of violence. Eleven year olds helped 6 year olds draw anti-violence posters, while 12 year olds cut violent photographs and headlines from newspapers and magazines to use in a collage, and kinder-garten children were given instruction by shelter (refuge) workers on how to call for help if their mother was being assaulted. The local newspaper reported daily on events in school and a range of community agencies and services offered support. Many other schools sought information on how to replicate the event, leading the original school to assemble a resource and information pack on violence for use elsewhere.

Most recently, the work in Ontario has been aimed at integrating learning about woman abuse into the mainstream curriculum (for example through a training pack: Sudermann *et al.*, 1994), as part of a 'violence-free schools policy' adopted in 1994, and linking it with policies on anti-racism and ethnocultural equity. Evaluation has shown that young people learn from such work and enjoy doing something positive to combat violence. It can also be helpful in giving a school and its local community a positive focus for anti-violence and anti-oppressive work.

Any or all of the above ideas could be tried in Britain, provided that the educators undertook their own training first and worked in close conjunction with organisations such as Women's Aid, both to develop appropriate teaching content and to handle the result of disclosures and newly raised awareness amongst children and their families. Social workers and probation officers could play a role in offering counselling during campaigns, in responding to disclosures, and in effective liaison with schools over pupils already known to have witnessed abuse.

Groupwork with parents

Mothers' groups

As was demonstrated earlier in describing the role of refuge childworkers, direct work with children can be supplemented by valuable work undertaken through their mothers. This can help women to understand the difficulties they may be experiencing with their children and to recognise many of these as stemming from natural reactions to living with abuse, rather than blaming themselves as 'bad mothers'.

In North America, some more formal work has been undertaken through groups helping abused women to focus on their role as mothers without forgetting their own needs (ideally running alongside groups that aim to meet those adult needs so as not to see women only in stereotypical mothering roles). In Duluth, Minnesota, for example, a parenting group offered as part of a co-ordinated raft of services gives women the opportunity to share experiences of contact, custody, court hearings involving the children, and ways in which their abusers have hurt them and continue to hurt them through the children. The group may also involve looking back to women's own childhood, and forward to the kind of childhood they now want to give their children. It can recognise and celebrate what women aspire to and achieve as mothers, without seeing this as their only purpose or sole existence (Pence *et al.*, undated).

Women come to the group feeling guilty that they have failed as mothers and the group helps them become aware that the system has colluded with this by blaming them also. The emphasis is always on empowering women to understand abuse in its wider context (from a feminist perspective) and to understand its effects on children, not as a mother's fault but as something around which she can take action. The groupworkers use as teaching tools a 'nurturing wheel' and an 'abuse wheel' based on the 'power and control' wheel seen in Chapter 2. This helps them make clear links between abusive ways of controlling people in adulthood and in childhood.

The Domestic Abuse Project in Minneapolis, Minnesota, also works at 'empowering battered women as mothers' (Bilinkoff, 1995). The aim of work there (relevant to both individual and group settings) is to develop a strong and confident feminist model of female lone parenting in the face of current social and political trends to portray single mothers as both deviant and inadequate. Women inevitably feel guilty in the face of such hostility and come to the project unsure as to whether they can give their children what they need. A similar mood in this country is compounded by child protection professionals judging whether women are 'fit mothers' or have 'failed to protect' their children against the impact of abuse, rather than naming and confronting the actions of the perpetrators. Bilinkoff and her staff help mothers coping alone to believe in themselves and to offer children who have lived with violence new stability and a new enjoyment of life. She writes (ibid., pp.102–3) about the creation of new family rituals and celebratory days chosen to replace those that have become associated with violence and distress. In a UK context, workers in refuges will often raise parenting issues in house meetings and aim to work with children through their mothers in a positive way. *Breaking Through* (1989) has a chapter on bringing up children (Chapter 9) which includes a focus on children's rights and material on how mother–child relationships are affected by abuse, for example towards greater protectiveness. There are power issues involved for women in taking over both the traditional gender roles that pose as much of a challenge to social workers' assumptions of good child care (Bilinkoff, 1995, p.104) as to those of the wider society.

Fathers' groups

British feminist observers, accustomed to the 'Families Need Fathers' style of lobbying and the manipulation of the system by abusive men, would no doubt want to see safeguards around any such initiative in Britain, but there have been valuable fathers' groups run, again in Duluth (Pence *et al.*, undated and pers. comms) and in St Paul (Mathews, 1995), for abusers to consider their role as fathers. Importantly, most of the men are court mandated to attend the groups; the courts are, in this way, recognising the impact of the men's abusiveness on their children, and their responsibilities as fathers rather than their 'rights' over their children.

Like other Duluth groups (Pence, 1987; Pence and Paymar, 1986), this one has a curriculum – with each group lasting for twelve weeks. Indeed, it follows the same curriculum as the mothers' group but meets quite separately because of the men's past and often continuing abusiveness to their partners. The two groups are very different in style, even though both may include court-mandated members. (There can be a tendency for courts to perceive woman abuse as 'mutual fighting': see Chapter 1, this volume, and to want to teach both partners to take better care of their children.) The mothers' group requires only one woman facilitator as a resource for women who readily discuss their role in meeting their children's needs and may, indeed, need pulling back from blaming everything on themselves. She helps them see that it has typically been their experience of abuse that has impeded their ability to care for their children as they would wish. The men's group, on the other hand, has two male facilitators who find that they have to work very hard to focus the men onto their own behaviour and responsibilities, and to keep them focused on their children's needs.

Because men are being referred by the courts all the time, they can join the group at any point, which makes cohesion more difficult. The facilitators are looking for motivation to change – they find that talking about their children can touch a sensitive nerve in the men. Perpetrators are often conscious at some level of their lack of relationship with their own children, or of the effect of their behaviour on their children, or of not wanting their children to act as they have done. Video vignettes of men and women acting abusively towards their children are used. The curriculum involves an intake week, then a session on family background when men talk rather reluctantly about their own experience with their fathers or their feelings about it now. They are asked what their relationship is like with their father and mother. It rarely occurs to them, without prompting, to make a link between that and how they want their relationship with their own children to be in twenty years' time, nor with the work they need to put into that relationship if they want it to be positive. Only the fathers' group asks men to focus in this way on their families of origin; the Duluth abusers' groups focus only on the present so as not to allow men to use the familiar 'cycle of violence' excuses for their current behaviour (see Chapter 2, this volume, and earlier section of this chapter).

Like any parenting curriculum, this one includes basic information on child development. The two sessions spent on this topic reveal that the men are often ignorant of basic facts. They do not know why 2 year olds say 'No!', or that small children in the parallel play stage are incapable of sharing toys. They expect far more of children than they are capable of, see displays of developing independence as wilfulness, and punish accordingly. A later session is devoted to nurturing and two to discipline – particularly learning to see it as education rather than punishment and considering non-violent ways of setting limits. One week focuses on communication, and a more upbeat session looks at fun ways of being involved with your children and giving them positive experiences. Week twelve is on co-parenting. Children do need boundaries, consistently set by both parents.

An intervening session is spent on definitions of abuse, particularly what constitutes an abuse of children. Since everyone in the group has acted abusively, the issue is to admit this and address it together – not to identify a few 'bad apples' and escape into blaming them for what they have done. This gives members the responsibility of talking about their own behaviour. The men are required to log a concrete example of abusive behaviour with children (as the abusers' groups do with behaviour towards women), and to bring it to the group. They must say what the action was, what were the feelings and actions involved, the impact and outcome. Bringing it back to the group reveals the wide divergence between intention and impact. Men have to face up to the ways they have hurt and are hurting their children.

In its early days, the group concentrated too much on getting through the curriculum and presenting the information; as it matures it is moving towards using the experiences the men bring. As with the abusers' groups, control logs are a valuable device in the group. Actual examples of currently abusive behaviour give opportunities to work on 'How could you have said that in a non-threatening, non-abusive way?', 'What communication skills could you develop to give your children realistic boundaries whilst also having fun together?' The group helps the men work on healing their relationships with their children. It is seen as important for them to acknowledge to the children that they, as fathers, were responsible for the abuse in the family – that they have not behaved as good, loving parents. Minimisation, denial and blaming others are a feature in this group as in the abusers' groups (see also Mathews, 1995, p.111). Common examples include: 'I never hit the kids so they're not affected' and 'They were always in the bedroom so they never saw it.' The video vignettes are of great importance because they illustrate the direct impact on children of living with abuse, whether or not they are directly abused or physically present. The group also requires members to recognise more direct abuse than they will at first admit. 'I only disciplined the child – I had a right to do it as a father' may reflect societal views about the ownership of children and what constitutes acceptable punishment, but these views can be questioned, particularly when they have been acted on within an abusive situation.

By this point in the group, some of the men have already started to question why they are behaving as they are. Their children are very important to them and they are hurt by their lack of a close relationship with them. Many do not understand the concept of intimacy and have to work on this both in this group and in the abusers' groups: 'Do you want your wife (or child) to do something because she is scared of you or because she wants to?' Nurturing, like intimacy, is a foreign language; it is a concept associated with women and gay men. These men have been socialised to see strength in domination. The group is based on the belief that they can be re-educated to see that it takes more strength to stop yourself than to give in to abusing your partner or your child. Groups can also work on concrete examples of non-abusive behaviour: 'When was the last time you had the opportunity to be abusive but were not? – What did you do that was different?' Men work hard in these groups. They are challenged to admit their failings and to build on their successes. They come expecting to be 'trashed', to be told how bad they are, but are told that the facilitators are not here to blame them but to help them change their life. It will be up to them to do the work which is also designed to build self-confidence; restraint is built on that.

CONCLUSION

Social work in Britain is only just beginning to link the issues of child care, child protection and woman abuse. Research and practice here and overseas have, in fact, told us a great deal about children's needs and reactions in situations of abuse, as well as suggesting constructive interventions that agencies could make available. It is an indictment of much of the child care provision in Britain – with the notable exceptions of Women's Aid and, more recently, the BBC Children in Need Appeal (in funding refuge child work), with some contribution, too, from the Children's Legal Centre and NCH Action for Children (in writing and researching on the topic) – that it has yet to rise fully to this challenge. Individual practitioners can add their voices to the call for more to be done while those who take the policy lead in relevant agencies can open up the debate about the urgent need for child- and woman-centred change.

Chapter 7

Social work and probation practice with families

The goal of all social work and probation intervention where there is or has been abuse should be to help make women and children safe, including by confronting men. The evidence that local authority child care work was not traditionally directed towards that goal, especially for women, was presented in Chapter 3. There is also a legacy to overcome in marital counselling in both the voluntary and statutory sectors; one classic text, for example, because it totally lacks a gender power analysis in relation to men's sexual violence, includes women's suicide attempts under coercive techniques employed by one partner against the other, on a par with men imprisoning and raping their wives (Mattinson and Sinclair, 1979, pp.120–1). Indeed, in all work with couples and families, including family court welfare work undertaken by the probation service, issues of women's safety have only belatedly and incompletely come to the fore. The growth of mediation between couples seeking a divorce could also reinforce power imbalances and dangers to women; even if all those disclosing assaults are successfully screened out, there are still risks for those not disclosing violence or experiencing other forms of abuse, as well as questions as to what is considered to constitute violence and who decides on this.

This chapter will outline the enormous challenge that has been posed to couples counselling, family therapy, and all work with families in recent years, including in the general child care field, by the recognition of widescale violence and by a broader feminist rethinking of the dangers inherent in intervention where the man is violent. In family court welfare work, which will receive separate attention within the chapter, this has directly resulted in changed policy concerning joint interviewing, although unfortunately there is no guarantee that practice has uniformly improved. In wider child care work, it will be shown that there has yet to be a consistent recognition of the ways in which women's safety needs and children's welfare and safety needs can be considered together, particularly in contexts where legislation and court practice too often favour the abusing men.

FAMILY WORK AND VIOLENCE: A FUNDAMENTAL CHANGE OF PERSPECTIVE

It is now widely accepted that family work as a specialism was relatively slow to recognise the challenge of feminism (e.g. Braverman, 1988, p.6; Perelberg, 1990, p.34). The greatest challenge of all was to acknowledge the dangers posed by the favoured theories of family therapists in situations involving abusive men. Once the message was received and understood, however, it began to result in some of the most dramatic recantations to be found anywhere in social work or related fields.

> *The most devastating consequence of family therapy's commitment to patriarchy has been its failure in the areas of wife-battering and incest ... leading approaches were wrongheaded and damaging to victims. It is feminists who have brought the subject of violence in the family to the fore, not only because feminists care about women, but because feminists, by definition, focus on power, including the power in marriage and family. From a feminist standpoint, any theory of family or therapy has to be measured against the case of violence, because if it cannot deal with the abuse of power, it cannot deal with power. If it cannot deal with power, then whatever else it may help or clarify, it works to keep inequity in place.*
> (Goodrich, 1991, pp.19–20)

The above passage is emphasised because it seems to reflect perfectly the fact that if we, as professionals, do not use the now readily available knowledge about sexual violence to become part of the solution, then we are part of the problem. A default decision – to opt out and make no change in ways of working – is actually a decision to collude with continued harm to women and children. The only moral option is to ally ourselves with active opposition to abuse and with positive work for safety. *And this must be true of every case where abuse is known or suspected.*

The changes demanded in prevailing thinking were huge: 'Without major restructuring, attempting to integrate feminism and family therapy may be a case of rearranging deck chairs on the *Titanic*' (Koss, 1993, pp.viii–ix). The restructuring has come from within, as feminist family therapists have reformulated fundamental concepts like interactional causality and neutrality on which their work was formerly based (see below) to take account of men's violent oppression of their partners. From the late 1970s in the USA (Hare-Mustin, 1978) and more recently in Britain (Perelberg and Miller, 1990; Burck and Speed, 1995; Reimers and Treacher, 1995), feminist challenges to, and recasting of, family therapy approaches have been appearing in the literature. (There are numerous summaries available; Avis, 1988, is a useful one.) Progress in changing practice can be expected to take longer, especially where practitioners do not identify themselves as family work specialists and do not keep up to date with developments in thinking. Although workers in statutory settings rarely employ formalised family therapy, they have been strongly influenced by its theoretical assumptions and its value base. Systemic work has exercised a particularly persuasive sway.

For students, social work methods are still often taught on qualifying programmes as if they were value free. There may be little opportunity to learn that some can be dangerous if used with the wrong people at the wrong time, especially if teaching on woman abuse is absent, or is confined to the feminist or social policy fringes of the curriculum without active links with practice contexts. Social work students may be led into supposing that family work is a generalised response they can apply in all situations, rather than one with clear limitations on its use and which has itself recently undergone a fundamental change from within as feminist critiques have gathered momentum.

Systemic work and circular causality

Initially, systemic family work itself was seen as a radicalising influence (Miller, 1990, p.8). It put a problem back into the whole context in which it was being experienced, in this case that of the family relationships, rather than allowing one family member to be scapegoated and hence expected to change or accept punishment on an individual basis. In some situations, such as those where a child offends or truants as a result of wider family problems, this can be a helpful approach. There are problems with it where abuse is concerned, however, because it can collude with a stronger person shifting at least part of the blame onto a weaker, and because the focus on the family can exclude an understanding of wider social forces.

Family systems theory, imported from the natural sciences into social science (see Walrond-Skinner, 1977, Chapter 2), generally views causality as a circular process – without beginning or end, without attributable reponsibility, and observable in the here and now rather than needing explorations of past events. In a popular textbook on social work methods, Coulshed illustrates circular causality by arguing that it may be too simplistic to see a husband's going to the pub as causing his wife's depression or her depression as causing him to go out to the pub. Rather, each reaction feeds into the other – again and again and again:

> Seeing events in this 'whole' or systems way reveals that each person is part of a circular system of action and reaction which can begin and end at any point and therefore there is little point in asking, 'Who started it?'
> (Coulshed, 1991, p.148)

In the first edition of her book, in 1988, Coulshed did not mention violence and had a longer version of the above quotation (which talked

about there being no real gainers and no victims) that sat very uncom-
fortably with situations of abuse. But there clearly are situations in which
women are victims and men *do* gain. By her 1991 edition, Coulshed had
moved from beginning to accept that 'one problem with this circular view
of causality is that it ignores the current unresolved power issues between
men and women in our society, which are reflected in relationships', to
naming violence against women as clearly resulting in winners and losers
and hence as requiring a complete feminist reframing of family work.

Adams outlines the more credible feedback loop without implicating the
female partner as responsible for the dynamic:

> For the man, violence gains compliance but also perpetuates his fears of
> her independence and anger about her noncompliance, which reinforces
> his attempts to control her. The woman cannot stop being afraid so long
> as the threat of violence is present. So long as this is so, neither can trust
> or openly communicate with each other.
>
> (Adams, 1988, p.188)

In other words, the violence is the cause, not a symptom, of the family's
problems (Leeds Inter-Agency Project, training materials). Furthermore,
the man is responsible for starting – and stopping – it. In traditional family
therapy, however, circular or interactional analysis regarded each person
as being helped to maintain his or her role position in the family through
the roles played by others (Walrond-Skinner, 1977, p.28). The abuser's
role kept his wife subservient but her subservience also kept him abusive.
Some of the blame was thrown onto her. Goldner (1985, p.22) sees this as
'confusing an elegant truth, that master and slave are psychologically
interdependent, with the morally repugnant and absurd notion that the two
are therefore equals'. Theorists saw the inter-relationship of roles not only
as sustaining the pattern of violence (Walker, 1979) – although, in fact,
women find it hard to leave for all the reasons outlined in Chapter 2
– but often as functional in sustaining the marriage itself (in critique by
Bograd, 1984, p.560). The assumed circularity of cause came to be reflected
in falsely gender-neutral terms like 'violent' or 'abusive families', 'spouse
abuse', or 'consort battering', which still pervade the entire literature of
social work. Such terminology fails entirely to attribute blame where it
belongs – to the abuser; consequently, it literally adds insult to injury for
the survivor. It also conveniently ignores the fact that men's physical force
over women is hugely more common, typically more dangerous, and bears
the additional risk of being likely to escalate into a pattern of dominance,
yet is more socially acceptable than anything women can do to men. This
is why it is never, ever acceptable for a man to hit back at a woman he
claims struck him first. Their actions do not equate with the matched
punches in a male fist fight and do not carry the same social messages or
the same subsequent dangers.

Worker neutrality

It was not only the terminology of abuse that was sanitised by false neutrality. The worker, too, was required to be neutral and 'not take sides'. Maynard quoted a social worker in her study as having written in the file, after visiting a woman who had recently been physically abused:

> I had again to explain my position to Mrs Blank. I said that I had to be seen to be neutral. I was there to help all members of the family. This I would be unable to do if the impression was given that I sided with any member of the family.
>
> (Maynard, 1985, p.130)

A serious problem with this response was that the woman's safety was not uppermost and her interests were not safeguarded. Likewise, her abuser's behaviour was not reported or challenged. Like other professionals, social workers are not infrequently ignorant of what is truly involved in domestic abuse and some are no more free of myths (such as the view that the woman learns to live with it or provokes it) than the general public. They may completely fail to recognise what danger they place a woman in by their failure to stand by her. Yet this was what family work training required.

I can remember my own gnawing feeling of anxiety, as a newly qualified worker, on packing a woman and her belongings into the car to take her to a refuge. It seemed to go against what I had been taught on my social work course about listening to each person's views and trying to help them work it out. I had not even met the husband at this point and had not heard his 'side' of the story. Yet another part of me knew that I had to get this woman to safety. There had been no theoretical or practical content in my training course giving me the analytical tools to work out this dilemma. I can now see that imbalances of power in relationships (never discussed in gender terms in my training – this was only a short time after the first refuge opened) can make couple and family work dangerous to those whose interests are silent or subsumed. Edleson and Tolman (1992, p.93) paint a graphic picture of a woman threatened with a gun before a therapy session who is hardly likely to voice her interests effectively with her partner present. To quote Maynard (1985, p.130) again, 'the "balanced view" approach to wife beating is part of general social worker attitudes and training. It is . . . rooted in a concern to treat most issues in terms of the family'. Only in the absence of a power analysis could such a view be considered 'balanced'. Once the power and control aspects of the relationship are seen for what they are and reveal abuse, it becomes obvious that neither non-intervention nor whole-family intervention is a neutral decision. Both side with the controller.

My personal example took place nearly twenty years ago but complacency should be challenged by a practice example gathered only recently, which shows the social worker struggling to keep a family together, ignoring a woman's safety needs, and allowing her abusive husband to speak for her. It also nicely illustrates the necessity to inform family casework with an adequate understanding of, and appropriate services for, Black and other minority ethnic service users.

Case example

A male duty social worker went into an Asian household, the 'C' family, under the child abuse procedures, after Mr C had beaten his 15-year-old daughter on the back with a slipper for misbehaviour reported to him by her school. The social worker could get by with Mr C's level of English but Mrs C spoke no English at all. She was not therefore involved in the interview, though present. The full procedures were operated with police, photographs of the injuries, and so on. The social worker realised Mrs C must have wondered what on earth was happening, but there had been no interpreter available at short notice. In later discussion with Mr C, the social worker suggested English evening classes for Mrs C so that she could go shopping, talk to the children's teachers, and so on, but Mr C said no, it would just give him more problems because she would understand more and he would lose even more of his control over his family's morals and welfare.

As work with the family progressed, it emerged that Mr C had been hitting his wife. Eventually she had had enough and walked out, leaving her four youngest children aged 2, 9, 11 and 15, and gone to stay with friends. The social worker interpreted her husband's refusal to let her attend classes as having been the last straw for her. It seems more likely to me that, knowing the social services were involved and would ensure the children were protected, Mrs C finally felt it was safe to escape. Seen in a cultural context, her leaving was a major statement about what she had undergone because it risked incurring the ostracism of her entire family and community and leaving her to fend alone in a hostile environment.

This was by now an allocated case, with the youngest child on the child protection register, so the social worker was able to put time into talking to husband and wife separately, in the latter case jointly with an Asian colleague. His comment, 'We eventually got the family back together again', was regarded as marking a real success. Dad was described as very sorry for his actions and Mum as sorry for walking out. After her return, Mrs C told the social workers she was no longer being hit. She was not asked about other forms of abuse.

Then Mr C went to Bangladesh and returned with his much younger second wife, whom no one had known about, and their four children. It transpired that he had been making trips to Bangladesh on his own for quite some time. The second wife began putting demands on the first wife to do things her way until the latter went to Mr C to complain. His violence against her then started again and continued even after he moved his second wife out into a flat of her own. Eventually, Mrs C had to go through all the trauma of leaving home again. This time, social services helped her. They negotiated with the homeless persons unit to place her in bed and breakfast accommodation with her four youngest children and successfully applied pressure for early allocation of a flat. At no time did they refer her to a refuge or any Asian women's support group. (Social services' main contact in the area was with an Asian family counselling project specialising in reconciliation and supported by male elders opposed to women leaving home yet often unwilling to confront abusive men.)

Nevertheless, by her own efforts, Mrs C is now 'doing very well'. She is attending English evening classes and was confident enough to attend hospital with her daughter and talk to the medical staff when the girl needed urgent treatment. Mrs C's 22-year-old son, who would never visit his parents' home while they were still together, now sees his mother regularly and is supporting her. Other family members and friends are also standing by her. She showed the resilience familiar to those who work in the field of domestic abuse. Unfortunately, she had to show even greater resilience, as do many others, while she withstood both inappropriate intervention from social workers and the continued abuse to which they persuaded her to return for a time.

Blaming the victim: implicating the woman through therapy

It took some courage for women therapists to start questioning the received truths about family work. At first, anyone who began to say that however helpless or subservient a wife's behaviour might appear to be it did not excuse her husband's hitting her, was 'dismissed as a feminist who was incapable of thinking interactionally' (Jones, 1990, p.67). Interactionists consider that both partners need to discuss 'marital communication, resolving conflict, and ending violence' (Adams, 1988, p.184, in a critique of the interactional approach), and that both partners in the relationship need to change. This may reinforce the woman's view that she is at fault. Indeed, it might be said to be intended to do so because of the concept of circular rather than linear causality, explored above:

> according to the interactionist perspective, battering is not characterized as one partner attempting to control or dominate the other but by the couple's combined communicational deficits and the attempts of both partners to coerce and otherwise incite the other.
>
> (ibid., p.185)

Any interactional approach will, by definition, emphasise the need to see both partners together. Work will be contracted between them that requires both to adjust their behaviour. This will involve the woman modifying or ending the behaviours the therapist sees as triggering the man's violence. (See Chapter 2 for a dismissal of the idea that women thus share blame by 'provoking' violence.) While her husband is advised to cool off in another room rather than become violent during arguments, for example (ibid., p.186), the wife is required 'to "suspend" her arguments (by not continuing to push her points or following him into the other room) until he has cooled down'. As Adams points out,

> Strongly implied in the assigning of such parallel tasks . . . is the message that the woman is partially responsible for the husband's subsequent violence should she fail to recognize his nonverbal cues accurately and desist from further argument.

> (ibid.)

Worse still, because women are socialised to work harder at relationships than men, are typically more open to change, more malleable in therapy settings (Bograd, 1984, p.565), and tend eventually to believe their abusers and blame themselves for what is not their fault (as opposed to the abusive man who persists in denying and minimising his responsibility), the notion of parallel tasks quickly slips over into the wife doing more of the work. Evidence of women accepting responsibility for relationship maintenance includes the far higher numbers of women who go alone to marriage guidance counsellors (to the London Marriage Guidance Council at more than twice the male rate during 1994/95, for example). In one example of counselling content from the contemporary but non-feminist family therapy literature (Hurvitz and Straus, 1991, p.46), the therapist clearly trades on the woman's willingness to take on responsibility and shared blame. Her commitment to an improved marriage is used to persuade her to work on her 'nagging' as the opening problem, firstly because it is the one most amenable to change (though not the most severe) and, secondly, because both parties agree it exists whereas the husband denies his abuse. In another case in the same book (p.104), the therapist (who openly disbelieves the extent of the man's abuse) decides to start by working on the wife smartening up the house and her own appearance for when her husband comes home from work, again because it is an easy place to start and both spouses agree about it. In this way, therapists collude with the man's control and the woman's disempowerment (Bograd, 1984, p.565). They also overlook the fact that women have typically already tried in every possible way they can to appease abusers (see pp.47–8, this volume), and that abusers persist in finding excuses to abuse long after their partners have become expert at reading their moods and behaviour.

Amongst the problems in the interactional approach (based on Adams, 1988, pp.186–7) are:

- the inaccurate or mixed messages the couple receive about responsibility for violence;
- the fact that the abuser may not commit himself to being non-violent if his partner does not make her agreed changes;
- portraying abuse as understandable;
- portraying it therefore as excusable;
- collusion with the abuser's denial of responsibility and attempts to justify his behaviour;
- reinforcing the abuser's efforts to divert attention from his actions;
- regarding the woman experiencing abuse as partly to blame when in fact she is an innocent party;
- leading her into accepting this blame;
- expecting her to read her abuser's cues;
- collusion with the myth of provocation;
- not allowing the woman to negotiate with her husband about her life or their shared life;
- setting up the situation that once he says the argument is over she is nagging;
- setting up the situation that if he fails to listen and she repeats herself she is nagging;
- silencing the woman.

Dangers and pointlessness in seeing couples and families jointly during current abuse

Many women are silenced before they reach professional intervention. They are terrorised into withholding the abuse from the therapist, who consequently leaves it out of account in assessment. When family work or couples counselling attempts to encourage each partner to identify and change how he or she contributes to a circular problem – for instance by equating 'the woman's withholding of sex, failure to state her own needs adequately, angry accusations, "nagging," or overinvolvement with the children' with 'the man's outbursts of temper, possessiveness, lack of responsibility for the children, and attempts to dominate' (ibid., p.185) – the woman's fear and the worker's orientation makes it impossible to identify that what could well be happening in this scenario is the woman experiencing sex as rape, having her own needs completely ignored, not daring to answer back, and being deprived even of the ability to offer her children basic protection. Her abuser hits and humiliates her, comfortable in the knowledge that he can force her to keep his behaviour quiet and that there are often still no effective legal sanctions against him.

To take a couple into counselling under such circumstances is both pointless and dangerous. It is not safe for a woman to open herself up to honest communication with a partner who is attempting to control her thoughts and actions and who is likely to retaliate against any deviation from what he is trying to impose. Adams sees this as placing the woman in an 'impossible bind' even where the violence is known to the therapist:

> Though she is expected to be open about her feelings, air her grievances, and report her husband's violence, to do any of these things places her in grave danger of continued violence. Many battered women report that past family therapy sessions were followed by violent episodes.
>
> (ibid., p.187)

The real extent of the abuse will be carefully concealed. The man will be plausible and the woman quiet – which can be misinterpreted either as co-operation (Bograd, 1984, p.564) or as defensiveness and resistance on her part. The latter can happen both in family therapy – 'Poor communication is seen by interaction therapists as a contributing factor, rather than as an inevitable *effect* of violence' (ibid.; emphasis in original) – and in family court conciliation:

> Mediation assumes some balance of power between parents, which is not possible when a mother lives in fear of the children's father . . . . Because the mediational process encourages cooperation and compromise, a battered woman may be put in the position of appearing rigid and un-cooperative because of her fear for the safety of herself and her children
>
> (Jaffe, *et al.*, 1990, p.109)

Only an interview with the woman alone, conducted in a sympathetic and believing way, will have any chance of getting at the truth, and even this can be extremely dangerous for her unless complete confidentiality and other safeguards are observed.

In the USA and Canada, there has been a move right away from family and couples work in abusive situations (Avis, 1988, p.23). In London, Ontario, the major children's mental health agency '*will work with the entire family only when the violence known to have occurred has stopped and the victim is not intimidated by her spouse*' (Madame Vanier Children's Services, 1990, pp.9–10, emphasis in original) and both they and the child protection agency routinely ask, at the beginning of contact, whether the child's mother has been abused. In work with adults, the agency guidelines for the Interagency Rehabilitation Project in Duluth, Minnesota, require participating organisations to agree that couples counselling will not be offered until at least three months after the violence has stopped. (See also Edleson and Tolman, 1992, p.102, advising that joint work is only possible after the man has worked to end his abuse and with a range of safety measures in place, as outlined below.) Such bodies recognise that, in a situation where a woman fears for her safety and often her life, a shared family resolution of problems or negotiated agreement over child care will never be possible – any decisions will have been coerced. Domestic violence cases are also screened out of wider conflict resolution work, for example in New York City where a wide range of criminal, civil and family work is referred to probation for mediation (Meteyard, 1995, p.26).

For similar reasons, it is now the policy of Relate (Marriage Guidance) in Britain not to work with couples where there is current violence, although their counsellors do not appear to be well trained in understanding men's abusive behaviour without assuming circular causality, or in how to apply the policy to keep women safe (pers. comms). Clear information is not routinely available about refuge provision, police, or other emergency responses. There is also confusion about when to apply the 'no current violence' policy, apparently based on the assumption against which Pressman warns (1989, p.29; see also Bograd, 1984, p.564), that domestic violence only relates to 'severe', physical abuse and that whatever the counsellor is seeing somehow happens to fall into a 'milder' category which does not rule out joint work. (Current research into family court welfare work by Hester, Radford, and their research colleagues [Hester and Radford, 1992; Hester and Pearson, 1993; Hester et al., 1994] has revealed a similar tendency to distance 'real' domestic violence, which might require special treatment, as something rarely seen or in the past; the researchers [pers. comm.] heard comments like: 'Well, he broke her arm three weeks ago but they've separated so it's all right now.') Pressman urges that no such distinctions be made, since men's abuse of women is always unacceptable, always harmful and debilitating, and typically escalates in frequency and level of injury (including after attempts at separation: see Chapter 2, this volume). It needs a particular response whenever and however it is seen. A man who has tried to strangle his wife 'a couple of times' but has not suffered any legal sanction for his behaviour, and a man who frightens his wife and their counsellor with his shouting in joint sessions should not come into couples counselling (pers. comm. with Relate Counsellor). Edleson and Tolman (1992, p.93) also state that a man's promises not to be violent during therapy frequently do not hold water. He must take active steps to change and give clear evidence of these over time before he is trusted.

As early as 1985 in Ontario, Canada (where there has been a widescale response to male violence), Sinclair wrote that:

Marriage counselling is a viable option only after the following conditions have been met:

1. the offender has accepted full responsibility for his violent behaviour and has made concerted efforts to change that behaviour.
2. the victim is clearly able to protect herself, measured by her understanding and willingness to assume responsibility for her protection.
3. the potential for further abuse is minimal (there is never a guarantee).
4. the degree of initimidation and fear felt by the victim is significantly reduced, so as not to interfere with open discussion of marital issues.

Make sure she does not think the issues she raises during the session will be used as an excuse by her husband to assault her after the session.

5. the goals of the couple are mutually agreed upon and couple work is entered into freely by both partners. Make sure he has not instructed her to remain silent on contentious issues.

(Sinclair, 1985, p.82)

Sinclair's good practice pointers are as relevant in child care or any other casework where both parents are being involved in the work as in the couples counselling Sinclair has in mind. Women cannot participate freely or openly in planning the future when threatening partners are present, nor, of course, can they state their fears in their abuser's presence. So being interviewed alone, often without the abuser's knowledge, is the only sure way to gauge the danger. This is not to suggest that the man should not be held to account for his abuse, or for his partnering and parenting responsibilities, under safe conditions in later work.

A residual role for conjoint family and couples work

Couples work is not completely rejected. Edleson and Tolman (1992, Chapter 5), after years of evaluative research of a range of interventions with abusing men (see also Chapter 9, this volume), write about 'cautious' and 'responsible' use of this mode of work. They still regard groupwork, separately for both abusers and the women they have abused, as the method of choice since groupwork, according to Edleson's extensive and rigorous research, can in some cases end violence. Couples work cannot realistically be expected to do so. They see it, therefore, as sometimes coming into play to repair the damage *after* the abuse has stopped, that is, after a significant period of attendance by the man at an abusers' group and after he has made a credible and proven commitment to living non-abusively, with a tested absence both of physical and psychological abuse over some period of time. The woman might still be well advised to have a safety plan worked out and there is no doubt that if she were also to attend an empowering women's group, or to obtain other benefit from a women's group or support network prior to the couple's counselling, it would help her not to blame herself for the abuse – even in part.

Purpose

If it does proceed safely, the roles of joint counselling can be:

- to address the impact of the abuse;
- to test out whether the couple can safely and rewardingly reunite or rebuild a relationship damaged by the man's abuse;

- to give the woman space safely to express pent up feelings, which need to be acknowledged and validated, so that she can heal and move forward;
- to demonstrate that the man can listen reflectively, without defending through anger or denial himself against the truth of what he did (though he may find it painful) but acknowledging what his partner went through and how she felt;

and, if those stages are successful:

- to allow her safely to express what she will need in a rebuilt relationship;
- to help him learn new relationship skills so as to remain non-abusive and be a caring and supportive partner;
- to help her regain her trust in him and be a caring partner without sacrificing herself to the relationship;
- to learn new communication and problem-solving skills together;
- to help them together resolve any problems in the relationship other than the abuse;
- to allow either or both of them to work on issues from the past. (Based on Edleson and Tolman, 1992, pp.97–102.)

This can only work in circumstances where each partner has separately decided in a supportive and honest environment that this is what he or she wants.

It is important to add that such work must not be subverted by the man for the purpose of satisfying a court, probation officer, or other criminal justice agent that he is working on his relationship and deserves leniency in dealing with his crimes of abuse or favourable treatment in deciding child care matters such as contact or residence. The high risk that he will try this constitutes a further reason for refusing to work with the couple until the man has taken responsibility for his own change process.

Safety measures

Couples work also requires specified safety criteria to be fulfilled (ibid., pp.95–6). Beyond the man's proven commitment to change and each partner's clear decision to try again, are required a counsellor who is sensitive to abuse and its effects (who will not be deceived or place the woman in greater danger), a female partner who has been supported to accept that she is not to blame for the abuse and to know that she does not control it through her actions or her part in the relationship, and special precautions for her safety. In particular, the woman needs a safety plan that she knows how to use and is prepared to use when necessary. In the British context, this could include an emergency refuge or helpline number, as well as details of how to call the police, an agreement with an employer to block the abuser's telephone access to her, and family or friends put on alert to offer help. Being able to draw on the support of a women's group or other service during this time can be invaluable. The man also needs a different kind of safety plan, one which covers what he must do when he feels the aggression and potential for abuse returning.

A crucial role of the work (ibid., p.102) may be to assist the woman to leave safely, having given the relationship every chance but realising that it is now dead or will always be too dangerous for her. The therapist must not rush her or she may be pushed back into an alliance with her partner against the therapist. Finally, conciliation may be needed with parting couples who need to agree about plans for the children or division of property. (See below for comments on mediation proposals in Britain.)

Content

The steps in counselling (ibid., pp.97–101) begin with addressing the abuse, normally missed in traditional couples work. This includes giving the woman a safe place to release her pent up anger against the abuser who has hurt and demeaned her and damaged a relationship that is clearly important to her or she would not be here. One way to start the work is to have several sessions just for her to tell him all this, based on her detailed memories of the abuse, what it did to her and the relationship, and how she feels about it now. Meanwhile, the man is expected to listen and to try and empathise, but not to argue back or defend himself. His denial levels will be clear from his success with this. Both the woman and the counsellor will be assessing the man's skills and progress from his groupwork experience during this stage. Individual debriefing may run in parallel with the joint sessions as part of this process and to review safety. If the man cannot safely listen to and show the skills to hear the woman's pain, then the partners are unlikely to be able to resume intimacy safely. Some couples part during or at the end of this stage and that is a successful outcome since it may help to prevent the woman being further abused. Sometimes the sessions must be stopped because the man's aggression is rising and it is no longer safe, even though both will have been warned that the process will be painful and difficult.

Only after this stage does the work focus on increasing positive and unsolicited caring behaviour and relationship skills. These include expressing feelings, general communication skills, developing problem-solving skills, and the use of time-out if feelings become too intense. Not until after all this does the worker turn to conflict resolution around particular areas of contention in the relationship such as the children, extended families, money, as well as issues of intimacy and affection between the partners. It will be the case that both partners will have issues to work on in the relationship but not in the abuse. That is the man's responsibility. McGregor (1990, p.69) also helpfully distinguishes between violence counselling, which is never appropriate between couples – since 'Violence is not primarily a relationship issue' – and relationship counselling, which may be appropriate but only after the violence has stopped. Edleson and Tolman emphasise (1992, pp.103–6) that there has been no sufficiently rigorous evaluation of couples work, including groups of couples seen together, to know whether it really works over time or on whose terms (see also Chapter 9, this volume). Certainly, the work must immediately stop if the woman experiences her partner as threatening – for example in a gesture – and focus on that, going back to earlier stages if necessary. It may be necessary to halt it altogether.

Principles

Deriving from criticisms of traditional work, the principles underpinning this work, which would be clearly shared with the couple, are that:

- the perpetrator is to blame for the abuse: the blame is not shared any more than it would be in a rape (the abuse not infrequently involves rape, of course);
- abuse is a crime and legal sanctions will be used when it occurs;
- violence between partners is like any other violence and will be tackled accordingly (as McGregor notes [1990, p.68], an embezzler is not expected to attend joint counselling with the employer from whom he has stolen, but is prosecuted);
- the violence must be named and confronted not minimised;
- preserving the couple's relationship and hence the family unit should not be a desired outcome held overtly or covertly by the counsellor independently of what the partners decide they want;
- a safe parting may be the most positive possible outcome.

(Based on Edleson and Tolman, 1992, pp.91–2)

Lessons for wider work

Once again, it must be stressed that the dangers of artificially neutral work are not inherent only in a formalised therapy model. They are also present every time a social worker or probation officer fails to tackle abuse and safety issues and resorts instead to excusing the man and focusing work elsewhere. One male social worker commented, for example: 'Any sort of violence in the home always, always has other complications. It never happens on its own. Usually there's a reason for the violence. Not something trivial but ongoing rent arrears, no money to have a night out or get a trolley-load of shopping. It's been building up and up over months and finally something goes.' This viewpoint, quite apart from ignoring the gender power dimension and the criminal behaviour involved, makes the violence sound understandable and even tolerable whilst, at the same time, failing to explain why every man with less money than he needs is not violent. The social work instinct – given this scenario and this analysis recorded, say, on a duty referral sheet or in a case transfer – is to sit and talk with the couple together (or, not infrequently, the woman alone) about budgeting, benefits, debt counselling – solutions to immediate practical problems that gloss over the man's abuse.

Any worker who is locked into looking at the family without regard for the societal, patriarchal context can end up blaming women for appearing to be inadequate wives and mothers. A feminist analysis may reveal these same women, on the contrary, to be managing a heroic struggle against physical and emotional harm, compounded by structural inequities in pay, opportunities and family responsibilities. Walters (1990, pp.20–1), for example, contrasts three separate social workers' views of a single mother in a child protection case as a disorganised and inconsistent parent providing insufficient protection and financial support for her five children (one sexually abused by her father, two others with disabilities) with her (Walter's) own feminist conclusion (when mother and children were referred to her for family therapy) that the woman was trapped between a harassing ex-partner, sparse and expensive day care provision, and poorly paid 'women's' work with unsocial hours. Whatever she did, within a limited and unsafe range of choices, would be regarded as unsatisfactory by the child care authorities unless they changed their frame of reference.

The whole context and content of family work needs to change. Even the way in which problems are defined has social and political connotations (Pilalis, 1987, p.13). Urry (1990, pp.106–7) describes the principles of a women's project where feminist family therapists work not only with openly acknowledged and challenged power imbalances in families (around housework, money, child care, gender roles; see also Avis, 1988, p.23), understood within a patriarchal social context, but also with re-examined therapist roles and values where the gender, age, race and profession of workers and clients are considered to be no more neutral than their language or behaviour. Empowering women and raising the consciousness of all parties are highlighted as part of the therapeutic process.

The change required from men in their assumptions and their practice will be particularly demanding. Bograd (1988a, p.76) has written about the way that subordinate groups have to learn the language and rules of the dominant class in order to survive. This operates for women both at the public level, where their 'service' role is exploited for low pay, and in the private domain, where Bograd describes the sensitivity women develop to nonverbal cues as a result of men's denial of their own vulnerabilities and weaknesses. Nowhere is this more true than in situations of abuse, as women learn to read the threats in atmospheres, gestures and looks. The challenge to male practitioners is how to undertake this painstaking learning in the opposite direction so as to understand what life is like for women subjected to abuse and be able to make appropriate responses that do not compound the insults and the harm. The front-line emergency services for women are better offered by women, but all men in relevant professions urgently need to think through their own position, whether they are social workers working with families, managers developing policies and allocating resources that could help make women safe, or educators who need to pass on enlightened ideas to their students. (I have twice recently, in different parts of the UK, had to overrule allegations of 'lack of balance' or 'bias' against women social work students who had mentioned feminism in assignments based on well-handled child care cases involving woman abuse.) The richness in Bograd's writing also creates resonances with the biculturalism required by Black people to survive in the UK, given that services tend always to be designed according to white norms and needs. Here again, the challenge to all white workers is to reverse the learning and strive to develop more relevant responses, free of racism. Equivalent arguments apply in relation to working-class gay and lesbian disabled and older service users.

The strongest message from this chapter so far must be that, where there is continuing violence, it is unsafe, unjust and pointless to do any work with the couple or family together that involves the abusive man in interviews. So what of situations in which a professional worker in a statutory context is required to be involved in resolving some question concerning the whole family and where abuse is or has been a major factor? How can the practitioner pay due account to the shift in awareness outlined above while still carrying out his or her duties to the court or employing agency? This has been a key question facing probation officers operating the family court welfare service. We shall now turn to consider the recent changes in their practice, which echo closely the concerns outlined above. Wider issues for work covered by child care legislation will also be considered later in the chapter.

FAMILY COURT WELFARE WORK

A key area of activity in which the probation service comes into contact with abusive men, their partners and children is family court welfare work. Its primary objective, according to Home Office National Standards (undated, para. 1.6, implemented in January 1995) is 'to help the courts in their task of serving the needs of children whose parents are involved in separation or divorce, or whose families are involved in disputes in private law'. Like child care in social services departments, it is covered by the general principles of the Children Act 1989. In addition, the National Standards require officers to pay particular attention to issues of gender, as well as race, culture and religion; to have regard to their service's equal opportunities policy; actively to address discrimination and its prevention; and to work with skilled interpreters, including for sign language, as well as providing written materials in a range of languages (paras 1.12–1.18).

Probation officers working as court welfare officers have run into criticism from those agencies most concerned with domestic abuse, particularly since a conciliation or mediation approach came to dominate the specialism. David Sleightholm, who represented the Association of Chief Officers of Probation (ACOP) on the Victim Support (1992) national working party on domestic violence, commented in his resulting discussion paper for ACOP's National Council:

> The area of civil work has provoked most controversy between myself and other members of the working party. It has been argued that probation services are cavalier in their approach to separated and divorced abused women, and that in particular our increasing preference for joint meetings with parents is sometimes pursued with little regard for the wishes or safety of women.
>
> (Sleightholm, 1991, p.5)

His resulting contribution to the Victim Support report gave careful consideration to these matters. ACOP incorporated the same material into its 'Position Statement on Domestic Violence' (Association of Chief Officers of Probation, 1992), approved by its National Council on 30th January 1992; section 4.7, on civil work, is identical (apart from minor details in the introductory and closing paragraphs to incorporate the material into its context) to the section on 'Security for Children' in the Victim Support report (1992, paras 5.23–5.32). The content refers back to 1989, when ACOP issued a position statement, agreed with the President of the Family Division of the High Court, favouring joint interviews by court welfare officers with separating couples, both to reach agreements to present to the court and as a foundation for 'continuing parental responsibility'. Already, at that date, it was acknowledged that the parties might prefer to be seen separately and that this should not adversely affect them:

> Invitations to couples to attend a joint meeting are accepted practice but parties may choose to be seen separately if they wish without detriment to their case. It is good practice to suggest that legal advice should be sought by either party if they are unsure of their position.
>
> (reproduced both in Victim Support, 1992, para. 5.27, and in para. 4.7.4 of the 1992 ACOP Position Statement)

The problem arises not in this reiteration of policy, then, but in actual practice. The Children's Legal Centre submission to the Home Affairs Committee (House of Commons, 1992a, p.3) states, for example:

The experience of our advice service would suggest that in many instances not only do court welfare officers fail to make clear to women that they have a choice about attending such [joint] meetings, but they apply considerable pressure to induce women to attend.

Women's Aid has also publicised this problem:

Women who have suffered abuse have often done so for a long time and finally gathered strength to leave. With a partner who has used violence and threats as a way to exert power and influence, a woman may be too intimidated and fearful to do justice to her perspective in such a joint meeting. While the Position Statement from ACOP, quoted above, clearly indicates that women can refuse without detriment to be seen jointly with their ex-partner, it is clear to Women's Aid that sometimes women do not know that they have a choice. We would ask ACOP to ensure that publicity is given to this aspect of their work.

(Victim Support, 1992, para. 5.28)

ACOP, perhaps in response to this, made the last sentence of paragraph 4.7.4 of its 1992 Position Statement (when separately issued) read: 'Probation Services (Court Welfare) need to ensure that publicity is given, so that women know they have this choice.'

WAFE was able to demonstrate that there was some way to travel:

many Court Welfare Officers are not operating under this guidance, do not inform a woman that she has a right to be seen separately, and in some cases, when challenged, still insisted that the joint interview was compulsory and refused to allow the woman concerned to have someone else present in the meeting for support.

(House of Commons, 1992b, Memorandum 22, para. 9.12)

This comment was based on a survey of 200 refuges in England, conducted by WAFE during 1992 to inform its response to the Home Affairs Committee, which generated 102 replies and the conclusion that 39 refuges knew of instances where a woman had been pressurised into having a joint interview (ibid., p.116).

More recently, the Home Office (undated) has added its weight, through its *National Standards for Probation Service Family Court Welfare Work*, in a similarly but yet more strongly phrased instruction:

4.12 Seeing parties together can be a valid method of report preparation which can promote continuing parental responsibility and can enable couples to reach agreements that can be reported to the court. But parties must be informed in writing, in plain terms, that they are free to choose to attend a joint meeting or be seen separately and that whatever choice they make it will not be to the detriment of their case. They should be advised to take legal advice if unsure of their position.

4.13 Court welfare officers must exercise particular care in cases in which violence between the parties has been alleged. A joint interview must not be convened if it can reasonably be foreseen that the safety or well-being of either party might be jeopardised.

Although the phraseology in this excerpt ('between the parties') betrays a lapse or blurring into the language of shared blame, as opposed to a clear understanding of the dangers of men's abuse of women, nevertheless it is admirably unequivocal in its call for safety to take precedence over a single, over-enthusiastically applied model of intervention. Safety considerations are also evident in the document's call for separate waiting areas (ibid., para. 1.21), although separate entrances to the building and panic buttons (Hester *et al.*, 1994, p.118) are ideally also needed (and too rarely provided: Radford, 1994, p.10), together with care in arranging staggered arrival and departure times. Some services attend to all or most of these things but there have been instances of physical attacks elsewhere, including a woman stabbed by her ex-partner in the corridor when leaving (ibid.). It needs to be remembered that Women's Aid and/or a housing authority may have moved the woman several times to evade her ex-partner's continued harassment. Care in keeping her address confidential and in preventing her abuser from following her home cannot be over-stressed.

Despite these advances, problems remain. The paragraphs cited above are taken from the chapter in the National Standards document on preparing welfare reports for the courts; this still leaves the whole area of mediation or conciliation requiring clarification. The purpose of mediation by a court welfare officer is specifically 'to encourage agreement between parties in disputes concerning the welfare of a child' (Home Office, undated, para. 3.2). Although both parties must give their 'informed consent' to entering into the process, and although the court is told only what both parties have agreed, it is not difficult to imagine circumstances where a woman who is fearful of, or overawed by, the court proceedings, or who is under pressure from her ex-partner, might go ahead without really being free to speak her mind in safety. Nothing is said about a separate meeting with the woman initially to check that she feels safe and is not under duress – and, indeed, separate interviewing goes against the conciliation methodology that has been developed by probation services in Britain (see, for example, Parkinson, 1986, pp.86–92; Howard and Shepherd, 1987, p.40). Yet there is much to be said for the probation officer checking with every woman who is referred, on an individual basis, that she is not encountering current abuse or threats of abuse to a level that is likely to impede her free and full participation in seeking a joint clarification and/or resolution of some or all of the questions relating to the children. Furthermore, there should also be careful thinking about the influence of emotional abuse and manipulation in such situations by men who have previously exhibited

patterns of intimidation. Most of the existing British literature on conciliation is wholly inadequate in relation to such imbalances of power (though
Roberts, 1988, p.107 does argue that domestic violence might make the
approach 'inappropriate or even unethical').

Taken in conjunction with wider indications of the dangers inherent in
couple and family work where abuse is involved (see above), and with calls
for experienced, independent child care practitioners rather than probation
officers to serve the family courts (Rickford, 1993; see also Hester *et al.*,
1994, pp.115–17, for problems in ascertaining children's wishes), these
concerns point to the need for a fairly fundamental rethinking of court
welfare practice in this country. Updating training, with the involvement of
Women's Aid, so that family court welfare officers know what questions
to ask about abuse and about considerations of safety – and ask them
routinely in every case – would be one positive way forward. Conciliation
interviews are not bound by the rules of evidence and need not confine
discussion to events the court is permitted to consider; consequently,
behaviour prior to the separation can be discussed. Women can be interviewed – and believed – in relation to domestic abuse, but only if a safe
opportunity is created by a professional who understands what he or she is
hearing and its full significance. Current research suggests that conciliators
and mediators in both probation and voluntary sector settings fail to make
clear enquiries about past or present abuse, fail to identify patterns of
abuse (associating it only with extreme physical violence – somehow
always worse than anything they themselves happen to be seeing), and
assume that women who are currently unsafe will not find their way into
the process (Hester and Pearson, 1993, pp.4–5) or that violence ends when
the relationship ends (Hester *et al.*, 1994, p.108). They compound the
dangers by assuming that their own presence in the interviews is sufficient
to make the process safe (Hester and Pearson, 1993, p.5), without allowing
for continued violence (e.g. father stabbing mother in the family court
welfare office in front of the children: Hester *et al.*, 1994, p.107) or for
subsequent consequences for women who may now be more likely to be
traced and reabused by partners whose wishes they have actively opposed
in the interview. North American writers are far more likely to conclude
that mediation under such circumstances should be avoided altogether
(Hart, 1990; Grillo, 1991, both cited in Hester and Pearson, 1993).

Everything that has been said above in relation to family court welfare
work in the UK can also be applied to mediation between divorcing
couples, a major feature of the Family Law Bill introduced into Parliament
in 1995 (and going through Parliament at the time of writing). The proposal
is for a move to 'no-fault' divorce, with a mandatory eighteen-month
waiting period for 'reflection' before the commencement of proceedings.
During that time, it is intended to ensure that far more couples use mediation to make arrangements concerning their children and/or finances; under

clause 12, the court has the power to direct couples to receive information about mediation services, and acceptance of mediation could become a condition of access to legal aid (unless 'good reason' for refusal could be demonstrated). It is not even clear as yet that mediation would not be required in some cases where women were seeking civil remedies against abusive men (WAFE, 1995, p.4, paras 4a and 4b). The White Paper preceding the Family Law Bill (Lord Chancellor's Department, 1995, Cm 2799) did acknowledge that divorcing spouses who have experienced domestic violence constitute a special category but failed to note that violence is, in fact, a widespread reason for divorce as opposed to a quite separate issue. Work in the USA has concluded that mediation is not appropriate where there has been or still is domestic violence (Brygger, 1990, p.48) and it is intended, under the proposed arrangements, that those disclosing domestic violence in the lead-up to divorce in Britain will be screened out of mediation. Nevertheless, this will be hard to achieve in a system that will be so firmly based on mediation and in the face of a problem so often hidden from outside scrutiny. WAFE (1995, p.4), in its briefing on the Bill, is calling for each spouse to receive information about mediation separately (so that women have real choices), and for it to be clearly stated that there is no compulsion to attend any joint meeting, since domestic violence may not, at that point, have been disclosed.

Even if the Bill fails, the trend towards mediation is likely to grow. Numerous agencies and projects, building on a strong base in the voluntary sector, will be involved in providing mediation services, and this fragmentation (as was suggested in Chapter 5 in relation to health and community care provision) may make it harder to ensure a consistent awareness of and attention to women's interests. Although National Family Mediation, an umbrella group of over 60 UK charities, circulates to its affiliates guidelines from America that advise against mediation where there is violence, most services here do not at present routinely screen for violence (Kaganas and Piper, 1994, p.272), so are scarcely in a position to follow the guidelines or to guarantee women's safety during the mediation process. Even if official guidance were to be issued requiring screening for violence, undisclosed or unrecognised violence, as well as other kinds of abuse and of power and control within relationships, would still leave women at a disadvantage in joint interviews. Mediators' actual practice would also be likely to be patchy, and to present another urgent need for training on woman abuse; their professional ethos of shared decision making does not sit comfortably with the need for women leaving abusive relationships to hold firm to their own understanding of events and for perpetrators' rationalisations to be utterly refuted. Yet refusing mediation may have adverse consequences for a woman in court; accepting it, on the other hand, may place her in physical danger, throw her back into emotional turmoil, and still result in an unfair outcome. The whole 'no-fault' climate of the divorce proposals is itself arguably tantamount to ignoring husbands' abusive behaviour and may mean that fewer women talk to their legal and other advisers about the abuse, leading to declining referrals for practical help (Women's Aid Federation England, undated a, para. 7.4).

CHILD CARE WORK, FAMILIES AND THE COURTS

The 1992 WAFE refuge survey (WAFE, 1992a, also available as House of Commons, 1992b, Memorandum 22), referred to earlier, revealed a range of practical problems creating or perpetuating dangers for women and/or children. These extend beyond family court welfare practice into the heart of the spirit and provisions of the Children Act – and are consequently of relevance to both social workers and probation officers. Child care work operates against a background of legislation that pays no regard to domestic violence as an issue. It leads practitioners in directions that increase the dangers for women subjected to abuse and fail to help them provide the level of safety and support they would wish for their children, including at times when they are not believed (because they are suspected of hidden agendas against ex-partners) or not supported.

The Children Act 1989 was hailed as giving increased rights to children because it made the welfare of the child the paramount consideration (s.1.1) and required that the child's wishes and feelings must be consulted (s.1.3). Because it was not based on an understanding of domestic violence or of gender power dynamics in men's abuse of women and children, however, it has failed to meet the needs of many children living with abuse in current relationships or after families have separated. What it has in fact done is greatly to strengthen the position of men, including the many men who abuse women and children, and increased their tendency to claim 'rights' over their children (Hester *et al.*, 1994, p.104). The problems this creates will be explored in detail below in relation to parental responsibility and section 8 orders under the 1989 Act.

Parental responsibility

Section 2(1) of the Children Act states that parents who were married at the time of the child's birth 'shall each have parental responsibility for the child'. (An unmarried father may also acquire parental responsibility along-side the mother, through a legal agreement with her or through a court order.) Parental responsibility is defined in section 3(1) of the Act as 'all the rights, duties, powers, responsibilities and authority which by law a parent of a child has in relation to the child and his property'. This assumption of joint parenting continues to operate after divorce, where courts no longer routinely make orders about the child's upbringing because there is no legal reason any longer to choose between the parents and because of the presumption in the Act against making unnecessary orders.

The Act is built on a concept of parents involved in divorce or child care hearings as reasonable people in a balanced relationship whose actions and decisions stem from the interests of their children. It ignores the gender power dynamics operating in relation to the large numbers of men who are driven by the pursuit of dominance and control to abuse women and/or children; it also ignores the way in which a patriarchal welfare and judicial system reinforces these dynamics. It neglects the abuse of women by men as a major reason for divorcing (Borkowski *et al.*, 1983), the likelihood of that abuse continuing after separation, and the misery and fear it causes. Thus, there is a mismatch between one of the key reasons for social work and court intervention in the lives of children on the one hand, and the issues tackled through that intervention on the other. The Act (particularly in the way it is interpreted in the courts) is inadequate as a means of tackling the power issues inherent in family relationships. Rather, it gives men new opportunities to abuse.

Harne and Radford (1994) give an important feminist analysis of the shift in the legal position of mothers and fathers after divorce. We were accustomed, not so long ago, to custody being granted predominantly to women following divorce or separation, although lesbian mothers disproportionately lost custody owing to the negative attitudes of the courts and the deliberate collusion of resentful husbands (Rights of Women Lesbian Custody Group, 1984). The campaigning by Families Need Fathers, formed in 1975, for joint custody and increased access glossed over domestic violence, child abuse, the relatively recent date of the acquisition by women of equal custody rights in law, and the fact that most men were content to leave unchallenged mothers who continued after divorce to have the major responsibility for the children (Harne and Radford, 1994, p.72). Nevertheless, calls for increased rights for men found favour from a male-dominated legislature, so that joint custody began to become more common and access for fathers to increase, culminating in the changes in the 1989 Act.

We should beware fathers' rights being dressed up as children's rights to be parented by or to have contact with their father, through an unquestioned assumption that children always benefit from this (there is now a presumption in favour of contact, set down in a leading case that went to the Court of Appeal) and that mothers only oppose it out of spite, revenge or selfishness. It is seen as axiomatic that children need two parents and that they need a male role model. In fact, children gain their role models from the whole family and the wider society. Boys raised by lone mothers or lesbian couples still learn how to be men. (If they learnt to be less controlling men, that would be all to the good.) Furthermore, research – brilliantly summarised by Hooper (1994) – indicates no clear findings about the supposed benefits of continuing contact with non-resident parents after divorce but 'much stronger evidence that the effectiveness of the resident parent and the protection of children from exposure to parental conflict are clearly related to better outcomes for children' (ibid., p.98). In other words, it is the non-abusing, caring parent who needs support and safety to care for the child. The debates about continued parental responsibility and contact simply have not engaged with the facts about men's abusive behaviour towards women and children, or its adverse effects on children (see Chapter 6, this volume) – including in the period following divorce, when it can continue and worsen.

Shared parental responsibility after separation or divorce is clearly problematic:

> While this approach may prove generally beneficial, it is likely that problems will continue to occur when it is applied to families where domestic violence has been a chronic feature. It is an approach that can make the plight of the abused woman even worse.
>
> (Victim Support, 1992, para. 5.23)

A school might, for example, reveal a child's home address to a father because he shares parental responsibility, or a housing authority may refuse to rehouse because it is not clear that the woman has sole responsibility for the children. These kinds of decisions actively allow abuse to continue or to recommence and hence are bad for women and children.

An oversight in the consultation leading to, and drafting of, the Act – caused by Britain's rigid demarcation between the child care 'establishment' and those who work with and understand domestic abuse – has caused this danger to children's well-being to be overlooked. Neither the Act nor the guidance governing its implementation makes any mention of domestic violence. Victim Support, in its national working party report in 1992 (para. 5.23), called for this omission to be rectified. Nevertheless, at the time of writing, the provision under section 1(1) of the 1989 Children Act, that the child's welfare is the paramount consideration for a court deciding about his or her upbringing, is frequently accompanied by a failure to understand what this means in contexts of woman abuse. In particular – despite the fact that the child's welfare may not be best served if the mother's safety is endangered – the court is not required to consider her safety, even in relation to her ability to care for the child, or any history of abuse of her by the father, and may decide that such matters are actively outside its remit. Looking at the situation solely from what a child care professional or a court considers to be the child's perspective may not be an adequate response to promoting and safeguarding the child's best interests (and see Hester *et al.*, 1994, pp.115–17 for a critique of the process of ascertaining children's wishes and feelings). It can only be hoped that any amendment to the Children Act that takes courts into the realm of removing abusers of women who also endanger children may assist the judicial and child care professions to learn to recognise the links between these two, inter-related forms of abuse (see Chapters 4 and 6, this volume), although it may have its own dangers of child care professionals removing choices from women.

Section 8 orders

Section 8 orders – covering residence, contact, 'prohibited steps' and 'specific issues' in the lives of children – may be made in any family proceedings. These include not only proceedings under the Children Act itself but those dealing with: adoption; divorce, judicial separation or nullity of marriage; maintenance; domestic violence, and occupation of the family home. This can mean, for example, that a woman going to court to obtain an injunction may become involved, without preparation, in proceedings concerning whether the children will have contact with her abuser for many years to come (ibid., p.111). She may accede to her ex-partner's, or his solicitor's, demands because she has not had time to think, or in order to get away from a frightening confrontation in court or a painful reliving of past events. There are general problems with men seeking section 8 orders for their own ends, not infrequently as a way of re-establishing contact with their ex-partners and recommencing their harassment and abuse. There are also problems with courts tending not to take women seriously, seeing them as vengeful and selfish rather than scared for themselves and their children. In short, the Act, and the practice that accompanies it, often make no clear distinction between the actions and motives of an abusing parent and those of a non-abusing parent, which leads to necessarily dubious decisions.

These inadequacies in the law are compounded by the fact that many women do not fully comprehend the language, the assumptions, or the behaviour of the courts for reasons of culture, race or class; that racism and homophobia remain rife in the justice system; and that the law typically operates through discussing incidents deemed to constitute evidence rather than understanding processes such as long-term patterns of abuse.

Residence orders

Twenty-two refuges in the WAFE survey (House of Commons, 1992b, Memorandum 22, p.116) knew of men obtaining residence orders against the expressed wishes of the woman and/or child. Conversely, ten knew of women having difficulty getting Income Support for the children or priority need rehousing because there was no residence order in *her* favour (i.e. she could not prove the need to maintain the children because they arguably could have gone to their father). Even if the woman has her child living with her on a residence order, she still shares parental responsibility with her abuser (where he is the father) and technically should obtain his agreement to any major decision affecting the child including schooling, moving, or medical treatment if he chooses to exercise that responsibility.

There is evidence of women encountering difficulty in obtaining a residence order while living in a refuge:

> In two cases known to Women's Aid in the past year, children as young as 10 months were returned to live with their father, where the reason given to the mother was that a refuge was not a suitable place for a child.
>
> (ibid., para. 9.10)

Court personnel need training to understand that a refuge is temporary – 'a point of departure' (Victim Support, 1992, para. 5.32) – not what the mother is offering the child as a permanent home, and that women only stay for extended periods because they encounter difficulties in getting rehoused (Malos and Hague, 1993, pp.58–9); also that refuges provide skilled support for children, at a difficult time, which is rarely available elsewhere (see Chapter 6, this volume).

Once again, the child's welfare requires fuller consideration:

> Courts should consider in particular the quality of the relationship between each child and each parent, and the long-term prospects for the child. The fact that the woman is presently living in a refuge should not be a consideration, but an indication that issues of violence require investigation.
>
> (Victim Support, 1992, para. 5.32)

A graphic case example is contained in Appendix 5 to WAFE's evidence to the Home Affairs Committee (House of Commons, 1992b, Memorandum 22, pp.122–3). A violent husband obtained an ex-parte interim residence order in respect of his two daughters, aged 8 months and 2 years, by alleging that their mother was a drug addict – although no evidence was produced other than allegations that both parents smoked cannabis. Ex-parte means that the mother was not present; in fact, she knew nothing about the proceedings until the court server and two male and two female police officers arrived at the refuge where the woman was living and threatened to break in and arrest everyone helping the woman unless she handed over the children. Clearly, the court had revealed her whereabouts – with profound effect on her, her children, and all the other residents who tried to hide and protect her. Refuge staff and the woman persuaded the father at the police station to let his wife go with him but he gave her the slip at the railway station. The baby had been being breast-fed and the electricity had been cut off at the house after the woman left so he had no means of feeding the baby. Social workers became implicated because social services had to pay for a reconnection and had to visit the children daily. At the next hearing, the judge said the children should stay with their father because of the allegations of drug abuse but refused evidence on the man's violent and abusive treatment of his wife as not relevant to the children's welfare. The children were finally returned to their mother, following a separation of approximately two months, after she had proved herself a fit mother during supervised contact sessions at the social services office. That her husband had not had to prove his fitness when he took the children is in line with a trend confirmed by Hester and Radford (1992, p.62, 1996a, 1996b): mothers' capacity to care is more readily questioned by professionals, and husbands play on this when they make allegations of mental health problems, alcohol or drug misuse. Conversely, it is by no means rare for judges not to question what the father will actually offer a child in the way of care. In one Canadian case where the judge felt the shelter (refuge) – was a bad environment for the children, life with father was preferred because he was in the family home and had the children's bicycles (pers. comm. with a staff member of the London Family Court Clinic, Ontario)!

Though legal detail is country specific, the wider issues commented on here are not confined to Britain but are the product of a patriarchal judicial system. Jaffe *et al.* (1990, pp.107–10) review literature conveying similar problems in North America and note 'a strong bias in many judges' minds about a father's rights to his children' (ibid., p.108), stoked by fathers' organisations; women feeling abused afresh by courts which are conned by the superficial charm of uninvolved and abusive fathers; women afraid to leave their abusers because they fear this outcome; judges and lawyers with inadequate knowledge and inappropriate attitudes; and reports prepared by professionals whose only acknowledgement of violence is as a factor that might be exaggerated by women to gain the advantage, and who attempt to mediate even where the imbalance of power puts the woman in real danger. The same authors give some examples of a better informed approach, with separate interviews to take a detailed history from each partner, including of any violence, and awareness of the child's resulting level of adjustment.

In Britain, mothers who have fled the violence alone may lose their children because the welfare checklist in the 1989 Children Act (s.1[3]) states that the court must take into account the likely effect on the child of any change in circumstances; taken in isolation (against the letter and spirit of other aspects of the Act) this has sometimes been interpreted to mean that it is better for children not to move home. This has led to residence orders in favour of violent men (where the mother has been forced to flee and the man has stayed in the family home) because of the court's failure to appreciate that 'The situation faced by some abused women is so severe and the options so limited that they may have left home unable to take the children with them' (Victim Support, 1992, para. 5.29). Furthermore,

the presumption that where possible a child should remain in the 'family home' has meant in the last year that many judges in particular have been ordering children to live with the father, even where this is against the wishes of the child concerned who is old enough to have an independent opinion.

(House of Commons, 1992b, Memorandum 22, para. 9.9).

Were courts to take a wider view of the remainder of the welfare checklist to determine opposed section 8 orders then: '(a) the ascertainable wishes and feelings of the child, (b) his [sic] physical, emotional and educational needs . . . (e) any harm which he has suffered or is at risk of suffering, and (f) how capable each of his parents . . . is of meeting his needs' might lead to very different decisions (1989 Children Act [s.i (3)]).

Contact orders

Over and above the assumption of joint parenting, which will often mean that contact continues with a father who has abused his wife and/or child, this contact can be enshrined in a court order. An assumption in favour of contact is not a new issue. Ogus *et al.* (1989, p. 363) noted, under the previous legislation (hence the out-of-date terminology): a 'consensus among professionals that . . . the access of the non-custodial parent is a "good thing" and to be encouraged (or insisted on)'. An equating of the child's best interests with contact with an absent father has been established through case law as the norm from which a court would need evidence to depart, whereas mothers who are forced to flee from violence and leave their children behind are often more punitively treated by the courts, with their children's interests sometimes seen as lying in a preservation of the status quo without them (Hester *et al.*, 1994, p.105). So strong is the emphasis on actual physical contact with fathers that it continues under supervision even with men who have killed the children's mother, some-times with the children watching (ibid., p.107, and pers. comms), and with fathers who have abused the children (ibid.). Contact through letters or other means is rarely explored or considered acceptable as an alternative, although it does fall within the legal understanding of contact.

A contact order under section 8 of the 1989 Children Act is defined in that section as

> an order requiring the person with whom a child lives, or is to live, to allow the child to visit or stay with the person named in the order, or for that person and the child otherwise to have contact with each other.

Since the child's welfare is paramount in the court's eyes, the emphasis is on the *child's* right to retain links with someone who is significant in his or her life – links that may include letters or telephone calls as well as or instead of face-to-face meetings. This may necessitate the *father's* knowing the child's address and telephone number – and consequently that of his ex-partner. Children's and mothers' interests may come into conflict here since many women remain terrified of their ex-partners – justifiably so when contact with the children and courts revealing addresses can be a direct cause of the man's renewing abuse (e.g. Binney *et al.*, 1988, pp.98–100). For example, a WAFE survey of refuges in September 1992 found that:

Less than a year since the Children Act has been in force, 50 refuges have had contact with at least one woman who after leaving a violent partner, has suffered further abuse, as a direct result of details of her whereabouts being revealed to her abuser as part of a Contact order. One woman was stabbed while taking the children to the contact visit as required by the court; another was beaten up at her new home, the address of which was given to her abuser by the court.

(WAFE, in House of Commons, 1992b, Memorandum 22, para. 9.5)

We also learn of 36 refuges' security being breached (ibid., p.116). Divulging refuge, or any, addresses in this way threatens the safety of many women and children who have fled to escape intolerable treatment. Singh (1991, para. 1.7) points out that this could have particularly severe repercussions for Asian refuges, where security has to be intense (because the workers are seen to be assisting women to defy cultural and religious proscriptions). She recommends asking for another address to be used on the order. The application form actually asks whether a woman is living in a refuge. This by itself could reveal her whereabouts if there is only one refuge nearby to which she is most likely to have gone initially.

Corroborating evidence of disclosures of women's whereabouts, including by social services departments and court welfare officers, comes from research into contact arrangements following domestic violence (presentation to British Sociological Association Violence Against Women Group by Marianne Hester; see also Hester and Radford, 1992; Hester and Pearson, 1993; Hester et al., 1994; Hester and Radford, 1996a, 1996b). The Child Benefit Agency can also be used as a means of men tracing their ex-partners. In the Scottish context, the Scottish Office has announced a change to the Children's Hearings Rules 1986, removing the obligation on Reporters to reveal children's addresses, after a man used this means to trace his estranged wife first to a refuge and then to a flat before stabbing her to death (Community Care, 23rd–29th March 1995, p.5, 'Stabbing prompts change'). It appears from reports that discretion will still apply, however, in judging whether there is an element of physical danger. The problem is that professionals appear often to be unaware of these dangers, or of the risks to women and children posed by breaches of confidentiality and by contact itself. It cannot help but have an adverse effect on children if their mothers are physically, sexually and/or emotionally abused at the beginning or end of a contact visit, if the children themselves are grilled for information about their mother's current social life, or used to relay threats, or kept longer than arranged to frighten their mother, or actually abducted – or otherwise used as pawns in their father's continued bid for control over their mother (Hester and Radford, 1992, p.61; Hester et al., 1994, pp.107–8). It is not uncommon for men to seek contact primarily to pursue ex-partners (ibid., p.106) and to let contact drop when thwarted.

Using children in such ways both before and after separation is a recognised part of men's abuse of women, to the point of occupying its own segment of the Duluth power and control wheel (see Chapter 2, this volume). More experienced legal and welfare professionals tend to be more pessimistic and more protective about contact in domestic violence cases, with more ability to see this from both the mother, and child's point of view (Hester and Radford, 1992, p.63). The London Borough of Hackney (1994, p.45) *Good Practice Guidelines* on domestic violence warn social workers to take women's safety into account, to consult the views of the children concerned, and to understand that contact is unlikely to be successful if the woman feels she has been pressurised into it and remains afraid of the children's father.

Children themselves are frequently at risk, over and above the harm inflicted on them by their father's actions towards their mother. The WAFE survey (House of Commons, 1992b, Memorandum 22, p.116) found that 22 refuges knew of child abuse occurring as a result of contact orders. Yet a biased professional or courtroom perspective can make it difficult for mothers to be believed when they report the child abuse or seek to obtain protection for their children (Nelson, 1994). Because the women themselves have been abused, they are seen as hitting back at partners through allegations concerning the children – or this is seen as a ploy to end the father's involvement in their lives. Courts are even using the term 'implacably hostile' to refer to women in this alleged situation, and are threatening women with payment of costs or imprisonment if they refuse to comply with contact orders once made. This perception of the woman's motivation leads to a lack of vigilance in pursuing investigations when she reports child abuse by her ex-partner. Yet it cannot be overstated that children whose mothers have been or are being abused constitute a group whose own risk of being abused by the men concerned is higher than average and who therefore require more, rather than less, protection (see Chapter 6, this volume for detailed research findings). In Forman's Scottish study of 20 cases where both child sexual abuse and woman abuse had occurred, 10 women who had separated from their partners reported that their children were sexually abused during access (Forman, 1995, p.28). Other reasons for close professional attention in such cases are that we know that children and/or their mothers may feel safe to reveal the child abuse only when no longer living with the abuser, and that the recent discovery of child abuse may have been the final catalyst for the woman to leave her abuser (e.g. ibid., p.30; Nelson, 1994, p.19).

Furthermore, as Nelson argues, it would not make logical sense for abused mothers who have their children living with them actively to seek to subject their households to social work enquiries, nor to incite partners whom most still fear (see also Hester and Radford, 1992, p.62), unless they had real concerns for their children's safety. In fact, mothers tend to pursue or oppose contact according to what they understand their children want, not according to their own preferences or interests. A large number attempting to comply with the court complain when men they would personally prefer not to see fail in their contact obligations (ibid.), while others risk further court proceedings against themselves to protect children from ill-judged court decisions (pp.63–4).

Still deeper problems lie in the reluctance of courts to view further contact negatively, even when they already know a child has been abused and when the child is actively opposed to the contact, and in a lack of support to help mothers prove continuing abuse – for example when children have been 'groomed' by their abusers to associate abuse with apparently harmless topics that can continue to be mentioned in letters and cards (O'Hara, 1990). If mothers are strongly resisting access, they generally have a good reason stemming from their close knowledge of the child (Hester and Radford, 1992, p.64), and they should always be listened to. Mothers are often critical of courts and related professionals for attempting various arrangements to make contact work in the face of children's suffering (ibid.), sometimes involving the abuser's family when they either deny the danger or are party to it (Hester *et al.*, 1994, p.113, and pers. comms with social workers). Contact centres may provide short-term help in some situations, particularly where children still have positive feelings for a father whom their mother fears, but the centres are not widespread, they provide only an artificial setting for meetings, they are typically staffed by volunteers or others who are not adequately trained in safety matters, and they are intended to be used only temporarily. They do not remove the need to ask more searching questions about when contact has a positive value and when it does not, nor to be very clear about the nature of the relationship between father and child and its meaning to the child. Furthermore, their staff (who are typically volunteers) are not in a formally supervisory role – the parent having contact is in charge of the child – and their training lacks a safety orientation (Hester and Radford 1996b).

Prohibited steps and specific issues orders

Although less discussed in the literature, these orders could be used positively to help women protect their children. One woman, who had previously been subjected to actual bodily harm, went back to court with a contact order to seek the imposition of conditions to stop the father periodically failing to return the child. The judge prohibited the man from seeing the child. This is a prime area in which Department of Health guidance on operating the Children Act in the context of domestic violence could help. Directions or conditions in any section 8 order could be used to help avoid violence and abuse, including abduction (Victim Support,

1992, para. 5.30). County and High Court judges can also support section 8 orders with injunctions. Social services departments could seek one or more orders to provide a legal framework in cases where children are not safe or where their emotional well-being needs to be safeguarded. A social worker known to the author who is holding responsibility for a case where the children's father is serving a prison sentence for killing their mother plans to seek the prohibition of unsupervised contact on his release. Overall, she considers it ironic that he will continue to share parental responsibility with the local authority (holding a care order), for children whose lives he has blighted in this way.

CONCLUSION

More careful attention to the welfare checklist in the 1989 Children Act, and a wider understanding of children's welfare as deeply connected with their mother's safety and her ability to interpret the wider situation, would help considerably to obviate the dangers in situations involving abusive men. At present, too many professional recommendations and court decisions play into the hands of men who manipulate the system in their own, not their children's, interests. Women and children who have survived years of abuse deserve a more robust defence of their interests. In particular, women must always be seen separately and directly asked about abuse of themselves and/or their children by practitioners trained to tailor their intervention safely according to the response. McKay (1994, p.35), for example, warns child protection workers to look out for men who resist allowing their wives to be seen or heard separately – and in fact urges workers to use this as evidence that the woman needs to be seen alone – closely echoing the National Standards which now require probation officers to undertake separate interviews in family court welfare work where there is a danger of violence. It is high time that family court practice began to show the same intolerance of the crime of domestic violence as is being noised in relation to criminal justice.

Worryingly, even though the message is coming over loud and clear from feminist and pro-feminist writers in Britain and overseas that joint interviews are pointless and dangerous where men are violent, there is evidence that practice can be remarkably resistant to change. Recent research in America has revealed that, in a survey of therapists and psychologists responding to case scenarios, 40 per cent failed to address overt violence at all and most of the rest dismissed it as 'mild' or 'moderate' (Harway and Hansen, 1993, p.44). Only eight out of 362 participants mentioned the possibility that the woman might be killed – which had actually happened in one of the cases used; over half did not think the violence required immediate action. Even when told of the fatal outcome, half of the 405 psychologists in a follow-up study failed to regard protecting the woman as the intervention of choice (ibid., pp.46–7). Yet 80 per cent of the total claimed to have been influenced by feminism (pp.45–6). Hundreds of these specialist practitioners, who knew the literature, were content to plough on with joint work and a few even blamed the woman for her partner's violence. In Britain, Malloch and Webb (1993, p.137) have shown that professionals favouring conciliation approaches in domestic abuse cases do less to protect the safety of women and children. And, even though the Home Office has given a strong lead, a small number of probation services appear to remain opposed to the national requirement not to interview couples together where there is violence, with some officers talking of 'getting round' this expectation (pers. comm. with an Assistant Chief Probation Officer). Women and children have less opportunity to 'get round' our ineptitude or intransigence – and some are harmed as a result. Clearly, then, there is still considerable work to be done, through training and agency policy development for example, to change welfare and court practice and practitioners' attitudes.

Chapter 8

The probation service and domestic violence

Two areas of probation work – family court welfare and groups for perpetrators (treated separately in Chapters 7 and 9) – have, to date, been the main sites of changed practice as far as domestic abuse is concerned. The challenge now is to extend this attention to the rest of the service's responsibilities. This will need to happen, of course, within a wider appreciation of gender oppression and its interaction with other forms of oppression – drawing, for example, on an awareness that Black women (e.g. Patel, 1990) and abused gay men and lesbians (e.g. Underwood, 1989) may be reluctant to use the criminal justice system for protection for fear of its inherent racism and homophobia against their partners or themselves. Similarly, women who do not speak English will be unable to seek police help unless interpreters are made more widely available, and women who fear deportation will be most unlikely to call the police under any circumstances.[1]

CURRENT ATTITUDES

As was mentioned in Chapter 1, the Association of Chief Officers of Probation (ACOP) has issued a position statement which now requires domestic violence to be treated on a par with other violent crime (Association of Chief Officers of Probation, 1992, updated in 1996). There is still some way to travel, however, in achieving this aim. Just as in social services departments (see Chapter 3) there has traditionally been a serious under-recording in probation settings of known abuse by men of their partners, linked to a failure to tackle the subject adequately, Swain (1986, p.132) found mention of domestic violence in only seven out of 300 files on random probation cases dealt with in 1983. She also found that, in examining files on cases where probation officers in interviews had specifically mentioned violence, the abusive incidents were rarely recorded. Reasons given in follow-up interviews with the officers concerned included avoiding the subject, or regarding it as not central to probation work, or not falling within their province. This at least suggests that ACOP policy of treating known domestic violence like any other violence may not be being followed. Swain further comments (p.133) that there was certainly additional violence that was hidden or went unrecognised.

Since abuse builds up over time, and since, as we shall see in the next section, persistent offenders can be sentenced more harshly, it is important to keep accurate records. Although, as will be discussed below, this may seem to cut across probation concerns for the offender's interests and probation opposition to imprisonment *per se*, there is also the victim to think about. She may benefit from or appreciate a sentence that at least makes a firm statement about what she has suffered, even if it does not deter reoffending, and that, if it removes her abuser for a period of time, keeps her safe while she deliberates on her options. This must, of course, be tempered with the concerns mentioned above about racism and homophobia in the criminal justice system, and with women's own views about what will help: there are certainly instances where a women knows her abuser will be more violent if criminal justice agencies intervene without guaranteeing her safety. Swain's respondents were not operating at this level of sophistication, however (see above), but appeared simply to be showing a lack of concern.

Certainly, the probation service is by no means free of the negative and false assumptions about domestic abusers and those they abuse that were discussed in Chapter 2. Some individual probation officers still overtly or covertly blame women for provoking, tolerating, asking for, enjoying, or seeking abuse, and have little or no understanding of why women stay with or return to their abusers (pers. comms with probation staff). This will inevitably influence their own work and may also set an atmosphere in a whole team – making any attempt to intervene with perpetrators, or to give practical assistance to the women they abuse, seem hopeless and a waste of valuable time. Swain (ibid., pp.132–3) commented both on flippant office talk and on responses in formal research interviews which revealed such attitudes (and sometimes attributed them to highly controversial psychological theories). Officers also knowingly or unintentionally collude with abusive men when they do not challenge denial or minimisation of the abuse or of its impact on the man's partner and on their children.

Perhaps the largest number of officers do condemn known violent abuse at the level of discussion, but see it as exceptional (the 'bad apple' scenario: see Chapter 2) and fail to look for it or act on it across their own caseloads. In fact, as we have seen in earlier chapters, domestic abuse is strikingly widespread and abusers are not lone monsters whose offending occurs in a vacuum. Rather, the roots of abuse lie in the social construction of masculinity and in the nature of male offending as often an extension of this. Socially constructed images of men and male sexuality that encourage men to think women exist to satisfy men's needs for sexual gratification and physical comfort, and often to hate women, lie behind all sexually violent offences – including domestic abuse. The abuser is not deviant in accepting these images but is carrying masculinity to its logical conclusion; his actions are illegal, but he may not consider them wrong and other men, including men in authority, may have sympathy with him. It is essential that *all* probation work addresses this gendered behaviour (see Bensted *et al.*, 1994, for a widely applicable groupwork approach which could be extended to discuss the abuse of women) and that wider work on confronting sexism amongst offenders always includes the topic of sexual violence within intimate adult relationships as well as against strangers.

This issue must also be seen within the context of the wider need for anti-sexist training and support for male and female staff. Male officers, in particular, need to consider carefully the gender dynamics of their role, and the impact of their own assumptions on their work and on the influence they have on others, but female officers too – partly in order to survive in a male-dominated environment – have often internalised patriarchal values and ways of working. Abusive behaviours by offenders, and collusion with them by staff, need to be challenged – both directly and indirectly, through every officer's language and attitudes, through the use of concrete legal steps, and through according higher priority to the victim's current and future safety than to the offender's choices, even where these affect his chances of lighter sentencing or temporary or early release from custody. At present, women perceive probation officers as concentrating on the male perpetrators and disregarding the women's own safety (McWilliams and McKiernan, 1993, p.96). There are implications in the above in relation to management support for both female and male staff who have a positive desire to introduce change, to the resourcing of training and practice priorities, and to the challenging of staff who persist in being 'part of the problem' through collusion with the negative attitudes held by abusers or failure to be adequately concerned with the safety of women and children.

Domestic violence needs, in fact, to become a prominent issue throughout probation practice. Probation officers work with many men who abuse their partners; sometimes the abuse constitutes an index offence – in other words, it may be the offence or one or more of the offences with which the officer is directly concerned in preparing a pre-sentence or other report for court, or in supervising a man on an order or on licence, or in seeking to evoke change, for example through running an offending behaviour group. More often, since prosecution is rare (ACOP in House of Commons, 1992b, Memorandum 6, p.37) – though ACOP expects it to increase as policing behaviour changes – the man is in contact with the probation service for another reason and discloses in the course of an interview that he is also abusing his partner – in other words, that he is committing criminal acts against her. The usual questions should arise: for example, are these additional crimes to be reported to the police; will they be taken to breach any good behaviour clause included in an order? If these offences are treated differently from others, then we are not serious in our claim to treat domestic violence as a crime, and as seriously as any other form of violence (e.g. ibid., p.38). Awareness of abuse and appropriate responses to it therefore need to be incorporated into the overall work of the service and into all its training – both in specialist courses and conferences and through a permeating approach designed to raise or tackle the issue appropriately as part of all individual work with men, all groupwork with or including men (whatever the substantive topic, e.g. alcohol, induction, offending behaviour, probation centre groups), all report preparation, all recording, and so on. There is also a direct relationship with increasing concerns about the safety of victims, for example how they should be consulted, warned or protected when their abuser is about to be released (e.g. Home Office Special Conferences Unit, 1994, para. 59), or is being considered for release from custody. The probation service has a role to play in this but, within the service, opinions differ as to how far that role should extend.

In recognition that it is women who predominantly suffer abuse and who should be our priority, this chapter will begin with a consideration of the probation role with them. It will then turn to a detailed consideration of general probation work with abusers.

THE PROBATION ROLE WITH WOMEN

As victims/survivors of abuse

Probation services already work with women who have been or who are being abused, either directly as service users or indirectly as partners and family members of offenders (as well as in family court welfare: see Chapter 7.) Throughout this work, officers need to take a believing approach, to make it clear that the man's behaviour is his responsibility, is criminal and unacceptable, and to place a high priority on the woman's safety by telling her about Women's Aid, respecting the vital confidentiality of her whereabouts when she is attempting to evade detection by her abuser, never passing on an address or even the location of a new school without her express permission, and so on. All the above applies to all probation staff, including those in hostels – who will clearly hear the man's side of the story and may be urged by him not to take his offence seriously, or requested to contact his partner regardless of bail or injunction conditions (ACOP, 1992, para. 4.5.2) – and administrative staff who might be contacted by the man or his solicitor for apparently innocent information. All service staff need proper support and training about the nature and dangers of abuse, and the role they can play in helping women and children to be safe. The women partners of defendants and of prisoners could be positively supported through the provision of general information about the criminal nature of abuse and the help available, for example in posters and leaflets for helplines and women's support agencies displayed in prison and court waiting areas and women's toilets. Probation could exert influence through liaison arrangements to achieve this. ACOP (ibid., para. 4.1.10) also advises the placing of posters in probation premises themselves, both to advertise sources of help and to indicate that the problem is being taken seriously. ACOP (ibid., para. 4.1) recognises that women will need to make different choices at different stages of the abuse and that it is unhelpful to hold, or impose, a view of what they 'ought' to do.

Tuck (1994, para. 23) is reported as seeing the national failure to provide sufficient refuge places as 'tantamount to aiding and abetting crime'; this argument could be extended to cover any failure by probation officers to help individual women who wish to do so to use refuges or other women's groups and support agencies, as well as any failure to confront their abusers. This is because domestic violence is typically a repeat crime (Lloyd, *et al.*, 1994, p.3; Morley and Mullender, 1994b, p.5) and active steps are needed to prevent it from continuing and escalating. Probation staff require a basic working knowledge of women's housing and benefits rights (or, at the very least, access to sound advice on these matters), as well as a willingness to play an advocacy role in obtaining these by providing letters or access to a telephone, together with personal support, for example. Women may also need advice and support in using the criminal law to deter abusers and/or the civil law to seek protection them from abusers. Police domestic violence units and other initiatives increasingly respond to the needs of victims, and the probation service could also strengthen its role considerably. For example, if an abused woman is being interviewed about her future safety during pre-sentence report preparation on her partner's violence towards her (Geraghty, 1994, para. 140), then the probation officer has a potential advisory and support role with the victim. It is important, however, not to usurp the role of specialist agencies in this respect, but to help women establish contact with others who have the experience most likely to meet their safety, legal or advocacy needs (e.g. Women's Aid, other women's organisations including those specifically for Black women, and sympathetic solicitors; see also Viney, 1994, para. 51).

Women should receive the same respectful and supportive approach, however many times it needs to be offered. Leaving an abuser is rarely straightforward or safe and many women are forced by the man or by practical obstacles to return on one or many occasions. Probation officers, like social workers, need a sympathetic understanding of this process and should never give in to feelings of despondency or of personal affront: 'after all I did for her ... '. It is not the officer who has to live with the threat of escalating violence, or the other pressures involved in near impossible decisions.

Considerable attention is currently being paid in probation circles to the agency's role in relation to victims generally, including the past victims of men in prison. Public interest in victims is being heightened by national reporting of cases, such as that on Christmas Day 1994 of a woman shot dead at home by her ex-husband (BBC Radio 4, 26th December 1994, *World at One*). Her killer, Philip Manning, had been released from prison two months earlier, after serving just over two years of a four-year sentence for her attempted murder (which followed her leaving him; she divorced him while he was in prison). The family knew Manning had been released because he tried to re-establish contact through his mother-in-law. Neither official warning of release nor police protection is routinely available in such cases; nor was there any scope to limit or refuse full remission of sentence for good behaviour, even though the perpetrator still posed a known threat to his victim (*Guardian*, 27th December 1994). The case also led to renewed calls for courts to be given new powers at the time of sentence to impose restrictions on offenders following release (Labour Party policy reported in the media, sources as above).

In the past, there have been accusations of direct probation implication in cases of repeat violence where abusers continued to pose a threat during or after a prison sentence. In 1990, for example, Keith Ward of Bradford, who had killed before, was sentenced to life imprisonment for murdering Valerie Middleton while on weekend home leave from a two-year prison sentence for wounding her (source: campaign group notes). A campaign group, formed after her death by the relatives of both Ward's victims, questioned the process by which the probation service came to nominate Valerie Middleton's address instead of a probation hostel for the leave, and whether any pressure had been placed upon her by an officer anxious to make viable arrangements for Ward's eventual release, given that she was frightened of Ward and had initially refused to see him. Prior to this, there had been no letters between them for some months. This was certainly a case with a very high risk factor and evidence of a woman thinking twice about the relationship, where extreme caution would have been advisable. The campaign group called for home leave never to be to a victim's home, not least so that she never has to take the responsibility for denying her abuser leave, and for leave always to be supervised. Wider evidence of women's complaints about probation assumptions that they will take back abusive partners, and about lack of consultation, come from research in Northern Ireland by McWilliams and McKiernan (1993, p.96). Women in that study particularly feared the release of their abusers from prison without warning. The ACOP position statement of 1992 recognised that women will be under pressure from their imprisoned abusers to continue relationships they themselves have decided to end. It states: 'Staff need to be very careful to ensure that in their concern to resettle prisoners on release, they do not themselves put pressure on abused women to have their partners home' (ACOP, 1992, para. 4.4.4). Conversely, it recognises the right of women to make their own choices whether or not to take men back, and to receive help in safety planning.

Considerations of risk to victims – in relation to requests for bail, remand visits, pre-sentence reports, supervision in the community, leave and parole applications, other release planning, and pre- and post-release supervision (including licence conditions) – are literally of life-and-death importance. Initial and ongoing assessments need to be scrupulously free of prejudices against women that feed into abusers' denial and minimisation of what they have done; they must also be based on taking men's threats seriously – never underestimating what abusers will do to exert control over women or, if that fails, to extract revenge. The ACOP position statement (1992, para. 4.4.8) warns probation officers, including those based in prisons, to be alert to the offence a remanded man is charged with, so as to avoid colluding with any attempt to contact a woman he has abused for the purpose of intimidating her into withdrawing co-operation with the prosecution process. Other safety considerations, in respect of bail, include the recommendation of a hostel or other accommodation away from the woman, or verification of any alternative address proposed by the man (para. 4.5.1). None of these options is as safe for the woman as the man being in custody.

As offenders

There may also be contact with women prosecuted and/or sentenced for offences of violence against a partner, male or female. The possibility should always be considered that her partner was abusing her and that she was defending herself or trying to stop the abuse from continuing to escalate (see section on 'mutual fighting' in Chapter 1). This is important because, even though the woman may now have been convicted as an offender, unless she has killed her partner, her safety could well still be at risk. The situation cannot just be dealt with on the simple basis that she is a perpetrator and he is a victim. ACOP (ibid., para. 4.1.9) recognises women's need for advice about Women's Aid and other sources of safety information, as well as the advisability of allocation to different supervising officers where both the woman and her abuser are supervisees. This overlapping of 'care' and 'control' functions was touched on by Walker (1994, p.32) at a Home Office conference, when contrasting his experience as Governor of Styal, a women's prison, with his previous work with male offenders. More than half the women at Styal had experienced abuse, in childhood or adulthood or both, so that most inmates were both victims *and* offenders (presumably often having committed far less serious crimes than they had suffered). Where the abuse was current or recent, prison in fact offered protection for the women – hence the remark by one woman who killed her abuser that she initially felt freer on a life sentence than she had in her relationship (*Women Who Kill*, broadcast on Network First, Yorkshire Television, 11th January 1994). This remark also puts into perspective the imprisoning nature of the isolation and control imposed on women by abusive men, which has been compared with slavery or 'involuntary servitude', against which harsher legal sanctions may be imposed (McConnell, 1991). Disclosures in prison of abuse have relevance to probation officers in their throughcare and aftercare work; women might well also need assistance to be safe after prison, which might involve information about Women's Aid, help with rehousing in another area, advice on the use of the civil law if the man reabuses, and so on.

Women may also be in contact with the probation service as a result of an offence of any kind, for example dishonesty, that was committed under duress – at the behest of the abuser. If the officer writing a pre-sentence report wins the woman's trust and this fact is revealed, the coercion or threats can be included in the report. Attention to the woman's safety needs, with the involvement of Women's Aid and/or the police if she so chooses, is likely to be particularly important under such circumstances unless (and only whilst) the abuser is in custody. This is by no means to collude with the stereotype that women offend because they are weak and cannot help themselves, but to recognise that there *are* incidences in which actual or threatened violence from an abuser plays a real causal role in a woman's behaviour. The law itself makes allowance for the fact that, although the woman retained choices about her own behaviour in such circumstances, those choices may have been constrained.

WORK WITH MEN

Sentencing[2]

Probation officers are not unused to representing a range of interests when they write pre-sentence reports. They clearly work to the courts, and hence to wider society. They do so in a climate increasingly politicised by a government determined not to be seen as 'soft' on crime. Commenting on seriousness, attitude to offence, risk, and the location of the victim require them to have regard for victims' safety and the wider public good. Where the offender is concerned, there is likely to be a balancing of many factors, including the researched impact of various sentencing options in reducing or increasing risk of further offending, and the consideration of community alternatives to custody where appropriate.

All reports on offences related to domestic abuse must reflect their seriousness (ACOP, 1992, para. 4.2.1), grounded not just in the nature and circumstances of the actions on this occasion but in an appreciation (see earlier chapters) of the unremitting terror and frequently escalating violence and sexual degradation to which women are subjected by their abusers. Particular knowledge and skill are needed in seeing through men's characteristic denial and minimisation in order to avoid collusion (ibid.). It may well be important to talk to the victim and/or witnesses in order to hear another side of the story. Reading a case study by a student recently, where she appeared to feel sorry for an offender who blamed his actions on the distress caused to him by his ex-partner's behaviour, I was not surprised to read a few pages later that the woman concerned had previously accused him of rape. The details of his account did not hang together and had all the hallmarks of a man combining denial of responsibility with victim blaming. This is not to say that we should prejudge, but that we should be sceptical and confronting. Had a report been needed on that particular man, related to abuse, it would have needed to start from the point that neither his feelings nor anything his partner might have done could excuse his behaviour towards her. Nor do external stress factors or personal weaknesses ever excuse men's abuse of women. A pre-sentence report should not be couched in terms that appear to legitimise the abuse by placing the blame anywhere other than with the man, or that minimise its seriousness for the victim, for any children in the household or for society, or that collude with victim blaming or other gender stereotyping. ACOP (ibid.) recognises the need 'to be vigilant to identify explanations and mitigation for the offence that demean women' and to obtain an account of it independent of the accused's. The position statement (ibid.) suggests that this vigilance may require a particular effort on the part of male officers because many abusers are 'plausible' and 'agreeable' in manner to other men and, of course, sexual violence is not an ever-present threat for most men as it is for women. Proposals in the report as to disposal need to be based on considerations of the victim's safety, in consultation with the woman herself, for example by recommending the man's residence in a probation hostel (ibid., para. 4.2.3). Other factors to consider are the seriousness of the particular offence and of this type of offence overall, and the best chance of changing the man's behaviour without placing the woman at risk in the meantime.

The establishment of groups for abusive men is beginning to offer a new sentencing option, although they are not uncontroversial (see Chapter 9, this volume). The debates as to how this option should be used were first thoroughly aired in Britain in relation to the CHANGE project in Stirling. Diversion from sentencing was rejected in that instance, even though the Procurator Fiscal (equivalent of the Crown Prosecution Service) had wanted it. Prosecution and stiffer sentences that reflect the seriousness of domestic abuse for the women concerned, and for all women, are already hard to achieve. Diversion from prosecution or sentencing is not acceptable in relation to crimes of sexual violence – precisely because the struggle to get the criminal justice system to take them seriously has not, as yet, been won (still only a tiny minority of offences lead to prosecution) – even though probation officers may properly argue for them in other circumstances. (This is a divergence from ACOP, 1992, para. 4.6.1, which accepts diversion on the same basis as for other crimes of violence, despite the differential prosecution and sentencing record which the document does recognise in the following paragraph.)

Diversion from custody has always been a fundamental aim of the probation service. It may cause controversy, therefore, when women's activists advocate prison for abusers (Dixon, 1992, p.40, responding to Horley, 1990), even if their aim is to see scarce community resources devoted to abused women rather than abusive men (see Chapter 9, this volume). In fact, prison is rarely the outcome of abuse, since, of the relatively few incidents that are prosecuted, typical outcomes have always been disproportionately light – for example, fines or binding over (Dixon, 1992, p.40). There are other reasons why women activists may advocate more custodial sentences. Firstly, prison does keep women safe from abusive men for a time (which is also relevant in respect of remand versus bail decisions, of course, and to the requests of remanded men for visits from their partners – which may be used to try and persuade or coerce the woman not to co-operate with prosecution: McWilliams and McKiernan, 1993, p.97). Secondly, imprisonment – as Britain's harshest sentence – can 'raise the stakes' and show domestic violence being taken more seriously by the courts.

However, this brings us up sharply against our knowledge of the impact of imprisonment. Prison currently does not change men or stop them re-offending; rather, it is likely to reaffirm sexist and controlling attitudes (ACOP, in House of Commons, 1992b, Memorandum 6, p.38). Walker admits (1994, p.32) to having been little concerned with victims during his work in male prisons (though there is no reason why this could not change; see section on throughcare, below). ACOP (in House of Commons, 1992b, Memorandum 6, p.38) would prefer to see probation officers undertaking work with abusers in the community and the men kept away from the negative influence of prison. If the woman can be helped to be safe and the man confronted to change without his going to prison, then diversion from custody is less controversial, since both seriousness and protection will have been considered (Geraghty, 1994, para. 140) – provided that the man is *required* to attend an abusers' group as part of a sentence supervised by the probation service (typically as a condition of a probation order) and subject to the critique of the ways in which groups are established and evaluated, as explored in Chapter 9, this volume. The reoffending rates of men in such groups, and the ineffectiveness of injunctions in protecting women when their abusers remain in the community, are both relevant in this regard and make it always a risky strategy.

The increasing move towards the probation service working in partnership with voluntary agencies is of relevance here, in that some abusers' groups (e.g. that offered by the Domestic Violence Intervention Project in London) are run by voluntary organisations but accept men who are required by the court to attend and who are supervised by a probation officer throughout the period of their attendance. It may be easier to have such groups run in conjunction with parallel services for women – both to meet specific needs and to help women stay safe while their partners are in the group – than to have probation-run groups that will need to build links with Women's Aid instead, and may be able to offer only limited contact with the men's partners.

Certainly, where a well-planned and monitored abusers' group is running, under whatever aegis, it can offer a useful additional sentencing option, including where prison would not have been considered by the court. (The evaluation of the CHANGE and Lothian abusers' programmes in Scotland is comparing their impact with that of other court disposals such as fines, probation and prison; the evaluation report is due from the Central Research Unit of the Scottish Office in June 1996: Dobash *et al*. 1996.) Anger control or management groups are not an acceptable alternative as they are not relevant to men's abuse of women (Geraghty, 1994, para. 146; see also Chapter 9, this volume); these men are fully in control of the victim they target, for example, and their so-called 'anger' is actually a need to dominate and control.

Probation officers making proposals to the courts do so in respect of specific offences. Domestic violence does not fit well into this model because, whereas offending is dealt with as an incident or a series of incidents that are punished, abuse is experienced as a process, protracted and compounded over time; this is partially reflected in recent thinking referring to it as 'the repeat crime par excellence' (Tuck, 1994, p.5). Probation officers may need to find ways to comment on this in their sentencing proposals (Perrott, 1994, p.138) and can draw on research in so doing (Lloyd *et al.*, 1994, p.3; summary in Morley and Mullender, 1994, p.5). The repeat nature of sexually violent crime is reflected in the exemption of violent and sex offences from the 1991 Criminal Justice Act policy of making sentences reflect the seriousness of the *specific* offences on which they are passed. Persistent offenders in these categories can be treated more punitively 'if this is necessary to protect the public from serious harm' (Home Office, 1990). This public need for protection might, however, be more apparent to the court in cases of stranger attacks on a series of victims than in intimate relationships where couples may still be assumed by lawyers and judges to contribute jointly to their problems (see Chapter 7, this volume). There is a need for monitoring of the application of this principle in sentencing and for the point to be argued in court in domestic abuse cases – if not through the agency of probation, then through the Crown Prosecution Service and the legal profession. For example, men pursue their earlier domestic abuse victims (with increased risks: see Chapter 2, this volume) *and* are abusive in subsequent relationships (e.g. Keith Ward: see above).

SUPERVISION

The probation officer supervising an offender has considerable freedom in the choice of theoretical model used and the development of a personal style of work. Everything in this book and in this chapter should be taken to indicate, however, that only a feminist (or, for men, pro-feminist) model of analysis and intervention can provide an adequate platform for work with domestic abusers. It is on this basis that a firm stand is urged in relation to abuse revealed during the course of supervision resulting from an unconnected offence (together with action to safeguard the victim). McWilliams and McKiernan (1993, p.96) report, for example, the anger of a woman who fled to a refuge during the time her partner was on probation who was never even contacted by his probation officer to ask about the assaults on her. Work done during the order, too, on accepting responsibility for criminal behaviour and working to change it, can encompass disclosures of abusiveness to a partner as well as the original offences (ACOP, 1992, para. 4.3.1; McWilliams and McKiernan, 1993, p.97). This is particularly valuable in respect of forms and patterns of abuse that do not lend themselves to intervention by other criminal justice agencies because they do not constitute one-off instances of identifiably assaultive violence.

Where the abuse is the index offence, it is equally crucial to keep the focus of work on the abuse as criminal behaviour and actively to resist collusion with denial of responsibility (including through victim blaming: 'She wound me up'; see Chapter 2, this volume) or minimisation of reported impact. Any such representations of what has occurred should be challenged in exactly the same way as an abusers' group would do – for example by making the man give details of precisely what happened, what he did, and how he harmed his partner (and often the children). Should any further incident of physical or sexual violence occur, or be revealed, during the currency of an order, then ACOP (1992, para. 4.3.2) advises that the officer should consider reporting it to the police on the same basis of 'seriousness' as would apply to any other offence. This is a contentious area, however, since judgements about degrees of seriousness may relate more to expectations of when the criminal justice system might be expected to take action than to the abuse itself, which is *always* serious in the context of a pattern of intimidation of the woman concerned. The officer can also consider initiating breach proceedings on the basis of failure to be of good behaviour. Both forms of response will convey to the man that abusive behaviour, as criminal behaviour, is unacceptable and will be treated as such.

There is, of course, no co-worker present in individual interviews, as there often is in groupwork, to help the officer hold to this confrontative style of work, so good supervision by a senior officer may be particularly important. Peer consultancy, special interest groups, training events and other measures may also assist staff to refine their skills and constantly to re-examine their own attitudes, including in working with Black abusers (whom staff may find it easier to blame) and with gay abusers (whose experience of homophobia puts their abuse in a particular context, whilst not excusing it: see Chapter 1, this volume). Male officers particularly may need challenging to avoid unintentional collusion with abusers (for example, when they deny full responsibility by alleging provocation: 'You know what women are like!'). Supervising officers also have personal support needs which can be met in the above variety of ways, and in single-sex and other groups. For female officers, and for female or gay male officers who have themselves been abused in intimate relationships, for example, the work will carry a particularly high personal price when the abuser speaks in a misogynist and/or homophobic tone, shows a lack of respect, or is directly verbally abusive to her or him. (See Perrott, 1994, pp.148–9 and *passim*, for a helpful development of the impact on, and issues for, women staff in working with sexual violence.)

Increasingly, officers will find themselves supervising men who are simultaneously working their way through an abusers' group (see Chapter 9, this volume). It will be important to reinforce the messages from the group, preferably by becoming well informed about the work undertaken there and the progress of this particular offender, so that the groupwork and the individual work reinforce each other's influence for change. The supervising officer may also have a role with the female partner during this time. Women whose abusers are being worked with by the CHANGE project in Scotland (which has no separate probation service), for example, are involved by the social workers holding the probation orders in reviewing the men's progress. Also, it is sometimes the social worker who takes the woman information about the men's group and the local help available to her.

Typically, groups resist allowing men to raise issues that can lead into excuses for the abuse, keeping the focus instead on the abuse itself and the responsibility for change. This usually includes avoiding discussion of the man's family of origin (so as to avert 'It's not my fault, I was abused as a child' diversions from the work in the here and now; see Chapter 2 for a questioning of this deterministic assumption). The supervising officer is free to undertake careful work on issues important to the man that the group does not or cannot cover, provided that this does not undermine the group. For example, work on current parenting behaviour may be informed by, but not pre-determined by, the man's own childhood memories (see description of parenting groups in Chapter 6), and could be undertaken with a man who might otherwise pose a risk of over-chastising his children. Similarly, many abusers' groups see alcohol use as an excuse for, not a cause of, domestic abuse (see Chapter 2) and consequently do not focus on it in the group. Work on alcohol misuse, including through referral to another group or programme, could therefore feature in supervision. (An exception to the above is the Lothian project which has responded to the very high rate of alcohol misuse in Scotland by building an element on it into the abusers' group; this does not constitute a full course of counselling or group treatment, however.)

If the supervising officer does refer the abuser to any group or resource other than an abusers' group, it is important to check that the messages conveyed are the same as his or her own. Anger management programmes are not appropriate for abusers because they often reinforce the perception that women 'trigger' abuse and that domestic abuse represents men's loss of control. In fact, it represents the epitome of control and of choice of target. It could be very relevant for the man to learn how to be assertive rather than aggressive, but not in any context that presents aggression as interactional. It might be safer to include assertiveness and other communication skills in individual work, and to locate the discussion within an analysis of, and challenge to, stereotypical gender power dynamics. Where family- or couple-related work is considered during the course of an order, all the warnings in Chapter 7 apply. Such work is not appropriate when the female partner is in current danger.

THROUGHCARE AND AFTERCARE

There have been calls for work on domestic violence in prisons (Home Office Special Conferences Unit, 1994, paras 59 and 165) and for work on sexual violence more widely with men in custody (Home Department *et al.*, 1993, Cm 2269, para. 71). There is no inherent reason why abusers' groups could not be run in prison (one example is in HM Prison Walton), and be jointly designed and/or run by probation staff. In this way, some of the concerns to be explored in Chapter 9 would be answered, for example victims would be safe while men were confronted, and money from budgets previously untapped for this purpose and not available for women's services would have to be found. Effectiveness would presumably be no less than in groups in the community, but would be harder to measure in the short-term because the victim is artificially protected and cannot provide the crucial perspective on behaviour change in the man; he will claim to have changed and may be judged primarily on level of compliance (Geraghty, 1994, para. 151). The major problem would therefore be accountability to women in the wider sense because it would be hard to keep such groups to a feminist agenda in male-dominated custodial settings.

Women may be less safe from their abusers while the latter are serving terms of imprisonment than in the past. Many prisoners now have access to telephone cards with unmonitored use and may use these to harass or threaten partners and ex-partners. Outgoing mail is no longer read and, similarly, may contain threats about what the man plans to do during his leave or on release. (An example of this was reported in the press in relation to a stranger attack: *Daily Express*, 20th April 1995, p.10.)

Although letters containing threats or abusive material breach prison guidelines, they can lead to loss of remission of sentence only if they come to official notice. The woman recipient may be too frightened to inform the prison authorities, but there may be times when a probation officer comes to hear about the matter and could take action. An alternative scenario is that the man may be writing or telephoning to make unrealistic promises to the woman, claiming to have changed in order to persuade her to take him back – with a high risk of reabuse. Membership of an abusers' group during a sentence could actually facilitate such claims, hence making it particularly important to keep female partners informed about membership of such groups, the work done in them, and their lack of guaranteed effectiveness (see Chapter 9). A probation officer who is in touch with a woman under such circumstances needs to inform her of the low success rates of abusers' groups, of the complete lack of predictable success in any individual case, of the continuing need for a safety plan in case of reabuse (who to call, where to go, whose help to enlist, and so on), and of the role and contact numbers of Women's Aid and other support organisations for women. Any woman whose partner goes through a group in prison should be given this information.

The National Inter-Agency Working Party on Domestic Violence (Victim Support, 1992, para. 2.52) called for sentence planning and release planning between the probation and prison services to begin from the date of imprisonment (see also ACOP, 1992, para. 4.4.3). Government moves towards longer sentences and a longer proportion of sentences to be served may give more opportunity to do this. The 1991 Criminal Justice Act in England and Wales made provision, for example, that in relation to offences involving sex, violence, drugs or arson, parole is only exceptionally granted and only for the last few months of sentence. Parole boards pay due attention to probation and other reports which comment not only on the offender's attitude towards the offence and the victim, but also on the attitudes of the victim or their family and of the local community towards releasing the offender on licence. Domestic abuse victims are amongst those it is most important to consult prior to home leave or release, and to keep informed. Home Office Circular 60/1990, a set of guidelines issued to all Chief Police Officers in England and Wales on the subject of domestic violence, recommended that, wherever possible, the police should advise a woman of her abuser's release from custody – thus recognising that she could well be in continued or even increased danger from him. Similarly, the ACOP *Position Statement on Domestic Violence* (1992, para. 4.4.1) refers to the high risk of women dying at the hands of their abusers. It calls for victims' safety and decisions for the future to be central factors in release planning and supervision and for threats by men imprisoned for offences of domestic violence to be taken seriously (paras 4.4.1–4.4.2). A man who has abused his wife for years may well blame her for his imprisonment or for any delay in leave or release. He may also be determined to continue his previous control over her life, and perhaps wish to extract vengeance if she has entered into another relationship. He is likely to place her in great danger unless measures are taken to prevent this, for example through the use of licence conditions. This danger may also extend to other family members. One perpetrator told his son on a contact visit following his release from prison for injuring his wife that he would kill the boy's grandparents. The man's ex-wife and the family's social worker saw undone all their good work of many months, while the man had been in prison, as the boy became very unsettled and began to have nightmares. His father later appeared outside the house while the whole family was there, brandishing a weapon.

Automatic conditional release now gives probation officers responsibility for supervising many offenders who have made no application for parole (which might have involved some element of choice about accepting restrictions and accountability for their actions). The terms of their licence may have conditions written into it that the officer is also responsible for supervising. These could be imposed in an attempt, for example, to keep a dangerous abuser away from his ex-partner and may raise safety implications both for her and for the officer supervising the man. Any threats the man makes while on supervision will need to be taken seriously and supervision should be geared to confronting him to accept responsibility for his abuse and for the need to change. This may involve partnership work with other agencies. The survivor of the man's abuse may also need to be contacted during this time and kept aware of the man's whereabouts and behaviour, as well as being helped to consider and meet her own safety needs. Research has highlighted women's fear of unnotified release (McWilliams and McKiernan, 1993, p.96), as well as their wish for their safety to be considered in release planning and for wives and partners of imprisoned abusers to have a contact point. (The Government's 'Victims' hotline' is intended to go some way towards providing this; the probation service could also have a role in this respect.) If reabuse does occur after release, or is threatened during or after the man's prison term, it should be treated extremely seriously and appropriate action taken, including breach where relevant.

All of the above section has relevance to women whose abusers go to prison for offences not connected with the abuse, making it essential that prison and probation staff should be aware of domestic violence in *all* sentence and release planning, and in relation to all contact between prisoners and their partners.

WAYS FORWARD: ACTION ON A SERVICE-WIDE LEVEL

The National Association of Probation Officers has been critically concerned with sexual violence and abuse since an AGM resolution in 1988, and local branches have established working groups, invited speakers (e.g Dixon, 1992, p.40, writing in London) and organised conferences; for example, the Otterburn conference organised by the Northumbria branch of the National Association of Probation Officers focused on domestic violence in 1995. This work needs to continue apace and to encompass every aspect of probation work, not just groups for abusers. Nationally, gender (and race) issues have been raised by section 95 of the 1991 Criminal Justice Act and by wider work in the service and in the Probation Inspectorate on developing appropriate services for women.

The ACOP position statement of 1992 represents major progress on domestic violence specifically, leading on from David Sleightholm's involvement in a national inter-agency working party (Victim Support, 1992), because it gives a lead to the whole service on taking men's abuse of women seriously as criminal behaviour. (Gaps remain because the ACOP position statement does not cover single-sex relationship abuse, or women who are charged with offences after injuring or killing their abusers, for example.) The next stage is to bring widescale attitudes and professional behaviour into line with the statement and, at the same time, to develop and disseminate best practice. Individual services need to begin by adopting one or all of the following: a policy, a strategy or action plan, and a set of good practice guidelines. The ACOP position statement suggests a form of words to underpin local policy that requires staff to treat domestic violence on a par with other violence and to promote women's safety. Overall, there has been a tangible increase in special initiatives relating to domestic violence during the 1990s (ACOP in House of Commons, 1992b, Memorandum 6, p.37).

Training for staff at all levels is of crucial importance and could be organised on a multi-agency basis; the judiciary, magistrates, solicitors and barristers, the Crown Prosecution Service, and the police are amongst those with overlapping training needs. It is always important to consult Women's Aid in designing training, and offering free places to their staff can improve the quality of discussion on courses whilst also giving something back to an under-resourced agency whose work underpins all attempts to respond to domestic abuse. There are now training and information packs available from sources such as the London Borough of Hammersmith and Fulham (1991) and the Leeds Inter-Agency Project (1993). Training can also make useful links with skills and knowledge used in working with sex offenders (Loewenstein, 1992; Hirst, 1994), currently a more widely recognised field of expertise in probation work. Training and policy making needs to encompass the way in which the service treats its own staff, who may be, firstly, the current victims or the survivors of domestic abuse (and hence may require advice and support, or may not wish to work with abusers) or, secondly, the perpetrators, because domestic abuse is such an under-reported, under-recorded and under-prosecuted offence.

The Association of Chief Officers of Probation has a Gender Action Group which, in turn, now has a working group on domestic violence (ACOP *Information Bulletin*, 25th March 1994, item 61/94). The group is establishing an information base and hopes to help services learn from one another. Some probation services, such as Merseyside and South Yorkshire (both represented on the working group), have assigned special responsibility within the service for domestic violence: Merseyside has two probation officers and a senior in this role, while South Yorkshire has linked their designated senior with family court welfare so that the concerns about abused women's safety reflected in National Standards (see Chapter 7, this volume) are brought across into criminal work. A range of action is possible; for example, Northumbria held a conference in March 1994, and concerned people in probation are writing on the subject, both specifically (e.g. Dixon, 1992; Stelman, 1993) and in the wider context of a feminist analysis of male abuse of women and children (Perrott, 1994). Though rarely the prime mover (Peterborough being one exception), probation is one of the statutory agencies most regularly and actively represented in inter-agency forums (see Chapter 10, this volume); this is often linked with the establishment of abusers' groups. Domestic abuse is also increasingly being taken up as a crime prevention issue, in relation to violence and violent death (ACOP written evidence in House of Commons, 1992b, Memorandum 6, pp.36 and 37; Geraghty, 1994, para. 151), with probation services working in conjunction with the police, local authority community safety units in some areas, voluntary sector agencies such as Crime Concern (Korn, 1993), and Safer Cities initiatives. Finally, probation research and information staff could play a key role in gathering and disseminating data to improve all aspects of practice in relation to domestic abuse, including that available from other agencies.

CONCLUSION

Domestic abuse remains a submerged issue in much of probation work, with negative or ambivalent attitudes still in evidence. Increasing national and local attention poses a timely challenge to reconsider its relevance throughout every aspect of the service's concerns, and not just in the well-publicised specialist initiatives such as the abusers' groups, which will be considered in the next chapter. Although perpetrators are typically resistant to change, it is vitally important that they are not supported in their abusive behaviour by the witting or unwitting collusion of probation officers. By persistently confronting the abuser's behaviour and attitudes through words and deeds, the probation officer will be sending an important message that society will no longer tolerate men's violent control of women. This will, of course, be all the more effective when criminal justice responses more generally have a greater impact on men who abuse women, by subjecting them to more serious charges and sentences (see Chapter 1). Probation officers, through their wider work with sex offenders, have a sound understanding of the processes of denial and minimisation which they can appropriately apply to domestic abusers. They can certainly become part of the solution to the problem of domestic violence.

Chapter 9

The men who abuse
What kind of intervention in groups?

Thus far, this book has clearly established men's responsibility for the grave and protracted abuse of large numbers of women in all sectors of society and throughout the world. It has also shown how this abuse causes untold suffering to the children who live with it and is often linked with direct child abuse. Given that we know this enormous harm is being perpetrated by men, it seems an indictment that, in the past, there has been so little concern or direct intervention focused on violent men. Now, this is beginning to alter. The $64,000 question is being asked in Britain: can anything effective be done to help, persuade or require these men to change their unacceptable behaviours and attitudes?

There are practical as well as ethical reasons for seeking such solutions. The criminal justice system is arresting and prosecuting increasing numbers of abusive men (though still only a tiny proportion of those who constitute the problem), in line with the decision to regard domestic violence as a crime like any other (see, for example, Home Department *et al.*, 1993, Cm 2269, para. 76 and Chapter 1, this volume), and consequently a greater range of disposals is needed to deal with them. Courts welcome more constructive sentencing options and, as a bonus, may learn more about domestic abuse through utilising them (Smith, 1989, p.70). Women may be more inclined to pursue incidents through the criminal justice system if they believe this will lead to treatment for their abusers (ibid., citing Canadian sources: Sinclair, 1985 and MacLeod, 1987). Probation officers in England and Wales, social workers in Scotland, workers in men's projects throughout the UK, and academic observers (Dominelli *et al.* 1995) also feel that something should be done about men who abuse and reabuse in the same or sequential relationships. As a result, practitioners are increasingly establishing groups and projects to which abusers can be sent by professional colleagues, by the courts, and/or by their own volition. Government backing has been given to a continuation and cautious increase of probation and related work with perpetrators, and to work with abusers in prisons (Home Department *et al.*, 1993, Cm 2269, paras 71 and 76–7, though see below for a discussion of problems with the model suggested).

This intervention is not uncontroversial, with key feminist concerns focusing around the methodology and philosophy underpinning groups, accountability to women, efficacy in achieving change in men in the shorter and longer term, and resourcing. With such work still in its infancy in Britain, this is an appropriate time to ask questions under each of these headings. Do the groups actively challenge the myths and denial that so characterise male abuse? Are they answerable to survivors and to women more widely for their standards? Do they genuinely help women to be safer? And do they take resources away from services to survivors, that is from women, in order to give them to men? It is certainly easier for male authorities in the political and criminal justice worlds to slot work with abusers under a law and order heading and to avoid considering the issues from a woman's (let alone a feminist) viewpoint, than to support services for, and hear the demands of, women. Founders of and workers in the men's projects, on the other hand, reply that women will never be safe unless work is undertaken with male perpetrators and that, without groups, no other sentencing option currently confronts men's attitudes or abusive behaviour.

THE CURRENT BRITISH CONTEXT

In Britain, the agencies most likely to establish projects for abusive men are voluntary bodies and probation settings. Currently, there are at least a dozen organisations actively running groups; group co-ordinators and others interested in establishing initiatives have been meeting in a loose network since May 1992. (Its mailing list is one source of the listing which follows, supplemented by personal contacts and other reporting, e.g. Lees and Lloyd, 1994, pp.48–51.) This network has recently produced a statement of principles to encourage best practice. They emphasise women's and children's safety, co-operation with services for women, and the lack of any guarantee that men will change, within a pro-feminist and anti-discriminatory framework.

Geographical locations of projects known to the author (though it must be recognised that, as relatively new developments, the list of these is constantly changing) cluster as follows. Scottish groups are: CHANGE in Central Region (voluntary sector, housed in Stirling University, taking court-mandated referrals); the Lothian Domestic Violence Probation Project (DVPP, sited in Lothian Social Work Department, Edinburgh, as part of its probation responsibilities); and Stop Male Violence (linked to Strathclyde Social Work Department in Glasgow). The London groups are all in the independent sector: the Everyman Centre is a men-only, self-referral initiative which initially received Urban Programme funding channelled through West Lambeth Health Authority (and may recently have foundered); the Men's Centre charges men considerable fees to attend groups and/or individual work with trained counsellors and psychotherapists; and the Violence Prevention Programme (VPP) for Men is part of the Domestic Violence Intervention Project (DVIP), a voluntary body which, together with a related Women's Support Service, is part of a multi-agency domestic violence forum. In the voluntary sector in the Midlands: PAX in Kidderminster is part of an inter-agency initiative and is contactable via the Community Health Council; Nottingham AGENDA is a men's group initiative which has made some response to early feminist criticism; and Fresh Start was set up to be coterminous with the West Midlands police area so as to combine court and probation with self-referrals. In the north, the main activity is in the voluntary sector with a number of MOVE (Men Overcoming Violence) men's self-help groups – the best known in Bolton (see Waring and Wilson, 1990), with others having run in Greater Manchester, Leeds and Dewsbury – as well as the Worth Project in Keighley, which is part of a domestic violence forum and hence the only one in this immediate region with formal links with women's groups. Working with its own clients, the Northumbria Probation Service is developing a programme within an inter-agency structure, whilst a Merseyside probation project also offers some support for the men's partners. Both are influenced by the need to challenge men's power and control. In the south-west, the voluntary sector is again to the fore: Everyman Plymouth operates short-term groups following individual sessions, along the lines of its namesake in London, and a Barnardo's project operating a Family Centre in Bristol sometimes offers groups. No doubt there are other developments elsewhere. The CHANGE project in Scotland is working on a directory of projects.

Differences in ethos and approach between groups include the source of referrals – ranging from CHANGE, with only court-mandated participation, to the self-referred men's groups (and some groups, such as the Violence Prevention Programme for Men of DVIP, combining both). Although most of the projects actually running are in the voluntary sector, new growth may well switch to probation now that there is Association of Chief Officers of Probation (ACOP) and Home Office backing for such work (Association of Chief Officers of Probation position paper dating from April 1992, with updated version in early 1996; and Home Department et al., 1993, Cm 2269). This may increase the link with the criminal justice system. At least a third of interested members of a nationwide network, with and without groups already running, have been coming from probation settings; these include Scottish social work departments, which encompass the functions of probation, and a prison (Barlinnie, which has a pioneering reputation for confrontative work with men). Rather more of the contact people work in the voluntary sector, but these include contexts linked with criminal justice such as Victim Support and an adult reparation bureau, as well as probation officers developing projects in their own time.

Another crucial difference between groups is the extent to which women have any say in how they are run. Amongst the fully established projects, there is sometimes only one in each region – DVIP, PAX, Worth – with formalised organisational integration with services for women, including Women's Aid. The men's projects are more of a law unto themselves – typically run by men for men. Although it is good to see men taking responsibility for working on men's violence and abuse, even when they claim to operate from a profeminist perspective many groups have few inbuilt safeguards against male collusion or empire building. Worse, many have not thought through the measures they should take to guarantee the safety of an abuser's partner during his membership of a group. In the statutory sector, male-dominated agendas may have something of the opposite effect in that men do not always show enough interest even to make unaccountable moves towards change. Many entries on the mailing list for those interested in setting up future abusers' groups in criminal justice agencies give a woman's name as the point of contact. This suggests that the probation service is leaving it to women to pursue this area of work, in what can be a very hostile environment for feminist ideals (Perrott, 1994). Here again, an inter-agency structure can prove the best way to link with and take a lead from women's organisations. The issues of accountability to women are complex and will be examined in greater detail later in this chapter.

METHODOLOGY AND PHILOSOPHY

The key issue in seeking a satisfactory groupwork model for abusers' groups is the extent to which they must work with men's denial and minimisation of what they have done. There is grave danger in adopting any approach that is not sufficiently confrontative in style and feminist in orientation to cope with the fact that much of what abusive men contribute in groups – until they are heavily challenged by the workers and by one another – is a gross distortion of reality.

Insight into the extent of this distortion and denial emerges from practice accounts and from research, such as the current study of men's perspectives on being violent to women being conducted in Bradford (Hearn, 1994). In a period of contact with 75 men and the agencies working with them, all but two of the men have talked to male interviewers about their violence. The focus includes not only who they are, what they have done and what has happened to them since, but also how they have made sense of events. Although their abuse runs the whole gamut – from shouting and written threats, to rape, kidnapping, torture, and murder – the men generally claim positive attitudes towards women. They also incorporate their abuse into their everyday lives: more than half in one account never found it hard to carry on with their usual activities between the attacks (ibid., p.52).

Denial and minimisation are of a high order and are shored up by the fact that expectations about women and heterosexual men are firmly rooted in wider social assumptions. Denial is shown to include forgetting, blanking out, and excluding particular sorts of abuse as not counting:

I wasn't violent, but she used to do my head in that much. I picked her up twice and threw her against the wall, and said 'Just leave it'. That's the only violence I've put towards her. I've never struck a woman, never, and I never will.

(ibid., p.6)

Only physical hitting tends to be acknowledged, not physical restraint, throwing, or sexual, verbal or emotional violence. Sexual violence is regarded not as violence but as sex, so is rarely mentioned; violence in response to her having sex elsewhere *is* violence but is understandable and hence normal. Minimisation includes playing down the definition, the extent, the frequency and the effects of abuse, for example the man's stating that he did less than he might have done, or than he is accused of doing, or than someone else would have done in his place. Other ploys include denying an abusive identity – 'I'm not a violent person', 'I'm not a wife beater' – or denying the intention: for example, claiming that the effects were worse because she ducked or fell down the steps. Violence may also be portayed as mutual fighting (see Chapter 1, this volume) and all the excuses we saw in Chapter 2 are employed: from abusive childhoods, drink, drugs, and psychiatric disturbance which explain away men's behaviour, to blaming it onto women's 'provocation' and failure to fulfil their allotted role, for example, being faithful, keeping the house and children and herself nice, and generally restricting her behaviour in ways he considers she should. What Hearn (1994, p.50) calls 'confessions' often lack remorse and merge into denial because they sound so normal; one man blamed the extent of his love. Men recruited to the study through abusers' groups were particularly prone to these confessions, which seriously calls into question how far they were really changing their attitudes as a result of group membership. Those research subjects recruited through individual contact with probation had gone less far, from outright denial into self-justification. These are men who believe themselves to be in the right and in the mainstream of social attitudes. As they progress through their careers of violence and their resulting contacts with the system (men who have escaped these are not in the study), they become more practised at telling their story and incorporating its internal inconsistencies into a widening repertoire of the mechanisms listed. It seems that agencies attempting direct work do get men to stop overt denial, i.e. to start talking about their violence, but not to believe in their responsibility for it (ibid., p.51). This may be the real challenge to those running abusers' groups: to ensure that their members are not just learning a new language with which to stay in control.

We also have confirmatory evidence from practice in Britain and North America that groups and practitioners dealing with individuals are battling at every turn with denial and minimisation of the most convoluted and entrenched kind. Jukes (1993, p.274), of the Men's Centre in London, writes:

> The extent of a batterer's denial, minimizing, projection and splitting, his capacity for self-deception, is quite something to see in an otherwise healthy man. It is not uncommon for a man to say during an initial consultation that he pushed his wife. Later, under persistent questioning, it will emerge that she happened to be at the top of the stairs at the time. Then, he will insist that he had not meant her to be so badly injured. When he begins to accept that maybe he had meant this, he will vehemently protest that she deserved it for the way she treated him.

Jukes has reached the conclusion from constant work with accounts of this kind that 'Any model which allows a battering man to evade responsibility for his violence will not succeed in helping him to stop' (ibid.). Only the most challenging of techniques are likely to work, whether these are utilised by professionals or peers (or both, since a good groupworker will draw on the confrontation of one member's lack of honesty by another). Some say it is easiest for the 'bullshit' to be confronted by ex-abusers (Waring and Wilson, 1990, e.g. p.102) and others consider that women groupworkers are hardest to con (pers. comms, e.g. with the Duluth-based Domestic Abuse Intervention Programme in the USA where two women sometimes co-lead groups). Women running a group in which they can utilise challenges from men who are beginning to change constitute a powerful combination; in one group the author observed, a participant remarked: 'If I can survive this, I can do anything!'

Male professionals, managers and policy makers are likely to have furthest to travel to see that abusers, although they do not believe themselves to be lying, are a million miles from telling the simple truth. We must be clear, with Jukes (1993, pp.272–3, giving an account of a therapist apparently persuaded to believe that a wife 'provoked' an attack in which her back was broken), that any lack of clarity in professional understanding feeds the denial. The only response must be constant and total challenge until the man accepts the reality of his behaviour, its consequences, and his direct responsibility for both. Official pronouncements are beginning to recognise this. A paper prepared for the National Council of Chief Officers of Probation (Sleightholm, 1991; this became the basis of the Association of Chief Officers of Probation position paper of 1992, updated in 1996) combines an emphasis on the urgent need for work with abusers to be undertaken with a clear statement that 'domestic violence cannot be addressed ... without dealing with the issue of male attitudes towards women. Domestic violence is an abuse of male power.'

Anyone seeking to establish a group for abusers is likely to look to

North America for models, because the work there has a 20-year history (Nosko and Wallace, 1988, p.33; Edleson and Tolman, 1992, pp.53–5) and is far more widespread, with around 500 programmes in the USA and over 100 in Canada by 1990 (Thorne-Finch, 1992, p.169). It is important not to adopt practice ideas unquestioningly from that context, however, not only because there are many approaches from which to choose but chiefly because, as has just been demonstrated, none is likely to be effective unless it is firmly grounded in the understanding about the nature and extent of male abuse emphasised in earlier chapters of this book. Furthermore, it is a matter of concern to find some projects now being established in Britain with little or no apparent awareness of the increasingly sophisticated critiques and evaluations of work with abusers that are becoming available in North America or the note of caution that they strike, for example concerning the fact that groupworkers and group members claim better rates of success than abused partners report (Edleson and Tolman, 1992, p.86; see below for a fuller discussion).

Models of intervention with abusive men

It is important for aspiring groupworkers to separate out the underpinning explanations upon which models for work with abusive men are based, the techniques they utilise (which of course betray underpinning explanations or assumptions), and the eventual aim they seek to achieve. When this is done, potentially confusing overlaps are revealed, but it becomes easier to recognise the models in the guises they have adopted in Britain – and hence to be able to judge the extent to which, for example, they interpret woman abuse as a male problem and women's safety as the first priority.

Three broad explanatory frameworks can be detected. Gelles and Straus (1979, cited in Pence and Shepard, 1988, p.284) list them as 'intraindividual', 'socio-psychological' and 'sociocultural'. Gondolf's division (1985, cited in Nosko and Wallace, 1988, p.34) into 'psychoanalytical', 'social learning' and 'sociopolitical' theories looks remarkably similar. Nosko and Wallace (ibid.) argue that, in practice, all three theories of male abuse can be combined because they simply represent different dimensions of human behaviour. We might categorise these as: feelings and relationships rooted in the past; learned behaviours and related thought processes; and the need to understand male and female roles within social systems. Groupwork is powerful, argue these authors, because it can engage people on all three levels. The social level of explanation is the most important from a feminist perspective, in the view of the present author, but, as probably the hardest to translate into existing models of groupwork intervention with oppressor groups (social action has traditionally targeted the oppressed: Mullender and Ward, 1991b, e.g. pp.3–5), it is often eclipsed in actual intervention – even by workers whose orientation is profoundly feminist or profeminist.

The three types of theory will now be explored in terms of their usefulness in groupwork with male abusers. Consideration will be given, too, to social action as a groupwork orientation that can lift men's efforts to take collective responsibility for violence beyond a sometimes indulgent focus on the self into female-directed activities to improve the social lot of women.

Social learning theory

It is interesting that each of the other two theoretical standpoints can be used to criticise the perspective of learned behaviour as incomplete on its own. Nosko and Wallace (1988, p.34), on the one hand, are critical of anger management work for falling into the masculine trap of underplaying emotions, while Pence and Shepard (1988, p.289), on the other, stress that it will do nothing to challenge men's domination over women unless it is accompanied by sociocultural re-education about stereotypical male and female roles and male domination.

Small wonder, then, that the male-dominated political and penal systems in this country have seized on anger management as their placatory response to concerns raised by women. Whereas the Home Affairs Committee report recommended 'the establishment, and wide dissemination, of programmes in prison which first encourage men to recognise their violent behaviour towards women and then to change it', and distinguished these from programmes teaching men to control their anger or their substance misuse (House of Commons, 1992a, para. 74), the Government response (Home Department *et al.*, 1993, Cm 2269, para. 71) refers only to an 'anger management programme', with 80 staff in 16 prisons already trained to deliver it and a commitment to extend this in 1993–94. This may be perfectly useful for other purposes but it misses the point as far as domestic violence is concerned. Anger management courses are not based on an understanding of men's abuse of women as any different from men's anger in the pub or the social security office (King, 1994, p.32). Nor would such a group necessarily distinguish between men's protracted, intimidating and escalating sexual abuse and violence and times when women may hit back at men, as demonstrated by the fact that a book can be called *The Hitting Habit: Anger Control for Battering Couples* (Deschner, 1984).

Sleightholm (1991, p.5) considers that one way forward might be for all anger management groups for men to work on concepts of masculinity, and how these relate to domestic violence. It is certainly a laudable aim to incorporate these issues into all work with male offenders, whether probation officers know the men have abused their partners or not, but it does not make anger management groups the best or safest response to male abusers. Sleightholm (ibid.) calls for evaluation of different ways of dealing with domestic violence so that this can be determined, and one cannot disagree other than to point to the considerable evaluative work that has already been done (see below) but not learnt from in Britain. Men who are convicted of offences involving the abuse of women and are mandated to attend groups, or those who admit such behaviour and seek help, require programmes that draw on all that we know about the phenomenon of men's abusiveness and ways of dealing with it, not a partial response taken out of context.

Gondolf and Russell (1986) argue the case against anger control programmes on grounds that include, firstly, men's tendency to learn the techniques as a set of gimmicks without undergoing real change and, secondly, their enhanced ability to persuade their wives to return – either with false claims that they have been 'cured', or with persuasion that they should be given one last chance because they are working hard to seek a cure. Even where violence has stopped or reduced, there can still be a strong tendency for threats and an atmosphere of fear and coercion to persist (see p.243, this volume). Wood and Middleman (1990, p.3) argue strongly that the whole model is flawed in its explanation of men's violence towards women; abusers actually have very good impulse control since they manage not to hit their employers but to go home and hit their female partners. We might say that this is the best controlled anger, not the least. Hearn's research bears this out. He states: 'men use *exactly* the amount of violence that is necessary to achieve their ends' (Hearn, 1993, p.14). Some speak of clear intentions to cause specific amounts of hurt and damage: 'I thumped her hard enough to hurt her, but not hard enough to knock her down, because I didn't want to hurt the baby. I knew what I was doing' pp.14–15. This leads Russell (1995) to argue for groupwork based on challenging men's beliefs – on seeking to achieve paradigm shifts from abuse as acceptable, even humorous, to abuse as unacceptable and criminal.

An overall objection to the concept of anger management is that it feeds into men's habitual denial and minimisation of their behaviour. A 'problem with my anger' can serve both as an excuse and as a natural-sounding and comfortable part of masculine behaviour (pers. comm. with Neil Blacklock, worker with the VPP of DVIP) – it does not sound criminal, unacceptable, or commensurate with the physical and emotional damage inflicted on women. It avoids focusing on the power and control inherent in the gendered dynamic of abuse. Hence it is dangerous to refer to anger management, even as a component of anti-violence work, because abusive men looking for an escape from confrontation will latch onto it. Government terminology is using the same exit-route (see above).

Despite these objections, Tolman and Edleson (1989) demonstrate that behavioural techniques have, in fact, become common to the majority of programmes, whatever their underlying theoretical orientation. Profeminist re-educational groups, for example, make heavy use of behavioural techniques but within a context of insisting that what has been learned can be unlearned by a man who is confronted to accept responsibility for his own actions. In other words, re-educational groups do not work with behaviourism in a deterministic way but with a strong cognitive overlay (i.e. regarding people as aware of what are they are doing and able to make choices). These groups also place far more weight on the social context within which men's violence is functional, intentional and purposeful and where it is upheld by the sociopolitical, economic and cultural context.

Intrapsychic models

Less threat is posed in abusers' programmes in Britain from an over-concentration on the intrapsychic level, although there are no doubt many psychiatrists, psychologists and counsellors in Britain still working from this orientation with individual men. Evidence for this comes from Jukes (1993, p.xxii) who became convinced over time that his own psychodynamic orientation was inadequate in the face of feminist experiences and understanding of male violence, and that confrontative techniques developed by feminist organisations in intervention with controlling abusive men were more effective than anything traditional therapy could offer.

The intrapsychic, or 'insight' model (Adams, 1988, in the context of a valuable critique) sees men's violence to women as rooted in earlier developmental problems (such as unresolved conflicts with violent parents: Schlesinger *et al.*, 1982; or unmet dependency needs: Beninati, 1989) – compounded by past or current stress – and takes the view that these problems need to be tackled before the violence itself will diminish. It does not take account of the full impact of violence (since the man's version of the 'truth' is accepted as the basis of therapy, and the woman is presumably left to suffer while the typically long-term treatment goes on); nor does it recognise the strength of men's denial, even after seeking treatment. Jukes (1993) – though he still uses his psychoanalytic training to inform his personal understanding of the underlying causes of what he refers to as men's hatred of women – in his work at the Men's Centre in London uses groups that are heavily confrontational in focusing chiefly on current behaviour; even in his long-term psychotherapy he works with current denial and actions as much as with deep-seated neuroses. The chief danger with failing to do this would lie in not insisting that men take responsibility for their own actions, as both the criminal justice system and the women's movement would expect them to do. Dwelling on the past could merely allow them to point to formative experiences outside their control as an excuse to feed into their denial without ending the violence. This is why feminist-inspired groups attempt to avoid any discussion of families of origin, i.e. past excuses for current responsibility. The workers in the Violence Prevention Programme of DVIP (also in London; pers. comm.), for example, consider that their earlier counselling and therapy training alone would have hooked them into empathy with the feelings of men whose partners have left them, or who had terrible childhoods, as opposed to an active confrontation of the men's currently abusive attitudes and behaviour. Where necessary, group members are offered individual sessions by the workers outside of the group to address other issues. This maintains the focus in the group programme on helping the man end his abusive behaviour by ensuring that he is not allowed to present or consider himself as a victim. He may have problems, but he can take responsibility for working on them and, crucially, for changing his behaviour.

Profeminist groups: the sociopolitical context

The profeminist stance regards men's abuse and denial – both of the impact of their behaviour and of their responsibility for it – as endemic in a patriarchal society and as needing to be actively confronted in intervention. In other words, its underpinning theory is sociocultural, not psychodynamic or behavioural:

> The process of education must constantly compare theory to the real experiences of women so that we do not operate from false assumptions. Such assumptions lead us to actions which do not result in changing the system ... [such as] ... hundreds of men's groups forming around the country which focus on teaching men who beat women into submission to reduce their stress level, to cope with anger differently, to express feelings differently rather than working with batterers on issues of power and dominance. These theories focus on the psychology of battering rather than on the political and social context of battering, and they analyze battering piecemeal. Our failure to deal with the full social and historical context in which battering occurs will result in a faulty agenda for our work.
>
> (Pence, 1987, p.22)

Profeminism is not a groupwork model, as such, but a set of beliefs and structures that give priority to a feminist understanding and feminist concerns. Whether a group is profeminist cannot be ascertained from the gender of the groupworkers, for example. Whilst a majority of groups are run jointly by a male/female co-worker team, profeminism can be seen in what was originally an all-male organisation – EMERGE in Cambridge, Massachusetts (Adams, 1988; Adams and McCormick, 1982) – while the Domestic Abuse Intervention Project in Duluth has had some men's groups run successfully by two women working together, initially accidentally when a male worker was unavailable but subsequently by choice. The women concerned feel less exposed and better supported; one of them at least will not now return to male/female working (pers. comm.) and the group members find their brand of confrontation very powerful.

Strictly speaking, the Duluth model developed in the Domestic Abuse Intervention Project – the one adopted and adapted most widely in Britain (e.g. by CHANGE in Central Region, where the number of group meetings has gradually extended to cover the material more thoroughly; by Lothian DVPP, where the video vignettes of violent incidents have been refilmed with Scottish dialogue; and by others – it can often be recognised from the now ubiquitous 'power and control wheel') – is a hybrid between cognitive behavioural work to achieve individual change, on the one hand, and education to put this into a sociocultural context, on the other (Pence and Shepard, 1988, pp.288–9; see also Pence and Paymar's manual on the approach, 1986). Hence the use of the term 'psychoeducational' for the model. Pence and Shepard reported that most men were being ordered by criminal or civil courts to attend 12 weeks of each kind of work in two different group settings. Workers take a directive approach in both groups. The 'psycho-' or counselling aspect uses cognitive behavioural work focused on anger management to teach men to use 'anger logs' to identify their own triggers, together with the internal dialogue or 'self talk' that escalated the incident, the feelings they were having at the time, and the points at which they could have behaved differently – for example by taking 'time out' from the situation. Although this work is not undertaken without a context, since the concepts of control and dominance are used throughout to explain the purpose and function of abuse, men may learn to avoid physical violence without becoming less pyschologically controlling. It is the educational groups that move onto male and female social and cultural roles. Violence stems not from anger but from a belief system wherein men are convinced they have a right to dominate and control, and men force their relationships to become deeply embedded in such assumptions (hence the need for empowerment groups for women as well as confrontative groups for men). Pence and Shepard (1988, p.289) recognise that the cognitive behavioural anger management and sociocultural re-education are 'in some ways, contradictory perspectives' but see them as needing to be combined so that men can both stop being violent and stop believing that women should be compliant.

It might be more accurate to see profeminist groups not as a subdivision in methodological terms – since the self-avowed profeminists include psychotherapists like Adam Jukes, cognitive behaviourists, and others – but to see profeminism as an essential prerequisite for all groups of abusive men. This should extend to their organisational framework, making them answerable to women for their standards as well as for content and process. In the British context, rooting a men's group project in an inter-agency structure where key women's organisations play an active role is one way of seeking to build in this accountability (as with DVIP in London, Worth in Keighley, and PAX in Kidderminster). Also, those projects that insist on court-mandated referrals – so as to stress the criminal nature of men's abusive behaviour – such as CHANGE and Lothian DVPP, can be seen to be working from a feminist analysis in this regard, engendered through keen debate with women's groups. All-female organisations such as Women's Aid do not, by definition and on principle, directly undertake work with men, so their involvement in setting agendas will always be at one remove. In Britain, some of the men's self-help groups have been accused of being insufficiently profeminist, particularly in relation to accountability to women (see below), and not all have sought or found ways of hearing women's demands. Their all-male structure can be a point of weakness here.

Social action

In the USA, on the contrary, some of the men's organisations working with self-referrals are amongst the most likely to extend beyond seeking individual change in abusers' groups into social action at a wider community level, often highlighting issues of men's violence and abusiveness and other matters put on the social agenda by women. This is largely because they were inspired by the women's movement to take responsibility, as men, for the problems of men. In this respect, groups of men can combine their efforts with the women they have hitherto oppressed (and from whose oppression they continue to obtain social advantage), but only after using groupwork to achieve change in themselves at the individual level and only if the overarching agenda of priorities and strategies for wider-scale action remains in women's hands. EMERGE was originally a men's collective. Its ethos was to support the women's cause, join campaigns, and not compete with women's projects for funding. It also works at a multi-systems level, for example to improve criminal justice and medical responses to domestic abuse (Smith, 1989, p.69), and, following a challenge to involve women in decision-making, now operates with 25 male/female management and staff offering 25 groups a week, largely to court-mandated male abusers. RAVEN (Rape and Violence End Now) in St Louis works to encourage all men to unlearn sexism and produces profeminist materials. Man Alive, in San Rafael, California, in a very long-term programme (up to two years), moves abusers on from intensive groupwork to involvement in community groups working on broader socio-economic issues; it is linked with the service for abused women in Marin County. Its guiding figure, Hamish Sinclair, combines a background as a therapist and as a former trade union organiser.

The Oakland Men's Project (Kivel, 1992) offers workshops and training to challenge male violence and the abuse of power inherent in gender stereotyping. These activities are not based on closed groups of abusers but are offered to young men in schools and to serving prisoners, for example. Oakland regards all men as having a responsibility to stop male violence, whether in themselves or others, and to break out of the patterns that uphold it. The approach, although it has a strong feel of personal growth and self-awareness, does overtly place anti-violence work in a social context that includes gay and lesbian liberation, anti-racism, class-based issues, and the environmental and peace movements (ibid., p.272). Control is seen as the key issue in men's lives: both controlling their own feelings (and sexuality) and gaining control over other people (p.83). The project seeks to replace 'power over' with 'power with', building communities for change. Kivel (pp.263–72) challenges the 1980s' men's groups – those that camp in the redwood forest, seeking to find the essence of masculinity and break away from the possessiveness of mothers (Bly, 1990; see also Armistead Maupin, 1989, for a revealing send-up) – as part of the male backlash against the 'social gains and political insights' (Kivel, 1992, p.272) achieved by women. The backlash groups are seen as aiming 'to shift our focus from eliminating inequality and violence to helping individual men become more powerful' (ibid.). And, of course, it must always be remembered that the power of groups is such that they can be an equally radical impetus for change in a progressive or retrograde direction.

Having examined the available theoretical models that abusers' groups can draw upon, this chapter will now explore key issues in the framework for such groups. These are accountability, evaluation and resources.

ACCOUNTABILITY TO WOMEN'S SAFETY, WOMEN'S PERSPECTIVES AND WOMEN'S PRIORITIES

Men's agendas and the risk of collusion

In Britain, men's self-help abusers' projects have been criticised as being insufficiently profeminist and some have initiated changes as a result. They include the MOVE groups, and Nottingham Agenda (which also derived initially from the MOVE model). Bolton MOVE is well known through its self-help manual (Waring and Wilson, 1990; other sources used here are Watts, 1990, and a presentation by Jim Wilson in Nottingham) and the high media profile of its instigator, Jim Wilson. Wilson admits to physically abusing his own wife for eight years and, after attending Manchester 'Men Against Sexism' for 18 months, was advised to start his own group, which he did in 1988. He believed it was essential to be able to draw on personal experience in this form of work: that 'those who had battered their partners, and who had found ways of overcoming their own violence were the best people to understand and to help others who wished to change their ways' (Waring and Wilson, 1990, Foreword). In fact, others may have much to offer. Ex-abusers are said to be unbeatable at spotting the tricks and denials employed by other abusers ('You can't con a con man': Watts, 1990, p.8, quoting Jim Wilson), but they are not the only ones who can do so. Any groupworker operating from a profeminist base learns this from talking to, or reading accounts written by, abused women. In particular, female workers in groups for violent men whose work also brings them into contact with the abused partners know that the men habitually underplay what they have done. The publicity material from the Worth group in Keighley, for example, states: 'Experience suggests that having a woman in the group helps the men stop bullshitting!' Male groupworkers, too, especially when teamed with a female co-worker and working hard to be non-sexist themselves, can draw on their own experience to see how sexist denial operates in the group.

The chief problem with the men's self-help model – by definition an all-male group with male groupworkers – would seem to be the lack of safeguards against collusion with the group members. One might look for a consultancy framework, for example. Most profeminist groups have support for the workers, and Worth in Keighley (which uses a re-educational model with a male/female groupworker team) interestingly includes a non-participant observer actually in the group as a consultant to the workers. The VPP men's group of the DVIP in London, because it happened to begin life with two male groupworkers, deliberately chose a female consultant to identify any collusion through, for example, certain kinds of male bonding and communication. It later moved to a mixed gender staff and volunteer team with, typically, male/female leadership of groups and an emphasis on equal co-working. This is not to argue that women never collude with men, but that men in groups tend to appeal to other men to back them up and that sensitive and skilled work is necessary to identify and avoid collusive traps. The VPP of DVIP also has minority ethnic members of its policy-making committees; race issues are tackled in the group within an integrated model of understanding oppression. One member stated that he had decided to learn his partner's first language which, if he did in fact follow this up, could be taken as a sign that the group helped him recognise the need to value her origins and heritage.

The idea of graduating from attending to running groups would also appear to draw an unrealistically sharp distinction between abusers and ex-abusers – as if it were possible to know when men are reliably violence-free, let alone free of abusive behaviours more generally. (Having said that, a male group 'graduate' is also a key groupworker in the definitively feminist programme in Duluth, but in an organisation run by women.) Women may be more likely to notice men's continuum of controlling behaviours and attitudes (see Chapter 1, this volume). The present author, for example, dislikes the fact that the further reading listed by Waring and Wilson (1990, p.104) is, with one exception, all by men, that the useful addresses are all men's groups, the acknowledgements in the foreword are only to men, and there is no statement that the material in the first chapter derives originally from the intervention of women activists and the theorising of women writers in response to men's violence against women. The main acknowledged source of groupwork content is Hamish Sinclair (of Man Alive), especially for a form of slow-motion role play of violent incidents called the 'Pekinpah Stills', but Sinclair's wider sociopolitical activism is missing (see 'Social action' section above).

Waring and Wilson are clear that violence against women is totally unacceptable and entirely the men's responsibility. It is seen as having its roots in male stereotypes that they have authority over and rights to services from women (Waring and Wilson, 1990, Foreword). The group aims to get men to accept the rights of their partners and to treat them as 'real, equal human beings' (ibid.). Yet the manual blurs the analysis, for example by recommending 'people', not men (p.1), who are violent in other friendships or relationships to use it. The entire summary of the programme (pp.9–10) (it is basically anger management) would stand just as well as a course in being less confrontational at work or in the pub (just replace the words 'your partner' with 'your colleagues' or 'your friends'). It is not so much that anything unacceptable is said about women in the manual – all the right arguments are there – as that they somehow feel tangential to the work. A man who learns to control his anger will not necessarily have had his sexist notions challenged (see the argument for the hybrid model in Duluth, above). This challenging does appear to feature more within the group itself (Watts, 1990) than is clear from the exercises in the manual. When I heard Jim Wilson speak, he appeared to agree that it takes place through peer confrontation in the group – for example in stressing that nothing a woman does warrants violence. The classic question asked in the group is 'What if I discover her in bed with someone else?' The reply is given that there is still no reason to hit her as it will do nothing to change the situation. There is also said to be work in the group on male identity and homosexuality which is not in the printed manual.

A further example of working from men's agendas appears to be that MOVE's group curriculum deliberately includes work on rebuilding relationships (as opposed to recognising the woman's threat to leave as her right and also as one of men's two major motivations for joining a group voluntarily, the other being fear of police involvement: Sone, 1993). Men are told that there are no guarantees and that an amicable parting is also a success, but it is possible that this message may not be heard. The problem is that, if groupworkers accept saving relationships as an aim, this could divert the group from the focus on ending abuse as their one purpose and remit, as well as diluting any commitment to women's freedom to choose how to be safe and whole. The local refuge (which is not affiliated to Women's Aid and allows men in on drop-in days) is used for couples counselling by a refuge worker and Jim Wilson. According to Wilson himself, a majority of men who go through the groups stay with their partners. He is reported as only rarely advising women who ring him for advice to leave home, for example when one had had her finger cut off by her husband (Watts, 1990, p.57). There is no mention of asking men to leave. Jukes, on the other hand (1993, p.323), gives an example of a man who repeated his violence and was told, after discussion between the group-workers and his partner, that he could only continue in the group if he agreed to leave home; he returned some months later, only with his partner's prior agreement.

Women's safety

This brings us to the all-important question of women's safety. It is, of course, good to see men taking responsibility for men's violence and, if even a proportion of men change as a result of groups, that is also to be welcomed. As will be seen later in this chapter, however, there are doubts about the overall efficacy of such intervention, and if it were to emerge that groups made men more dangerous, or dangerous in different ways – perhaps under a veneer of having changed – then this would give grave cause for concern. This means that a top priority of men's programmes should be to ensure women's safety and that no one should ever assume any individual man is 'safe' during or after attendance at a group.

Contact with women during their partners' membership of a group is essential: to build in measures for their safety, to give them an objective picture of the group (including its lack of guarantees of success), and to offer them access to support. (See Morley, 1993, p.187, for a neat summary of the feminist agenda here.) When a man is referred to the CHANGE project in Central Region (which has accepted and assesed over 170 referrals since April 1990), for example, the female co-ordinator contacts his partner. If they are separated and she can receive her own mail in confidence, the woman is sent a letter giving a 24-hour telephone number. However, if the couple is still living together, the female co-ordinator telephones the woman while her partner is with the other co-ordinator or his social worker, to ensure that he does not know she has been contacted or what has been said. If the woman is not on the telephone, the social worker who is completing the report for court (carrying out Scottish probation functions) and is recommending the group as a sentencing option, contacts her.

Through one of these means, the woman is informed that her partner is being considered for the programme (he may or may not have told her himself – this is never assumed), and she is given an information pack that has been jointly developed by CHANGE, Women's Aid and the Social Work Department. The woman is asked if she will agree to follow-up contact. Approximately half agree, meeting either at home or in the social work office. The woman is assured complete confidentiality and often, of course, gives a conflicting story to the man's. She is told that there can be no guarantee of success but that she will get feedback on the work done with him. She is also told the ethos of the programme, that she bears no responsibility for the violence, and that her safety is a prime consideration. However, her views on whether he should go on the programme, though consulted, are not necessarily followed. (By this stage, the man is being prosecuted and sentenced; victims of crime might be more punitive or more forgiving than the court. It is to be hoped that their safety is at least fully considered in formulating the recommendation for sentence.)

All the women contacted are advised to get in touch with Women's Aid for support, and at all meetings a visit from Women's Aid is offered. Women's Aid agreed to this because the CHANGE worker takes the message out to the woman; Women's Aid have a policy of not being pro-active because they cannot guarantee either the woman's safety or their own. Some women initially refuse contact with the programme but change their minds after talking it over with Women's Aid and deciding that the project does have their safety in mind. A one-off group meeting for female partners is held once men have started on the programme, at which CHANGE, Women's Aid and the Social Work Department are all repre-sented, and the women are sent a series of information leaflets about the content of the groupwork being done with the men as it proceeds, inviting them to telephone if they would like further information. Increasingly, it has become the case that female partners are involved with the probation order by the social worker concerned, for example having the right to attend reviews.

The Lothian Domestic Violence Probation Project in Edinburgh, which began taking referrals shortly after CHANGE, consulted with Women's Aid, separately as well as through the representation on its advisory group, about women's safety. One result of this was a call for a partner check to be built into the programme; another has been a search for funding for a full-scale partner support network in the voluntary sector to parallel the work the Social Work Department is doing with the men in its probation capacity.

The Domestic Violence Intervention Project (DVIP, operational since November 1992) in London, because it has established parallel services for men (the VPP) and women, can offer contact to female partners within its own resources. When a man is referred to the group, one of the conditions of joining is to give his partner's address and telephone number, if he knows it, to the men's worker, who passes it to the Women's Support Service (WSS) but does not file it in his own office. In the early days, the women's worker then wrote to the woman and sent a leaflet explaining the service for women within the context of the project as a whole. As few made contact, there has been a move towards being more proactive and following this up with a telephone call, though there is no wish to be intrusive where women have made a new life for themselves.

The purpose of contacting the woman is to offer her support, to tell her there is a worker for her to talk to in confidence, and to explain the project so that she is not dependent on the man's version. She is given details of the content of the men's programme, as well as information designed to aid her in maximising her own safety, which is well to the fore. Men are offered a limited form of confidentiality which gives the men's worker the right to contact the women's service, to warn the partner if the man's demeanour in the group (or talk of discovery of her whereabouts or of expiry of an injunction, for example) makes him appear a threat, and also the police if specific threats are voiced. The women's worker informs the woman if her partner fails to attend or is excluded from the group, so that he cannot mislead her, and she is advised that the WSS is still there to support her if required, quite separately from the question of his group membership.

The issue of alternative sanctions to the somewhat self-defeating exclusion of a man from a group for reabusing – such as insisting on his starting the group programme again or on a guilty plea to charges, or having him agree to place money and a signed confession at his partner's disposal for future use should she eventually decide to leave, or collecting donations for the local shelter (refuge) – has been interestingly developed by the PIVOT group in Houston, Texas (Myers, 1993). The emphasis is on the woman, and on women more generally, benefiting from the sanction imposed on the man, and on his not escaping the continuing challenge to him to accept full responsibility for his actions and for his partner's safety, through the group. Probation officers and groupworkers working with abusive men in any context need a similar sensitivity to safety issues. It is also important not to get into bargaining with the men about sanctions.

Wider accountability to women

Any men's project should be accountable to a wider structure, where work with women and women's viewpoints are central components, and should   not be set up in potentially collusive isolation. Live issues in planning the Worth group, for example (Keighley Domestic Violence Forum, 1993, p.16), include the safety of partners, safety of facilitators, follow-up of non-attenders, and wider accountability. This project has a very clearly structured integration into the Keighley Domestic Violence Forum with the same Management Committee responsible for the Worth men's group, the women's support group, the Asian women's group, and a youth education project. This Management Committee is directly responsible to the full forum, and issues of policy and broad practice requiring decision would go to those bodies for discussion and decision. Morley (1993, p.187) emphasises how critically important it is that there always be a strong women's voice, representing the perspective of those who work with and those who have survived violence, in the planning, implementation, monitoring and evaluation of men's programmes.

CHANGE debated the question of accountability to women during its planning phase (source: personal interviews). Women's perspectives on the past performance of all the relevant legal and welfare agencies, including specific criticisms of the criminal justice system, resulted in an emphasis on the criminality of abusive behaviour (men are referred to throughout CHANGE literature as 'offenders') and the invocation of legal sanctions. The local procurator fiscal, the equivalent of the Crown Prosecution Service, who prepares cases for court, initially proposed pre-trial diversion to the programme where prosecution was difficult. The planning group saw too little sanction in such a course, however, since the threat of prosecution might not hold water if the man failed to complete the programme; they stood firm for a non-diversionary court referral system and have continued to do so, with the support of the local Social Work Department (carrying the probation function in the Scottish court system). This does not mean that the issue has gone away for good. At the time of writing, for example, the Scottish Office is again looking at diversion more generally.

The stand taken on non-diversion pre-trial has, of course, created tensions in its turn because it gives CHANGE formal accountability to the courts as well as to feminist agendas. The project is answerable to the Sheriff's Courts, and to the social workers holding the probation orders under which men are required to attend the group, as well as to its own Management Committee and, in a broader way, to abused women. (Women's Aid is represented on its Advisory Committee, for example.) Each man joining the programme signs an agreement to participate in the group at a three-way meeting with the social worker holding his probation order and one of the project workers. The Sheriff is formally notified that the man understands the agreement and feels able to comply with it. Strict rules cover attendance, time keeping, sobriety and confidentiality. Each man is individually tracked through the group, with a progress report written after every meeting using the homework he has done and his participation in exercises and discussions during the sessions, to assess his changing view of the severity, frequency and cause of his violence. His social worker is kept informed of his progress and attendance but, as earlier chapters have indicated, there may well be inconsistency in the extent to which individual workers back up the work being done with the men or understand the confidentiality and safety needs of the women.

Since the tension between accountability to the courts and accountability to women is hard enough to hold in balance when there has been careful planning, no local probation service or voluntary agency should launch into establishing a programme for abusers with referrals from the courts without formalising the links with women's organisations (including Black women's organisations), for example through an inter-agency forum and a representative management committee. It was important to CHANGE, for example, that an independent management committee, including women activists among its members, was able to debate the issue of pre-trial diversion and consider it from the perspective of women's best interests. The criminal justice system had a quite different agenda. A forum with strong women's membership can also keep men's workers in touch, for example, with the need not to make overstated claims for what they can achieve and the imperative of keeping women's safety to the fore. Those referring men to groups – whether probation officers, social workers, or voluntary sector staff and volunteers in Relate and elsewhere – should also question those groups about their procedures for keeping female partners safe and the wider framework within which they operate and to which operational problems and dilemmas will be reported.

EFFICACY

Practitioners favouring any of the theoretical bases outlined earlier in this chapter can offer case studies which claim to illustrate success, but very few are involved in rigorously monitoring their favoured model at work. In North America, there is a proliferation of papers arguing the efficacy or otherwise of work with male abusers, although the majority of programmes have no follow-up evaluation (Shupe et al., 1987). It is, of course, crucial to know whether violent men can change as a result of intervention because, even if their partners leave, there are frequent reconciliations, and abusers are also often violent in a series of relationships (Gondolf, 1987, p.96). Ideally, no new programmes should be set up without evaluation being built in.

In Britain, the results of the two Scottish court-mandated programmes have been measured, over three years, by Russell and Rebecca Dobash and their co-researchers; their findings are currently awaited (Dobash et al., 1996). Those projects are, of course, working with a tiny minority of abusers, not only because there are so few programmes available but because they recruit only men who have been reported, arrested, charged, prosecuted, who have pleaded or been found guilty and then sentenced high enough up the tariff to attend the group. Clearly, there are many more at each of these stages with whom no work of this kind is being done. As this is the case everywhere, we know little about the potential for change of the generality of abusers.

There is no published evidence that the more informally established work in Britain has been researched in any rigorous way, although Jim Wilson verbally claims 60 per cent of men violence-free after 12 months. It is crucially important for any professional referring a man to a group to remember that – quite apart from the fact that some men will not be assessed as suitable for the group, some may drop out when they realise what is involved, or may be asked to leave for breaking their contracts (e.g. attending while drunk, using violence or threats in the agency, failing to attend) – success can never be guaranteed with any individual. In fact, on close examination of groupwork programmes, it becomes quite difficult even to define success, as work overseas has shown. Eisikovits and Edleson (1989, pp.392–400) review a literature of more than 50 publications on groups for men who abuse their female partners and conclude that, although sophistication is increasing, there are still severe methodological shortcomings (pp.407–8). The problems that they and others cite include the issues of:

- the weak link between interventive models and the theoretical literature on the causes of violence (ibid.);
- the mix of techniques used in groups, making it hard to isolate those which work, if any (p.394);
- the source of the study: too often this is the same person who ran the programme, giving no guarantee of objectivity (Chen et. al., 1989, p.310; Eisikovits and Edleson, 1989, p.407);
- the source of the data: since it is well established that female partners report more incidents of abuse than their abusers (Edleson and Brygger, 1986; Poynter, 1989, p.138), it is essential to go beyond male self-report (Eisikovits and Edleson, 1989, p.396) and ask the woman what has happened since her partner started or stopped attending the programme;
- defining violence: there is evidence that whereas physical abuse may decline or stop, threats of abuse continue or even escalate so that the woman still lives in fear (Edleson and Grusznski, 1989, pp.20–21; Eisikovits and Edleson, 1989, pp.396 and 397, reviewing a range of studies, and discussion on p.399; Edleson, 1990, pp.134 and 141). One would hesitate to call this 'success' (Brygger and Edleson, 1987, p.334) and, indeed, the gravest fear about abusers' programmes is that they may replace physical violence with emotional terrorisation or other forms of abuse. Yet several studies have used a measure of conflict that incorporates only physical violence (Poynter, 1989, p.134);
- the lack of control groups in many studies (Chen et al., 1989, p.310; Tolman and Edleson, 1989, p.187);
- their frequent vagueness over key information such as the source of follow-up reports (Edleson, 1990, pp.133 and 135);
- the risk that a positive effect may have resulted from some other factor, such as the threat of a return to court, the partner having left, or other sources of support, rather than the programme of intervention itself (Eisikovits and Edleson, 1989, p.408);

- low response rates, low recruitment, and high drop-out from programmes (Chen *et al.*, 1989, pp.310–11) which mean that those whose response is measured may not be typical, together with the fact that those sentenced to attend may not resemble those who do so voluntarily. Certainly, those who come through the criminal justice system tend to be from the lower educational and occupational strata of society (Johnson and Kanzler, 1990, p.21) while some ethnic groups are over- or under-represented in abusers' groups or poorly served by them (Williams, 1993 and 1994; Williams and Becker, 1994);
- the difficulty of measuring the rate of abuse where the partners are no longer together (Edleson and Grusznski, 1989, p.20) since, on the one hand, this may give less opportunity for violence but, on the other, men can indulge in severe harassment at such times, together with the difficulty that studies may not distinguish the separated from the other couples and they may separate and reunite more than once;
- the fact that contact with a programme itself sensitises both partners to the issue of abuse and may make them more likely to report it at follow-up (ibid.);
- the fact that evaluation studies have mainly been underfunded and hence small and not necessarily systematic (Edleson, 1990, p.144);
- the need for far longer periods of follow-up before we know whether positive effects really are maintained over time (Poynter, 1989, p.141), particularly since the whole pull within society is towards male domination of women. Periods of three or six months are far too short; we are going to need to know what is happening years later. We already know that the picture can change fairly radically between a 6-month and an 18-month follow-up on the basis of a study that had first proclaimed self-help groups less effective than educational, particularly in ending threatening behaviour, but later found that the latter's results improved to a surprising degree over time, as did those offering a more intensive frequency of meetings (Domestic Abuse Project, 1989, pp.1–3, and 1991, pp.1–3; Edleson and Syers, 1990 and 1991).

Taken together, then, although many studies do report successes in reducing overt violence – in the region of 53 to 85 per cent according to a review by Edleson and Tolman (1992, p.86) – the evidence is as yet far from firm and total success is rarely achieved in giving women a life free of the fear of these men. A more sobering finding, for example, comes from the Domestic Abuse Project (Minnesota, USA) comparison of six types of group, with randomised allocation, at 6- and 18-month follow-up. Although two-thirds of completers were reported non-violent at the 18-month point, most persisted with controlling or threatening behaviour (Edleson and Syers, 1991, p.240). Worse still, taking the original large pool of over 500 men who contacted the agency (of whom 283 were allocated to groups and

153 completed at least 80 per cent of their assigned sessions; most exclusions were men who had been in a similar programme before), only a small minority of this larger total (approximately 20 per cent) went all the way through to completion of a programme and then to being reported non-violent at follow-up. This is especially worrying in that women may be more likely to return to a man who has at least sought help, even if he has dropped out of the group or failed to respond to it. 'For some women, returning to their partners may be a safe decision; however, treatment groups for batterers will surely fail most victims' expectations' (ibid., p.242). Those involved with court-mandated programmes may wish to note that involvement with the courts at intake was one of only two variables in this study that were predictive of lower rates of violence at follow-up, the other being an absence of prior mental health treatment (ibid.). All workers involved in working with or referring to any kind of men's programme need to be keenly aware of these low success rates – particularly in warning men's partners not to expect too much and to keep in place a safety plan for themselves and their children. The poor record of success could also be a factor for professionals when making decisions about where best to devote scarce or contested resources (see next section).

The danger involved in the lack of guaranteed success is a very strong reason for never setting up a men's project in isolation. It needs to be linked with other services (and social policy changes) that are designed to help women be safe, and to grow in the confidence required to seek safety or outside intervention when necessary. It also needs a clear communication channel whereby women can alert the co-ordinators if the man's involvement in the group is having any adverse effect on his treatment of her and whereby they, in turn, can warn her if they believe her to be in danger. Ideally, the programme would also be taking the initiative to check with her periodically about her safety and would find ways, with her consent, to build her views into its evaluation of its own success.

RESOURCING

Work with abusers, then, should only ever be one plank of a co-ordinated and structured approach to the problem of male violence towards women in intimate relationships. Priority still needs to be given to direct services for women and children because their health and safety are directly endangered. Men's work should form one part of an overall response, as happens in the Domestic Abuse Intervention Project in Duluth and the Domestic Abuse Project in Minneapolis, Minnesota, for example. This is also what the best developed inter-agency domestic forums are hoping to achieve in Britain. The Keighley structure, which includes the Worth project, and the Domestic Violence Intervention Project in London are, as yet, amongst the very few with parallel services for men and women;

elsewhere, some groups for abusive men work in more or less close conjunction with local Women's Aid groups.

Men's groups are not infrequently accused of competing for funding with women's organisations, or of being the political 'flavour of the month' and so attracting resources more easily or more generously. (Perhaps they are seen as less contentious than women's groups because the latter are popularly identified with splitting up families; in fact, most women want to save their relationships in the early days if only the abuse would stop, but later despair in the face of escalating violence from their male partners.) Bolton MOVE claims a policy of not competing with Women's Aid for money and so tries to ascertain what funders are being approached; it is not always told, however, because, without formalised links, it is not always trusted not to approach the source divulged. This suspicion is understandable given that the high media profile of this men's group does not seem to have been used to boost women's work locally. Also, Women's Aid in the region appears to have been by passed. Cross-referrals are made between Bolton MOVE and Chiswick Family Rescue in London, the latter the legacy of Erin Pizzey's solitary campaign outside the Women's Aid Federation and as self-promoting an organisation as MOVE itself. In Nottingham, it did not go unobserved that the grants obtained from Safer Cities and from the Equal Opportunities Unit of the County Council by the self-help men's project, Nottingham Agenda, were both larger than those that had gone to any women's project locally.

Even those projects that are most profeminist in philosophy and intent still give rise to contention. The court-mandated programmes in Scotland, for example, represent a new and relatively unproven area of work. Women's Aid locally had been struggling for nearly two decades on a shoe-string when the first, new and extensively publicised men's project obtained major funding for its operation at only the third attempt, followed by extension funding and a further large grant from the Home Office and the Scottish Office for evaluation purposes. This caused some irritation, even though the project's founders have been active in women's interests for decades and their aims are unimpeachable. It is the lack of a funding-base for work with women which is at fault and which needs to be the focus of major campaigning.

The question of money reverberates right through the system. For example, court-mandated projects can work with only a minority even of known abusers, owing to low prosecution rates, and this leaves work with men vulnerable in refunding bids. Police and prosecutors in turn blame the low figures of men successfully prosecuted on female partners who are 'unreliable witnesses' (though no doubt they themselves could do far more). Meanwhile, the low funding base for work with women means that many have no access to support to remain safe and strong while the case against their partner comes before the courts. Very few examples of the

North American model of women's advocacy services exist in Britain (see Chapter 10, this volume) and there is no money available even to consider creating more while basic emergency provision for women and children is still underfunded. Thus the process remains unsatisfactory from all perspectives.

CHANGE argues that the criminal justice system should fund work with offenders whilst local government should resource work with survivors in statutory and voluntary settings, with co-ordination and no competition for funding. But this is clearly not the case at present with no secure funding base for any of the work and no national commitment to establishing one. Clearly, women who have been abused need as much or more help than their abusers; empowerment groups and advocacy services for women, running alongside a men's programme, with adequate funding for fares and child care, are the least they should be able to expect. Women's Aid could be well placed to extend into such outreach work if adequate resources were made available but, at present, it has to be recognised that even refuges are still struggling to survive.

CONCLUSION

Any practitioners wanting to take action to reduce male violence towards women need, then, more than a wish to help. Also essential are a willingness to take the trouble to read the evaluative American material that has been cited here; a rigorous analysis of the causes of violence; the adoption of a model that builds on this; a structure through which their project will be made accountable to women, particularly abused women, and to the wider community; a published and enforceable commitment not to compete for funding with the front-line efforts of preventative women's work; and an in-built, continuing and rigorous evaluation that gives abused women a voice, particularly in defining and measuring positive outcomes. Some of the models that enthusiasts might happen to light on can be positively dangerous; all can feed into unrealistic expectations. Concerned professionals have a responsibility to maintain an active debate about them.

Starting a men's programme from scratch is far from easy. We know from the CHANGE and Lothian projects in Scotland, and from DVIP in London, for example, that setting one up requires a long lead in, which may well extend over years rather than months since it needs to cover detailed planning, the creation of an infrastructure, winning the trust of the courts who will refer to the programme as a sentencing option, and developing a programme relevant to the local context. Most importantly, it needs to be located within a multi-agency framework where Women's Aid has a strong voice, since domestic violence forums are a crucial way of broadening policy influence beyond the male-dominated agendas of probation and the criminal justice system.

Whilst increasing numbers of probation officers and others are becoming committed to groups taking action against men's abuse of women, this must not be at the expense of support or safety for women. Men's work is new and fashionable; it feeds into central Government concerns with law and order, as well as probation preferences for diverting from custody (Perrott, 1994, pp.139–41). But it is dangerous. If it assumes a higher profile and attracts funds more readily than work with women, including refuge provision, it will leave large numbers of women at risk from precisely the kind of abuse such groups aim to eliminate – but which they can only hope to stop in a very few cases. Furthermore, there is some evidence that groups, in their minority of successful completers, replace gross physical abuse with subtler forms of control (see next chapter) – perhaps, even, that they teach men how to dominate in less detectable or in non-punishable ways, or how to make acceptable explanations. Accountability – to individual women through the contact policies of groups, including during follow-up periods, and to the women's movement through integrated structures of management and policy making – is crucial, as is independent, long-term, sophisticated evaluation of groups' effectiveness.

Finally, it must be remembered that, even if some abusive men do change for the better, they will still be living in a society that condones the physical and sexual exploitation of women. Abusers' groups must be seen as only one part of a wider move towards changing the way the criminal and civil justice system treats women and their abusers, and, in turn, as only one element of the social activism needed to combat oppression and create a more just and equal life for women.

Chapter 10

Working together for change

The wider context and the empowerment of women

Earlier chapters of this book aimed to improve detailed policy and practice in social services departments and probation services in relation to domestic abuse. They have called on professionals and their managers to put on a new pair of spectacles – just as had to happen when the widespread nature of child abuse began to be fully realised – to see men's violence to women as already present in every category of work and as urgently requiring an improved response. Improvements in the ability of agencies to offer women practical assistance and empowering emotional support, and to help prevent further violence, will have an immediate impact. There is also a need for a more proactive approach, to plan new ways of harnessing social work and probation skills so as to make life easier for women and children and harder for abusive men.

Current thinking leads towards the view that pooling efforts with others in multi-agency activity is the best way forward. It is certainly the only possible means by which services for women, children and male perpetrators can be integrated in Britain, given that there are not the resources to design interlinked responses from scratch. Rather, we need to build on what we already have. We also need this to happen within the context of a community that takes overall responsibility for raising public awareness that domestic abuse is widespread and that it will not be tolerated. Political support, private sector funding and local community activities can all play a part in this. Whatever action is taken needs to be clearly informed by a feminist analysis and a woman-centred approach that keeps women's perspectives, safety and choices to the fore. Ensuring that Women's Aid plays a central role in any service planning and campaigning is a key way of holding to this essential focus, as is providing the necessary services to help women rebuild their confidence and their lives. To achieve the latter, women need the opportunity to come together in informal groups and formally constituted organisations to develop a positive view of their own capabilities and strengths in the face of an often hostile and still deeply sexist social environment.

This chapter will explore the development and role of inter-agency forums, public education programmes, and confidence-building groups for women. All of these need to form part of the wider context in which social work and probation efforts to tackle abuse and its aftermath will make most sense. The chapter, and the book, will conclude by arguing that the overriding concern of workers in all settings must always be to empower women.

INTER-AGENCY FORUMS

In order to be part of the solution rather than part of the problem, then, agencies including social services and probation need to move forward together, with each developing a clear underpinning policy and a positive programme for change. This is necessary not least because women often have to approach many different agencies before they receive an appropriate response (Binney *et al.*, 1988, p.12: 4 per cent had approached ten or more sources of help; see also Chapter 2, this volume), and because the most helpful response of all is multi-faceted but well co-ordinated. Most of the best practice in social work and probation settings, referred to in earlier chapters, has been developed in a context of inter-agency co-operation. Increasingly, such co-operation is being formalised in inter-agency domestic violence forums, with a wide range of statutory and voluntary agencies in membership.

Where they work well, such forums are a constructive way of improving the services abused women receive, by pressing each member agency to be more rigorous in its response to the issue and by co-ordinating overall responses to women, children and men. At their best, they can identify and tackle the organisational obstacles to confronting male power and empowering women, forge alliances for change, and highlight practice that needs to improve and points at which responses fall down between agencies (for example, social workers cannot effectively help women and children who have nowhere to live, and groupworkers who run court-mandated programmes for men rely on the criminal justice system to arrest and prosecute). In other words, a central aim of any forum must be to avoid the situation where 'because no one [statutory] agency or professional group owns the problem, it has not been a focus for policy development, staff training or data collection' (Mugford, 1990, pp.4–5, citing the Queensland Domestic Violence Task Force). Women's Aid, of course, does 'own' the problem of domestic abuse in that it was set up precisely in response to it, but it looks to other agencies to put their own houses in order by sharing a high level of concern.

Although these forums are a popular and almost certainly an important way forward (research currently being undertaken by the Domestic Violence Research Group at the University of Bristol is evaluating their effectiveness: Hague *et al.*, 1995, 1996), there are at least four major dangers that forums need to guard against. Firstly, they could slip into being the latest bandwagon or mere talking-shops. The National Association of Local Government Women's Committees (NALGWC, undated, pp.6–7) refers to possible tendencies to overstate achievements, court free publicity, and generally appear concerned while being unwilling to make real changes. To counteract these risks, they advise a clear purpose and stated aims or terms of reference (see also Hague *et al.*, 1995, p.14), a shared sense of responsibility, and good central co-ordination and organisation (NALGWC, undated, p.7). To this might be added action plans with clear timescales, such as the one in Nottinghamshire that identified the links between domestic violence and child abuse as a priority concern in 1993/94. Further negative manifestations of talking-shops can be seen when agencies 'pat each other on the back' in acknowledgment of small advances instead of keeping up the pressure for change, or sympathise with the obstacles each is encountering instead of co-operating in a search for solutions. A second danger in the establishment of forums is that they could drain resources away from emergency and other direct services from women and children, in terms of either cash or the professional time that goes into attending all the meetings involved, while, thirdly, they could fail to accord Women's Aid the central influence which its expertise and experience merits. The views of other women's groups, too, need to be heard and not swamped by the louder voices of the large statutory agencies which 'discovered' domestic abuse so much more recently than they did. Fourthly, returning to the NALGWC advice (pp.6–7), there can be a conflict of interests between agencies and/or departments that may result, for example, in a mistrust of one another's motives. An example of this in the early days was a somewhat negative attitude towards the police, owing to their deliberate history of non-involvement in 'domestics' and rather sudden change of policy (see Chapter 1, this volume, and Morley, 1993), which made it ironic and sometimes unhelpful that they were at that time prime movers in initiating forums. Conflicting interests are also in evidence in relation to resource shortfalls that lead to tight gatekeeping and to sending women from one agency to another as each agency passes the buck. Problems such as housing authorities insisting on injunctions or residence orders before giving women assistance, for example, should be thrashed out by having sympathetic solicitors and senior housing and homelessness officials present in a forum together, ideally resulting in altered priorities (which recognise that women's lives are at risk) and in tight codes of practice. Those who attend any multi-agency forum need to be aware of all the potential pitfalls outlined here and to take all possible measures to avoid them. External monitoring and evaluation of the work of a forum may be a useful adjunct to internal awareness of good standards.

Domestic violence forums are proliferating now in Britain. There are over 100 established inter-agency projects and more than 50 others in the pipeline (Hague *et al.*, 1995, p.10). Government and other national encouragement for this kind of initiative (Victim Support, 1992, para. 7.7; House of Commons, 1992a, para. 133; Home Department *et al.*, 1993, p.17, Recommendation 41) has been formally reiterated in an inter-agency circular (Home Office and Welsh Office, 1995). This outlines the role and responsibilities of key statutory and voluntary services, outlining the Government's approach to domestic violence as a 'serious crime which must not be tolerated' (p.9), and suggesting ways to improve co-operation. Some of the major ways in which domestic violence forums have begun have been through police instigation (pursuing Home Office policy; see Hague *et al.*, 1995, p.11 for examples of this which include forums throughout the West Midlands), or, perhaps most commonly, a major conference or similar event on domestic violence or women's safety more broadly, beginning in Leeds in 1985 and followed, for example, by North Tyneside, Wolverhampton, Birmingham, Keighley and Nottinghamshire (National Association of Local Government Women's Committees, undated, p.7; Nottinghamshire County Council, 1990; information leaflet from Keighley Domestic Violence Forum). The key role of women's organisations should be recognised in this whole sphere of work, from Women's Aid's pioneering attempts throughout its existence to bring agencies together in meetings and conferences to take woman abuse seriously, to the energy and influence exerted through forums such as those in North Wales and in Cleveland. The most successful forums are often those in which women with a background in the women's voluntary sector have taken on a co-ordinating role, contributing, especially, relevant experience and skills and credibility with a wide range of statutory and voluntary (including Black-run) agencies.

From the start, the local probation and social services have been invited onto the majority of forums, although it has not infrequently been a struggle to get them fully involved. Local authorities have often taken a less active role through social services than through their women's or equal opportunities or community safety units. The latter played an initiating role in Hammersmith and Fulham and in Sheffield, as did the Women's Equality Unit in Islington, with various forums in Scotland originating from equal opportunities' responsibilities (Hague *et al.*, 1995, p.12). Housing departments, too, have perhaps been more readily recognised as very centrally involved than have social services. It is rare for either social services or probation to have played a key initiating role in setting up a forum, though, in Leeds, social services is one of the originating funders of the Inter-Agency Project (see below), and probation was the prime mover in Peterborough and in Staffordshire (ibid.). Probation has tended to be more to the fore where a forum has been established with a view to offering or supporting work with abusing men, for example in Derby (ibid.).

Increasing specialisation can tend to mean that social services departments are unsure even whom to send when invited to join a forum, being often still at the stage of recognising no 'statutory' obligation in respect of domestic violence. (The quotes refer, firstly, to the fact that *all* social services work is actually conducted under statute and secondly, as discussed in earlier chapters, to the move towards local authorities being required to establish their own definitions and priorities in respect of community care and child care need. Of course local authorities have precise duties in child protection but not in woman abuse.) Some departments have begun thinking about the relevance of woman abuse for child protection *or* for community care, so may send a representative of one or other of these spheres, but there is very rarely an across-the-board acknowledgement of its importance in the lives of service users. Those local authorities that have produced clear policies and guidelines for social workers on domestic abuse tend to be amongst those with the most active inter-agency links; Nottinghamshire was early in the field on both counts (guidelines in 1989, see Chapter 4, this volume, and a conference which spawned its forum in 1990; Nottinghamshire County Council, 1989 and 1990). While no active inter-agency forum can afford not to involve social services in meetings and in multi-agency training in view of the scope of its work (see earlier chapters and Hague *et al.*, 1995, p.13) a challenge remains to get a commitment from social services departments at a high level (Hague *et al.*, 1996, paras 15–17).

Some examples

Hammersmith and Fulham

One of the first local authorities to take up the issue of domestic abuse, and a good example of a corporate approach, was the London Borough of Hammersmith and Fulham. From a community safety perspective, it began to look at domestic abuse in the context of crime and policing as early as 1985 (National Association of Local Government Women's Committees, undated, p.6). The Borough commissioned a study of all its relevant services in 1987 (McGibbon *et al.*, 1989) and, from then on, concentrated on borough-wide policy in a Corporate Domestic Violence Programme, launched in October 1989, which encompassed all departments. The report included considerable detail of the work done and the changes needed in social services (ibid., pp.56–72). The corporate policy was based on five areas of service delivery: support for 'victims', provision of safe alternative accommodation, action against perpetrators, provision of information and advice, and training and service enhancement. This co-ordinated response to policy making and monitoring remains an important model for local authorities, where lack of effective liaison between different departments even of the same council can cause inexcusable problems for which women and children pay the price. Without doubt, it is a positive model for social services departments and their staff to work within, as has been recognised more recently in Newham, Newcastle and numerous other authorities.

In Hammersmith and Fulham, the policy was based on recognising that the complexity of domestic abuse can bring it into the working sphere of virtually any member of staff:

> for example, a Play Service worker ... may become involved in a domestic violence issue when an abusive man comes looking for his children and partner at the former's play centre; or where a social worker from SSD visits a home to find distinct signs that a man is being abusive to his partner but is (not yet) abusing the children; or when a woman approaches the Housing Department for emergency re-housing in order to flee a violent situation.
>
> (Housing Committee papers, 'Review of Domestic Violence Policy', HC 3434, 21st November 1990)

A Corporate Domestic Violence Working Group guided the development of action plans by each relevant service department, with a working group within each for implementation purposes. At a yet wider level, the Council's membership of a Multi-Agency Domestic Violence Group convened by the Hammersmith and Fulham Association of Community Organisations takes the impetus beyond local authority concerns, for example in respect of the collection and presentation of police statistics, though with decision making and accountability initially harder to establish owing to the greater diversity of ownership.

Leeds

Perhaps the best known and most highly developed multi-agency forum is the Leeds Inter-Agency Forum which manages the Leeds Inter-Agency Project (Women and Violence). This Project combines being large and ambitious with being soundly gender-based in its analysis of abuse and live to other oppressions, particularly racism. Included in the links with approximately 60 agencies (including several that are women-only or Black-only projects, or both), are close links with Women's Aid and with Sahara, a Black women's refuge. The ethos of the Leeds work, as well as emphasising men's violence against women as a crime and as prevalent across society, acknowledges 'the non-judgemental models of work developed by women's voluntary sector organisations ... as the most helpful current models to meet the needs of abused women and their children' (Leeds Inter-Agency Project, 1993, ch. 1, p.3). Part of the challenge to statutory agencies has to be to take this message on board and learn from it. The climate in which the Project was able to take root and flourish was one where the women's movement was already strong and active and where women's issues were being forced onto the agenda of the police and other agencies, not least because of the 'Yorkshire Ripper' murders and the Keith Ward case (referred to in Chapter 8). There is a parallel here with the development of responses to woman abuse in Canada, partly in the wake of the 'Montreal massacre': the selective shooting of fourteen women at the University of Montreal on 6th December 1989 by a man shouting that he hated feminists; see, for example, Malette and Chalouh, 1991.

Having grown out of a city-wide forum established the year before (with impetus from the City Council's Women's Committee and the police, amongst others), its three originating funders in 1990 were the City Council's Social Services Department alongside Housing Services and the Equal Opportunities Unit Women's Section. Beginning with one staff member and administrative support, the Project now has around 15 staff and sessional workers. It aims to 'help and support agencies in developing "good practice"' (Leeds Inter-Agency Project, 1993, ch. 1, p.1). Its emphases include multi-agency training (and training the trainers) where statutory workers and those from women's organisations can learn together, including about one another's work, policy development in individual agencies and departments and a corporate basis for the whole City Council, information exchange, and some collaboration in demonstration projects. There is a general stress on inter-agency co-operation and on the service needs of Black women, tackled, for example, through the employment of outreach workers.

The Leeds Inter-Agency Project has made advances in virtually all the fields highlighted in this book as requiring attention. In respect of adult services, for example, the Project manages a Community Care Partnership Adviser, who works specifically with social services and health, and has a subforum on 'Care in the Community: Women and Violence'. Excellent work has been done in fostering joint work by health, social services and the voluntary sector, leading to the inclusion of a specific volume on 'Women Experiencing Violence by Known Men' in the Community Care Plan for Leeds (see Chapter 5, this volume). In addition, the Project has placed confidential counsellors in GP surgeries (again, see Chapter 5, this volume) because many women seek treatment or advice from that source, and has recognised that a negative impact on women's mental health is one of the observable results of violence and abuse, frequently leading to misdiagnosis (Leeds Inter-Agency Project, 1993, ch. 4, p.1). On the child care side, the Inter-Agency Project's Steering Group (ibid.) has emphasised the 'vulnerability of children living in violent homes and the need for co-ordinated safety strategies with child protection agencies and schools'. The latter leads to an acceptance of responsibilty to 'link work to offer support to children, with protection and support for the non-abusing parent', as well as the recognition that abused women may themselves be survivors of child abuse. There are also a Schools Project and an Education Working Group within the Inter-Agency Project. Naturally, the permeating view throughout the

Project of men's violence as criminal behaviour that cannot be tolerated, and of the criminal justice system as vital to women's safety, is vitally important to probation officers, as is the appointment in March 1993 of a Co-ordinator for Women, Violence, Civil and Criminal Justice (Leeds Inter-Agency Project, 1993, ch. 2, p.4) and the existence of a subforum on civil and criminal justice. Of interest to social workers and probation officers in all settings are the inclusiveness of the list of women whose needs are recognised in Leeds, including 'black women, disabled women, older women, lesbians, travellers and women involved in the sex industry' (ch. 4, p.2), together with the Black Women's subforum and outreach work. Above all, all organisations are seen as having a role to play in 'preventing violence and abuse of women by men known to them' and in 'making women's safety a reality in Leeds'. They are also able to look to the Inter-Agency Project for information, for example an Information Pack, multi-agency training and support with particularly complicated cases (source: 'Inter-Agency Work [Women and Violence]: Introductory Leaflet').

Cleveland[1]

A more recent development, again of keen interest to social workers, is the Cleveland Multi-Agency Domestic Violence Forum which also operates a county-wide Zero Tolerance awareness campaign (see next section on public education). Since 1994, it has employed a co-ordinator (source of information: pers. comm.) who is managerially hosted by the Social Services Department, though located in an outreach building alongside two other voluntary projects. In Cleveland, social services' interest (personal and professional) has been forthcoming from a very senior managerial and elected member level, and through an active representation on the Forum – matching the co-ordinator's high expectations of co-operation and pace of progress. She began her task by auditing the current situation and what needed to change. It was immediately apparent that a clear policy and guidelines for best practice by staff were essential, and these were approved in 1995. They are regarded as a crucially important foundation for a complete change of attitude within the delivery of professional services. With the same aim in mind, the co-ordinator reached agreement that a member of the training division of social services would be assigned to the Forum. The approach taken was to train this trainer, who would then be able to take responsibility for training at least one immediate colleague with whom to share the task of instituting a thorough-going programme of in-house training. This will be backed up by the preparation of an advice pack, along the lines of materials produced in Hammersmith and Fulham (London Borough of Hammersmith and Fulham, 1991). Input has also been offered, by the co-ordinator herself, to local social work qualifying and post-qualifying programmes.

The issue of men's abuse of women and its wider impact is now firmly on the agenda in Cleveland. As a result of inter-agency work, including through a Children's Sub-Group of the Forum, Cleveland's Area Child Protection Committee has established a Domestic Violence Task Group which has developed and published inter-agency practice guidance (Cleveland Area Child Protection Committee, 1995) on domestic violence. This offers enlightened information on the experiences of women and children as well as the roles and responsibilities of a range of voluntary and statutory agencies.

Keighley

A forum can set up an independently constituted project which employs its own co-ordinator and other workers, becoming a voluntary sector agency in its own right, as seen, for example, in Leeds. In Keighley, this has led to the provision of new forms of service delivery that were previously missing. This is perhaps closer to the model of the Domestic Abuse Project and of the Domestic Abuse Intervention Project (respectively in Minneapolis and Duluth, Minnesota, USA), where one large not-for-profit agency (on a far larger scale than here) runs men's groups, women's groups and children's groups as well as other services.

Under the auspices of Keighley Domestic Violence Forum (see its 1993 publication), and growing mainly out of Safer Cities funding, are provided Keighley Women's Support Group for survivors of domestic abuse, an Education Support Group which provides a focal point for teachers and employs a Youth Education Worker (funded by the Home Office Programme Development Unit), an Asian Women's Group which is raising awareness and referring women on to appropriate services while seeking funding for direct service provision through a Black outreach worker, and the Worth Project which runs groups for male abusers. The latter has had a link with probation through an officer paid sessionally to act as one of the groupworkers.

Overview

Amongst 150 initiatives (Hague *et al.* 1996, p.17), the above are necessarily only examples, with some attempt to emphasise social work and probation-related activity and relevance. Whilst they are not unproblematic, co-ordinated inter-agency responses can clearly assist in the establishment of formal policies and recording/data collection procedures, in multi-agency training, in fostering best practice, and in improved collaboration and liaison in many settings, including social work and probation. They can also instigate new services for women, children and/or men where this is seen to be needed.

They could achieve far more than has yet been the case, however. If child protection collaboration can achieve fast-track housing transfers (in a multiple abuse case in London), and automatic two-way notification and checking of records by police and social services in respect of known danger-ous men, then there should be no reason why inter-agency collaboration cannot similarly raise the stakes in relation to woman abuse. Certainly, a planned and integrated approach to the safety of women and their children could represent a major improvement on the *ad hoc* situation that still prevails in most parts of the country, provided that it took a lead from women's organisations in being woman-centred as well as child-centred, and non-judgemental of women making near impossible choices in life-threatening circumstances. It could also debate, and perhaps resolve, dilemmas highlighted elsewhere in this book, such as the need for agencies to take confidentiality and safety more seriously in their internal and collaborative working. As there is nothing like one agency for spotting all the shortcomings in the work of another agency, a really searching and honest interchange in a forum – with mutual support to recognise that no one is perfect and everyone needs to improve their services – could lead to far-reaching improvements that could help a woman experiencing or fleeing abuse to feel confident that all the agencies involved will support her and understand her needs at every stage of the process of seeking to become safe.

Since men are in the majority in some agencies (police, probation) and in the senior management of others (social services), there will need to be special efforts to keep women's, and particularly feminist, agendas to the fore. One forum has concentrated on the 'women's voluntary sector' as its constituency (Preston Women and Violence Forum: see Hague *et al.*, 1995, p.13), while Hounslow's has a women-only membership, and inter-agency projects tend to employ women staff except to co-run groups for men. Forums need to secure a situation in which work with men does not overshadow or replace direct services for women and their children but is complementary to and non-competitive with these, yet in which there is a clear focus on men taking responsibility for their behaviour. The Nottinghamshire Domestic Violence Forum, for example, included within the responsibilities of its Steering Group: 'to ensure that schemes, projects and service developments do not negatively affect funding for Women's Aid' and this later became a commitment 'to ensure that the Steering Group and the forum give priority to support for women's aid'.

For similar reasons of white domination in the majority of agencies, issues for Black women and children require special attention through mechanisms such as the Black Women's Forum of the Leeds Inter-Agency Forum (Women and Violence) and the Asian Women's Subgroup of the Keighley Domestic Violence Forum.

Clearly, it is easier to organise inter-agency structures and to meet together frequently in urban areas – where transport is easier, distances less great, and voluntary agencies typically more developed – with the result that large cities, metropolitan areas, conurbations and shire counties focused on cities have seen the most extensive developments to date. Rural areas pose a greater challenge. They may require different models of communication, based less on regular face-to-face meetings and more on occasional large events interspersed with more localised activity, or perhaps even contact via new technology, as is increasingly used for distance learning and information transfer. Any consideration of high expenditure on travel or communication equipment, however, should serve to remind us that we are still not seeing anything like enough basic investment even in emergency services for women and children or assistance to survivors in this country, and that women and children in rural areas are also isolated by distance, cost and poor transport provision from what few sources of help do exist. Nevertheless, not everything modern costs more or drains resources: telephone conferencing can be cheaper than meeting face to face, for example, while well-publicised conferences can generate income to subsidise year-round work, and high-tech firms could be approached to make capital donations of equipment.

PUBLIC EDUCATION

If we look beyond the professional world to the wider context of community and general public awareness, we note that recent years have seen a number of public education campaigns on domestic violence, or sexual violence more generally, at both a national and local level in Britain and, on a smaller scale so far, in schools. The aims of this kind of activity can encompass prevention at every level. By teaching young people or the general public that male abuse is unacceptable and will not be tolerated, there may be a primary prevention role in preventing some abuse from ever happening. Social workers and probation officers who spread Zero Tolerance attitudes in all their contact with service users and the general public, including in groupwork and projects with young people, can play a role here. Secondary prevention can also occur as a result of educational activities if some women and children are encouraged to seek help, if professionals' awareness is raised to make the help more effective, and if some men's behaviour is challenged so that abuse that has previously been happening comes to an end. This level of prevention covers virtually all the criminal justice and health and welfare intervention included in this book. Tertiary prevention, making the impact of abuse less severe, comes through making agencies and the wider community more responsive to the needs of those women and children who have been abused or who have lived with abuse. Direct work with women and children can come into this category. In the UK, self-help support in refuges and other women-only settings, together with child work in refuges, are the major resource under this heading. Enlightened counselling services could also be used in this way. Elsewhere, in Canada for example, groupwork programmes both for women and for children devote far more attention to this recovery phase.

Campaigns can be pitched, then, at raising the broad issues and changing widescale attitudes towards both abusive men and abused women, at educating the community on how to respond, at indicating to men that their behaviour will not be tolerated, and/or at encouraging women to seek help. Recent efforts in Britain have, between them, tried all of these, though certainly not on the scale of some other countries where far more money has been made available and a higher political profile adopted. It may help concerned social workers and probation officers to feel supported in their efforts to tackle abuse if they know they are doing so in a climate of official backing and generally heightened awareness.

The role of the community in determining attitudes

Communities have traditionally had an involvement in regulating relationships between men and women, though less markedly so during this century when, for white couples at least, their peer group and the media have become the major opinion formers, alongside immediate family members. Dobash and Dobash (1981) give details of ways in which, historically, husbands who failed to dominate and control their wives, and wives who failed to live by this accepted order of things, were humiliated in public parades and other ceremonies involving the whole village – the woman being also punished, for example by ducking. Beating their children, wives and servants was normal behaviour for men, and women were expected to obey their husbands' orders and whims. Interestingly, however, there were 'limits of community tolerance' (p.568) and, in nineteenth-century England, a man who became simply too brutal might be publicly shamed by a procession to his door, with loud singing and banging on pans and other utensils (ibid.). Such public involvement in private violence became submerged beneath the rise of legislative justice and institutionally determined norms and sanctions, leaving women relatively defenceless during a long period when the police and courts were reluctant to intervene. In many minority ethnic contexts in Britian, however, the views of religious and community leaders, and the actions and attitudes of whole communities, have remained important in relation to abuse (Imam, 1994). It is also interesting to note that a contemporary leaflet from a Native American domestic abuse programme (from the Fond du Lac Reservation, close to Duluth) gives advice on what to do 'if you see a woman being beaten or attacked' which includes trying to gather people to move towards an assault taking place in public, or going to knock on the door if a woman is heard screaming indoors.

Only recently have communities across the board, typically prompted

by women's or equivalent units of their elected councils, once again begun
to be seen as needing to take a view about men's treatment of women
in intimate relationships. This could go a great deal further than it has
to date with, for example, employers taking a stand against employees who
are known to be violent (one police officer ceased his domestic violence
overnight when threatened with dismissal), and a whole range of organisations – from churches and other faith-related groups to evening classes
and sports clubs – assisting women with safety planning by refusing
simultaneous (or all) access to abusive ex-partners. Neighbours already
play a significant role in summoning the police to domestic disturbances,
though their position at this private/public interface is awkward and
sometimes dangerous as well as hugely inconsistent (source: research interviewers). Public education campaigns could assist communities to feel
more justified and more supported in offering help to women experiencing
abuse.

Local government action: Zero Tolerance

At the local government level, the then Edinburgh District Council was
one of the first in Britain to use widespread public education to confront
domestic abuse. It drew inspiration from Canada to run a Zero Tolerance
campaign, launched by its Women's Committee in November 1992 (Foley,
1993). This covered not just domestic violence but the whole continuum
of men's criminal abuse of power, using the slogan 'working for zero tolerance of violence against women' with an upper-case 'Z' as a logo. Posters
referring specifically to child sexual abuse, to domestic abuse, and then
to rape were released in three phases – placed on billboards all over the city
and in a range of other highly visible locations, such as pubs and doctors'
surgeries. Community groups and local organisations, together with
academics, worked with the council to run public conferences and debates
during the period of the poster campaign in 1992/93, and agency responses
as well as public attitudes were challenged (Lloyd, 1995, pp.170–1). The
publicity campaign also used official statistics on women assaulted and
killed by partners and raped by men known to them – for example on bookmarks given away in public libraries and on glossy leaflets with returnable
cards to register support – to raise general awareness and challenge
complacence.

Many survivors of sexual violence and intimidation felt they were
receiving public validation of their perspective in the campaign's open
challenge to men to take responsibility for their abuse, as opposed to the
more typical calls to women and children to keep themselves safe (see
below) – and they found this an empowering experience (Foley, 1993,
p.16). The wording on the domestic abuse poster made it clear that all
abusive men were being confronted and not only those in stereotypically

262 Rethinking Domestic Violence

recognised groups: 'She lives with a successful businessman, loving father and respected member of the community. Last week he hospitalised her.' Women's organisations were consulted in the design of the campaign, and the local Asian women's refuge asked not to have Asian women portrayed (pp.18–19). Wider public support for the campaign was also forthcoming: it attracted a considerable unsolicited postal response and its impact was monitored through street surveys which showed it to have been generally well received (p.19), to have attracted attention and generated debate (Lloyd, 1995, p.171). It also established a context of heightened awareness within which the media took more interest in sexual assaults and women's services from a woman's perspective. Many women identified with, and felt heartened by, the campaign. There were stories, for example (Foley, 1993, p.18), of women telling their male harassers to 'Z off' (rather than to 'F*** off'), summing up in the symbolism of this single letter 'Z' an entire social construction of men's abuse and of changing attitudes towards it.

There was some backlash. The 'No man has the right' poster attracted negative responses from men who identified it with the 'Every man is a potential rapist' slogan (ibid.), which many take as a personal insult; in fact, the point of the latter is that a woman never knows when she meets a man whether he may turn out to be a rapist, not that every man actually is likely to become one. Also, some of the smaller sized posters displayed within reach had the word 'male' crossed out of the slogan 'Emotional, physical, sexual, male abuse of power is a crime' (ibid.).

On the positive side, although the posters portrayed women and children, they clearly spoke of men's abuse and men's responsibility. The formal launch of the campaign involved prominent men in signing a public pledge of support that named women and children as usually the targets and men and boys as usually the perpetrators, and set the prevention of crimes of violence against women as a priority for political activity (p. 17). The words 'Male abuse of power is a crime' appeared on the three initial posters. Interestingly, the Edinburgh work began with a study in local secondary schools which revealed that boys in particular widely tolerated violence against women and held many misconceptions about it. Once again, this demonstrates that it is males who need to change and it also links with the role of public education work in schools which is just beginning in Britain and is well established in Canada, for example (see Chapter 6, this volume and also Mullender, 1994b). Following the initiative in Edinburgh, a number of other local authorities in Scotland and England have run Zero Tolerance campaigns, using similar or different materials and usually with the same feminist agenda, although one London borough blurred it into a message about more general abuse in the home, including elder abuse (Foley, 1993, p.19). The National Association of Local Government Women's Committees and women's activist groups such as Rights of Women have worked to co-ordinate, support and evaluate the campaign as a major community education initiative. Public education work by local authorities should not, of course, be regarded as acquitting them of their responsibilities to take many forms of action over domestic abuse, notably in funding adequate services for women and their children.

National Government: 'Don't Stand For It'

At the national level in England, the Home Office, appointed in 1992 as the lead department to co-ordinate governmental responses to domestic violence, funded a poster and leaflet campaign in 1994 aimed at raising awareness of domestic violence as a serious crime, with the slogan 'Don't Stand For It'. The materials were displayed and distributed in public places such as libraries, and were accompanied by advertisements shown in cinemas over a three-month period. The campaign appears to have made less impression than local Zero Tolerance initiatives, and was not widely picked up by the media. It has also been criticised by feminists for targeting women rather than men to take the initiative for change by reporting incidents ('Don't Stand For It' rather than 'No Man Has The Right'), and for representing far less in terms of financial outlay than higher impact public education campaigns on drunk-driving (where, incidentally, there is no difficulty in targeting the offender rather than the victim). It is widely felt that central government should be prepared to devote a similar level of resources to promoting women's safety. Central, state and provincial governments in Australia, Canada and Papua New Guinea have all done far more than has been attempted in England (Morley, undated). The Ministry of Education in the province of Ontario, Canada, for example, has alone spent millions of dollars over a decade or so.

In Scotland, a media campaign funded by the Scottish Office also ran in the second half of 1994, in the form of posters and a television commercial with a follow-up giving the number of a telephone information service. The broad aims of the campaign were to make male perpetrators think about the implications and consequences of their violence, to foster a view of men's violence to women as socially unacceptable, and to give women the confidence to report assaults to the police (Scottish Office Central Research Unit, 1995, p.2). Independent research by Strathclyde University into the impact of the campaign revealed that, when a photo-prompt was used, 9 out of 10 people could recall having seen the commercial, with 97 per cent of young adults aged 16 to 24 having seen it, although only 30 per cent of all respondents felt they had been told something new (p.vii). The television advertisement was the first Government broadcast ever to have to be shown after the 9 p.m. 'watershed' (transmissions earlier in the evening are judged to be acceptable for children to watch without parental guidance), owing to the scenes of violence portrayed, yet it related to a common event in the lives of thousands of people including children. Again, there has been criticism of the campaign. Scottish Women's Aid has argued that Government attempts to encourage more women to seek help are of little use unless they are accompanied by funding of comprehensive services for women and children escaping violence. As in England, one of the aims of the campaign was to encourage women to have the confidence to report abuse – thus placing the onus on them to take action. It does seem to have resulted in an increase in requests for help received by Women's Aid groups in Scotland (which rose from 26,000 to 35,000 in 1995 according to news reporting in *Community Care*, 15–21 February 1996, p.4) but was not accompanied by any increase in resources to women's organisations or any assurances for the future from the Scottish Office. The campaign was not effective in encouraging perpetrators to change their behaviour and, despite a growing climate of disapproval, it did not lead to men directly receiving adverse comment from others (p.68). Publicity aimed at the general public may work better if it offers practical guidance on what to do and combats collusion in the form of inappropriate remarks and misdirected humour (ibid.). Subsequently, the public education work in the Scottish Office has moved on to the dangers of fire and of young drivers (*Today*, BBC Radio 4, 25th August 1995), leaving the need for public education and attitude change on domestic abuse very far from satisfied. Sustained work for change is perhaps becoming harder to publicise in the age of the sound-bite.

Private sector

It is not just central and local government in the UK that have taken public stands against men's violence, or could do far more in policy terms. The private sector – industry, commerce, and the privatised utilities – has also been involved in a small way through donating money (Allied Dunbar has given corporate support to a number of local Women's Aid groups), considering the implications of its product ranges (British Telecommunications), or undertaking outright campaigning (The Body Shop).

British Telecommunications (BT), in offering two new telephone services, for example, has had to design them with an awareness of their potential impact on women harassed by ex-partners or other abusers, amongst other customers in dangerous circumstances. New, low-cost telephone equipment with the 'caller display' service shows the number from which a call is being received. This could make abused women reluctant to call formal or informal sources of help because they can no longer be assured of anonymity. In fact, the caller can prevent the number being revealed by dialling 141 first, or making a special arrangement with BT – possibilities which probably require greater publicity. The 'call return' service, on the other hand, gives the number of the last call received, if the call's recipient dials 1471. Refuges have had to reassure women that they do not trace incoming calls, as well as arranging for their own number to be automatically withheld from outgoing calls (e.g. *Evening News*, Worcester, 1st December 1994, p.11). On the plus side, a woman who can afford to, could invest in the call display facility and an answerphone in order to decide whether to answer her telephone in person – only doing so when the number is recognisably that of someone she trusts. Although her abuser could easily circumvent her precaution by dialling 141 before calling her, she could include this in the category of calls for which she would not pick up the receiver. There might also be uses for the call return service in discovering where abusers are calling from, assuming the 141 block had not been utilised.

A socially active involvement in the issue of the continuum of violence against women comes from The Body Shop, a company that takes a strong ethical stand on a wide variety of human rights and environmental issues. In Canada, the company's shops have turned a range of items into public education materials opposing woman abuse, such as carrier bags, bookmarks and T-shirts, have distributed information, and contributed a portion of profits from certain goods to relevant women's organisations. The Body Shop Canada also incorporated into a broadsheet a list of ten ways customers could work locally for women's safety, and four steps to support political action. These focused predominantly on supporting and publicising emergency and support services for women, with just one mention of protesting at inadequate disposals for violent offenders. Similarly, in Britain, WAFE has worked with The Body Shop to raise awareness of domestic violence issues through a *Women's Rights* broadsheet (Women's Aid Federation England, 1993/94) and a wider campaign launched in September 1995 based around a petition, a leaflet, a paper bag to wrap purchased goods that carries the campaign's slogan, logo and petition, and a lapel sticker, as well as window displays in the company's shops. The campaign slogan, '1 in 5 women suffer domestic violence', backs a call for increased refuge provision. In 1996, this has moved on to leaflets carrying a call to 'Blow the whistle on Domestic Violence', together with protest postcards to be sent to the Lord Chancellor seeking amendments to the Family Law Bill to provide better protection for all women, married and unmarried (see Chapter 2, this volume).

There are, in fact, implications for the economy both in women taking sick leave as a result of injuries or stress, or being forced to leave jobs to move away from the abuser, and in abusers increasingly missing time from work if more are arrested and if sentences more regularly include imprisonment. There is every reason for employers' organisations to follow the lead of some trades unions, for example the former NALGO (now Unison) in its National Women's Committee's leaflet entitled: 'You Are Not Alone: Domestic Violence is a Trade Union Issue'. This covered campaigning, awareness, support for members, and also negotiation with employers for job security and flexibility, for example over confidential redeployment, no penalising of sick leave resulting from abuse (the present author has just heard of a nurse on a temporary contract dismissed by an NHS Trust for this reason), availability of paid leave or irregular hours, and free counselling and other support. Employer and employee organisations need to become more aware of domestic abuse and advise their members on how to respond to it constructively.

No substitute for services

There must, of course, be a note of caution in respect of public education and awareness campaigns. While resources remain scarce, the first priority must always be to spend far more on direct emergency and outreach services for women and children. It is galling and often dangerous for women to be told to seek help when refuges are full and other alternatives scarce, however hard Women's Aid works to make all contacts from women helpful and supportive. There must never be any hint of diverting funds away from direct services, nor away from women's organisations more generally, into the educational or other work. A poster does not make a woman and her children safe.

Furthermore, evaluations of campaigns undertaken overseas suggest that, to work effectively, public education materials require careful planning and targeting, considerable funding, multi-media and multi-lingual distribution, an intensive impact with regular repeats to keep interest alive, and co-ordination with a wider programme of services for prevention (Morley, unpublished). Most of these factors were present in the Edinburgh Zero Tolerance campaign, for example, which was certainly carefully thought through with local women's groups (Foley, 1993, pp.18–19), although there is nowhere in Britain that can claim co-ordination of agency and community services for women, children and men to the degree that this exists in places like London, Ontario (Canada) and Duluth, Minnesota (USA).

Nevertheless, it is good to see 'Zero Tolerance' and similar posters displayed in public spaces, and providing backing for those professionals, like the more aware social workers and probation officers, who are trying to confront men's complacence and women's feelings of fear, stigma and isolation.

THE OVERALL AIM: THE EMPOWERMENT OF WOMEN

As has been shown in earlier chapters, the single most empowering thing any practitioner can offer a woman who is being abused is to take her seriously and to assist her to become safe, in whatever way feels best to her when she considers her own and her children's needs and knows the options available. Assisting in such a decision inevitably requires a good knowledge of practical sources of help and effective liaison to back this up, through links with Women's Aid, Black women's groups, the police, solicitors, and local housing agencies for example. It also requires an empowering approach to supporting women in the choices they make. This is certainly needed in the individual cases taken on in social service and probation settings, but it can often be most effectively achieved in the longer term through collective work in women's groups and organisations, including those for Black women, lesbian women, disabled and older women.

As was suggested in Chapter 5, all contexts in which groups of women meet together, including social services provided or funded settings, could also employ the techniques of discussion and empowerment in women-only groups to help women disclose current or past abuse, regain a strong sense of self, and decide what actions to take and what help to seek. At present, there is far less awareness in statutory agencies of this kind of possibility than of the need to begin planning responses for children and for abusive men. It is as if the women at the heart of woman abuse were invisible.

Renewal and regrowth: the role of mutual support in refuges

In fact, once a woman feels that the immediate danger is less, because she or her abuser has left or because legal remedies have been used against him – and always because she has a safety plan to follow – she needs time and space to regain some equilibrium and to decide what kind of life she wants to make for herself. Although there are likely to be continuing anxieties – for example as to whether her partner will find her or continue to make trouble, and/or whether she will be able to make ends meet or find suitable housing – there is much that can be positive about this time of renewal and rediscovery.

Women in refuges, because of the self-help and mutual support ethos and the woman-centred approach offered there – operating from women's own perspective and choices – typically find great support from one another and from the workers. They attend house meetings, at which mutual solutions are sought to problems of group living, and gain strength from the realisation that many other women have lived through similar horrors which, self-evidently therefore, *cannot* have individual causes: 'If me, her and her have all been battered, it can't be all us faults' (abused woman, during women's group meeting attended by the author; see also Clifton, 1985, pp.51–2; Condonis *et al.*, 1989, pp.8–9). All the verbal abuse from the ex-partner, making it sound as if the problems were the woman's own fault and as if she were no good, can be identified as just another part of his campaign of belittlement and control. Nevertheless, they will have taken a personal toll by sapping self-esteem and self-confidence. It can take time to build or rebuild a positive, assertive self-image. There is some evidence that group support like that in refuges is more effective than therapy in assisting women to rebuild their emotional strength (Rodriguez, 1988, p.242) by reducing feelings of guilt and stigma and explaining abuse as part of a wider social problem.

It is also clear that women meeting together in specialist Black refuges find them invaluable in understanding their own particular experiences of abuse, for example as lived within a South Asian, African Caribbean, Latin American or Chinese family and community structure, as well as the way in which problems are compounded by the inappropriate and racist responses of British welfare and criminal justice agencies, for instance in offering rehousing to areas where racial attacks are common, or demanding to see passports (Guru, 1986, pp.162–3). Such groups can support women in withstanding racism and, for those who are unlikely to be accepted back or who would find no safety in traditional communities, they can help in building a new identity and new support networks (p.163).

Outreach, support after the refuge, and other services for women

The mutual help found in refuges already continues into the community on many occasions, but this is not consistent owing to lack of funding. Rather, it happens when ex-residents live near enough to keep in touch or in other *ad hoc* ways. Nevertheless, Binney *et al.* (1988, p.172) found that 83 per cent of women re-interviewed eighteen months after their initial survey felt they had benefited from staying in a refuge rather than being rehoused immediately on leaving the abuse, 'often because of continuing contact with the refuge and friends made while they were living there'. Writing about Asian women, Guru (1986, p.164) describes a Birmingham refuge where 'A vital development has been the support offered to the residents by women who have left the refuge and now live independently.'

Community-based groups could be offered in a more organised way for women who have been through refuges as well as for other women, if the money were available. In New South Wales (Noesjirwan, 1985, pp.84–5) a need has been identified for coherent follow-up programmes and funded worker time to run them. Suggestions include a regular ex-residents' day at each refuge and liaison between refuges to offer a network of support groups as women are rehoused into different areas. The same publication identifies the need to target rural areas where refuges might take on a range of extra roles, if suitably funded, to cover the shortfall in support, for example, around issues of rape and incest. Wilson *et al.* (1989, p.282), based on research on readmissions to shelters, regard continual contact with former residents as a crucial supportive network in preventing the woman returning to further abuse as well as helping with reintegration into the community. Refuge workers in Britain are very aware that, when a woman moves on, she can benefit from help to locate the local resources, groups and forms of support that she will need to 'make a go' of her new life and that may make all the difference to her. One woman tried leaving home eight times in three months because, after 25 years as a housewife, she found the hurdles of police, courts, housing, poll tax, schools, and the social security office too much to cope with. With adequate support from refuge workers, however, she is now rehoused and is doing voluntary work in her local community as a precursor to seeking employment.

There are examples from the USA of projects that offer a whole range of services to help rebuild women's strength and confidence. Groups are a fundamental part of this:

> When a woman walks into a group of ten other women who share the common experience of being physically abused, the silence imposed upon her by her assailant and by the community is broken . . . we begin to understand how our lives have been shaped by other people's self-interests. . . . With few exceptions, batterers attempt to cut women off from other people, places, ideas and resources that would help her understand what is happening to her.
>
> (Pence, 1987, pp.2 and 15)

This is part of maintaining his power over her while convincing her that it is all her fault. Group membership cuts through this 'closed system' (ibid.) and helps the woman to re-evaluate her life and begin making her own decisions. Pence writes of having five different community-based groups running every week as well as one in the shelter (refuge) (p.1). Three are neighbourhood educational groups, including one specifically for Native American women. A fourth runs alongside a court-mandated abusers' programme, and the last is an action group mainly consisting of women who are now separated. The same project offers active outreach to women still living in abusive relationships, with child care costs paid where necessary, transport arranged for them to attend groups, and individual befriending used to overcome isolation prior to first attending a group. Group members also offer newer members help and companionship through legal processes, in the same way as refuge residents and workers do in Britain. In some places, such as Duluth, legal advocacy services for women offer volunteer support throughout periods of court hearings related to abuse (including child care cases) and also monitor court statistics to gauge how women are being treated, leading to lobbying and training of the judiciary. Advocacy has been slower to develop in Britain, though there are examples. In Mansfield, Nottinghamshire, a voluntary group called ASSET (Advice, Service, Support and Escort Team) has been formed to support a woman through all stages of the legal process if she chooses to pursue that route (Nottinghamshire County Council Social Services et al., 1993/94, p.176). In

Islington, one aim of the Home Office-funded Domestic Violence Matters project is to offer an immediate crisis intervention response to women, delivered by an independent service working in close conjunction with the police and able to respond when the police are called. Many more such services are needed.

Women's Aid groups and other women's organisations in the UK have, from the beginning, been acutely aware of the need to provide a wider range of services and to create non-threatening ways to access these. Imaginative examples include a weekly drop-in which ran in a shopping centre in Bristol – offering cheap tea and coffee, a chance for women experiencing abuse to seek information safely, and for women who had been through refuges to get back together for a chat – and the operation now of a number of charity shops which combine low-cost goods with freely available advice in a safe location. Additional funding sources have been tapped and the roles played by workers rethought in order to meet the needs of a continually widening range of women. Currently, for instance, Hereford Women's Aid runs three advice surgeries in nearby market towns, part-funded as a rural development initiative. In Greenwich, a support group runs in the local housing office. Around a third of refuges have separate advice centres or contact points and all Women's Aid groups extend beyond pure refuge provision, notably into informal advice giving, drop-in and after-care, but often also into second stage housing or other formalised services. Over 30 outreach workers meet in a national support group; their roles include training other agencies' staff and keeping them up to date with information, and making contact with women through solicitors, police, social workers and other bodies. Developing this kind of work comprehensively is possible only where there are designated workers, since it is extremely time-consuming, especially when agency demand builds up. Every Women's Aid group responds to emergencies on a 24-hour basis and gives considerable informal help and advice over the telephone in office hours. Help-lines involving the police and other agencies also have a role to play in supplementing the likelihood of women successfully contacting someone who can listen, believe and respond to them and their immediate circumstances. The lack of resources is the only real obstacle to continued expansion of an ever-increasing range of activity by Women's Aid and other women's groups, but it is a very real one.

Mugford (1990, p.4) refers to the crucial need for 24-hour crisis intervention services. Existing services, including those in the statutory sector, are often not geared up to deal with domestic violence appropriately and are often not available at the most necessary times. Such crisis services should include a help-line, with responses available in a range of languages, backed up with posters and other public education (see above) also in a range of languages and in appropriate media, including the ethnic press. There are now many models available from various countries of information materials, attractively presented and very readable, from book length (National Collective of Independent Women's Refuges Inc., 1988) to the tiny and easily concealed *Advice Card for Women: Legal Advice and Information for Women Experiencing Violence in the Home* (Attwood, 1990), produced by CAPA, a voluntary agency in East London. More attention still needs to be given to ways of conveying information to disabled women, for example through posters in accessible toilets and through disability organisations, an issue that some local authorities – such as Hounslow and Islington – have begun to recognise.

The content of women's groups

In countries where there are co-ordinated programmes of response to domestic violence, groupwork offered by women to women, and run on feminist principles, is always a key element of the support offered, particularly after separation from the abusive man. A number of the programmes have produced manuals about their groups. Although the work in Duluth, Minnesota, is better known in Britain for its groups for abusive men, the help given to women is actually the bedrock of a raft of services there. The women's group manual by Ellen Pence (1987) – *In Our Best Interest: A Process for Personal and Social Change* – deserves to be far more widely known and used. It draws on the same 'power and control' wheel as the men's groups, now familiar to many in Britain (see Chapter 2, this volume). Other examples of women's group publications include a guide by Condonis *et al.* (1989) – *The Mutual-Help Group: A Therapeutic Program for Women Who Have Been Abused* – which developed from work in the Macarthur Region of Sydney, New South Wales, and another, the *Women's Therapy Handbook*, from the Women's Therapy Team of the Domestic Abuse Project (DAP) in Minneapolis, Minnesota (Domestic Abuse Project Women's Therapy Team, 1991).

Groups like these aim at a process of healing and growth. They are not simply support groups, although they are supportive, but tend to be organised to a pre-set programme or curriculum and to be run by group facilitators. Terms like 'therapeutic group' (Condonis *et al.*, 1989, p.8) and 'treatment' (DAP Women's Therapy Team, 1991) tend to be used more freely in American and American-influenced settings than in Britain, and need not imply a clinical setting. The Duluth subtitle (Pence, 1987), which refers to 'personal and social change', is probably the one with which UK readers can feel most comfortable.

The Duluth groupwork model focuses on helping women to understand abuse as a man's individual responsibility located within a society-wide (and worldwide) framework of oppression, works on supporting women to name their own reality of having been trapped in the abuse, and moves towards building the confidence for an independent life – with the potential of remaining involved in groupwork for social and community action if participants so choose. The manual includes group exercises, homework assignments, women's stories and poems, guidance and discussion papers for facilitators, and accounts of running and belonging to groups, all organised within ten themes covering the causes and effects of men's abuse and control tactics, as well as women's enforced submission, survival, anger and energy for change. It emphasises internalised oppression and cultural expectations as amongst the reasons women stay in a bad relationship. This is not a superficial 'how-to-do-it' text but a rich and densely argued (though highly readable) source of critical rethinking on women's experiences. It also includes accounts of other women's groups, such as one for Native American women, and is stronger on the integration of a range of oppressions (e.g. class, age, race) than many American sources, particularly of its date. It also constructively combines individual affirmation ('I am a lovable person, I deserve to be treated well') with the scope for external change ('What can we do that will make a difference?').

Lacking the exercises and direct groupwork content because it was not written as a groupwork manual, but equally strong on personal accounts (this time British), art and poetry, analysis of the experience of abuse (and leaving it) and debunking of myths – and hence another possible source for groupwork content provided the facilitators can improvise implementation – is *Breaking Through* (1989). This could be usefully combined with the Duluth manual (Pence, 1987).

Although there may currently seem to be little scope for groupwork with women in social work and probation settings in the UK (it has, if anything, been cut back), this is unfortunate because social workers, provided their approach is a fundamentally feminist one, do have many of the necessary skills and a useful tradition on which to draw (Donnelly, 1986; Dominelli, 1990; Butler and Wintram, 1991). In recognition of this, the London Borough of Hackney *Good Practice Guidelines* (1994, p.46) state: 'Social workers who wish to run groups for women who are or who have experienced domestic violence will be encouraged to do so by the Department.' Also in a local authority setting, but taking a different approach to meeting the need, Islington's Women's Unit (*Community Care*, 19th–25th May 1994, p.28) has trained volunteers to facilitate support groups for survivors of domestic violence. Earlier chapters of this book have already suggested that there may be many other opportunities than are currently being used – in group care, nursery and numerous other settings – for social services staff to facilitate supportive discussion wherever women gather together. Groups for women whose children have been identified as having child care needs, for example (Fleming and Ward, 1992; Butler, 1994) will always include women who are being or have been abused, and can be a fruitful location for meeting women's as well as children's needs if approached in the right vein. Probation officers had a fine tradition of offering groups to women clients, prisoners' wives, and so on, which would be worth fighting to revive. Suggesting and supporting such work in the visitors' centres attached to prisons might be one way forward.

Community work and youthwork settings are, of course, ideal for women's groups because they are free of the 'statutory' role and stigma of social services and leave women freer to set their own agendas along self-help lines or to take up opportunities to attend groups offered by others. In North Derbyshire, for example, women who were formerly refuge residents have taken the initiative to meet fortnightly in a community centre as the TASK group – 'Talk, Advice, Support and Knowledge' – to empower one another to build new lives, a stage that can be the hardest part of leaving or separating. In Toronto, Canada, paid workers take referrals for a twelve-week programme for women who have been abused in childhood and/or adulthood (source: group literature, YWCA of Metropolitan Toronto). Groups are run both in the evenings and daytime, child care is provided, fares are paid, and the venue is wheelchair accessible. Meetings begin with music and a 'check-in time' to deal with current feelings; they then give each woman individual space and also the chance to participate in pre-planned discussion topics, and finish with music and a feelings 'check-out' at the end. One of the most important topics is women's anger – how to name it, how to give yourself permission (despite social conventions) to express it, how to use it as part of a process towards change. It is not uncommon for women in the group to be experiencing disturbances of mood, sleep patterns, memory, or identity which might easily have led them into the typically far less self-enhancing setting of individual therapy or clinical treatment for mental health problems if the group had not been available.

Guidance is available on both self-help and worker facilitated models of groupwork. Hammersmith and Fulham (McGibbon and Kelly, 1989, section 13) has a two-page guide to starting a support group in its *Abuse of Women in the Home* pack, for example, and there are professional group-work texts that are useful (e.g. Mullender and Ward, 1991b), provided they are combined with ample reading on domestic abuse. Similar background reading is also strongly advised for the volunteers or workers in any group that brings women together with the stated aim or the potential to explore the issues in their lives because abuse will typically be on the agenda. Whether it meets as a drop-in in a community centre, a sewing session for Muslim women, a women and health class in a family centre, or discussion time in an adult education setting, any women-only group can constitute an opportunity to offer useful support and advice to women living with or women who have left abuse, and to make available suitable resource materials, as well as to validate women's experiences, feelings and aspirations for the future.

Women who have belonged to women-only groups frequently report deriving great benefit from them, making tremendous strides in personal terms, as these quotations from group members in the UK show: 'It's just amazing that someone else is saying the same as happened to you – it's a really unbelievable experience and instantly brings you out of yourself' and 'You know that you're no longer on your own, that others feel the same way – that you're not mad, or, if you are, so is everyone.' A woman who had been through a group in Duluth said (at a training event for professionals) that discussion in the group helped her see her abuser not just as her husband and the father of her children, on whom she tended to keep taking pity, but as part of a bigger picture where so many men abuse women and get away with it that it is important for action to be taken against individual men whenever this is safe for women. She also pointed out that women's groups are full of fun and intimate moments, as well as shared pain. Although the emotional content is high and many terrible memories are recalled, these groups are marvellously rewarding to work with, whereas in men's groups there is always the question of their untested effectiveness with any individual man. Workers vary as to how easy they feel with either the pain or the uncertainty, i.e. with women's groups or men's groups, and some women groupworkers in large projects or in the course of a career move between the two, getting fired up by women's accounts of abuse and refreshed by women's survival strengths to go back and challenge abusive men. Of course, male workers only have the option of operating in men's groups and therefore have to try harder, through reading, discussion and self-confrontation, to understand what their work means to individual women and to the collectivity of women.

A framework for empowerment

An empowering approach to women who have survived domestic abuse can stem from a generic model of empowerment. An appropriate one from the social work literature, for example, is that by Mullender and Ward (1991b). This is based on a model incorporating six principles for practice (expanded from the original five: see Mullender and Ward, 1991a and 1991b, pp.30 –1) that are most relevant to a groupwork approach but also have wider applicability. Indeed, the model can serve to sum up the approach taken throughout this book and can also be used as a good test to apply to work in any setting to see whether it is grounded in enlightened attitudes.

Adapting the language and coverage of the principles for the present context, these could read as follows:

1. We need to take a view of each woman experiencing abuse that refuses to accept any negative labels applied to her by her abuser or by other agencies because of the abuse or her reaction to it, and recognises her instead as a person with strengths, survival strategies, skills, understanding and ability.

2. Women who experience abuse have rights, including the right to be heard and the right to control their own lives. It follows that they also have the right to choose what kinds of intervention to accept in their lives. No one should try to make choices or decisions for an abused woman, such as whether she should leave or stay, whether it would be more or less safe to arrest and prosecute the abuser. She is the expert on his dangerousness and on her own safety. If she is invited to join an empowerment group, she has the right to decide whether or not to participate, and the right to help define the issues on which the group will take action.

3. The problem of men's abuse of women is complex, with its roots in a patriarchal society and other structures of oppression, so responses to it always need to reflect this. Neither men's actions nor women's responses can ever be fully understood if they are seen solely as a result of personal inadequacies. Issues of social oppression, and social policy responses, are major contributory factors in what happens to women, including those who are trying to rebuild their lives as a result of abuse. This also reminds us that, however skilled we may be as individual professionals, we cannot help women properly unless houses, incomes, child care facilities, civil law and criminal justice remedies, and so on, are adequate. Therefore we should also work to improve these.

4. Practice can most effectively be built on the knowledge that women acting together can be powerful. Women who feel they lack power can gain it through working together in groups and collectivities. Women's organisations are effective because they work collectively to help women be safe and strong.

5. Facilitators of groups and organisations run along feminist lines do not 'lead' them in traditional ways, but assist women in making decisions for themselves and in taking control of whatever outcomes ensue. Though experienced workers and group facilitators do employ particular skills and knowledge, these are often based on life experience (including of abuse), do not accord privilege, and are shared with the group. The most empowering settings for women are women-only organisations run along collective lines, such as Women's Aid and Rape Crisis. They, in turn, can be most effective if they are supported and consulted – not undermined – by other agencies, which means understanding their philosophy and co-operating with it.

6. All work in the field of domestic abuse, as in any other, must challenge oppression whether by reason of gender, sexuality, race, age, class, disability or any other form of spurious social differentiation, and challenge, too, the abuses of power on which such oppression is based. Patriarchal power is seen as the cause of domestic abuse, but the interaction of oppressive dynamics in families, groups, communities, organisations and societies is complex and must be considered in its entirety.

Asking the question 'Why?': not an individual problem

Another important feature of the empowerment model analysed and described by Mullender and Ward (1991b) is that groups are taken through the questions 'What?', Why?' and 'How?' Most social work practice has a tendency to move straight from asking '*What* is the problem?' to deciding *how* to tackle it. The function of the question 'Why?' is to give pause to consider *why* this problem exists. In work connected with domestic abuse, asking 'Why?' leads into the explanations explored in Chapter 2 which emphasise social structural – patriarchal – explanations rather than individual weaknesses in the abuser or the woman experiencing abuse. Though individual men must take responsibility for their actions, and need to change their attitudes and behaviour, this will happen on a wide scale only when the wider society and its institutions cease to tolerate and condone abuse. This asking 'Why?' is very close to what happens in the Duluth women's groups where women start by sharing their current issues and are helped by the facilitators to analyse these in terms of personal, institutional and cultural realities of men's abuse. Poems, songs, television clips on video, and any other materials brought into the group are used in this way to find the underlying themes about the position of men and women in society and the options for change.

As this book has attempted to show, if social workers and probation officers do not develop a clear understanding of the inadequacies of many of the popular assumptions and myths about men's violence, they may be side-tracked into all manner of inappropriate responses. These can include attempting couple or family work when the woman is in current danger (see Chapter 7), or believing that an anger control or alcohol group on its own will stop a man from abusing his partner (see Chapters 8 and 9) or, perhaps, assuming that the woman must find the abuse tolerable because she does not leave or has previously left and returned (see Chapter 2). A clear understanding of *why* men abuse women, based on an analysis of men's social power, leads to quite different responses which emphasise safety and empowerment for women and children – so that women can make the safest available choices at their own pace – as well as intervention to hold men accountable for their actions and to require them to stop their abuse. We need to find as many ways as possible of listening to women and children, responding to women and children, and challenging the men who abuse women and children, in a manner informed by an understanding of the operation of male power in society.

CONCLUSION

We have been living, over the last few years, through a resurgence of interest in the subject of men's abuse of women in the context of relationships and family life. Sometimes salacious and voyeuristic, this interest has been reflected throughout the media, from long-running soap operas to studio audience participation shows, and in multi-professional attempts to be seen to be doing something in response. Like the journalists and media researchers, the health, welfare and criminal justice professionals involved in confronting the issue are having to rethink their tendency to regard 'serious' domestic abuse as something exceptional. The best estimates at gathering statistics and the devastation that abuse can be seen to be causing in the lives of many thousands of women and children are shocking. As the statistics are still almost certainly an understatement, and as many of those who need it are still not receiving help, we should be spurred into the action necessary to give women and children real options to live in safety.

Within each agency, and with co-ordination between agencies, this means developing clear policies and setting priorities focused on the needs of women and children, gathering data and collating information, outlining what is currently considered to be best practice, and being answerable for all these improvements to a wider grouping which includes a strong voice for women's organisations. Above all, it means ensuring that every woman who takes the risk of seeking help finds that risk worthwhile.

All social workers and probation officers, and their agencies, need to take a lead from Women's Aid and to base their work with women who have been abused on a believing, supportive and empowering approach underpinned by a feminist analysis. In this way, they *can* confront domestic violence far more constructively and cease to be part of the problem.

Notes

1 THE TERMS OF THE DEBATE

1 There are also refuges not affiliated to Women's Aid.
2 An earlier wave of action was marked by a Select Committee, established by Parliament to examine all aspects of 'violence in marriage' (House of Commons, 1975). This led to some changes in the civil law, following which the issue largely disappeared from view until the late 1980s.
3 The term 'Black' is used in a political sense to denote the commonality of experience of all those who suffer racisim because of skin colour. It is acknowledged that there are also many differences between minority ethnic communities and individuals.

2 WHAT DO WE KNOW ABOUT DOMESTIC VIOLENCE?

1 There is clearly a risk of voyeurism and of repeat victimisation in including the experiences of particular women in this chapter. However, the main intended audience for this book, social workers and probation officers, are accustomed to dealing with people's lives and may not be moved to action by a purely statistical or technical account. Readers are asked to remember the personal distress and resilience that lie behind the facts on these pages and not to slip into the complacency of regarding these simply as 'case histories'.
2 Dowry was formerly a substitute for inheritance but now passes directly to the new husband's family and may include continuing expectations of, or dissatisfactions with payment. Indian brides go to live in their husbands' families and are most at risk during the first few years of marriage and when they are totally economically dependent. Continuing torture and abuse are also reported. Dowry has been illegal in India since 1961 (Heise, 1989, p.5), with the law tightened since (Prasad and Vijayalakshmi, 1988, pp.276–7), but persists there across all caste, religious, class and regional groupings (ibid., p.271). It is not illegal in Britain.

8 THE PROBATION SERVICE AND DOMESTIC VIOLENCE

1 Stelman (1993, p.196) has called for both ACOP and the National Association of Probation Officers (NAPO) to express their concern about the primary

purpose rule whereby women who come to Britain to marry or join their spouses must normally 'prove' that their marriage is genuine by staying with their husbands for one year before they can apply in their own right to remain permanently. They have no recourse to public funds during this time.

2 See Pence *et al*. 1989 for a useful comparison with a well-developed American context.

10   WORKING TOGETHER FOR CHANGE

1 On 1st April 1996, Cleveland County Council was replaced by four unitary authorities, leaving the Forum with the decision as to whether (and how) to rename itself.

References

Abrahams, C. (1994) *The Hidden Victims: Children and Domestic Violence*, London: NCH Action for Children

Adams, D. (1988) 'Treatment models of men who batter: a profeminist analysis' in Yllö, K. and Bograd, M. *Feminist Perspectives on Wife Abuse*, Newbury Park, CA: Sage

Adams, D. and McCormick, A.J. (1982) 'Men unlearning violence: a group approach based on the collective model' in Roy, M. (ed.) *The Abusive Partner: An Analysis of Domestic Battering*, New York: Van Nostrand Reinhold

Ahmad, B. (1990) *Black Perspectives in Social Work*, Birmingham: Venture Press

Ahmad, S. (1990) 'Domestic violence in Malaysia', *The Law Institute Journal*, June, 64(6), pp.527–9

Ahmed, S. (1986) 'Cultural racism in work with Asian women and girls' in Ahmed, S., Chetham, J. and Small, J., *Social Work with Black Children and Their Families*, London: Batsford

Alibhai, Y. (1989) 'For better or worse', *New Statesman and Society*, 6th January, pp.22–3

Andrews, B. and Brown, G.W. (1988) 'Marital violence in the community: a biographical approach', *British Journal of Psychiatry*, 153, pp.305–12

Andrews, C., Nadirshaw, Z., Curtis, Z. and Ellis, J. (1994) *Women, Mental Health and Good Practice*, Brighton: Pavilion Publishing

Association of Chief Officers of Probation (1992) *Position Statement on Domestic Violence*, London: ACOP (Also available as House of Commons Home Affairs Committee, 1992b, *Domestic Violence. Memoranda of Evidence*, Memorandum 6. NB. Original author: David Sleightholm). Under revision in 1996

Attwood, B. (1990) *Advice Card for Women: Legal Advice and Information for Women Experiencing Violence in the Home*, London: CAPA (East London)

Au, S. and Banu, H. (1991) 'Hope after hospital', *Social Work Today*, 14th November, p.18

Avis, J. M. (1988) 'Deepening awareness: a private study guide to feminism and family therapy' in Braverman, L. (ed.) *A Guide to Feminist Family Therapy*, New York: Harrington

Ball, M. (1990) *Children's Workers in Women's Aid Refuges: A Report on the Experience of Nine Refuges in England*, London: National Council for Voluntary Child Care Organisations

Ball, M. (1994) *Funding Refuge Services: A Study of Refuge Support Services for Women and Children Experiencing Domestic Violence*, Bristol: Women's Aid Federation England

Ball, M. (1995) *Domestic Violence and Social Care: A Report on Conferences Held by the Social Services Inspectorate in London and Leeds, Spring 1995*, London: Social Services Inspectorate

Barman, M.R. (1981) 'One hospital's very workable approach to battering', *RN*, October, pp.23–8 and 102

Barnes, M. and Maple, N. (1992) *Women and Mental Health: Challenging the Stereotypes*, Birmingham: Venture Press

Barnett, O.W. and LaViolette, A.D. (1993) *It Could Happen to Anyone: Why Battered Women Stay*, Newbury Park, CA: Sage

Barron, J. (1990) *Not Worth the Paper*, Bristol: Women's Aid Federation England

Barron, J. and Harwin, N. (1994) 'The myth of the battered husband', *ROW Bulletin*, Spring, pp.5–7

Beninati, J. (1989) 'Pilot project for male batterers', *Social Work with Groups*, 12(2), pp.63–74

Bensted, J., Brown, A., Forbes, C. and Wall, R. (1994) 'Men working with men in groups: masculinity and crime', *Groupwork*, 7(1), pp.37–49

Berk, R.A., Berk, S.F., Loseke, D.R. and Rauma, D. (1983) 'Mutual combat and other family violence myths' in Finkelhor, D., Gelles, R.J., Hotaling, G.T. and Straus, M.A. (eds) *The Dark Side of Families: Current Family Violence Research*, Beverly Hills, CA: Sage

Bilinkoff, J. (1995) 'Empowering battered women as mothers' in Peled, E., Jaffe, P.G. and Edleson, J.L. (eds) *Ending the Cycle of Violence: Community Responses to Children of Battered Women*, Thousand Oaks, CA: Sage

Binney, V., Harkell, G. and Nixon, J. (1985) 'Refuges and housing for battered women' in Pahl, J. (ed.) *Private Violence and Public Policy: The Needs of Battered Women and the Response of the Public Services*, London: Routledge & Kegan Paul

Binney, V., Harkell, G. and Nixon, J. (1988 reprint of a 1981 text) *Leaving Violent Men: A Study of Refuges and Housing for Abused Women*, Leeds: Women's Aid Federation England. Reprinted, Bristol: Women's Aid Federation England, 1988, with new foreword. (Page references are to the 1988 reprint.)

Bly, R. (1990) *Iron John: A Book About Men*, Reading, MA: Addison Wesley

Bograd, M. (1984) 'Family systems approaches to wife battering: a feminist critique', *American Journal of Orthopsychiatry*, 54(4), October, pp.558–68

Bograd, M. (1988a) 'Enmeshment, fusion or relatedness? A conceptual analysis' in Braverman, L. (ed.) *A Guide to Feminist Family Therapy*, New York: Harrington

Bograd, M. (1988b) 'Feminist perspectives on wife abuse: an introduction' in Yllö, K. and Bograd, M. *Feminist Perspectives on Wife Abuse*, Newbury Park, CA: Sage

Borkowski, M., Murch, M. and Walker, V. (1983) *Marital Violence: The Community Response*, London: Tavistock

Bowker, L. H. (1983) *Beating Wife-Beating*, Lexington, MA: Lexington Books, D.C. Heath

Bowker, L. H. and Maurer, L. (1987) 'The medical treatment of battered wives', *Women and Health*, 12(1), pp.25–45

Bowker, L. H., Arbitell, M. and McFerron, J. R. (1988) 'On the relationship between wife beating and child abuse' in Yllö, K. and Bograd, M. *Feminist Perspectives on Wife Abuse*, Newbury Park, CA: Sage

Bradley, C. (1994) 'Why male violence against women is a development issue: reflections from Papua New Guinea' in Davies, M. *Women and Violence: Realities and Responses Worldwide*, London: Zed Books

Brand, P.A. and Kidd, A.H. (1986) 'Frequency of physical aggression in heterosexual and female homosexual dyads', *Psychological Reports*, 59, pp.1307–13

Braverman, L. (1988) 'Feminism and family therapy: friends or foes' in Braverman, L. (ed.) *A Guide to Feminist Family Therapy*, New York: Harrington

Breaking Through: Women Surviving Male Violence (1989) Bristol: Women's Aid Federation (England)

Bridge Child Care Consultancy Service (1991) *Sukina: An Evaluation of the Circumstances Leading to Her Death*, London: Bridge Child Care Consultancy Service

Broverman, I., Broverman, D., Clarkson, F., Rosenkrantz, P. and Vogal, S. (1970) 'Sex-role stereotypes and clinical judgements of mental health', *Journal of Consulting and Clinical Psychology*, 34, pp.1–7

Browne, A. (1987) *When Battered Women Kill*, New York: Free Press

Browne, A. and Williams, K.R. (1989) 'Exploring the effect of resource availability and the likelihood of female-precipitated homicides', *Law and Society Review*, 23(1), pp.75–94

Bryan, B., Dadzie, S. and Scafe, S. (1985) *The Heart of the Race: Black Women's Lives in Britain*, London: Virago

Brygger, M.P. (1990) 'Domestic violence: the dark side of divorce', *Family Advocate*, 13(1), pp.48–51

Brygger, M.P. and Edleson, J.L. (1987) 'The Domestic Abuse Project: a multi-systems intervention in woman battering', *Journal of Interpersonal Violence*, 2(3), pp.324–36

Bunch, C. and Carrillo, R. (1992) *Gender Violence: A Development and Human Rights Issue*, Dublin: Attic Press.

Burck, C. and Speed, B. (eds) (1995) *Gender, Power and Relationships*, London: Routledge

Burstow, B. (1992) *Radical Feminist Therapy: Working in the Context of Violence*, Newbury Park, CA: Sage

Butler, S. (1994) '"All I've got in my purse is mothballs!" The social action women's group', *Groupwork*, 7(2), pp.163–79

Butler, S. and Wintram, C. (1991) *Feminist Groupwork*, London: Sage

Carlson, B.E. (1992) 'Questioning the party line on family violence', *Affilia*, 7(2), pp.94–110

Casey, M. (1987) *Domestic Violence Against Women*, Dublin: Dublin Federation of Refuges

Cervi, B. (1993) 'Attack on worker focuses dangers', *Community Care*, 2nd September, p.5

Champagne, C., Lapp, R. and Lee, J. (1994) *Assisting Abused Lesbians: A Guide for Health Professionals and Service Providers*, 69 Wellington Street, London, Ontario, N6B 2K4: London Battered Women's Advocacy Centre (Pamphlet)

Chen, H., Bersani, C., Myers, S.C. and Denton, R. (1989) 'Evaluating the effectiveness of a court sponsored abuser treatment program', *Journal of Family Violence*, 4(4), pp.309–22

Children's Subcommittee of the London Coordinating Committee to End Woman Abuse, London, Ontario (1994) *Make A Difference: How to Respond to Child Witnesses of Woman Abuse* in Mullender, A. and Morley, R (eds) *Children Living with Domestic Violence: Putting Men's Abuse of Women on the Child Care Agenda*, London: Whiting & Birch

City of Bradford Metropolitan Council, Bradford Health Authority and Bradford Family Health Services Authority (1995/96) *Bradford Community Care Plan 1995/96*, Bradford: City of Bradford Social Services Department

Clark, A. (1988) *Women's Silence, Men's Violence: Sexual Assault in England 1770–1845*, London: Pandora

Cleveland Area Child Protection Committee (1995) *CAPC Practice Guidance. Domestic Violence: Whose Problem Is It?* Middlesbrough: Cleveland ACPC

Clifton, J. (1985) 'Refuges and self-help' in Johnson, N. (ed.) *Marital Violence*, London: Routledge & Kegan Paul

Condonis, M., Paroissien, K. and Aldrich, B. (1989) *The Mutual Self-Help Group: A Therapeutic Program for Women Who Have Been Abused*, 67 Smith Street, Wollongong, NSW 2500, Australia: Cider Press. Funded by the Office of the Status of Women.

Corob, A. (1987) *Working with Depressed Women: A Feminist Approach*, Aldershot: Gower

Coulshed, V. (1988) *Social Work Practice: An Introduction*, Basingstoke, Macmillan

Coulshed, V. (1991) *Social Work Practice: An Introduction*, Basingstoke, Macmillan. Second edition

Davidoff, L. and Dowds, L. (1989) 'Recent trends in crimes of violence against the person in England and Wales', in Home Office Research and Planning Unit, *Research Bulletin*, 27, London: HMSO

Davies, M. (1994) *Women and Violence: Realities and Responses Worldwide*, London: Zed Books

Debbonaire, T. (1994) 'Work with children in Women's Aid refuges and after' in Mullender, A. and Morley, R. (eds) *Children Living with Domestic Violence: Putting Men's Abuse of Women on the Child Care Agenda*, London: Whiting & Birch

Department of Health (1991) *The Health of the Nation: A Consultative Document for Health in England*, London: HMSO. Cm 1523

Department of Health (1995) *Child Protection: Messages from Research*, London: HMSO

Department of Health Social Services Inspectorate (1991) *Women in Social Services: A Neglected Resource*, London: HMSO

Department of Health Social Services Inspectorate (1992) *Promoting Women: Management, Development and Training for Women in Social Services Departments*, London: HMSO

Department of Health Social Services Inspectorate and Scottish Office Social Work Services Group (1991) *Care Management and Assessment: Practitioners' Guide*, London: HMSO

Derbyshire County Council (1993) *Care in the Community: Derbyshire Community Care Plan 1993/94*, Matlock: Derbyshire County Council Social Services Department

Deschner, J. (1984) *The Hitting Habit: Anger Control for Battering Couples*, New York: Free Press

Dixon, L. (1992) 'An effective challenge to women abuse', *Probation Journal*, 39(1), March, pp.40–2

Dobash, R.E. and Dobash, R.P. (1979) *Violence Against Wives*, New York: The Free Press (Also available in a 1980 edition from Shepton Mallet, Somerset: Open Books.)

Dobash, R.E. and Dobash, R.P. (1992) *Women, Violence and Social Change*, London and New York: Routledge

Dobash, R.E., Dobash, R.P. and Cavanagh, K. (1985) 'The contact between battered women and social and medical agencies' in Pahl, J. *Private Violence and Public Policy: The Needs of Battered Women and the Response of the Public Services*, London: Routledge & Kegan Paul

Dobash, R. P. and Dobash, R.E. (1981) 'Community response to violence against wives: charivari, abstract justice and patriarchy', *Social Problems*, 28(5), pp.563–81

Dobash, R.P. and Dobash, R.E. (1984) 'The nature and antecedents of violent events', *British Journal of Criminology*, 24(3), pp.269–88

Dobash, R.P., Dobash, R.E., Cavanagh, K. and Lewis, R. (1994) 'Research evaluation of programmes for violent men', paper presented at two Social Services Inspectorate conferences in London and Leeds, March 1995

Dobash, R.P., Dobash, R.E., Cavanagh, K. and Lewis, R. (1996) *A Research Evaluation of Programmes for Violent Men*, Edinburgh: Scottish Office, Central Research Unit.

Domestic Abuse Project (1989) *Research Update*, number 2, June, Minneapolis, MN: Domestic Abuse Project Inc.

Domestic Abuse Project (1991) *Research Update*, number 3, Winter, Minneapolis, MN: Domestic Abuse Project Inc.

Domestic Abuse Project Women's Therapy Team (1991) *Women's Therapy Handbook. March 1991*, Minneapolis, MN: Domestic Abuse Project Inc.

Dominelli, L. (1990) *Women and Community Action*, Birmingham: Venture Press

Dominelli, L., Mullender, A. and Orme, J. (1995) 'Working with violent men from a feminist social work perspective', paper presented at the IASSW Symposium at the Non-Governmental Organisations Forum of the UN Conference on Women, Beijing.

Donnelly, A. (1986) *Feminist Social Work with a Women's Group*, Norwich: University of East Anglia, Social Work Monograph 41

Downey, R. (1992) 'Behind closed doors', *Social Work Today*, 23rd July, p.11

Edleson, J.L. (1990) 'Judging the success of interventions with men who batter' in Besharov, D.J. (ed.) *Family Violence: Research and Public Policy Issues*, Washington, DC: AEI Press

Edleson, J.L. and Brygger, M.P. (1986) 'Gender differences in reporting of battering incidences', *Family Relations*, 35, July, pp.377–82

Edleson, J.L. and Grusznski, R.J. (1989) 'Treating men who batter: four years of outcome data from the Domestic Abuse Project', *Journal of Social Service Research*, 12(1/2), pp.3–22

Edleson, J.L. and Syers, M. (1990) 'The relative effectiveness of group treatment for men who batter', *Social Work Research and Abstracts*, 26, pp.10–17

Edleson, J.L. and Syers, M. (1991) 'The effects of group treatment for men who batter: an 18-month follow-up study', *Research in Social Work Practice*, 1, pp.227–43

Edleson, J.L. and Tolman, R.M. (1992) *Intervention for Men Who Batter: An Ecological Approach*, Newbury Park, CA: Sage

Edwards, S.S.M. (1986a) *The Police Response to Domestic Violence in London*, London: Central London Polytechnic

Edwards, S.S.M. (1986b) 'Police attitudes and dispositions in domestic disputes: the London Study', *Police Journal*, July, pp.230–41.

Edwards, S.S.M. (1989) *Policing 'Domestic' Violence: Women, the Law and the State*, London: Sage

Eisikovits, Z.C. and Edleson, J.L. (1989) 'Intervening with men who batter: a critical review of the literature', *Social Services Review*, 63(3), pp.384–414

Ellis, B. (1994) *Disabled Women's Project Report*, London: Greater London Association of Disabled People

Ellis, B. (1995) *Findings: The Experiences of Disabled Women*, York: Joseph Rowntree Foundation. Social Policy Research 81

Ernst, S. and Goodison, L. (1981) *In Our Own Hands: A Book of Self-Help Therapy*, London: The Women's Press

Evason, E. (1982) *Hidden Violence*, Belfast: Farset Press

Ewing, C.P. (1987) *Battered Women Who Kill: Psychological Self-Defense as Legal Justification*, Lexington, MA: D.C. Heath

Farmer, E. and Owen, M. (1995) *Child Protection Practice: Private Risks and Public Remedies*, London: HMSO

Farnham, M. (1992) 'Still working against the grain', *Trouble and Strife*, 23, Spring, pp.41–52

Fisher, M., Marsh, P. and Phillips, D. with Sainsbury, E. (1986) *In and Out of Care: The Experiences of Children, Parents and Social Workers*, London: Batsford

Fleming, C. (1989/90) 'A Falkirk woman writes . . . ', *Scottish Women's Aid Annual Report*, Edinburgh: Scottish Women's Aid

Fleming, J. and Ward, D. (1992) '*For the Children to Be Alright, Their Mothers Need to Be Alright'. An Alternative to Removing the Child – the Radford Shared Care Project. An Evaluation From the Participants' Viewpoints*, Nottingham: University of Nottingham, Centre for Social Action

Foley, R. (1993) 'Zero Tolerance', *Trouble and Strife*, 27, Winter, pp.16–20

Forman, J. (1995) *Is There a Correlation between Child Sexual Abuse and Domestic Violence? An Exploratory Study of the Links between Child Sexual Abuse and Domestic Violence in a Sample of Intrafamilial Child Sexual Abuse Cases*, Lawson's Building, 1700 London Road, Glasgow G32 8XD: Women's Support Project (Reprint of an earlier, undated report)

Freeman, M.D.A. (1979) *Violence in the Home*, Farnborough: Saxon House

Frieze, I. (1980) 'Causes and consequences of marital rape', paper presented at the American Psychological Association Meetings, Montreal, Canada, September

Frieze, I.H. (1983) 'Investigating the causes and consequences of marital rape', *Signs*, 8(3), pp.532–3

Gayford, J.J. (1975) 'Wife battering: a preliminary survey of 100 cases', *British Medical Journal*, 25th January, pp.194–7

Geller, J. (1982) 'Conjoint therapy: staff training and treatment of the abuser and the abused' in Roy, M. (ed.) *The Abusive Partner: An Analysis of Domestic Battering*, New York: van Nostrand Reinhold

Gelles, R.J. (1974) *The Violent Home*, Beverly Hills, CA: Sage

Gelles, R.J. (1983) 'An exchange/social control theory of family violence' in Finkelhor, D., Gelles, R.J., Hotaling, G.T. and Straus M.A. (eds) *The Dark Side of Families: Current Family Research*, Beverly Hills, CA: Sage

Gelles, R. and Straus, M. (1979) 'Determinants of violence in the family: toward a theoretical integration' in Burr, W.R., Hill, R., Nye, F.I. and Reiss, I.L. (eds) *Contemporary Theories about the Family*, New York: The Free Press. Vol. 1

Geraghty, J. (1994) 'Responding to offenders (ii)' in Home Office Special Conferences Unit, *Criminal Justice Conference. A Conference Report. Hall Garth Hotel 15–17 March 1994*, Liverpool: HOSCU, paras 139–53

Ghattaora, S. (ed.) (1992) *Forwarding the Struggle: Conference Report*, Nottingham: Roshni (Nottingham Asian Women's Aid) Ltd

Glass, D. (1995) 'Why women stay', paper presented to the Sixty-First Otterburn Conference, organised by the Northumbria Branch of the National Association of Probation Officers, 19th–21st May

Goldner, V. (1985) 'Warning: family therapy may be hazardous to your health', *Family Therapy Networker*, 9(6), pp.18–23

Gondolf, E.W. (1985) 'Fighting for control: a clinical assessment of men who batter', *Social Casework*, January, pp.48–54

Gondolf, E.W. (1987) 'Evaluating programs for men who batter: problems and prospects', *Journal of Family Violence*, 2(1), pp.95–108

Gondolf, E.W. and Russell, D. (1986) 'The case against anger control treatment programs for batterers', *Response*, 9(3), pp.2–5

Good Practices in Mental Health (1994) *Women and Mental Health: An*

Information Pack of Mental Health Services for Women in the United Kingdom, London: GPMH Publications

Goodrich, T.J. (1991) 'Women, power, and family therapy: what's wrong with this picture?' in Goodrich, T.J. (ed.) *Women and Power: Perspectives for Family Therapy*, New York: Norton

Gorman, J. (1992) *Out of the Shadows*, London: MIND Publications

Gove, W. R. (1972) 'The relationship between sex roles, marital status and mental illness', *Social Forces*, 51(1), pp.34–44

Governor's Battered Women's Working Group (1985) 'Violent crime in the family: enforcement of the Massachusetts Abuse Prevention Law', unpublished monograph

Graham, D.L.R., Rawlings, E. and Rimini, N. (1988) 'Survivors of terror: battered women, hostages and the Stockholm syndrome', in Yllö, K. and Bograd, M. *Feminist Perspectives on Wife Abuse*, Newbury Park, CA: Sage

Gray, A. (1989) 'Family violence: a background paper', paper prepared for the Family Violence Prevention Project, Department of Social Welfare, Wellington, New Zealand

Greater London Association of Disabled People (1995) *Report on 'Our Right to be Safe': A Conference for Disabled Women*, 20th March, London: GLAD

Grillo, T. (1991) 'The mediation alternative: process dangers for women', *Yale Law Journal*, 100(1545), pp.1545–1600

Grunsell, A. (1990) *'Let's Talk About' RACISM*, London: Franklin Watts

Guru, S. (1986) 'An Asian women's refuge' in Ahmed, S., Cheetham, J. and Small, J. *Social Work with Black Children and Their Families*, London: Batsford

Hague, G. and Malos, E. (1994) *Domestic VIolence: Action for Change*, Cheltenham: New Clarion Press

Hague, G., Kelly, L., Malos, E. and Mullender, A. (1996) *Children, Domestic Violence and Refuges: A Study of Needs and Responses*, Bristol: Women's Aid Federation (England)

Hague, G., Malos, E. and Dear, W. (1995) *Against Domestic Violence: Inter-Agency Initiatives*, Bristol: School for Advanced Urban Studies, University of Bristol

Hague, G., Malos, E. and Dear, W. (1996) *Inter-Agency Approaches to Domestic Violence*, Bristol: University of Bristol, School for Policy Studies.

Hall, A. (1992) 'Abuse in lesbian relationships', *Trouble and Strife*, 23, Spring, pp.38–40

Hall, R.E. (1985) *Ask Any Woman: A London Enquiry into Rape and Sexual Assault*, Bristol: Falling Wall Press

Hammond, N. (1989) 'Lesbian victims of relationship violence', *Women and Therapy*, 8, pp.89–105

Hanmer, J. (1990) *Women, Violence and Crime Prevention: A Study of Changes in Police Policy and Practices in West Yorkshire*, Violence, Abuse and Gender Relations Unit Research Paper No. 1, Bradford: Department of Applied Social Studies, University of Bradford

Hanmer, J. (1993) 'Women and violence: commonalities and diversities', paper presented at a one-day conference on 'Women, Men, Children – Violence and Abuse', held at the University of Bradford on 28th June

Hanmer, J. and Saunders, S. (1984) *Well-Founded Fear: A Community Study of Violence to Women*, London: Hutchinson

Hanmer, J. and Stanko, E. (1985) 'Stripping away the rhetoric of protection: violence to women, law and the state in Britain and the USA', *International Journal of the Sociology of Law*, 13(4), pp.357–74

Hanmer, J. and Statham, D. (1988) *Women and Social Work: Towards a Woman-Centred Practice*, Basingstoke: Macmillan

Hare-Mustin, R. (1978) 'A feminist approach to family therapy', *Family Process*, 17, pp.181–94

Harne, L. and Radford, J. (1994) 'Reinstating patriarchy: the politics of the family and the new legislation' in Mullender, A. and Morley, R. (eds) *Children Living with Domestic Violence: Putting Men's Abuse of Women on the Child Care Agenda*, London: Whiting & Birch

Hart, B. (1990) 'The further endangerment of battered women and children in custody mediation', *Mediation Quarterly*, 7(3), pp.278–91

Harway, M. (1993) 'Battered women: characteristics and causes', in Hansen, M. and Harway, M. *Battering and Family Therapy: A Feminist Perspective*, Newbury Park, CA: Sage

Harway, M. and Hansen, M. (1993) 'Therapist perceptions of family violence' in Hansen, M. and Harway, M., *Battering and Family Therapy: A Feminist Perspective*, Newbury Park, CA: Sage

Health Gain Commissioning Team on Domestic Violence (1995) 'Preliminary report to the Director of Public Health', March, Glasgow: Department of Public Health

Hearn, J. (1993) 'Men's violence to known women', paper presented at a one-day conference on 'Women, Men, Children – Violence and Abuse', held at the University of Bradford on 28th June

Hearn, J. (1994) 'Men's violence to women' in Featherstone, B., Fawcett, B. and Toft, C. *Violence, Gender and Social Work*, Bradford: University of Bradford, Department of Applied Social Studies

Hearn, J. (forthcoming) *The Violences of Men*, London: Sage

Heise, L. (1989) 'International dimensions of violence against women', *Response to the Victimization of Women and Children*, 12(1), pp.3–11

Heise, L. *et al.* (1994) *Violence Against Women: The Hidden Burden*, Washington: World Bank

Helton, A.S, Anderson, E. and McFarlane, J. (1987) 'Battered and pregnant: a prevalence study with intervention measures', *American Journal of Public Health*, 77, pp.1337–9

Hester, M. and Pearson, C. (1993) 'Domestic violence, mediation and child contact arrangements: issues from current research', *Family Mediation*, 3(2), pp.3–6

Hester, M. and Radford, L. (1992) 'Domestic violence and access arrangements for children in Denmark and Britain', *Journal of Social Welfare and Family Law*, 1, pp.57–70

Hester, M. and Radford, L. (1996a) 'Contradictions and compromises: the impact of the Children Act on women and children's safety', in Hester, M., Kelly, L. and Radford, J. (eds) *Women, Violence and Male Power*, Buckingham: Open University Press

Hester, M. and Radford, L. (1996b) *Domestic Violence and Child Contact in England and Denmark*, Bristol: Policy Press

Hester, M., Humphries, J., Pearson, C., Qaiser, K., Radford, L. and Woodfield, K.-S. (1994) 'Domestic violence and child contact' in Mullender, A. and Morley, R. (eds) *Children Living with Domestic Violence: Putting Men's Abuse of Women on the Child Care Agenda*, London: Whiting & Birch

Higgins, G. (1994) 'Hammersmith Women's Aid Childwork Development Project' in Mullender and Morley, R. (eds) *Children Living with Domestic Violence: Putting Men's Abuse of Women on the Child Care Agenda*, London: Whiting & Birch

Hilberman, E. and Munson, K. (1978) 'Sixty battered women', *Victimology*, 2, pp.460–70

Hirst, G. (1994) 'Laying the foundations for working with those who commit sex offences', *Social Work Education*, 13(1), pp.32–46

Hirst, J. (1996) 'House of power', *Community Care*, 29th February–6th March, p.21.

Hoff, L.A. (1990) *Battered Women as Survivors*, London and New York: Routledge

Holder, R., Kelly, L. and Singh, T. (1994) *Suffering in Silence: Children and Young People Who Witness Domestic Violence*, London: Hammersmith and Fulham Domestic Violence Forum (Available from Community Safety Unit, Hammersmith Town Hall, King Street, London W6 9JU)

Home, A. (1991–92) 'Responding to domestic violence: a comparison of social workers' and police officers' interventions', *Social Work and Social Sciences Review*, 3(2), pp.150–62

Home Affairs Committee *see* House of Commons Home Affairs Committee

Home Department, Lord Chancellor's Department and Attorney General's Deparment (1993) *The Government Reply to the Third Report from the Home Affairs Committee Session 1992–93 HC 245*, Cm 2269, London: HMSO

Home Office (1990) *Partnership in Dealing with Offenders in the Community*, London: HMSO

Home Office (1992) *Criminal Statistics: England and Wales 1990*, London: HMSO

Home Office (undated) *National Standards for Probation Service Family Court Welfare Work*, London: HMSO

Home Office and Welsh Office (1995) *Inter-Agency Circular: Inter-Agency Co-ordination to Tackle Domestic Violence*, London: Home Office Public Relations Branch.

Home Office Special Conferences Unit (1994) *Criminal Justice Conference. A Conference Report. Hall Garth Hotel 15–17 March 1994*, Liverpool: Home Office Special Conferences Unit (The topic was domestic violence.)

Homer, M, Leonard, A.E. and Taylor, M.P. (1984) *Private Violence: Public Shame*, Middlesbrough: Cleveland Refuge and Aid for Women and Children

Hooper, C.-A. (1992) *Mothers Surviving Child Sexual Abuse*, London: Routledge

Hooper, C.-A. (1994) 'Do families need fathers? The impact of divorce on children' in Mullender, A. and Morley, R. (eds) *Children Living with Domestic Violence: Putting Men's Abuse of Women on the Child Care Agenda*, London: Whiting & Birch

Horley, S. (1990) 'A shame and a disgrace', *Social Work Today*, 21st June, pp.16–17

Hough, M. and Mayhew, P. (1983) *The British Crime Survey: First Report*, London: HMSO. Home Office Research Study no. 76.

House of Commons (1975) *Report from the Select Committee on Violence in Marriage, Together with the Proceedings of the Committee*, session 1974–75. Vol. 1, Report, HC 553–i and vol. 2, Minutes of Evidence and Appendices, 553–II, London: HMSO

House of Commons Home Affairs Committee (1992a) *Domestic Violence. Volume I. Report Together with the Proceedings of the Committee*, Session 1992–93. 245–I, London: HMSO

House of Commons Home Affairs Committee (1992b) *Domestic Violence. Memoranda of Evidence*, Session 1992–93. 245–i, London: HMSO

Howard, J. and Shepherd, G. (1987) *Conciliation, Children and Divorce*, London: Batsford

Hughes, B. and Mtezuka, M. (1992) 'Social work and older women: where have older women gone?' in Langan, M. and Day, L. (eds) *Women, Oppression and Social Work: Issues in Anti-Discriminatory Practice*, London: Routledge

Hughes, H. (1992) 'Impact of spouse abuse on children of battered women', *Violence Update*, August, 1, pp.9–11

Hughes, H.M. and Marshall, M. (1995) 'Advocacy for children of battered women' in Peled, E., Jaffe, P.G. and Edleson, J.L. (eds) *Ending the Cycle of Violence:*

Community Responses to Children of Battered Women, Thousand Oaks, CA: Sage

Hughes, H. M., Parkinson, D. and Vargo, M. (1989) 'Witnessing spouse abuse and experiencing physical abuse: a "double whammy"?', *Journal of Family Violence*, 4(2), pp.197–209

Hurvitz, N. and Straus, R.A. (1991) *Marriage and Family Therapy: A Sociocognitive Approach*, Binghamton, NY: Haworth Press

Imam, U.F. (1994) 'Asian children and domestic violence' in Mullender, A. and Morley, R. (eds) *Children Living with Domestic Violence: Putting Men's Abuse of Women on the Child Care Agenda*, London: Whiting & Birch

Ingram, R. (1993/94) 'Violence from known men', *OpenMind*, 66, December/January, pp.18–19

Island, D. and Letellier, P. (1991) *Men Who Beat the Men Who Love Them: Battered Gay Men and Domestic Violence*, Binghamton, NY: Harrington Park Press (Haworth)

Jacobson, A. and Richardson, B. (1987) 'Assault experience of 100 psychiatric inpatients: evidence of need for routine inquiry', *American Journal of Psychiatry*, 144(7), pp.908–13.

Jacobson, A., Koehler, J.E. and Jones-Brown, C. (1987) 'The failure of routine assessment to detect histories of assault experienced by psychiatric patients', *Hospital and Community Psychiatry*, 38(4), pp.386–9.

Jaffe, P.G., Wolfe, D. Wilson, S. and Zak, L. (1986) 'Family violence and child adjustment: a comparative analysis of girls' and boys' behavioral symptoms', *American Journal of Psychiatry*, 143(1), pp.74–7

Jaffe, P.G., Wolfe, D.A. and Wilson, S.K. (1990) *Children of Battered Women*, Newbury Park, CA: Sage

Jervis, M. (1986) 'Why Asian women need a helping hand', *Social Work Today*, 18th August, 17(49), pp.7–8

Johnson, J.M. and Kanzler, D.J. (1990) 'Treating domestic violence: evaluating the effectiveness of a domestic violence diversion program', paper presented at the Tenth Annual Symposium on Social Work with Groups, Miami, Florida, October

Johnson, N. (1985) ' Police, social work and medical responses to battered women' in Johnson, N. (ed.) *Marital Violence*, London: Routledge & Kegan Paul

Jones, A. (1980) *Women Who Kill*, New York: Fawcett Columbine.

Jones, A. and Schechter, S. (1992) *When Love Goes Wrong: What to Do When You Can't Do Anything Right*, London: Victor Gollancz

Jones, E. (1990) 'Feminism and family therapy: can mixed marriages work?' in Perelberg, R.J. and Miller, A.C. (eds) *Gender and Power in Families*, London: Tavistock/Routledge

Jones, T., MacLean, B. and Young, J. (1986) *The Islington Crime Survey: Crime, Victimization and Policing in Inner-City London*, Aldershot: Gower

Jukes, A. (1990) 'Making women safe', *Social Work Today*, 21(41), 21st June, pp.14–15

Jukes, A. (1993) *Why Men Hate Women*, London: Free Association Books

Kaganas, F. and Piper, C. (1994) 'Domestic violence and divorce mediation', *Journal of Social Welfare and Family Law*, 3, pp.265–78

Kaufman, J. and Zigler, E. (1987) 'Do abused children become abusive parents?', *American Journal of Orthopsychiatry*, 57(2), pp.186–92

Kaufman Kantor, G. and Straus, M.A. (1987) 'The "drunken bum" theory of wife beating', *Social Problems*, 34(3), pp.213–30

Keighley Domestic Violence Forum (1993) 'Review Day Report', 20 January

Kelly, L. (1988a) 'How women define their experiences of violence' in Yllö, K. and Bograd, M. *Feminist Perspectives on Wife Abuse*, Newbury Park, CA: Sage

Kelly, L. (1988b) *Surviving Sexual Violence*, Cambridge: Polity Press

Kelly, L. (1991) 'Unspeakable acts: abuse by and between women', *Trouble and Strife*, 21, pp.13–20

Kelly, L. (1994) 'The interconnectedness of domestic violence and child abuse: challenges for research, policy and practice' in Mullender, A. and Morley, R. (eds) *Children Living with Domestic Violence: Putting Men's Abuse of Women on the Child Care Agenda*, London: Whiting & Birch

Kelly, L. (1995/96) 'Zero commitment', *Trouble and Strife*, 32, pp.9–16.

Kemp, A., Green, B.L., Hovanitz, C. and Rawlings, E. I. (1995) 'Incidence and correlates of posttraumatic stress disorder in battered women: shelter and community samples', *Journal of Interpersonal Violence*, 10(1), pp.43–55

Kennedy, H. (1992) *Eve Was Framed: Women and British Justice*, London: Chatto & Windus

King, J. (1994) 'Out of control', *Community Care*, 30th April, pp.31–2

Kirkwood, C. (1993) *Leaving Abusive Partners: From the Scars of Survival to the Wisdom for Change*, London: Sage

Kivel, P. (1992) *Men's Work: How to Stop the Violence that Tears Our Lives Apart*, Center City, MN: Hazelden Educational Materials

Korn, Y. (1993) *Inspirations for Action: A Practical Guide to Women's Safety*, Swindon: Cr!me Concern

Koss, M.P. (1993) 'Foreword' in Hansen, M. and Harway, M. (eds) *Battering and Family Therapy: A Feminist Perspective*, Newbury Park, CA: Sage

Krzowski, S. and Land, P. (eds) (1988) *In Our Experience: Workshops at the Women's Therapy Centre*, London: The Women's Press

Kurz, D. (1987) 'Emergency department responses to battered women: resistance to medicalization', *Social Problems*, February 34(1), pp.69–81

Kurz, D. and Stark, E. (1988) 'Not-so-benign neglect: the medical response to battering' in Yllö, K. and Bograd, M. *Feminist Perspectives on Wife Abuse*, Newbury Park, CA: Sage

Labour Party (1995) *Peace at Home: A Labour Party Consultation on the Elimination of Domestic and Sexual Violence Against Women*, London: Labour Party

Law Commission (1992a) *Criminal Law: Rape Within Marriage*, Law Com. No. 205, London: HMSO

Law Commission (1992b) *Family Law: Domestic Violence and the Occupation of the Family Home*, Law Com. No. 207, London: HMSO

Leeds City Council Department of Social Service (undated) *Good Practice Guidelines: Women Experiencing Violence from Known Men*, Leeds: Leeds City Council

Leeds City Council, Leeds Health Authority, Leeds Family Health Services Authority, and Voluntary Action Leeds (1992) *Women Subject to Violence by a Known Man: An Overarching Theme*, Leeds

Leeds City Council, Leeds Health Authority, Leeds Family Health Services Authority, and Voluntary Action Leeds (1992/93) *Final Draft Community Care Plan for Women Subject to Violence by a Known Man*, Leeds

Leeds City Council, Leeds Health Authority, Leeds Family Health Services Authority, and Voluntary Action Leeds (1993/94) *Women Subject to Violence by a Known Man: Community Care Plan Update*, Leeds

Leeds Inter-Agency Project (1993) *Information Pack*, c/o CHEL, 26 Roundhay Road, Leeds LS7 1AB: Leeds Inter-Agency Project

Leeds Joint Planning (1994) *Community Care Plan 1994/95*, Leeds (Available from Leeds Social Services)

Lees, J. and Lloyd, T. (1994) *Working with Men Who Batter Their Partners: An Introductory Text*, London: Working with Men/The B Team

Lent, B. (ed.) (1991) *Reports on Wife Assault*, Ontario: Ontario Medical Association Committee on Wife Assault

Leonard, P. and McLeod, E. (1980) *Marital Violence: Social Construction and Social Service Response. A Pilot Study Report*, Coventry: Department of Applied Social Studies, University of Warwick

Lloyd, S., Farrell, G. and Pease, K. (1994) *Preventing Repeated Domestic Violence: A Demonstration Project on Merseyside*, Police Research Group, Crime Prevention Unit Series: Paper 49, London: Home Office Police Department

Lloyd, S. (1995) 'Social work and domestic violence' in Kingston, P. and Penhape, B. (eds) *Family Violence and the Caring Professions*, Basingstoke: Macmillan

Loewenstein, P. (ed.) (1992) *Changing Men: A Practice Guide to Working with Adult Male Sex Offenders*, Nottingham: Nottinghamsire Probation Service

London Borough of Hackney (1993) *The Links between Domestic Violence and Child Abuse: Developing Services*, London: London Borough of Hackney

London Borough of Hackney (1993/1994) *The Hackney Community Care Plan 1993/1994*, London: London Borough of Hackney, Social Services Department

London Borough of Hackney (1994) *Good Practice Guidelines: Responding to Domestic Violence*, London: London Borough of Hackney, Women's Unit

London Borough of Hammersmith and Fulham (1991a) *Challenging Domestic Violence: A Training and Resource Pack for Anyone Who Wants to Address Domestic Violence in Their Work or Community Setting*, London: London Borough of Hammersmith and Fulham, Community Safety Unit

London Borough of Hammersmith and Fulham (1991b) *Women and Domestic Violence*, London: London Borough of Hammersmith and Fulham, Community and Police Committee and Women's Committee (Third edition)

London Borough of Hammersmith and Fulham (1992) *Abuse of Women in the Home*, London: London Borough of Hammersmith and Fulham

London Borough of Hammersmith and Fulham Environment Department Research Group (1993) *Crime and Harassment: A Survey of its Impact on People with Disabilities*, London: London Borough of Hammersmith and Fulham. Research Report Number 81

London Borough of Hounslow (1994) *Domestic Violence: Help, Advice and Information for Disabled Women*, London: London Borough of Hounslow

London Borough of Islington (1992, revised 1995) *Working with Those Who Have Experienced Domestic Violence: A Good Practice Guide*, London: London Borough of Islington, Women's Equality Unit

London Borough of Islington (1995) *STOP: Schools Take on Preventing Domestic Violence*, London: London Borough of Islington, Women's Equality Unit

London Borough of Newham, Newham Health Authority, City and East London Family Health Services Authority (1993–96) *Unitary Community Care Plan, 1993–96*, London: London Borough of Newham, Social Services Department

London Borough of Southwark (1993/94) *Community Care Plan 1993/94. Volume 7, Services for Women Experiencing Domestic Violence*, London: London Borough of Southwark, Social Services Department

Loosley, S. (1994) 'Women's Community House children's program: a model in perspective' in Mullender, R. and Morley, R. (eds) *Children Living with Domestic Violence: Putting Men's Abuse of Women on the Child Care Agenda*, London: Whiting & Birch

Loraine, K. (1981) 'Battered women: the ways you can help', *RN*, October, 44, pp.23–8 and 102

Lord Chancellor's Department (1995) *Looking to the Future: Mediation and the Ground for Divorce*, Cm 2799, London: HMSO

McCarthy, M. (1991) 'The politics of sex education', *Community Care*, 21st November, pp.15–17

McCarthy, M. (1994) 'Against all odds: HIV and safer sex education for women with learning difficulties' in Doyal, L., Naidoo, J. and Wilton, T. (eds) *AIDS: Setting a Feminist Agenda*, London: Taylor & Francis

McConnell, J.E. (1991) 'Beyond metaphor: battered women, involuntary servitude and the thirteenth amendment', paper given at the joint international conference of the Law and Society Association and Research Committee on the Sociology of Law of the International Sociological Association, Amsterdam, June 1991

Macdonald, B. with Rich, C. (1983) *Look Me in the Eye: Old Women, Ageing and Ageism*, London: The Women's Press

McFarlane, J. (1991) 'Violence during teen pregnancy: health consequences for mother and child' in Levy, B. (ed.) *Dating Violence: Young Women in Danger*, Seattle, Washington State: Seal Press

McGibbon, A. and Kelly, L. (1989) *Abuse of Women in the Home: Advice and Information*, London: London Borough of Hammersmith and Fulham

McGibbon, A., Cooper, L. and Kelly, L. (1989) *'What Support?' Hammersmith and Fulham Council Community Police Committee Domestic Violence Project. An Exploratory Study of Council Policy and Practice, and Local Support Services in the Area of Domestic Violence within Hammersmith and Fulham. Final Report*, London: Child Abuse Studies Unit, Polytechnic of North London

McGregor, H. (1990) 'Conceptualising male violence against female partners', *Australia and New Zealand Journal of Family Therapy*, 11(2), pp.65–70

McKay, M.M. (1994) 'The link between domestic violence and child abuse: assessment and treatment considerations', *Child Welfare*, 73(1), January/February, pp.29–39

MacLeod, L. (1987) *Battered But Not Beaten . . . Preventing Wife Battering in Canada*, Ottawa: Canadian Advisory Council on the Status of Women

MacLeod, L. (1989) 'Wife battering and the web of hope: progress, dilemmas and visions of prevention', discussion paper for Working Together: 1989 National Forum on Family Violence, Ottawa, Ontario: The National Clearinghouse on Family Violence

McWilliams, M. and McKiernan, J. (1993) *Bringing It Out in the Open: Domestic Violence in Northern Ireland*, Belfast: HMSO

Madame Vanier Children's Services 'Child Victim/Witness to Wife Assault Working Group' (1990) *Madame Vanier Children's Services' Response to Wife Assault*, London, Ontario: MVCS

Maguire, S. (1988) '"Sorry love": violence against women in the home and the state response', *Critical Social Policy*, Autumn, 8(2), issue 23, pp.34–45

Malette, L. and Chalouh, M. (eds) (1991) *The Montreal Massacre*, Charlottetown, Prince Edward Island, Canada: Gynergy Books (Translated by Wildeman, M.)

Malloch, M.S. and Webb, S.A. (1993) 'Intervening with male batterers: a study of social workers' perceptions of domestic violence', *Social Work and Social Sciences Review*, 4(2), pp.119–47

Malos, E. and Hague, G. (1993) *Domestic Violence and Housing: Local Authority Responses to Women and Children Escaping from Violence in the Home*, Bristol: Women's Aid Federation England and University of Bristol, School of Applied Social Studies

Mama, A. (1989) *The Hidden Struggle: Statutory and Voluntary Sector Responses to Violence against Black Women in the Home*, London: The London Race and Housing Research Unit. To be reissued by Whiting & Birch, London

Mama, A. (1993) 'Black women and the police: a place where the law is not upheld' in James, W. and Harris, C. *Inside Babylon: The Caribbean Diaspora in Britain*, London: Verso

Martin, D. (1976) *Battered Wives*, San Francisco: Glide Publications

Mathews, D.J. (1995) 'Parenting groups for men who batter' in Peled, E., Jaffe, P.G. and Edleson, J.L. (eds) *Ending the Cycle of Violence: Community Responses to Children of Battered Women*, Thousand Oaks, CA: Sage

Mattinson, J. and Sinclair, I. (1979) *Mate and Stalemate: Working with Marital Problems in a Social Services Department*, Oxford: Basil Blackwell

Maupin, A. (1989) *Significant Others*, London: Black Swan

May, M. (1978) 'Violence in the family: an historical perspective' in Martin, J. (ed.) *Violence and the Family*, Chichester: John Wiley & Sons

Maynard, M. (1985) 'The response of social workers to domestic violence' in Pahl, J. (ed.) *Private Violence and Public Policy: The Needs of Battered Women and the Response of the Public Services*, London: Routledge & Regan Paul

Maynard, M. (1993) 'Violence towards women' in Richardson, D. and Robinson, V. (eds) *Introducing Women's Studies*, Basingstoke: Macmillan

Meteyard, B. (1995) 'The Inbetweener', *Community Care*, 9th–15th March, pp.26–7

Miles, A. (1988) *Women and Mental Illness: The Social Context of Female Neurosis*, Brighton: Wheatsheaf

Miles, J. (1981) 'Sexism in social work', *Social Work Today*, 8th September, 13(1), pp.14–15

Miller, A.C. (1990) 'Introduction II' in Perelberg, R.J. and Miller, A.C. (eds) *Gender and Power in Families*, London: Tavistock/Routledge

MIND (1992) *Stress on Women*, London: MIND (pack)

MIND (1994) *Eve Fights Back: Report on MIND's 'Stress on Women' Campaign*, London: MIND

Mooney, J. (1994) *The Hidden Figure: Domestic Violence in North London*, London: London Borough of Islington, Police and Crime Prevention Unit

Morley, R. (undated) 'Public education and primary prevention', unpublished paper

Morley, R. (1993) 'Recent responses to "domestic violence" against women: a feminist critique' in Page, R. and Baldock, J. (eds) *Social Policy Review 5: The Evolving State of Welfare*, Canterbury: Social Policy Association

Morley, R. and Mullender, A. (1994a) 'Domestic violence and children: what do we know from research?' in Mullender, A. and Morley, R (eds) *Children Living with Domestic Violence: Putting Men's Abuse of Women on the Child Care Agenda*, London: Whiting & Birch

Morley, R. and Mullender, A. (1994b) *Preventing Domestic Violence to Women*, Police Research Group, Crime Prevention Unit Series: Paper 48, London: Home Office Police Department

Morris, T. (undated) *Putting a Stop to Domestic Violence: A Practical Guide for All Advisers*, West Bridgford, Nottingham: Nottinghamshire County Council

Mugford, J. (1990) 'Domestic violence in Australia: policies, practices and politics', paper presented at the conference of the American Society for Criminology, Baltimore, November 1990

Mullender, A. (1994a) 'Groups for child witnesses of woman abuse' in Mullender, A. and Morley, R (eds) *Children Living with Domestic Violence: Putting Men's Abuse of Women on the Child Care Agenda*, London: Whiting & Birch

Mullender, A. (1994b) 'School-based work: education for prevention' in Mullender, A. and Morley, R (eds) *Children Living with Domestic Violence: Putting Men's Abuse of Women on the Child Care Agenda*, London: Whiting & Birch

Mullender, A. (1995) 'Groups for children who have lived with domestic violence: learning from North America', *Groupwork*, 8(1), pp.79–98

Mullender, A. and Morley, R. (eds) (1994) *Children Living with Domestic Violence: Putting Men's Abuse of Women on the Child Care Agenda*, London: Whiting & Birch

Mullender, A. and Ward, D. (1991a) *The Practice Principles of Self-Directed Groupwork: Establishing a Value-Base for Empowerment*, Nottingham: Centre for Social Action, University of Nottingham

Mullender, A. and Ward, D. (1991b) *Self-Directed Groupwork: Users Take Action for Empowerment*, London: Whiting & Birch

Myers, T. (1993) 'Reoffending in battering programs', *Violence Update*, 4(3), November, pp.3 and 8

Nadirshaw, Z. (1992) 'The promotion of mental health for black women users' in Trent, D.R. and Reed, C. *The Promotion of Mental Health*, vol.2, Aldershot: Ashgate

National Association of Local Government Women's Committees (undated, published in 1990) *Responding with Authority: Local Authority Initiatives to Counter Violence Against Women*, The Pankhurst Centre, Chorlton-on-Medlock, Manchester M13 9WP: NALGWC

National Collective of Independent Women's Refuges Inc. (undated) *Home Is Where the Hurt Is*, Wellington, New Zealand: National Collective of Independent Women's Refuges Inc. (leaflet)

NCH Action for Children (1994) *see* Abrahams, C. (1994)

Nelson, S. (1994) 'Catch-22', *Community Care*, 14th April, pp.18–19

NiCarthy, G. (1990) *Getting Free: A Handbook for Women in Abusive Situations*, London: Journeyman. Revised edition, edited and adapted by Jane Hutt

Noesjirwan, J. (1985) *Ten Years On. 1975–1985. Evaluation of Women's Refuges in NSW*, New South Wales, Australia: publisher unstated

North Eastern Legal Action Group Women's Section and N.E. Women's Aid (1992) *'It's Just a Domestic . . . ' A Report on Domestic Violence Injunctions*, Newcastle upon Tyne: North East Legal Action Group – Women's Section

Norwood, R. (1985) *Women Who Love Too Much*, New York: Pocket Books

Norwood, R. (1988) *Letters from Women Who Love Too Much: A Closer Look at Relationship Addiction and Recovery*, London: Arrow Books

Nosko, A. and Wallace, B. (1988) 'Group work with abusive men: a multi-dimensional model', *Social Work with Groups*, 11(3), pp.33–52

Nottinghamshire County Council (1989) *Domestic Violence: Guide to Practice. Practice Guidelines to Assist Staff Dealing with Situations Involving Domestic Violence*, West Bridgford, Nottingham: Nottinghamshire County Council

Nottinghamshire County Council (1990) *Domestic Violence Conference Report*, West Bridgford, Nottingham: Nottinghamshire County Council

Nottinghamshire County Council Social Services, North Nottinghamshire Health Authority, Nottingham Health Authority, Nottinghamshire Family Health Services Authority (1993/94) *Caring for People: The Nottinghamshire Community Care Plan 1993–1994*, West Bridgford, Nottingham: Nottinghamshire County Council Social Services Department

Novello, A.C., Rosenberg, M., Saltzman, L. and Shosky, J. (1992) 'From the Surgeon General, US Public Health Service', *Journal of the American Medical Association*, 267(23), 17th June, p.3132

Ogus, A., Walker, J. and Jones-Lee, M. (1989) *Report of the Conciliation Project Unit, University of Newcastle upon Tyne to the Lord Chancellor on the Costs and Effectiveness of Conciliation in England and Wales*, Newcastle upon Tyne: University of Newcastle upon Tyne

O'Hara, M. (1990) 'Access visits that betray an abused child's trust', *Childright*, 70, October, pp.17–18

O'Hara, M. (1992) 'Child protection and domestic violence: making the links', *Childright*, 88, pp.4–5

O'Hara, M. (1993) 'Child protection and domestic violence: changing policy and practice' in London Borough of Hackney *The Links between Domestic Violence and Child Abuse: Developing Services*, London: London Borough of Hackney

O'Hara, M. (1994) 'Child deaths in contexts of domestic violence: implications for professional practice' in Mullender, A. and Morley, R (eds) *Children Living with Domestic Violence: Putting Men's Abuse of Women on the Child Care Agenda*, London: Whiting & Birch

Okun, L. (1986) *Woman Abuse; Facts Replacing Myths*, Albany, New York: State University of New York Press

Ontario Medical Association (1990) *Curriculum Guidelines for the Medical Management of Wife Abuse for Undergraduate Medical Students*, Ontario: OMA Board of Directors

Pagelow, M.D. (1981) *Woman-Battering: Victims and Their Experiences*, Beverly Hills, CA: Sage

Pagelow, M.D. (1984) *Family Violence*, New York: Praeger

Pagelow, M.D. (1992) 'Adult victims of domestic violence: battered women', *Journal of Interpersonal Violence*, 7(1), March, pp.87–120

Pahl, J. (1978) *A Refuge for Battered Women*, London: HMSO

Pahl, J. (1979) 'The general practitioner and the problems of battered women', *Journal of Medical Ethics*, 5, pp.117–23

Pahl, J. (1982) 'Men who assault their wives: what can health visitors do to help?', *Health Visitor*, October, 55, pp.528–60

Pahl, J. (ed.) (1985a) *Private Violence and Public Policy: The Needs of Battered Women and the Response of the Public Services*, London: Routledge & Kegan Paul

Pahl, J. (1985b) 'Refuges for battered women: ideology and action', *Feminist Review*, 19, March, pp.25–43

Pahl, J. (1993) 'Money matters', *Community Care*, 22nd July, p.15

Painter, K. (1991) *Wife Rape, Marriage and the Law. Survey Report: Key Findings and Recommendations*, Manchester: Department of Social Policy and Social Work, University of Manchester

Parkinson, L. (1986) *Conciliation in Separation and Divorce*, Beckenham: Croom Helm

Patel, P. (1990) 'Southall Boys', in Southall Black Sisters, *Against the Grain*, Southall, Middlesex: Southall Black Sisters

Pease, K., Sampson, A., Croft, L., Phillips, C. and Farrell, G. (1991) 'Strategy for the Manchester University Violent Crime Prevention Project', August

Peled, E. and Edleson, J.L. (1995) 'Process and outcome in small groups for children of battered women' in Peled, E., Jaffe, P.G. and Edleson, J.L. (eds.) *Ending the Cycle of Violence: Community Responses to Children of Battered Women*, Thousand Oaks, CA: Sage

Peled, E., Jaffe, P.G. and Edleson, J.L. (eds) (1995) *Ending the Cycle of Violence: Community Responses to Children of Battered Women*, Thousand Oaks, CA: Sage

Penal Affairs Consortium (1996) *The Mandatory Life Sentence: Submissions by the Penal Affairs Consortium to the House of Commons Home Affairs Committee in December 1994 and January 1996*, London: Penal Affairs Consortium

Pence, E. (1987) *In Our Best Interest: A Process for Personal and Social Change*, Duluth, MN: Minnesota Program Development Inc.

Pence, E. and Paymar, M. (1986) *Power and Control: Tactics of Men Who Batter. An Educational Curriculum*, revised 1990, Duluth, MN: Minnesota Program Development, Inc. (206 West Fourth Street, Duluth, MN 55806, USA)

Pence, E. and Shepard, M. (1988) 'Integrating feminist theory and practice: the challenge of the battered women's movement' in Yllö, K. and Bograd, M. *Femininst Perspectives on Wife Abuse*, Newbury Park, CA: Sage

Pence, E. with Duprey, M., Paymar, M. and McDonnell, C. (1989) *The Justice System's Response to Domestic Assault Cases: A Guide for Policy Development*, Duluth, MN: Domestic Abuse Intervention Project (Revised edition)

Pence, E., Hardesty, L., Steil, K., Soderberg, J. and Ottman, L. (undated) *What about the Kids? Community Intervention in Domestic Assault Cases: A Focus on Children*, Duluth, MN: Duluth Domestic Abuse Intervention Project

Perelberg, R.J. (1990) 'Equality, asymmetry, and diversity: on conceptualizations of gender' in Perelberg, R. J. and Miller, A.C. (eds) *Gender and Power in Families*, London: Tavistock/Routledge

Perelberg, R.J. and Miller, A.C. (eds) (1990) *Gender and Power in Families*, London: Tavistock/Routledge

Perrott, S. (1994) 'Working with men who abuse women and children' in Lupton, C. and Gillespie, T. (eds) *Working with Violence*, Basingstoke: Macmillan

Pilalis, J. (1987) 'Consciousness-raising and family therapy', paper presented at the Fifth New Zealand Family Therapy Conference, Hamilton, 14th–17th May

Pizzey, E. and Shapiro, J. (1982) *Prone to Violence*, London: Hamlyn

Pleck, E. (1987) *Domestic Tyranny*, Oxford: Oxford University Press

Poynter, T.L. (1989) 'An evaluation of a group programme for male perpetrators of domestic violence', *Australian Journal of Sex, Marriage and Family*, 10(3), pp.133–42

Prasad, B.D. and Vijayalakshmi, B. (1988) 'Dowry-related violence towards women: some issues', *Indian Journal of Social Work*, July, 49(3), pp.271–80

Pressman, B. (1989) 'Wife-abused couples: the need for comprehensive theoretical perspectives and integrated treatment models', *Journal of Feminist Family Therapy*, 1(1), pp.23–43

Pringle, K. (1995) *Men, Masculinities and Social Welfare*, London: UCL Press

Ptacek, J. (1988) 'Why do men batter their wives?' in Yllö, K. and Bograd, M. *Feminist Perspectives on Wife Abuse*, Newbury Park, CA: Sage

Queensland Domestic Violence Council (1990) *Update*, 3, July (newsletter)

Radford, J. and Russell, D.E.H. (1992) *Femicide: The Politics of Woman Killing*, Buckingham: Open University Press

Radford, L. (1994) 'Domestic violence, child contact and mediation', *Rights of Women Bulletin*, Autumn/Winter, pp.7–11

Reimers, S. and Treacher, A. (1995) 'User-friendliness and theories of family therapy: the contribution of second-order thinking and feminism' in Reimers, S. and Treacher A. *Introducing User-Friendly Family Therapy*, London: Routledge

Renzetti, C.M. (1992) *Violent Betrayal: Partner Abuse in Lesbian Relationships*, Newbury Park, CA: Sage

Research Committee and Staff of London Battered Women's Advocacy Centre (1993) *Confronting Lesbian Battering*, 69 Wellington Street, London, Ontario, N6B 2K4: London Battered Women's Advocacy Centre (Pamphlet)

Rickford, F. (1993) 'Court welfare under fire' and 'A private function', *Community Care*, 14th January, pp.4 and 16–18

Rights of Women (1994) 'Council of Europe initiative on violence against women', *ROW Bulletin*, Autumn/Winter, pp.18–23

Rights of Women Lesbian Custody Group (1984) *Lesbian Mothers on Trial: A Report on Lesbian Mothers and Child Custody*, London: Rights of Women

Roberts, M. (1988) *Mediation in Family Disputes*, Aldershot: Wildwood House

Rodriguez, N.M. (1988) 'A successful feminist shelter: a case study of the Family Crisis Shelter in Hawaii', *Journal of Applied Behavioral Science*, 24(3), pp.235–50

Rosewater, L.B. (1988) 'Battered or schizophrenic? Pyschological tests can't tell' in Ylló, K. and Bograd, M. *Feminist Perspectives on Wife Abuse*, Newbury Park, CA: Sage

Rounsaville, B. and Weissman, M.M. (1977–78), 'Battered women: a medical problem requiring detection', *International Journal of Psychiatry in Medicine*, 8 (2), pp.191–202

ROW Bulletin (1994) 'Council of Europe Initiative on Violence Against Women', Autumn/Winter, pp.18–23

Russell, D.E.H. (1990) *Rape in Marriage*, Bloomington: Indiana University Press. Revised edition

Ryan, W. (1971) *Blaming the Victim*, New York: Pantheon and London: Orbach and Chambers (There is also a 1976 revised edition from Vintage Books)

Saunders, A. (1994) 'Children in women's refuges: a retrospective study' in Mullender, A. and Morley, R. (eds) *Children Living with Domestic Violence: Putting Men's Abuse of Women on the Child Care Agenda*, London: Whiting & Birch

Saunders, A. with Epstein, C., Keep, G. and Debbonaire, T. (1995) *'It Hurts Me Too': Children's Experiences of Domestic Violence and Refuge Life*, Bristol: WAFE/London: NISW/London: ChildLine

Saunders, D.G. (1984) 'Helping husbands who batter', *Social Casework*, June, pp.347–53

Saunders, D.G. (1988) 'Wife abuse, husband abuse, or mutual combat? A feminist perspective on the empirical findings' in Ylló, K. and Bograd, M. *Feminist Perspectives on Wife Abuse*, Newbury Park, CA: Sage

Saunders, D. G. (1995) 'The tendency to arrest victims of domestic violence: a preliminary analysis of officer characteristics', *Journal of Interpersonal Violence*, 10(2), June, pp.147–58

Schlesinger, L.B., Benson, M. and Zornitzer, M. (1982) 'Classification of violent behaviour for purposes of treatment planning: a three-pronged approach' in Roy, M. (ed.) *The Abusive Partner: An Analysis of Domestic Battering*, New York: van Nostrand Reinhold

Schlesinger, P., Dobash, R.E., Dobash, R.P. and Weaver, C.K. (1992) *Women Viewing Violence*, London: British Film Institute

Scottish Office Central Research Unit (1995) *An Evaluation of the Scottish Office Domestic Violence Media Campaign*, HMSO

Scottish Women's Aid (1989a) 'Bill of Rights for Women', Edinburgh: Scottish Women's Aid

Scottish Women's Aid (1989b) 'Social workers: working with abused women and their children', Edinburgh: Scottish Women's Aid (Leaflet)

Scottish Women's Aid (undated a) 'Battered women: the myths exploded', Edinburgh: Scottish Women's Aid (Leaflet)

Scottish Women's Aid (undated b) *Children, Equality and Respect: Children and Young People's Experience of Domestic Violence*, Edinburgh: Scottish Women's Aid

Scottish Women's Aid (undated c) 'Getting over the fear', Edinburgh: Scottish Women's Aid (Leaflet publicising a video)

Scottish Women's Aid (undated d) 'Going to a new house?', Edinburgh: Scottish Women's Aid (Leaflet)

Scottish Women's Aid (undated e) 'Moving on with your kids', Edinburgh: Scottish Women's Aid (Leaflet)

Scottish Women's Aid (undated f) 'To – general practitioners', Edinburgh: Scottish Women's Aid (Leaflet)

Scottish Women's Aid (undated g) 'To – health visitors', Edinburgh: Scottish Women's Aid (Leaflet)

Shainess, N. (1984) *Sweet Suffering: Woman as Victim*, New York: Pocket Books

Shefali, M. (1988) 'Women in rural areas and domestic violence in Bangladesh', paper presented at the First International Women's Aid Conference, Cardiff, 21st to 23rd October

Shupe, A., Stacey, W.A. and Hazlewood, L. (1987) *Violent Men/Violent Couples: The Dynamics of Domestic Violence*, Lexington, MA: Lexington Books

Sinclair, D. (1985) *Understanding Wife Assault: A Training Manual for Counsellors and Advocates*, Toronto, Ontario (from Ontario Government Bookstore, Publications Services Section, 880 Bay Street, Toronto, Ontario M7A 1N8)

Singh, T. (1991) *'Working Together under the Children Act': WAFE Submission to the Department of Health*, Bristol: Women's Aid Federation England

Skrobanek, S. (1986) 'Violence against women in the family: the case of Thailand', Bangkok: Women's Information Centre

Sleightholm, D. (1991) 'Domestic violence', paper prepared for discussion by the National Council of the Association of Chief Officers of Probation (*see also* Association of Chief Officers of Probation, 1992)

Smith, L. (1989) *Domestic Violence: An Overview of the Literature. Home Office Research Study 107*, London: HMSO

Smith, S., Baker, D., Buchan, A. and Bodiwala, G. (1992) 'Adult domestic violence', *Health Trends*, 24(3), pp.97–9

Sone, K. (1993) 'Challenging behaviour', *Community Care*, 14th October, p.20

Sone, K. (1995) 'Lack of conviction', *Community Care*, 8th–14th June, pp.22–3

Southall Black Sisters (1990) *Against the Grain: A Celebration of Survival and Struggle, 1979–1989*, Southall, Middlesex: Southall Black Sisters

Stanko, E.A. (1985) *Intimate Intrusions: Women's Experience of Male Violence*, London: Routledge & Kegan Paul

Stark, E. and Flitcraft, A. (1985) 'Woman-battering, child abuse and social heredity: what is the relationship?' in Johnson, N. (ed.) *Marital Violence*, London: Routledge & Kegan Paul

Stark, E. and Flitcraft, A. (1988) 'Women and children at risk: a feminist perspective on child abuse', *International Journal of Health Services*, 18(1), pp.97–118

Stark, E. and Flitcraft, A. (1996) *Women at Risk: Domestic Violence and Women's Health*, Thousand Oak, Calif.: Sage

Stark, E., Flitcraft, A. and Frazier, W. (1979) 'Medicine and patriarchal violence: the social construction of a "private" event', *International Journal of Health Services*, 9(3), pp.461–93

Stark, E., Flitcraft, A., Zuckerman, D. *et al.* (1981) *Wife Abuse in the Medical Setting: An Introduction for Health Personnel*, Domestic Violence Monograph No. 7, April

Stelman, A. (1993) 'Domestic violence: old crime, sudden interest', *Probation Journal*, 40(4), December, pp.193–8

Stout, K.D. (1995) 'Legal and social differences between men and women who kill intimate partners', *Affilia*, 10(2), Summer, pp.194–205

Straus, M.A. (1980) 'Victims and aggressors in marital violence', *American Behavioral Scientist*, 23(5), pp.681–704

Straus, M.A. and Gelles, R.J. (1986) 'Societal change and change in family violence, 1975 to 1985, as revealed in two national surveys', *Journal of Marriage and the Family*, August, 48, pp.465–79

Straus, M.A., Gelles, R.J. and Steinmetz, S.K. (1980) *Behind Closed Doors: Violence in the American Family*, New York: Anchor

Sudermann, M., Jaffe, P.G. and Hastings, E., with Watson, L., Greer, G. and Lehmann, P. (1994) *ASAP: A School-Based Anti-Violence Programme*. Revised preview edition, London, Ontario: London Family Court Clinic

Swain, K. (1986) 'Probation attitudes to battered women: apathy, error and avoidance?', *Probation Journal*, 33(4), pp.132–4

Tayside Women and Violence Group (1994) *Hit or Miss: An Exploratory Study of the Provision for Women Subjected to Domestic Violence in Tayside Region*, Dundee: Tayside Regional Council, Equal Opportunities Unit

Teevan, S. (1991) *Women Who Are Abused by Their Therapists*, London: MIND

Thorne-Finch, R. (1992) *Ending the Silence: The Origins and Treatment of Male Violence against Women*, Toronto: University of Toronto Press

Tolman, R.M. and Edleson, J.L. (1989) 'Cognitive-behavioral intervention with men who batter' in Thyer, B.A. (ed.) *Behavioral Family Therapy*, Springfield, IL: Charles E. Thomas

Tomes, N. (1978) 'A torrent of abuse: causes of violence between working class men and women in London 1840–1975', *Journal of Social History*, 11(3), pp.329–45

Tuck, M. (1994) 'Scene setting' in Home Office Special Conferences Unit, *Criminal Justice Conference. A Conference Report. Hall Garth Hotel 15–17 March 1994*, Liverpool: HOSCU, paras 11–28

Underwood, J. (1989) *Lesbians' Experiences of Crime and Policing*, London: Polytechnic of North London

United Leeds Teaching Hospitals NHS Trust (1994) *Practice Guidelines: Providing Health Care for Women Who Are Experiencing Violence from Known Men*, April, Leeds: United Leeds Teaching Hospitals NHS Trust

United Nations (1986) 'The evolution of the work of the United Nations and its concern on the question of violence in the family, 1975–1986', New York: United Nations. Document BAW/EGM/86/BP.1

United Nations (1988) 'Efforts to eradicate violence against women within the family and society. Report to the Secretary general', E/CN.6/1988/6.

United Nations (1994) 'Understanding the problem' (from the United Nations resource manual *Strategies for Confronting Domestic Violence*) in Davies, M. *Women and Violence: Realities and Responses Worldwide*, London: Zed Books

United Nations (1995) *Beijing Declaration and Platform for Action, Adopted by the Fourth World Conference on Women: Action for Equality, Development and Peace* (unedited advance text), available from Women's National Commission, Level 4, Caxton House, Tothill Street, London SW1H 9NF

United States Department of Health, Education and Welfare (1980) *Domestic Violence*, Washington, DC: US Government Printing Office

Urry, A. (1990) 'The struggle towards a feminist practice in family therapy: premisses' in Perelberg, R.J. and Miller, A.C. (eds) *Gender and Power in Families*, London: Tavistock/Routledge

Ussher, J. (1991) *Women's Madness: Misogyny or Mental Illness?* Brighton: Harvester Wheatsheaf

Victim Support (1992) *Domestic Violence: Report of a National Inter-Agency Working Party on Domestic Violence Convened by Victim Support*, London: Victim Support

Viney, A. (1994) contribution to Home Office Special Conferences Unit, *Criminal Justice Conference. A Conference Report. Hall Garth Hotel 15–17 March*, Liverpool: HOSCU, paras 48–57

WAFE *see* Women's Aid Federation England

Walby, S. (1990) *Theorising Patriarchy*, Oxford: Blackwell

Walker, G. (1994) contribution to Home Office Special Conferences Unit, *Criminal Justice Conference. A Conference Report. Hall Garth Hotel 15–17 March*, paras 154–66

Walker, L.E.A. (1977–8) 'Battered women and learned helplessness', *Victimology*, 2(3–4), 525–34

Walker, L.E.A. (1979) *The Battered Woman*, New York: Harper & Row

Walker, L.E.A. (1983) 'The battered woman syndrome' in Finkelhor, D., Gelles, R.J., Hotaling, G.T. and Straus, M.A. (eds) *The Dark Side of Families: Current Family Research*, Newbury Park, CA: Sage

Walrond-Skinner, S. (1977) *Family Therapy: The Treatment of Natural Systems*, revised edition, London: Routledge & Kegan Paul

Walters, M. (1990) 'A feminist perspective in family therapy' in Perelberg, R.J. and Miller, A.C. (eds) *Gender and Power in Families*, London: Tavistock/Routledge

Waring, T. and Wilson, J. (1990) *Be Safe! A Self Help Manual for Domestic Violence*, Bolton, Lancashire: MOVE

Warshaw, C. (1989) 'Limitations of the medical model in the care of battered women', *Gender and Society*, 3(4), December, pp.506–17

Warshaw, C. (1993) 'Limitations of the medical model in the care of battered women', in Bart, P.B. and Moran, E.G. *Violence against Women: The Bloody Footprints*, Newbury Park, CA: Sage

Watts, J. (1990) 'Wifebeaters: men say why they batter women', *Observer*, 25th February, pp.57–8

Widom, C.S. (1989) 'Does violence beget violence? A critical examination of the literature', *Psychological Bulletin*, 106, pp.3–28

Williams, F. (1992) 'Women with learning difficulties are women too', in Langan, M. and Day, L. (eds) *Women, Oppression and Social Work: Issues in Anti-Discriminatory Practice*, London: Routledge

Williams, J., Watson., G., Smith, H., Copperman, J. and Wood, D. (1993) *Purchasing Effective Mental Health Services for Women*, London: MIND

Williams, O.J. (1993) 'Are partner abuse programmes prepared to work with African American men who batter?' Minneapolis, MN: University of Minnesota School of Social Work (Monograph)

Williams, O.J. (1994) 'Group work with African American men who batter: toward more ethnically sensitive practice', *Journal of Comparative Family Studies*, 25(1), pp.91–103

Williams, O.J. and Becker, L.R. (1994) 'Partner abuse programs and cultural competence: the results of a national study', *Violence and Victims*, 9(3), pp.287–96

Wilson, S.K., Cameron, S., Jaffe, P. and Wolfe, D. (1986) *Manual for a Group Program for Children Exposed to Wife Abuse*, London, Ontario: London Family Court Clinic

Wilson, M.N., Baglioni, A.J. and Downing, D. (1989) 'Analyzing factors influencing readmission to a battered women's shelter', *Journal of Family Violence*, 4(3), pp.275–84

Wilton, Tamsin (undated) *My Colouring Book of the Refuge*, Bristol: Women's Aid Federation England

Winfield, M. (ed.) (1988) *Domestic Violence: A Step-by-Step Guide for Social Workers and Others*, London: Family Service Units

Wolfe, D.A. and Gough, B.A. (1994) *Promoting Healthy, Non-Violent Relationships: A Group Approach with Adolescents for the Prevention of Woman Abuse and Interpersonal Violence*, London, Ontario: University of Western Ontario, Youth Relationships Project

Wolverhampton Council (1995) *Wolverhampton's Joint Community Care Plan*, Wolverhampton: Wolverhampton Council

Women and Children in Refuges (undated) *You Can't Beat a Woman*, Bristol: Women's Aid Federation England

Women Experiencing Violence by Known Men Service Planning Team, Leeds City Council (1994) Notes of an 'Information Briefing' held on 24th February

Women in MIND (1986) *Finding Our Own Solutions: Women's Experience of Mental Health Care*, London: MIND

Women's Aid Federation England (1992a) *Report to Home Affairs Committee Inquiry into Domestic Violence*, Bristol: WAFE (Also available as House of Commons Home Affairs Committee, 1992b, *Domestic Violence. Memoranda of Evidence*, Session 1992–93. 245–i, London: HMSO, Memorandum 22)

Women's Aid Federation England (1992b) *A Women's Aid Approach to Working with Children: An Information Pack for Women Working with Children in Refuges*, Bristol: WAFE

Women's Aid Federation England (1993/94) *Action against Domestic Violence. Annual Report*, Bristol: WAFE

Women's Aid Federation England (1995) *Family Law Bill: Briefing from the Women's Aid Federation England*, Bristol: WAFE

Women's Aid Federation England (undated a) 'Response by Women's Aid Federation England to: "Looking to the Future: Mediation and the Ground for Divorce"', Bristol: WAFE

Women's Aid Federation England (undated b) 'Unhelpful myths and stereotypes about domestic violence', Bristol: WAFE (Leaflet)

Wood, G.G. and Middleman, R. (1990) 'Re-casting the die: a small group approach to giving batterers a chance to change', paper presented at the Tenth Annual Symposium on Social Work with Groups, Miami, FL, October 1990

Worrall, A. and Pease, K. (1986) 'Personal crime against women: evidence from the 1982 British Crime Survey', *Howard Journal*, 25(2), pp.118–24

Yllö, K. and Bograd, M. (1988) *Feminist Perspectives on Wife Abuse*, Newbury Park, CA: Sage

Name index

Abrahams, C. 70, 73, 83, 96, 140, 141, 142, 145
Adams, D. 172, 175, 176–7, 178, 231
Ahluwalia, Kiranjit 5, 28, 52, 53
Ahmad, B. 29, 77
Ahmed, S. 77
Alibhai, Y. 52
Andrews, B. 32, 35, 45, 50, 118, 120, 123, 124, 126
Attwood, B. 271
Au, S. 120, 121
Avis, J. M. 170, 178, 184

Ball, M. 57, 59, 60, 82, 153, 154, 242
Banu, H. 120, 121
Barman, M. R. 126, 128
Barnes, Marian 118, 121
Barnett, O. W. 55
Barron, J. 11, 57
Becker, L. R. 244
Beninati, J. 231
Bensted, J. 205
Berk, R. A. 13
Bilinkoff, J. 164–5
Binney, V. 20, 21, 24, 50, 59, 61, 66, 69, 70, 71, 72, 74, 75, 77, 79, 80, 109, 197, 250, 268
Bisla, Rajinder 46
Blacklock, Neil 230
Bly, R. 235
Bograd, M. 10, 38, 40, 45, 49, 50, 62, 63, 172, 176, 178, 179, 184, 185
Borkowski, M. 35, 68, 71, 113, 192
Bowker, L. H. 15, 61, 67, 80, 102, 124, 126, 146, 147, 149
Brand, P. A. 22
Braverman, L. 170

Broverman, I. 120
Brown, G. W. 32, 35, 45, 50, 124, 146
Brown, Hilary 12, 138
Brown, P. 12
Browne, A. 21, 35, 36, 61
Bryan, B. 77
Brygger, M. P. 190, 243
Burck, C. 170
Burstow, B. 15, 17, 18, 21, 22
Butler, S. 272

Carlson, B. E. 13
Casey, M. 145
Cervi, B. 76
Chalouh, M. 255
Champagne, C. 16, 17, 18
Chavrimootoo, Prakash 52
Chen, H. 244
Clark, A. 29
Clifton, J. 267
Cobbe, Frances Power 30
Condonis, M. 267, 271
Corob, A. 121
Coulshed, V. 171–2

Davidoff, L. 34
Davies, M. 28, 63
Debbonaire, T. 91, 153, 154
Deschner, J. 229
Dixon, L. 212, 218, 220
Dobash, R. E. 3, 13, 14, 20, 21, 23, 25, 26, 30, 31, 33, 35, 37, 38, 40, 46, 49, 50, 55, 61, 66, 67, 70, 73, 74, 76, 80, 111, 112, 113, 114, 117, 124, 141, 152, 213, 242, 260
Dobash, R. P. 3, 13, 14, 20, 21, 23, 25, 28, 30, 32, 33, 35, 37, 38, 40, 46, 49,

50, 55, 61, 66, 67, 70 73, 74, 76, 80, 109, 111, 112, 113, 114, 117, 124, 141, 152, 213, 242, 260
Dominelli, L. 222, 272
Donnelly, A. 272
Dowds, L. 34
Downey, R. 85

Edleson, J. L. 160, 173, 178, 179, 180–2, 183, 228, 230, 243, 244
Edwards, S. S. M. 34, 36
Eisikovits, Z. C. 243
Ellis, B. 136
Ernst, S. 122
Evason, E. 31, 35, 57, 63, 141, 142

Farmer, E. 97–8
Farnham, M. 53
Fisher, M. 102
Fleming, Carol 22, 272
Flitcraft, A. 40, 42, 148–9
Foley, R. 261, 262, 266
Forman, J. 145, 199
Freeman, M. D. A. 29
Frieze, I. H. 22, 23

Gayford, J. J. 50
Gelles, R. J. 13, 43, 44, 228
Geraghty, J. 207, 212, 213, 216, 220
Ghattaora, S. 60, 78
Glass, D. 5, 34
Goldner, V. 172
Gondolf, E. W. 228, 230, 242
Goodison, L. 122
Goodrich, T. J. 170
Gorman, J. 121
Gough, B. A. 140
Gove, W. R. 121
Graham, D. L. R. 25
Gray, A. 26
Grillo, T. 190
Grunsell, A. 157
Grusznski, R. J. 243
Guru, S. 53, 268

Hague, G. 2, 4, 31, 56, 57, 140, 156, 195, 250, 251, 252, 253, 258
Hall, A. 16
Hall, R. E. 23
Hammond, N. 17
Hammond, Sukina 149
Hanmer, J. 20, 28, 33, 35, 76, 77, 78, 80, 116, 117

Hansen, M. 201
Hare-Mustin, R. 170
Harne, L. 192
Hart, B. 189
Harway, M. 37, 201
Harwin, N. 11
Hearn, J. 11, 36, 45, 47, 225–6, 230
Hearn, 36
Heise, L. 26, 29, 109
Helton, A. S. 124
Hester, M. 198, 199, 200, 140, 179, 188, 189, 191, 192, 196, 197
Higgins, G. 161
Hilberman, E. 112–13, 116
Hirst, G. 138, 219
Hoff, L. A. 20, 22, 50, 54, 61, 141, 143, 146, 150, 152
Holder, R. 139
Home, A. 95
Homer, M. 61
Hooper, C.-A. 150, 192–3
Horley, S. 212
Hough, M. 14, 33
Howard, J. 188
Hughes, B. 131
Hughes, H. 141
Hughes, H. M. 144, 158
Humphreys, Emma 5, 6
Hurvitz, N. 176

Imam, U. F. 28, 52, 68, 78, 152, 153, 260
Ingram, R. 116
Island, D. 15, 16

Jacobson, A. 123
Jaffe, Peter 139, 142, 143, 161, 178, 196
Jervis, M. 53
Johnson, J. M. 244
Johnson, N. 72, 112
Jones, A. 62
Jones, Ann 55
Jones, E. 175
Jones, T. 20, 33
Joseph, Sir Keith 40
Jukes, A. 227, 231, 237

Kaganas, F. 190
Kantor, G. 43–4
Kanzler, D. J. 244
Kaufman, J. 40, 43–4
Kelly, L. vii, 9, 10, 13, 16, 17, 21, 23, 24,

26, 32, 33, 43, 50, 55, 59, 61, 62, 147,
  150, 273
Kemp, A. 49
Kennedy, A. 5, 12, 26, 33, 46, 50, 52, 55
Kennedy, H. 117
Kidd, A. H. 22
King, J. 229
Kirkwood, C. 61
Kivel, P. 235
Korn, Y. 220
Koss, M. P. 170
Krzowski, S. 122
Kurz, D. 109, 126, 127, 128

Land, P. 122
LaViolette, A. D. 55
Lees, J. 223
Lent, B. 114, 116, 124, 125, 127, 129
Leonard, P. 68, 71, 76
Letellier, P. 15, 16
Lloyd, S. 35, 207, 213, 261, 262
Lloyd, T. 223
Loewenstein, P. 219
Loosley, S. 99, 58
Loraine, K. 125, 127, 129

McCarthy, M. 137
McConnell, J. E. 25, 124, 210
Macdonald, B. 131
McFarlane, J. 124
McGibbon, A. 13, 32, 43, 54–5, 59, 60,
  62, 68, 74, 76, 79, 88, 89, 101, 102,
  116, 118–19, 131–2, 133, 134, 253, 273
McGrail, Joseph 46
McGregor, H. 182–3
McKay, M. M. 201
McKiernan, J. 56, 65, 67, 71, 72, 73, 74,
  75, 77, 88, 90, 92, 116, 132, 205, 208,
  212, 214, 218
Maclean, David 34
McLeod, E. 68, 71, 76
MacLeod, L. 28, 222
McWilliams, M. 56, 65, 67, 71, 72, 73,
  74, 75, 77, 88, 90, 92, 116, 132, 205,
  208, 212, 214, 218
Maguire, S. 9, 50
Malette, L. 255
Malloch, M. S. 202
Malos, E. 4, 31, 56, 57, 195
Mama, A. 5, 33, 45, 68, 71, 77, 104–5,
  112, 156
Manning, Philip 208
Maple, Norma 118, 121

Marshall, M. 158
Martin, D. 48, 51
Mathews, D. J. 165, 167
Mattinson, J. 169
Maupin, Armistead 235
Maurer, L. 124, 126, 146
May, M. 29
Mayhew, P. 14, 33
Maynard, M. 9, 10, 23, 29, 37, 38, 44,
  45–6, 47, 55, 63, 69, 72, 73, 74, 75, 76,
  79, 149, 173
Meteyard, B. 179
Middleman, R. 230
Middleton, Valerie 208
Miles, A. 121
Miles, J. 73
Miller, A. C. 170, 171
Mooney, J. 32, 35, 44, 45
Morley, R. 4, 21, 34, 36, 96, 129, 139,
  143, 145, 207, 213, 238, 240, 251,
  266
Morris, T. 84
Mtezuka, M. 131
Mugford, J. 250, 270
Mullender, A. 21, 34, 36, 96, 106, 129,
  139, 143, 145, 160, 162, 207, 213, 228,
  263, 273, 274–6
Munson, J. 112–13, 116
Myers, T. 240

Nadirshaw, Z. 121
Neffield, Margaret 29
Nelson, S. 199–200
NiCarthy, G. 62
Noesjirwan, J. 268
Norwood, R. 50
Nosko, A. 228, 229
Novello, A. C. 109

Ogus, A. 197
O'Hara, M. 102, 145, 149, 200
Okun, L. 40
Owen, M. 97–8

Pagelow, M. D. 13, 37, 40, 45, 50–1,
  146
Pahl, J. 10, 14, 20, 21, 25, 29, 31, 32, 33,
  35, 43, 44, 50, 51, 56, 62, 63, 66, 69,
  70, 72, 79, 95, 109, 111, 112, 115–16,
  125, 132, 144–5, 146, 153
Painter, K. 35
Parkinson, L. 188
Patel, P. 203

Patel, Vandana 53
Paymar, M. 138, 165, 233
Pearson, C. 179, 189, 198
Pease, K. 14, 33, 35
Peled, E. 139, 160
Pence, Ellen 15, 22, 27, 38, 42, 62, 140,
   164, 165, 229, 232, 233, 269, 271, 270
Perelberg, R. J. 170
Perrott, S. 213, 215, 220, 225, 247
Pilalis, J. 184
Piper, C. 190
Pizzey, Erin 40, 50, 246
Pleck, E. 29
Poynter, T. L. 243, 244
Prasad, B. D. 28, 55
Pressman, B. 179
Pringle, K. 63
Ptacek, J. 14, 20, 36–7, 38, 39, 40, 42,
   43, 46–7, 64

Radford, J. 18, 63, 196
Radford, L. 179, 188, 196, 198, 199,
   200
Reimers, S. 170
Renzetti, C. M. 15, 16
Rich, C. 131
Richardson, B. 123
Rickford, F. 189
Roberts, M. 189
Rodriguez, N. M. 268
Rosewater, L. B. 118
Rounsaville, B. 125
Russell, D. E. H. 18, 21, 23, 63, 230
Ryan, William 37, 40, 46, 63

Saunders, A. 156
Saunders, D. G. 12, 13, 14
Saunders, S. 33, 116, 117
Schechter, S. 62
Schlesinger, L. B. 231
Schlesinger, P. 48, 51
Shainess, N. 49
Shapiro, J. 50
Shefali, M. 28
Shepard, M. 229, 233
Shepherd, G. 188
Shupe, A. 242
Sinclair, D. 142, 143, 150, 179–80
Sinclair, Hamish 234, 237
Sinclair, I. 169
Singh, T. 91, 198
Skrobanek, S. 28
Sleightholm, David 186, 219, 229

Smith, L. 10, 13, 20, 25, 29–30, 33, 34,
   43, 44, 59, 110, 146, 152, 222, 234
Smith, S. 11
Sone, K. 137, 237
Speed, B. 170
Stanko, E. A. 10, 26, 33, 35
Stark, E. 20, 33, 40, 42, 56, 113, 116,
   125, 127, 128, 148–9
Statham, D. 76, 77, 78, 80
Stelman, A. 220
Stout, K. D. 12
Straus, M. A. 13, 40, 42, 43–4, 228
Straus, R. A. 176
Sudermann, M. 140
Swain, K. 203–4
Syers, M. 244

Teevan, S. 121
Thorne-Finch, R. 228
Thornton, Sarah 5, 6
Tolman, R. M. 173, 178, 179, 180–2,
   183, 228, 230, 243, 244
Tomes, N. 29
Treacher, A. 170
Tuck, M. 207, 213
Tulloch, Shirley 34

Underwood, J. 203
Urry, A. 184
Ussher, J. 118

Vijayalakshmi, B. 28, 55
Viney, A. 207

Walby, S. 45
Walker, G. 209
Walker, L. E. A. 24, 26, 49, 117, 172
Wallace, B. 228, 229
Walrond-Skinner, S. 171, 172
Walters, M. 184
Ward, D. 228, 272, 274–6
Ward, Keith 51, 208
Waring, T. 224, 227, 235, 237
Warshaw, C. 116, 125, 126
Watts, J. 235, 237
Webb, S. A. 202
Weissman, M. M. 125
Widom, C. S. 40
Williams, F. 137
Williams, J. 121
Williams, K. R. 36
Williams, O. J. 244
Wilson, Jim 224, 227, 235, 237, 242

Wilson, M. N. 268
Wilson, S. K. 161
Wilton, Tamsin 155
Winfield, M. 83–4
Wintram, C. 272

Wolfe, D. A. 140
Wood, G. G. 230
Worrall, A. 14, 33

Zigler, E. 40

General index

abduction of children 99, 200
abusers' groups 39, 138, 180, 211, 212–13, 215, 222–48; compared with women's 274; in prison 216, 217, 229
accident and emergency departments (A & E) 125–8
accountability issues 235–41, 247
ACOP *see* Association of Chief Officers of Probation
advocacy: for children 158; for women 117, 207, 269–70
African Caribbean women 28; contact with social services 68, 71, 77
aftercare and throughcare 216–18
alcohol: as alleged cause of abuse 40–2; alcohol misuse 215
Allied Dunbar 264
America *see* North America; USA
American Medical Association 109
anger management 39, 213, 216, 229–30; use in profeminist groups 230, 233
anti-oppressive work with children 156–8
approved social workers (ASWs) 117–18, 121
Area Child Protection Committees 91, 96
Asian women: Bengali mental health group 121; contact with social services, 68, 71–2, 78, 129–30, 174-5; dowry deaths 28, 278n; and general practitioners 112; help from children 152; and refuges 79, 198, 262, 268; alleged 'toleration' of abuse 52–3
Asian Women's Group, Keighley 257, 258

Asian Women's Project, Newham 90, 108
ASSET (Advice, Support, Service and Escort Team), Nottinghamshire 270
Association of Chief Officers of Probation (ACOP): Gender Action Group 220; *Position Statement on Domestic Violence* (1992, updated 1996) (also available as House of Commons Home Affairs Committee, 1992b, Memorandum 6) 6, 186, 187, 203, 205, 206, 207, 208, 209, 210, 211, 212, 214, 217, 219, 220, 224, 227

Barlinnie prison 224
'battered husbands' 11, 13
'battered wives'/'battered woman syndrome' 10, 26, 49–50, 117
BBC Children in Need Appeal 154, 168
behavioural theory of abuse 229–30; use in profeminist groups 230, 233
Black abusers 214
Black communities: biculturalism required 185; and police 5, 44–5; victim blaming 46
Black women 86, 203; contact with social services 68, 77–9, 86, 92, 104–5; elders 133; interpreter support 93, 112; liaison with groups 90, 105, 254; and medical services 112; mental health issues 119, 120, 121, 122–3; and police 5, 45; and refuges 78, 156, 254, 268
Black Women's Forum, Leeds Inter-Agency Forum, 256, 258
Black workers 77, 79, 87, 93, 119, 123, 257

blaming the victim *see* victim blaming
Boadicea 136
Body Shop 265
Bolton MOVE 224, 235, 245–6
Bradford: liaison work 90; male
    violence study (1994) 225–6
Breaking Through (WAFE) 165, 272
Bridge Child Care Consultancy Service
    149
Bristol: drop-in centre 270; marital
    violence study (1983) 35, 112
British Association of Social Workers
    (BASW): Memorandum of Evidence
    submission (1992) 82; 'Women and
    Mental Health' conference (1993)
    121
British Crime Survey 33, 34, 35
British Telecommunications (BT)
    264–5
Brookside 6

Canada 28, 54, 227, 260; Body Shop
    Canada 265; child witness work 139,
    140, 142, 159–60; gender of abusers
    research 14; judge's view of refuges
    196; 'Montreal massacre' 255; refuge
    referral study (1991–2) 69; women's
    groups 273 *see also* Ontario
CAPA: *Advice Card for Women: Legal
    Advice and Information for Women
    Experiencing Violence in the Home*
    271
care management 107–10; and disabled
    women 134, 135, 136; in health care
    settings, 111, 113, 115, 119; and older
    women 131
caseloads, woman abuse cases 68–9
causation 36–62; circular causality
    171–2
CHANGE project, Stirling 211, 213,
    215, 223, 224, 233, 239, 241–2, 246,
    247; evaluation 242
child abuse: and contact orders
    199–200; links with woman abuse
    97–9, 105–6, 144–51, 193–4, 199;
    physical 145–51; protection and
    welfare work 89, 96–106, 255, 257;
    sexual 91, 123, 145, 199
Child Benefit Agency 198
Child Support Act (1991) 60
ChildLine 140, 152
children 139–68; child care work,
    families and courts 191–201; direct
    work with 159–67; of disabled
    mothers 134, impact of woman abuse
    on 96–7, 141–53, 255; interests
    placed above women's 73–5;
    labelling mothers 'unstable' 117; in
    refuges 153–9; and women's
    difficulties in leaving abusers 55–6,
    74–5
Children Act (1989) 4, 96, 98–9, 106,
    107, 185, 191–201; section 17 support
    95, 100–1, 103, 154, 257
Children of Battered Women (Jaffe)
    139
Children (Scotland) Act (1995) 99
Children's Legal Centre 168;
    submission to Home Affairs
    Committee (1992) 186–7
childwork in refuges 154–9
Chiswick Family Rescue, London 246
Cleveland Area Child Protection
    Committee 100, 257; Domestic
    Violence Task Group 257
collusion: in abusers' groups 235–7; by
    probation officers 210–11, 214, 215
community, role of 260–1
community-based groups 268–9
Community Care 12, 52, 121, 138, 198,
    264, 272
community care planning 10, 107–8,
    255; for disabled women 135, 136; in
    health care settings 111,123, 125, 128,
    255
Community Mental Health Trust 118
conciliation, and family court welfare
    work 188–9
confidentiality 87, 92, 93; in accident
    and emergency departments 126;
    and child sexual abuse 91; and
    contact orders 197–8; in health care
    111; and probation service 206
contact: orders 197–200; supposed
    benefits of 192–3
couples counselling: and abusers'
    groups 237; dangers of 177–80;
    residual role for 180–3
Council of Europe: Committee on
    Violence Against Women 1994 29
courts: accountability issues 240–1;
    advocacy services 269–70; attitude to
    female killers 5, 12, 50; attitude to
    male killers 46–7; effects of Children
    Act (1989) 191–201; family court
    welfare work 178, 185–91, 201;

historical responses 30; mandates to abusers' groups 15, 165, 211, 212–13, 233, 244, 246; marital rape 5, 9; sentencing 210–13; usefulness of medical evidence 115

Criminal Justice Act (1991) 213, 217, 219

criminal justice system 4–5, 9, 12, 46–7, 50, 203–21, 222, 229, 246, 255–6; accountability issues 240–1; advocacy services 269–70; and people with learning difficulties 137, 138; sanctioning of abuse 63–4; treatment of arrested women 14–15

criminality of abuse 4, 33, 34, 35, 203, 205–6, 214, 219, 222, 240, 255–6, 262; of marital rape 5, 9, 22

crisis intervention 270, 271

Crown Prosecution Service 5, 137, 213

custody (of children) 192

custody (prison) *see* prison

'cycle of violence' (transgenerational transmission) 40–2, 84, 96, 151–2

'cycle of violence' (Walker's three stage theory) 49

Daily Express 216

denial and minimisation 36–7, 225–7, 230

Department of Health research (1995) 101, 103, 150

Department of Health Social Services Inspectorate 73, 82

deportation and immigration 5, 28, 52, 93, 105, 203, 278n

disability 133–8; in children, caused by abuse 146; refuge access 94, 135, 137; women's need for information 271

Disabled Persons (Services, Consultation, and Representation) Act (1986) 135

disclosure work with children 159–60

divorce and mediation 189–91

Domestic Abuse Intervention Project (DAIP), Duluth, 236, 245, 257; abusers' groups 138, 165–7, 227, 232; parenting groups 164; power and control wheel 26, 27, 164, 199, 271 *What About the Kids?* 140; women's groups 271, 274, 276

Domestic Abuse Project (DAP), Minneapolis 164–5, 244, 245, 257, 271

Domestic Violence Intervention Project (DVIP), London, 212, 224, 233, 245, 247; Violence Prevention Programme 223, 224, 231, 236, 239

Domestic Violence Units (DVUs) 4

'Don't Stand For It' campaign 263

dowry deaths 28, 278n

Duluth: Interagency Rehabilitation Project 178 *see also* Domestic Abuse Intervention Project (DAIP)

duty work 92–5

Edinburgh District Council Zero Tolerance campaign 261–3, 266

education: profeminist re-educational groups 230, 233 *see also* public education; schools EMERGE, Boston 232, 234

emotional abuse 24–6

empowerment 59–60, 62, 106, 267–77; of Black women 105; of disabled women 136; framework for 274–6; and mental health 119–20; of women as mothers 149, 150, 164–5

European Regional Council of the World Federation for Mental Health (ERC/WFMH) 122–3

evaluation, of abusers' groups 242–5

Everyman Centre, London 223

Everyman Plymouth 224

Families Need Fathers 12, 165, 192

Family Health Service Authorities 111

Family Homes and Domestic Violence Bill (withdrawn 1995) 58, 99

Family Law Bill (1995) 58, 189–90, 265

Family Service Units (FSUs): *Domestic Violence: A Step-by-Step Guide for Social Workers and Others* (1988) 83–4

family therapy: dangers of 177–80; family systems theory 171–2; influence of feminism 170–1, 172; interactional approach and victim-blaming 175–7; residual role for 180–3

family work 169–202; changing perspective 170–85; family court welfare work 178, 185–91, 201; effects of Children Act (1989) 191–201

fathers' groups 165–7

feminist perspective 3, 79, 214, 249; on

abusers' groups 222–3, 228, 231; in accident and emergency departments 128; on custody rights 192; on family work 170–1, 172, 184–5, 201; on gender inequalities 45, 63; on lesbian abuse 16–17; in mothers' groups 164; on public education 263; of Women's Aid 69–70 see also profeminist groups Fresh Start, West Midlands 224

gay men: abusive relationships 15–17, 18, 203; supervision of abusers 214–15
gender, and children's reactions to woman abuse 142–3, 152
gender roles in child abuse 150
gender stereotyping 120–1, 211, 234, 236–7
gendered power dynamics 37, 45; and abusers' groups 227, 229, 230, 233, 234; and concept of masculinity 17–18, 63, 204–5; and family work 171–2, 173; ignored by Children's Act (1989) 192; in probation officers' roles 205; and Zero Tolerance 262–3
general practitioner (GP) services 110–15, 255
Glasgow Health Gain Commissioning Team on Domestic Violence 110, 130
global experience of abuse 26–9
good practice guidelines 83–7
Government response 4, 5–6, 222, 229; encouragement for inter-agency initiatives 252; health issues 109; housing policy 4, 56–7; law and order concerns 210, 247; public education work 263–4; sentencing policy 217; terminology 230
Governor's Battered Women Working Group, 64
Greater London Association of Disabled People (GLAD) 136
groupwork: with children 155–6, 160–1; with parents 164–7; see also abusers' groups; women's groups
Guardian, The 32, 208

Hackney, London Borough of: caseload study 69; The Links Between Domestic Violence and Child Abuse (1993) 139; Women's

Unit 161–2: Good Practice Guidelines: Responding to Domestic Violence (1994) 86, 99, 104, 105, 118, 123, 132, 133, 199, 272
Hammersmith and Fulham, London Borough of: Abuse of Women in the Home pack 273; abuse statistics 32; inter-agency work 91–2, 252, 253–4; Social Services support groups 101; Suffering in Silence: Children and Young People Who Witness Domestic Violence 139; training and information packs 219, 256
health care settings 110–30
health services 107–38, 255
Hereford Women's Aid 270
historical experience of abuse 29–30, 260–1
Home Affairs Committee see House of Commons Home Affairs Committee
Home Department, 1993 response to Home Affairs Committee report (1992a) 6, 28, 52, 60, 216, 222, 224, 229, 252
Home Office: Circular 60/1990 (police guidelines) 4, 217; and deportation threats 52; 'Domestic Violence Factsheet' (1995) 33, 34, 35, 57; 'Don't Stand For It' campaign 263; Research Study on Domestic Violence (1989) 109–10 see also National Standards
Home Office and Welsh Office inter-agency circular (1995) 252
Home Office Special Conferences Unit (1994) 206, 216
homelessness see housing and homelessness
homophobia 16, 17, 119, 156, 203, 214
homosexuality see gay men, lesbians
hospital settings 123–30
Hounslow, London Borough of 258; Domestic Violence – Help, Advice and Information for Disabled Women 133–4
House of Commons Home Affairs Committee enquiry report: 1992a 5, 229, 252; 1992b 5, 82, Memorandum 6 see under Association of Chief Officers of Probation, Memorandum 22 see under Women's Aid Federation England

House of Commons Housing
Committee papers (1990) 254
House of Commons Select Committee
on Violence in Marriage 30, 278n;
1975 Report 20, 21, 30, 31
housing and homelessness 4, 56–7,
104–5, 251

immigration and deportation 5, 28, 52,
93, 105, 203, 278n
*In Our Best Interest: A Process for
Personal and Social Change* (Pence)
271, 272
information provision 92, 113, 124–5,
206–7, 271
injunctions 57–8
inter-agency work 250–9; and abusers'
groups 212–13, 225, 233, 241, 245,
247; with children 100, 158, 160–1;
and health care 108–9, 110–11, 115,
125, 128, 129, 130; liaison and
co-ordination 90–2, 95; probation
service 212–13, 219–20; training 89,
111, 219, 255, 256
Interagency Rehabilitation Project,
Duluth 178
interpreter support 79, 93, 112, 118,
203; for deaf women 135
intervention models 228–35
intrapsychic models of intervention
231
Islington, London Borough of: abuse
statistics 32; Domestic Violence
Matters project 270; educational
pack (1995) 140; Women's Equality
Unit 161–2, 252, 272: *Working With
Those Who Have Experienced
Domestic Violence – A Good
Practice Guide* (1992) 85

Joint Commission on Hospital
Accreditation, USA 109
joint meetings 186–9, 201–2 *see also*
couples counselling
Joseph Rowntree Foundation 136
Justice for Women 12

Keighley Domestic Violence Forum
90, 240, 245, 252, 257, 259 *see also*
Worth Project killing: of abusive
men, by women 5, 6, 12, 21–2, 50, 55,
117, 124, 209; of children, by abusive
men 149–50; of women, by abusive

men 21, 36, 46, 51, 55, 104, 124, 197,
198, 201, 208

Law Commission reports (1992a and
1992b) 5
'learned helplessness' 26, 49, 117
learning difficulties 137–8
leaving: assistance through family work
182; obstacles to 54–62, 207, 269; by
older women 132; and residence
orders 196; social workers' responses
to 71–2, 74–5, 173, 174–5
Leeds City Council: community care
plans 10, 88, 111, 115, 118, 255;
Women Experiencing Violence by
Known Men Service Planning Team
31, 111
Leeds City Council Department of
Social Services *Good Practice
Guidelines* 86–7, 93, 99, 101, 106,
118, 131, 132, 134, 135
Leeds General Infirmary 128
Leeds Inter-Agency Forum 254, 259
Leeds Inter-Agency Project 89, 90–1,
119, 135, 172, 219, 252, 254–6
Leeds Joint Planning 111, 113, 118
Legal Aid 58
Leicestershire Royal Infirmary 11
lesbians: abusive relationships 15–17,
18, 203; anti-oppressive work with
children 156; and custody 55–6, 192;
mental health issues 119, 122–3
local authorities: interagency work
252–7; public education 261–3
London: abuse statistics 32–3, 34, 35;
abusers' groups 223 *see also*
Hackney, Hammersmith and
Fulham, Hounslow, Islington,
Newham
London Battered Women's Advocacy
Centre (Ontario) 16, 17, 18 loss of
control models 39–40
Lothian Domestic Violence Probation
Project (DVPP) 213, 215, 223, 233,
239, 247; evaluation 242

Madame Vanier Children's Services
178
Man Alive, San Rafael, California 234
Manchester University, police statistics
research (1991) 35
marital rape 5, 9, 22, 23; links with
child abuse 147; of older women 131

Marriage Guidance *see* Relate
masculinity 17, 63, 204–5, 229, 234
masochism 49
Matrimonial Causes Act (1878) 30
mediation: and divorce 189–91; and
family court welfare work 178, 186,
188–9
men: alleged abuse of 11–15; fathers'
groups 165–7; male workers 25, 70–1,
78, 79, 184–5, 205, 211, 215, 227, 274;
probation work with 210–18; social
workers' failure to confront 76–7;
theories about causation of abuse
37–45 *see also* abusers' groups
Men's Centre, London 223, 226–7, 231
mental health 26, 115–23, 255
Mental Health Act (1983) 118, 123
mental illness, as alleged case of abuse
37–8
Metropolitan Police 4, 34
MIND 121
minority ethnic groups 56, 78, 156, 236,
261
mothers' groups 164–5
MOVE (Men Overcoming Violence)
groups 224, 235, 237, 246
multi-agency work *see* inter-agency
work
mutual fighting 13–15
*Mutual-Help Group, The: A
Therapeutic Program for Women
Who Have Been Abused* (Condonis
et al.) 271
My Colouring Book of the Refuge
(Wilton) 155

NALGO (now Unison) 265–6
National Association of Local
Government Women's Committees
(NALGWC) 251, 252, 253, 263
National Association of Probation
Officers (NAPO) 218–19
National Family Mediation 190
National Society for the Prevention of
Cruelty to Children 100
*National Standards for Probation
Service Family Court Welfare Work*
185–6, 187–8, 201, 220
Native American women 29, 261, 269
NCH Action for Children 168; 1994
study 70, 83, 140, 141, 142, 145
neutrality of social workers 173–5
New South Wales 268–9, 271

Newham, London Borough of: Asian
Women's Project 90, 108; liaison
work 90
NHS and Community Care Act (1990)
108, 111, 135
North America 28, 37, 105, 115–16,
189, 242, 246; abusers' groups 227–8;
accident and emergency departments
127–8; child witness work 139, 140,
144, 151; residence issues 196
Northern Echo 104
Northern Ireland domestic violence
studies: (1992) 31, 35, 141, 142;
(1993) 71, 208
Northumbria Probation Service 224
Not Worth the Paper (Barron) 57
Nottingham AGENDA 224, 235, 246
Nottinghamshire ASSET 269
Nottinghamshire County Council 90,
251, 252, 253; *Domestic
Violence – Guide to Practice:
Practice Guidelines to Assist Staff
Dealing with Situations Involving
Domestic Violence* (1989) 84–5
Nottinghamshire Inter-Agency
Domestic Violence Forum 100, 258

Oakland Men's Project 234
obstetric services 123–5, 146
older women 122–3, 131–3
Ontario, Canada 9–10, 105;
'Community Group Treatment
Program for Child Witnesses of
Woman Abuse' 160–1; family and
couples work 178, 179–80; London
Family Court Clinic 196; medical
training 114–15; preventive
educational work 162–3, 263
Ontario Medical Association 114
Ontario Ministry of Education 162–3,
263
Otterburn conference (NAPO, 1995)
219
outreach work 269, 270

parental responsibility, under Children
Act (1989) 191–4
PAX group, Kidderminster 224, 233
'Peace at Home' 5
'Pekinpah Stills' 236
physical abuse: of children 145–51; of
women 19–22
physical disabilities 133–7

PIVOT group, Houston, Texas 240
playwork 154–5
police: advising women on abuser's
  release from custody 217; arrest of
  women 14–15; and domestic
  disturbances 8, 131, 251, 261;
  improvements in response 4–5; and
  inter-agency work 251, 252; policing
  of poor and Black communities 5,
  45; statistics 33–6
policy development and statistics 88–9
power and control wheel 26, 27, 164,
  199, 271
Powerhouse group 137
pre-sentence reports 210–11
pregnancy 115, 123–5, 146
Preston Women and Violence Forum
  258
prevalence of abuse 30–6
primary health care teams 110–15
prison 229; advocated by women
  activists 212; impact of 212;
  throughcare and aftercare 216–18;
  women prisoners 209–10
private sector involvement 264–6
Procurators Fiscal 211, 240
profeminist groups for abusers 230,
  232–3, 236
prohibited steps orders 200–1
provocation: as alleged cause of male
  abuse 46–9; as women's legal
  defence 5, 12
pychodynamic theory of abuse 231
psychological theories of causation:
  men 37–44; women 49–51, 117
psychosocial theories of causation 44–5
public education 259–66

racism 53, 120, 123, 157, 203, 236, 254,
  268 71; inverted/reverse 53, 77–8
Rape Crisis 24, 275
RAVEN (Rape and Violence End
  Now), St Louis 234
record keeping: by doctors 114–15; by
  probation officers 204; by social
  workers 93
refuges 3, 30, 66; and contact orders
  197–8; disabled access 94, 135, 137;
  extended services 270; follow-up
  work 268–9; funding 31, 60, 154;
  importance of 59–60; and lesbian
  abusers 17; liaison with community
  psychiatric nurses 119–20; men's

11–12; mutual support 260, 267–8;
  and obstetric services 124; referrals
  by social workers 69–70; and
  residence orders 195; shortage of
  places 31, 59, 207, 266; specialist 28,
  53, 60, 78, 79, 119, 198, 254, 262, 268;
  tracing of telephone calls 265; work
  with children 153–9, 260
Relate Marriage Guidance 151, 179
residence orders 194–7
resource prioritisation 245–6, 247, 251,
  258–9, 266
Rights of Women (ROW) 12, 263;
  Bulletin (Autumn/Winter 1994) 5,
  12, 47, 50; *Newsletter* (July 1995) 52
Rights of Women Lesbian Custody
  Group 55–6, 192
rural areas 259, 269

safety: and abusers' groups 237–40,
  245; in accident and emergency
  departments 126; of Asian women
  53, 198; and contact orders 197–200;
  during imprisonment of abusers 51,
  212, 216–17; in family court work
  169, 181–2, 188, 189: good practice
  87, 93; planning 60–1, 93–4, 103, 134,
  160; and probation work (general)
  205, 209; and release of abusers from
  custody 206, 208, 217–18; after
  separation 35–6; of social work staff
  76–7, 87; of women offenders 209–10
schools: boys' attitudes in 262–3;
  liaison with refuge workers 158;
  work in 161–3, 255
Scotland: abusers' groups 223, 224, 242;
  inter-agency work 252; public
  education 261–3, 263–4, 266; social
  work contact research (1985) 66–8;
  spouse assault study (1974) 14;
  woman and child abuse study (1995)
  145, 199 *see also* CHANGE project;
  Lothian Domestic Violence
  Probation Project; Tayside Women
  and Violence Group
Scottish Office: changes to Children's
  Hearing Rules (1986) 198; policing
  policy 4–5
Scottish Office Central Research Unit
  263
Scottish Women's Aid 31, 49, 51, 55,
  61, 83; 'Bill of Rights for Women'
  (1989a) 47–8; *Children, Equality and*

Respect: Children and Young People's Experience of Domestic Violence 139; criticism of public education campaign 264; *Going to a New House?* 155; *Moving on with Your Kids* 155; 'To – General Practitioners' 113
Section 8 orders 194–201
Select Committee on Violence in Marriage *see under* House of Commons
self-help model of intervention 235–7
sentencing 210–13
sexism 17, 157–8, 205
sexual abuse and violence 9, 22–4, 226; child 91, 123, 145, 199; and disabled women 136; in older women 131; and probation work 204–5, 218–19; in psychiatric settings 121; sentencing 211, 213; and women with learning difficulties 137
Sheffield inter-agency work 252
Shelter News Release 57
sin, as alleged cause of abuse 38
social action 234–5
social class 31–2, 44–5
social learning model of intervention 229–30
sociocultural theory of abuse 232–2
Southall Black Sisters 6, 29, 52, 53, 78
specific issues orders 200–1
statistics: police 33–6; and policy development 88–9; prevalence of abuse 32–3; proportion of abused women seen by social workers 66–9
Stop Male Violence, Glasgow 223
Strathclyde University, public education research 264
Styal prison 209
suicide 55, 56, 113, 116
supervision orders 213–16
systemic family work 171–2

TASK group, North Derbyshire 273
Tayside Women and Violence Group, 1994 study 69, 70–1, 141, 142, 143, 146, 152
terminology 8–10, 172, 230
The Time, The Place (ITV) 34
throughcare and aftercare 216–18
Today (BBC Radio) 264
'toleration' of abuse 51–3
training: family court welfare officers

189, 190; health care 111, 118 122–3, 125; inter-agency 89, 111, 219, 255, 256; probation service 189, 205, 206, 219; social work 71, 89–90, 103, 118
tranquilliser use 112, 113, 122, 126–7
transgenerational transmission *see* 'cycle of violence'

Unison 266
United Leeds Teaching Hospitals NHS Trust: *Practice Guidelines* (1994) 110, 125
United Nations 109; Decade for Women 29; World Conference on Women, 1995 28, 109
University of Bristol Domestic Violence Research Group 250
USA 43, 49–50, 67, 178, 190, 227; alleged abuse by women 12, 13, 14–15; health care 109, 112–13; marital rape study (1990) 23; sanctioning of abuse 63–4; social action 234–5; social class and abuse 32; survey of therapists' attitudes (1993) 201–2; woman and child abuse studies (1988) 146–9; women's groups 269–70, 271–2 *see also* Domestic Abuse Intervention Project, Duluth; Domestic Abuse Project, Minneapolis

victim blaming 10, 37, 45–56; in family therapy 175–7; and mental health problems 117; by probation officers 204, 211; amongst social workers, 75–6
Victim Support, National Inter-Agency Working Party Report on Domestic Violence (1992) 6, 8, 54, 186, 187, 193, 195, 196, 200, 217, 252
Violence Prevention Programme (VPP) of the Domestic Violence Intervention Project (DVIP), London 224, 231, 236, 239
voluntary sector: abusers' groups 212–13, 223–4; importance of liaison with 91; and mental health 121–2

weapons, use of 20, 28
Wolverhampton Domestic Violence Forum 108
women: abuse of children 104–6, 193; accountability to 235–41; alleged

abuse of men 11–15; fear of social workers 101–2; mothers' groups 164–5; negative aspects of social work help 72–80; positive aspects of social work help 70–72; probation role with 206–10; running abusers' groups 227, 232, 235, 236; theories about causation of abuse 45–62

Women and Children in Refuges 61

Women Experiencing Violence by Known Men Service Planning Team 110, 255

Women in Learning Diificulties (WILD) 137

Women Who Kill (Yorkshire Television) 124, 209

Women's Aid 3, 4, 22, 30, 65, 66, 94, 135, 139, 168, 206, 213, 250, 275, 277; and abusers' groups 224, 233, 239, 245–6, 247; childwork 153–4; extended services 270; funding 29, 60, 154, 245–6, 259, 266, 270; and inter-agency work 89, 90, 100, 247, 249, 251, 252, 254, 259; philosophy 59–60; referrals by social workers 69–70; views on joint meetings 187; work in schools 161

Women's Aid Federation England (WAFE), 24, 25, 31, 49, 54, 83, 191; annual report (1993/4) 56, 60, 153; *Breaking Through* 165, 272; briefing on Family Law Bill (1995) 58, 190; information pack (1992b), 154, 157; refuge survey (1992a, also available as House of Commons, 1992b Memorandum 22) 12, 51, 59–60, 143, 187, 191, 194–5, 197–8, 199; research project on children 140; *Womens Rights* broadsheet 265

women's groups 267–77, for women as abusers 15; for disabled women 136; for older women 133; for women with learning difficulties 137

Women's Support Service (WSS), London 223, 239

Women's Therapy Handbook (Domestic Abuse Project Women's Therapy Team) 271

World At One (BBC Radio) 208

World Health Organisation 109

Worth Project, Keighley 224, 233, 236, 240, 257

Zero Tolerance 256, 259–60, 261–3, 266